NEW FORMS OF LABOUR ADMINISTRATION: ACTORS IN DEVELOPMENT

NEW FORMS OF LABOUR ADMINISTRATION: ACTORS IN DEVELOPMENT

Edited by Normand Lécuyer
General editor: Jean Courdouan

International Labour Office   Geneva

Lécuyer, N. (editor); Courdouan, J. (general editor)
New forms of labour administration: Actors in development
Geneva, International Labour Office, 2002

Labour administration/./administrative reform/./developed country/./developing country.
04.03.05
ISBN 92-2-106480-8

First published in French: *Les nouvelles administrations du travail: des acteurs du développement*
(ISBN 92-2-206537-9)

ILO Cataloguing-in-Publication Data

Photocomposed by the ILO, Geneva, Switze   PAO
Printed in Austria   HOL

Preface

Far-reaching and rapid changes in the world of labour and employment are taking place in countries the world over, changes that constitute significant challenges for labour administrations. What are the latter doing in order to take these changes on board and to contribute to the economic and social development of their countries? This volume seeks to answer this question, in the context of globalization, with an emphasis on the valuable contribution that labour administrations make to creating an environment conducive to economic and social development, to the introduction and development of democracy, and to the legal and social protection of workers.

The authors' analysis of the prerequisites for success, based of actual examples of effective and innovative practices that have been implemented by labour administrations to meet the needs of their users and clients, points to new organizational practices and new internal and external operational processes: definition of objectives, organizational choices, management of resources, and partnership with the other actors in the system.

The present study[1] is addressed, in the first instance, to heads of labour administrations and other agencies, but also to the various partners of these administrations, especially the social partners (employees' and workers' organizations). It is also meant for heads of other public administrations because the modernization of labour administration is part of the wider issue of public service reform. Finally, it aims to provide specialists in international organizations and researchers with a better understanding of this particular field of public activity.

We would like to thank the specialists who worked with us, in numerous ways, on the preparation of this volume: Philippe Bernoux, Yves C. Gagnon, Jean-Marie Laneyrie, Normand Lécuyer, Bernard Lust and Jean-François Robinet, as well as Naziha Gaham-Boumechal and Anne Lakowleff. We also wish to acknowledge the contribution made by the many national experts who wrote the case studies that served, in whole or in part, to compile the analytical files on labour administration practices in the areas of work, employment and vocational training, industrial relations, and evaluation in more than 20 countries around the world. Last, we are grateful to all of our colleagues

---

[1] This English edition is based on the French version, *Les nouvelles administrations du travail: des acteurs du développement*, first published in 2000.

in headquarters and on the multidisciplinary teams whose advice has contributed to the completion of this study, edited by Normand Lécuyer, a specialist in labour administration at the International Labour Office.

Jean Courdouan,
Director,
Department for Government and Labour Law
and Administration

Contents

General introduction

Despite the adoption by the International Labour Organization (ILO) in 1978 of the Labour Administration Convention (No. 150), and its accompanying Recommendation (No. 158),[1] the past two decades have seen very few studies dealing with this subject at the international level. This glaring lack of interest by specialists unfortunately reflects the situation that labour administrations often face.

Although some labour administrations have developed the capacity to intervene in national economic decisions and exercise their powers to the satisfaction of users, government authorities and the social partners, many others are weak and isolated and have very little impact on the social fabric of their country. In exceptional cases the Minister of Labour might be ranked second to the Prime Minister in terms of protocol, but it is more usual for his or her name to appear at the bottom of the list of Cabinet members. Similarly, although there are examples of labour administration departments that possess modern and adequate operational tools and are staffed by competent civil servants whose protected status allows them to fulfil their mission without having undue influence placed upon them, in most cases the everyday reality is quite different.

This heterogeneity could have dissuaded the ILO from developing universally applicable standards in this area, but in the 1970s it in fact appeared useful for the Organization to deal with these issues in depth, notably on the basis of a number of observations made in 1973 by the Meeting of Experts on Labour Administration:

— first, the formulation of international standards would help certain countries to solve to some extent their difficulties in this field;

— second, they would afford a form of protection to any national systems of labour administration that were still weak;

— third, such standards would fill a gap in the International Labour Code by taking into account the important role that labour administration systems can play in the development, implementation, and control of labour policy.[2]

Although the number of countries that have ratified Convention No. 150 (52 as of July 2001) has not been as high as its unanimous adoption would have led one to expect, the text is more relevant than ever. The world has continued to change, often at a rapid pace, and many of those in charge of labour administration do not have the means they need to play the role that workers and employers expect of them and that the provisions of the Convention defined for them.

We therefore considered it necessary to take stock of the current situation and to put forward some elements for thought and action on how best to strengthen the functions of labour administrations, as identified by the 1978 Convention and confirmed in their entirety some 20 years later (in 1997) by the ILO Committee of Experts on the Application of Conventions and Recommendations. [3]

Some of the contents of the Convention are discussed at the end of Chapter 1, such as the definition of the terms "labour administration" and "system of labour administration", the latter including, besides public administration bodies, any institutional structures (including those managed by parapublic agencies or by the social partners) that are involved in national labour policy.

The present study is wholly in keeping with the view that all the actors in the system have a role to play and that public administration bodies should not have a monopoly but should function within a partnership. It aims to describe the activities of labour administration, to demonstrate its usefulness for the society in which it operates, to promote its modernization and thereby to contribute to the strengthening of the system as a whole.

Although there are some systems of labour administration in which the major actors (labour administration and the social partners) are strong and experienced, there are many in which all of these actors are weak and do not share a legacy of joint relationships and achievements.

Anyone unfamiliar with the 1978 Convention might find it paradoxical that in the conclusions of the preparatory report for the 61st Session of the International Labour Conference that had to consider its adoption, the ILO experts specifically stressed the decisive role of employers' and workers' organizations in labour policy. [4] In fact, much of the substance of the Convention is embodied in this seeming paradox, one that has only been amplified by democratic developments.

The role of the social partners – which for historical reasons varies from one country to another, and ranges from law-making to administration – is essential and must be recognized as such in the actions undertaken by public administration bodies.

The subject is well set out in Convention No. 150: while some functions should be exercised on behalf of society as a whole, for the benefit of workers and enterprises, the State should make sure not to go it alone, but should affirm the right of existence and the autonomy of the social actors, encourage dialogue between them, and respect their fields of activity.

The different roles therefore do not compete with each other, but are complementary. Transitory weakness of one actor can be temporarily compensated by the strength of the other, but the overall aim of strengthening each of the actors in the social dialogue must be maintained. When accepted by everyone, this arrangement should allow for cooperation and mutual support, which is useful to all parties, especially to those whom the social partners represent and to users.

This study was written with those in charge of labour administration in developing countries uppermost in mind. But it is also addressed to decision-makers and influential persons, particularly within employers' and workers' organizations, who might find in it an unexploited potential that might support, or indeed amplify their efforts. Finally, it calls on the leaders of developed countries to share their experience, not by trying to impose their own models on others, but by being empathetic and rigorous in helping other labour administrations to fashion their own future.

Rather than seeking to set out a series of broad considerations or, conversely, to offer a set of recipes to be faithfully copied, *we wanted to underpin our analysis with specific information*, with proven experiments and with "good practices" that we were able to identify, though without passing any value judgements on them. Although they are representative of the functions, objectives, and methods of labour administrations, the examples we have chosen (which may well have changed since we studied them) are neither exceptional nor exhaustive, and should certainly not be copied slavishly.

* * *

A series of examples would be of very little interest, however, if they were not accompanied by a wider consideration of the dynamics that drive the activities of labour administrations in the changing world that surrounds them. This is precisely the subject of the three chapters comprising Part I of the study.

Chapter 1 deals with the changes that in a few short years have altered the very foundations of public administration: users, partners, problems, expectations, and ways of thinking. Moreover the State, to which the public administration is answerable, has to deal with new issues, with political and financial constraints and a host of other changes; these problems will only be overcome if its contribution to the process is made more visible and if the measures it takes are improved – two key elements for its credibility and the taxes that it imposes.

This environment is a given that must be taken into account, within the framework of specific national characteristics, in order to make it possible to re-examine essential questions that are buried under administrative routine and the sheer weight of day-to-day tasks. The discussion of the changes affecting the environment will reveal their scale, their frequency, and their impact on labour administrations.

On the basis of specific examples studied, Chapter 2 goes to the heart of the process: the management, organization, and internal functioning of labour administration. For example, if there is no clear policy and no proper internal management, the training of field personnel will not yield visible and durable results. Traditional thinking along the lines of "Labour inspectors don't do a good job, so let's train them and things will get better" has been shown to be inadequate. The repeated failures of this type of "solution" make it important to discuss internal operations (i.e. strategy, policies, aims, management of internal human resources, management, leadership, and so on), not in order to proffer a universal solution, but to identify the issues that need close and high-priority attention.

Chapter 3 examines a long and arduous process: the management of change. All leaders of labour administrations aspire to make their organizations more effective and useful. To this end, the chapter puts forward a few subjects for reflection and discusses several of the methods used in various organizations. However, these proposals can be used only once it has been recognized that the initial situation must be assessed so as to compare it to the desired end result, and so long as a realistic approach in terms of timing and content is followed.

Although it can be used by interested labour administrations, this approach to modernization may, for a host of reasons, require external support.

Part II of the study examines the "good practices" that we hope will fuel an exchange of ideas between labour administrations, allowing each to provide information about its initiatives or aspects of its practices, to benefit from the experience of others, and to enter into contact with those responsible for practices that might be relevant in their own countries.

Once again, we must stress that the present study does not seek to provide recipes or to decree what must be done. It is aimed at managers who want to make their labour administrations actors in development, that is, a source of initiatives geared to national priorities and characteristics. We emphasize this objective because we believe it is essential for putting labour administrations on the right track.

The majority of labour administrations were established to deal with the most serious social problems (child labour, life-threatening conditions in factories, etc.), and they must continue to play this essential protective role in occupational health and safety, and in industrial relations more generally. But they have also frequently demonstrated, in all of these areas, a capacity to anticipate and to avert problems that are costly in human, social and economic terms.

Labour administrations are instruments of growth in many developed countries, even though they are not always perceived as such. They have a hand in formulating and applying stable, clear, and accepted legal rules because of their aptitude for dialogue with the social partners. This is also a necessary condition for encouraging domestic and foreign investment. They prepare and implement policies of intervention in the best conditions, thereby creating elements of security that are useful to all.

Labour administrations make labour markets more transparent and fluid by means of employment services that are increasingly able to respond to the needs of firms and workers. They encourage the adjustment of vocational training systems and are sometimes able to anticipate trends, thus helping to match workers' skills and employers' needs in a timely manner. They contribute to the modernization of industrial relations by encouraging a constructive social dialogue, particularly by putting in place the conditions needed to foster the growth of social actors that are active and representative of workers and employers.

Finally, we should add that, as a result of the functions noted above, labour administrations play an indispensable role in consolidating democratic relations within a country.

Much remains to be done, but it is especially in developing, transition or newly industrializing countries that this dimension of labour administration as an actor in development can take on its full meaning and contribute to the reconstruction (and sometimes the construction) of a system in which governments will find it in their interest to invest because it is clearly useful to their projects and supported by the social partners.

Notes

[1] ILO: Labour Administration Convention, 1978 (No. 150); Labour Administration Recommendation, 1978 (No. 158), in *International labour Conventions and Recommendations 1919-1995*, Vol. 3 (Geneva, 1996), pp. 35-51.

[2] idem: *Labour administration: Role, functions and organisation*, Report V(1), International Labour Conference, 61st Session, Geneva, 1976, pp. 5-6.

[3] idem: *Labour administration*, Report III (Part 1B), International Labour Conference, 85th Session, Geneva, 1997.

[4] idem: *Labour administration: Role, functions and organisation*, op. cit., p. 158.

Part I

A state of upheaval

1

The context in which public administrations operate has changed immensely over the last few decades because of technological, economic and political developments, as well as the globalization of trade, forcing public administrations to review their role, organization and operational methods.

Labour administrations have not been exempt from this trend. It has actually often given them new justification for their existence and development, and has helped some of them play a more dynamic role once again. In fact, since labour administrations were created in response to changing expectations, they may actively contribute to national development by tackling the problems that hinder it. Some of them, however, seem to have lost their influence and their raison d'être and need to rediscover, notably by means of tripartism, ways of redefining an intervention strategy and an organization that will enable them to fulfil their mission.

To meet the new challenges, all labour administrations have a common conceptual framework at their disposal, one that is formed by international standards yet respects their diversity.

1.1 Some major developments

The twentieth century, which began with a spiral of change set in motion by the Industrial Revolution, has been marked by all kinds of upheaval. In addition to two world wars that have remodelled the way in which different groups of people interact, most countries throughout the world have witnessed changes in their political, economic and even moral systems, notably with the collapse of traditional constraints which, in some instances, have not been replaced by other values. In certain cases the transformation has been reasonably smooth, thanks to the adaptability of individuals and institutions, but it has been more difficult in others, especially when accompanied by revolutions, economic collapse and national strikes. The one constant has been change, which has accelerated over the last 20 to 30 years.

The question is no longer simply one of the development or adaptation of economies, but of a significant transformation or mutation of societies, that is to say, a more far-reaching and marked movement for the future. These changes go by the names of globalization, new technologies, new forms and new organization of labour, deregulation (removal of tariff barriers, decentralization), opening up of markets (unrestrained competition), political and trade union pluralism, free enterprise economy, new public management and governance. They affect workers and firms alike. They also impose continuous adjustment and increased flexibility on institutions, particularly those operating in the field of labour administration.

In short, this is the challenge faced by labour administrations. They must act both as a safety net for workers and firms (by implementing regulations and means of protection in labour matters) and as an instrument of progress that supports workers and firms in their development and initiates appropriate changes. Their role as a safety net originated in the late nineteenth century, when the State first took steps to regulate labour issues. "Governments began to enact legislation regulating the employment of women and children, reducing hours of work, helping the poor and needy, granting subsidies to the earliest forms of private social assistance, aiding the unemployed."[1] This form of regulation was then enriched by activities in areas such as vocational training and active employment measures, so that today the State is undeniably involved in development.

This study does not aim to analyse all these developments which test the adaptability of the different actors in society,[2] but to consider those observed notably within the immediate or more remote environment of labour administrations, those that have direct consequences on these administrations, their client groups, their approach to problems, their activities and the way in which they operate.

1.1.1 Economic and technological developments

1.1.1.1 Workforce distribution

Economic activity has changed significantly since the nineteenth century, when it was concentrated mainly in the agricultural sector. The early twentieth century was marked by a shift towards the manufacturing sector as the result of industrialization and the necessity of meeting basic needs in developed countries, bringing about more and more pronounced urbanization. The subsequent development of new technologies and means of communication, improved means of production and new forms of labour contributed to the emergence of new activities and attracted a large part of the workforce towards the services sector.

This concentration of activities in the services sector has been noted throughout the world, but it has progressed much more slowly on the African continent, as shown by the comparative data in table 1.1. Between 1980 and 1997, activities in the agricultural sector fell by 6 per cent in Africa, and by as much as 13 per cent in the Americas. A large part of this activity was transferred to the services sector, with a rise of 5 per cent in Africa and as much as 15 per cent in Europe. The industrial sector remained relatively stable, except

Table 1.1.   Workforce distribution by region and sector, 1980-97 (%)

Region	Agriculture		Industry		Services	
	1980	1997	1980	1997	1980	1997
Africa	76	70	8	9	16	21
Americas	33	20	23	23	44	57
Asia	47	35	20	22	33	43
Europe	20	10	37	32	43	58

Note: In "G7" countries, over the 1970-94 period jobs in the services sector as an average percentage of total civilian employment (which is understood to cover all non-military occupations) increased from 49.4 to 66.6 per cent (OECD, *Statistics Directorate: Services–Statistics on value added and employment*, Summary tables 1 and 11 (Paris, 1996)).
Source: ILO: *World Employment Report 1998-99: Employability in the global economy – How training matters* (Geneva, 1998), Statistical annex, pp. 221-224.

in Europe, where it fell by 5 per cent. Movement towards the services sector, in Africa especially, is partly linked to the growing incidence of work performed outside any regulatory framework providing workers with social protection, either immediate (illness, maternity, accident at work) or deferred (retirement). This type of work is generally described by the terms "clandestine labour" or "informal work".

Since the 1970s, the structure of this predominant tertiary sector has been marked in particular by new atypical forms of employment and an increase in the number of small and medium-sized enterprises (SMEs).[3] In the countries of the Organisation for Economic Co-operation and Development (OECD), SMEs "account for almost 95 per cent of all enterprises, for between 60 and 70 per cent of employment, and for between 30 per cent and 70 per cent of total output".[4] These enterprises appear as a flexible and efficient means of production and partly explain the development of the "informal sector" in developing countries, in particular throughout Africa, where employment in this sector accounts for over 60 per cent of total urban employment.[5] In the countries for which statistical data are available, including African countries, these figures are 57 per cent in Bolivia and Madagascar, 56 per cent in the United Republic of Tanzania, 53 per cent in Colombia, 48 per cent in Thailand and 46 per cent in Venezuela.[6] The informal sector (see section 1.3.2.2 below) in 13 Latin American countries – Argentina, Bolivia, Brazil, Chile, Colombia, Costa Rica, Ecuador, Mexico, Panama, Paraguay, Peru, Uruguay and Venezuela – employs an ever-increasing share of the non-agricultural workforce. Between 1990 and 1996 the average increase was 5 per cent in more than half of these countries (from 1 per cent in Chile to as much as 8.9 per cent in Venezuela).[7]

In addition to this move of a significant proportion of the workforce from one sector to another, the authors of the ILO's *World Employment Report 1998-99* noted a new distribution of tasks within each sector of activity. The mechanization of basic activities in industry in particular and the computerization of production processes have led to a specialization of tasks and a fall in the demand for less-skilled personnel. According to the OECD, "[a] major characteristic of the transition towards a knowledge-based economy is that output is growing fastest in the manufacturing and service sectors that develop and use technology most intensively and have the highest skill requirements".[8] Production becomes more efficient, thereby reducing the need for less-skilled work, and new products and services are developed in order to meet or even create better targeted demand. Even in the services sector this phenomenon is noticeable and is sometimes striking: in the insurance industry, for example, staff reductions can reach as much as 40 per cent.[9]

The characteristics of the workforce and of firms have thus changed significantly. They now require the involvement and intervention of labour administration in sectors that were hitherto non-existent or ignored, such as the informal sector or clandestine labour (see Part II, Peru, Senegal, Argentina, etc.).

1.1.1.2 New products and services

One of the features of recent economic and technological development is the *arrival en masse of new products and services on the market,* partly as the result of investment in research and development. In OECD countries this type of investment was substantial during the 1980s; it has since stabilized and in certain cases even fallen. Some studies show that in industry applied research is supplanting basic research, the main aim being the creation and development of products. Furthermore, the passage from traditional and more stable sectors of production to the services sector which, as already mentioned, is evolving more rapidly and demands ever-shorter research time "may suggest a more applied focus, but may also be a sign of greater efficiency".[10] Research and development now centres on new technologies, information and communication, health and life sciences (biotechnology, genetic studies, combinatorial chemistry), robotics, the development of new materials, the application of biotechnology to the environment, new sources of energy and so on, all of which focus on the creation of new products and services.

A second factor conducive to the arrival of new products and services is the introduction of new information technologies to assist the production-consumption chain for the packaged consumer goods sector. It has resulted in enormous gains through a better knowledge of the markets, assisted production, product management (bar codes) and reduction of stock (tight flow), which often obviate the need for intermediaries. In addition to profit made by firms, consumers have also benefited from a much wider range of products: for example, the number of items per supermarket in the United States rose from 2,200 in 1950 to 29,000 in 1995.[11]

Finally, *the new forms of labour and the number of working hours, the entry of vast numbers of women into the labour market*[12] and *higher life expectancy* have also increased demand for new products and services, particularly for products directly or indirectly connected with the leisure industry in developed countries.

All these changes in demand and supply entail changes in the organization of the market and of production processes, forcing the workforce to adapt and labour administrations to diversify their activities in order to respond to these new needs. This is the case, for example, in the United States and China in the field of employment, and in Hungary with regard to collective bargaining (see Chapter 2, section 2.2.2.2).

1.1.1.3 Development of computer technology

New technologies promote globalization in particular by accelerating communications; by giving rise to increasingly fierce competition, globalization, in turn, prompts economic actors to invest in new technologies in order to preserve their markets or conquer new ones. These new information technologies (IT) modify and improve production processes (product quantity, quality and cost), change work and enterprise organization, relations with clients, worldwide distribution of economic activity and, consequently, the way in which labour administrations operate (see Chapter 3 and Part II). To meet new expectations, labour administration must bring its organization, equipment and means of communication into line with those of its users.

The OECD notes that "the world IT market (hardware, software, and computer services) grew at an annual rate of 10 per cent between 1987 and 1995 – nearly twice that of world GDP".[13] In 1994, IT accounted for 11 per cent of international trade, compared with less than 4 per cent in 1980.

The production of computer goods has increased considerably over the last few years and prices have fallen, but the acquisition of this material by individuals and institutions is reserved for minorities, even if these are becoming increasingly large. In seven OECD countries by the mid-1990s a quarter of households or more had a computer.[14] In certain countries the penetration rate of computers in schools has been particularly positive. In the United States, for instance, the proportion of pupils having access to a computer at school rose from 28 per cent in 1984 to 60 per cent in 1993. Similarly, the number of pupils per computer fell between 1992 and 1996 from 25 to 12 in Denmark and from 42 to 28 in Finland. In developing countries, however, new technologies are being introduced in education more slowly, keeping them at a disadvantage in relation to other parts of the world. Indeed, according to the United Nations Educational, Scientific and Cultural Organization (UNESCO), these countries experience specific problems, namely: "(a) impact on culture, (b) impact on communities, (c) authority and control, (d) creation of school programmes and access, (e) type of school, (f) competence of the teacher and (g) equity and social justice".[15]

Although the large-scale development of powerful equipment offers an undeniable advantage to economies and to firms in particular, it is the development of interconnections and networks which over the last few years has greatly speeded up the progress made in the business and knowledge spheres. "As the word 'Internet' becomes a common part of our vocabulary, it is a clear indication that OECD economies are well into the third stage of computing:

network computing". [16] In some countries the networks are so sophisticated as to provide users with direct access to various labour administration services, as is the case with employment services in the United States (see Part II). An illustration of this may be found on the ILO website, which provides a list of servers of national labour administrations (ADMITRA-ATLAS). Powerful networks also make it possible to cut labour costs by decentralizing activities like management data processing (accounting) or even the administrative management of personnel, thereby accelerating globalization and offering countries in which labour is less expensive the opportunity to engage in new economic activities. Less-developed countries may also envisage possible integration into global markets, as has been the case in the past few years for India and some South-East Asian countries.

1.1.1.4 Rising levels of education

The transformation of societies and the reorganization of their institutions are also the result of higher levels of education and training of individuals. Political liberalization, democratization, access to new jobs, the mobility of individuals, technological progress, the boom in creativity – these are all direct or indirect consequences of investment in education and training within a country. While it admittedly aims to meet the needs of firms, this investment is also directed at improving the quality of life of the individuals that make up these societies.

In order to remain competitive or to expand, firms need qualified personnel; countries wishing to strengthen their economic activities and attract new firms must therefore develop their education and training systems to produce a more and more qualified workforce. The level of qualification and labour costs are two reasons often cited for choosing the location of a new firm or for relocating to another country. It is therefore necessary to regularly update data concerning the demand for and the supply of personnel and notably their current and future training needs (see Part II, France and the United States respectively). Nevertheless, trying to strike the right balance between supply and demand does not always produce the expected results; there have been attempts to use other methods (analysis of occupations and competencies, projected labour requirements), notably on account of the time lag between the time when needs become apparent and the actual response provided by teaching and training institutions. This shows the importance of projecting requirements over a longer period (see Part II, United States).

Demand for qualified personnel has evolved in recent years. As already noted, in both developed and developing countries there has been a marked rise in demand in the services sector, due to the latter's expansion over the past few years. Employment in this sector is also marked by sharp contrast between activities requiring a high degree of knowledge and information, and those that are labour-intensive and poorly paid. [17] The former are to be found for example in banks, insurance companies and, up to a point, in transport and communications. However, the most significant advance in developed countries, and to a lesser extent in developing countries, has taken place in the scientific, technical and liberal professions. From 1981 to 1996,[18] for example, rises exceeding 5 per cent were noted in Canada, Spain, Brazil, the Republic of Korea, Thailand, Pakistan and Malaysia.

Education and training were a governmental priority in several countries during the 1960s and 1970s, and it is undeniable that they drained a considerable proportion of those countries' gross domestic product (GDP).[19] Already in 1970, at least eight OECD countries were devoting over 4.5 per cent of their GDP to education. Since then the growth has stopped, however; according to the OECD, "[o]verall, as a proportion of GDP, public educational expenditure roughly held its ground, but the data suggest a convergence of public educational expenditure among OECD countries".[20]

The general level of education has therefore improved and there has been a "large increase over the past thirty years in the numbers completing various levels of education beyond compulsory schooling [and] a narrowing of country differences".[21] The rate of success in secondary schools rose on average from 54 per cent in the 1960s to 69 per cent in the 1980s, while the proportion of university graduates increased from 19 to 23 per cent over the same period.

In non-OECD countries the level of instruction, although lower than in OECD member States, has also improved over the last few years. Between 1960 and 1994 the average duration of schooling[22] for OECD countries increased from 7.3 to 9.8 years. For the same period, in certain Asian countries it soared from 2.7 to 7.5 years.

A good level of basic training is, however, no longer enough. Constant change requires individuals to continually update their skills and sometimes even to make major career changes. Education systems must adapt to these new needs and bring education, apprenticeship and continuous training programmes into line with demands at the international level. This means that the problem of matching demand and supply must be approached somewhat differently. Indeed, many countries already take account of the concept of lifelong learning when drawing up their education and training policies.[23] But who is better suited to tackle the ever-growing needs for vocational training – labour administrations or education ministries? The question is not clear-cut and arises especially in countries where vocational training programmes do not take sufficient account of the needs of the labour market, an area normally controlled by labour administrations.

The new needs of the economy as well as new users, who are better trained and demand better quality of service, force labour administrations to continually reassess themselves by regularly evaluating their services (see Part II, Canada (Province of Quebec), France, United Kingdom, and Chapter 2, section 2.8) and making the necessary adjustments.

1.1.2 Globalization

The term globalization "refers to the transborder operations undertaken by firms to organise their development, production, sourcing, marketing and financing activities".[24] This generic term is used primarily in connection with the phenomenon of business dealings between firms from different countries. One could also talk about "globalizations" in the plural, first because each field of activity has its own method of functioning, even if this is strongly influenced by external factors, and second because globalization affects not only firms, but also people and societies – it has an effect on the way people think and on their relations with others, as well as on nations' relations, especially political and economic, with their neighbours. In order to better understand the impact of this phenomenon on labour administrations, we will group some of these "globalizations" into three categories: those affecting trade and activities of enterprises, those concerning information, and those relating to the regulations (adjustments, conformities) that societies impose on themselves.

1.1.2.1 The economy

In national economies, decisions concerning the ownership of capital and means of production fall less and less under the direct influence of States since they are often taken outside state territory or by bodies which obey their own mechanisms. They therefore have unforeseeable consequences on economic activity and repercussions that labour administrations must deal with urgently, as in the case of industrial redeployments (see Part II, Austria, China). They also create insecurity, to which governments must respond by introducing reforms in order to offset their social consequences, such as unemployment, as during the recent crisis in Asia.

Capital

The closer links and interaction between economies and markets are two important points to be borne in mind where globalization is concerned. With the return to the global economy of transition countries (this expression is generally understood to mean countries with a centralized economy which have recently chosen the market economy system), notably in the loan and bond markets, financial integration is being achieved. According to the OECD, "the increasing integration of the international financial system is evident in the rapid expansion of foreign exchange markets".[25] This partly explains the influences and the domino effect of one system on another. Financial crises affecting a country or a continent (Mexico, 1995; Asia, 1997) are examples of interaction or integration between economies that can stop or slow down economic recovery and the development of the labour market in other countries or indeed the world over.

In addition to the integration of financial markets, attention must be drawn to the rapidity of trade, due to more sophisticated means of communication and to its growing volume. The annual growth rate of global trade between 1980 and 1997 (in inflation-adjusted dollars), for example, increased from 4.4 per cent on average between 1980 and 1989 to 9.4 per cent in 1997, while the annual net flow of private capital into developing countries increased from 16.2 billion dollars between 1984 and 1989 to 139.3 billion dollars in 1997.[26] According to a report published by the United Nations Conference for Trade and Development (UNCTAD), developing countries accounted for nearly one-third of the global inward foreign direct investment (FDI) stock in 1997, up from one-fifth in 1990.[27]

Certainly, there have been other financial crises during the course of the twentieth century. However, owing to the new factors mentioned previously, contemporary financial upheavals have such a profound impact that they could paralyse democratic political power in certain countries. As stated in a recent ILO paper, "it appears to many workers that these trends have enabled capital markets to capture control of the political process and their demands now drive the decision making process. Governments, regardless of their political persuasion, appear increasingly powerless to take decisions on economic or social policy".[28]

Production and distribution

Among the visible and sometimes spectacular globalizing activities of the late 1990s, we can cite numerous mergers and acquisitions between competitors or in firms upstream or downstream of their activities. These decisions are taken primarily in order to help create synergies in research and production, provide access to (foreign) markets protected by protectionist regulations, and allow firms to streamline their activities and reduce costs, in particular labour costs, sometimes by relocating certain activities. All countries are affected, either directly or indirectly, as are all sectors of economic activity: services (banks, insurance, civil aviation), research (chemistry, pharmacology), production (automobile industry), distribution (petrol), and so on.

Such concentrations of activities may, however, be considered "abusive" when they tend to become monopolistic, prompting action by consumer protection bodies and restrictive procedures by the anti-trust authorities, when the latter have the power and the means to act in order to curb monopolies' negative effects.

1.1.2.2 Information

Improved communications make for much faster circulation of information and ideas, and this facilitates exchanges. The rate of progress is unequal, however, since access to information sources is also unequal. It has been said that the world is turning into a global village. The Internet, for instance, which allows computer owners, or the increasing number of people having access to a public terminal (see section 1.1.1.3 above) to communicate with other people throughout the world, opens up almost unlimited possibilities for exchanging information. According to the OECD, the number of Internet users has been growing exponentially over the last 15 years,[29] from 213 users in 1983 to more than 16.1 million in January 1997; at that rate, it was set to pass the 1 billion mark by the year 2000. Looking at the breakdown by type of user, between 1991 and July 1996 significant increases can be noted in the field of commercial applications, followed, in descending order, by universities and scientific applications, households, and so on. By contrast, there has been little change in the number of governmental services with their own Internet site. The establishment of computer networks is making it possible to bring together enormous amounts of stored data and, at least in theory, to access it from anywhere in the world: for example, online databases are available, more and more electronic library projects are being developed, and so on.

It thus becomes possible to engage in comparisons of approaches, methods, processes, products and services. Just like the new demands by clients, consumers and users for products and services that meet their expectations – including those provided by labour administrations – such comparisons help to put administrations under scrutiny and stimulate the search for new solutions.

1.1.2.3 Regulations

Action – or inaction – by governments when it comes to monitoring economic activities on their territory sometimes has such an impact on their immediate neighbours, or even on the world as a whole, that in some pressing cases it has become necessary to establish a set of common rules. In the context of globalization, a laissez-faire approach leads to abuses, in particular with regard to competition, the environment and human rights.

Numerous States have therefore felt the need to join forces, firstly to establish a dialogue and then to conclude agreements on matters of common interest. The number of regional groupings has multiplied over the last few decades, whereas the creation of international organizations has been staggered throughout the twentieth century.

At the regional level

Over the past three decades, in all parts of the world numerous countries have joined forces for economic, political or other reasons. Although their degree of involvement in a common regional project varies from case to case, it demonstrates a real desire on the part of such countries to act in order to protect and/or develop the communities that they cover. They have developed supranational arrangements that lead them, in certain cases, to define common rules, implement common policies, create permanent exchanges and increase cooperation, thus transcending certain hitherto sacrosanct national competencies such as currency, immigration, transport, the environment, consumer goods regulations, and labour. Even if they do not necessarily lead to identical national legislation, these rules streamline approaches and eliminate causes of conflict between neighbours. They bring order to the factors of unrestrained competition. Finally, they offer larger and more homogeneous markets to foreign investors. An UNCTAD report points out that membership in regional integration groupings is among policy factors that can have a direct influence on FDI. [30]

Regional groupings may be found in all parts of the globe:

— In *Europe*, the European Union (EU) currently includes 15 countries, with at least ten other applicant countries wishing to join. Its strong points include the stability pact for controlling public deficits, the strengthening and consolidation of the convergence criteria fixed by the Maastricht Treaty concerning inflation, borrowing and debt, the creation of a European Central Bank and agreement on a single currency. Outside the EU framework, European countries are working to ensure that new legislation, in particular labour legislation, conforms to the European Economic Area (EEA) agreements (see Part II, Austria).

— In *Asia*, the Asia-Pacific Economic Cooperation Council (APEC) comprises more than 20 members and, in 1998, accounted for more than 55 per cent of global GDP. One of its priorities is the establishment of a free-trade area. However, for the time being at least, its achievements have been few. The Association of Southeast Asian Nations (ASEAN), for its part, aims to promote economic, commercial, scientific and political cooperation between its (currently ten) member countries.

— In *North America*, the North American Free Trade Agreement (NAFTA) brings together Canada, the United States and Mexico in a free-trade area.

— In *Latin America*, the Southern Common Market (MERCOSUR) groups four countries (Argentina, Brazil, Paraguay and Uruguay) aiming to operate as a real common market by the year 2000; the founding agreement has been completed by a declaration on social and labour issues.

— In *Africa*, the Organization of African Unity (OAU) comprises 53 independent States whose goal is to strengthen regional unity, solidarity and stability. Economic objectives are pursued by various other groupings of different sizes, such as the West African Economic and Monetary Union (WAEMU) and the African Development Bank (ADB).

— In *Eastern Europe*, following the end of the Second World War, the Soviet bloc countries sought economic integration in parallel with their political unity, setting up in 1956 the Council for Mutual Economic Assistance, commonly known as Comecon. This supranational body, which comprised the Soviet Union and most Eastern European countries, had jurisdiction over economic matters and was charged with coordinating the planning of national economies by allocating production and trade; however, it was not able to withstand the global change initiated in these countries in the late 1980s.

Certain countries belong to several bodies and therefore participate in discussions that affect huge numbers of individuals and volumes of trade. Cooperation agreements have been concluded between certain groups and integration is even envisaged, as in the case of a possible free-trade area of the Americas.

At the international level

Over the course of the twentieth century, various international organizations have been created for different reasons and with different aims, ranging from simple meeting forums to organizations regulating political, economic and social affairs.

Some of these organizations are of primarily political import. The first to appear on the world scene, following the First World War, was the League of Nations. In the aftermath of the Second World War it became the United Nations, which now groups almost all the countries of the world in pursuit of the organization's mandate of promoting justice, peace, freedom and human rights. The United Nations system includes more than 35 specialized agencies that have been set up over the years. One of them is the International Labour Organization (ILO), which was actually created in 1919 under the Treaty of Versailles. Its mission is to promote social justice and, in particular, to ensure that human rights are respected in the field of labour. United Nations agencies have different functions and cover sectors of activity as diverse as health, education, labour, standardization, meteorology, and so on. Some of them play a significant economic role, such as the World Trade Organization (WTO), or the World Intellectual Property Organization (WIPO), which ensures patent protection (the magnitude of infringement problems in the trading of luxury goods, for example, demonstrates the importance of the establishment of international regulations in this field).

Other organizations have jurisdiction over monetary activities and have become increasingly important over the years. At the end of the Second World War, the Bretton Woods agreements (1944) provided for the creation of the International Monetary Fund (IMF), the World Bank, at the time also called the International Bank for Reconstruction and Development (IBRD), and the International Trade Organization (ITO). The IMF, which now has over 180 members, worked to defend the international monetary system, and the IBRD devoted itself to post-war reconstruction. The World Bank now comprises several agencies, including the IBRD and the International Development Association (IDA), which covers developing countries. Intervention by the World Bank and the IMF is not limited simply to providing economic assistance, because aid and aid programmes are subject to preconditions that tend to mould the organizations or systems affected. They thus play a more positive role in some cases than in others, depending on their repercussions on social protection in the context of globalization.

There is also international trade. The WTO – the successor to the General Agreement on Tariffs and Trade (GATT), a temporary agreement originating from the Bretton Woods agreements – is an international body charged with applying global regulations that govern trade between countries. Its main function is to encourage as much as possible the smooth functioning, predictability, fairness and free trade of goods and services. Today it has 136 members and serves as a forum for negotiating international agreements on trade, settles trade disputes between countries, and provides support to its members and developing countries in general to help them establish a national trade policy.

Since they are dependent on economic and technological developments and on globalization trends, public administrations will continue – just as they have in the past – to be buffeted by change: there are new technologies, new needs and new user demands, the harmonization of regulations, upheavals in the financial markets and oil crises which over the past few decades have led to shortages of some resources and affected national economies, notably as regards public expenditure. In many countries economic downturns and falling tax revenues have led to cutbacks in public expenditure. Questions concerning state intervention and the obligation to produce results have affected staffing levels in particular. In order to maintain and/or improve the services provided to users, numerous administrations have attempted, often as a result of comparisons made with foreign administrations, to modernize, notably by making greater use of IT. The degree of success of these experiments differs in each case, depending on whether the changes introduced were accompanied by a reorganization of services and a change in attitude towards users. In the case of IT, however, they have generally led to improved services by stimulating local IT markets and boosting economic activity and, above all, allowed cost reductions to be made. According to the OECD, "recent evidence suggests that, in the longer run, government investments in IT result in significant increases in productivity and reduced labour costs".[31] Public administrations too have been profoundly affected by globalization.

1.1.3. Political changes

The fall of the Berlin Wall and the dissolution of the communist bloc in the late twentieth century signalled the end of polarization in international politics; most of the world's countries rallied round similar ideas on forms of government, freedom of expression and individual action. Although in many countries it was not achieved easily, this new openness favours the advent of globalization in its many forms.

1.1.3.1 Parliamentary democracy and trade union pluralism

The break-up of single-party regimes in recent years has favoured the expansion of the free-market economy and trade globalization. The spread of information has contributed to the development of democracy in these countries, notably as a result of the penetration and impact of means of communication and improved access to information.

Progress has been uneven, however. Establishing governmental institutions that combine different political tendencies, creating bodies where partners are consulted in order to reach more consensual agreement, taking into account the opposition between employers and trade unions, both of which are subject to pluralistic pressures – all these factors disrupt systems in place. Moreover, indiscriminate adoption of foreign models or hasty implementation of changes are dangerous and in certain cases have impeded progress. The new democracies that appear to have obtained the best results are those that were able to use the strengths within their society and involve all the parties in reaching a consensus on a system based on their resources, their specific features (cultural, religious, etc.) and their needs.

1.1.3.2 Market economy and privatization of production

Countries which have embraced representative democracy have also opted for the free-market economy system. Those which have kept a single-party political regime have adjusted their systems by becoming more market-economy oriented and abandoning a totally state-run system. These choices have resulted in major disruptions to domestic systems of production since the arrival of competition has dealt a fatal blow to firms that are inefficient, outdated, overstaffed and ill-equipped. Comecon, for instance, provided for distribution of markets among its members; its dissolution has opened up these countries to external markets, which operate in a highly competitive environment.

In market economy countries there has also been a significant wave of privatizations of state-run enterprises so as to disengage the State from non-profitable activities. This has had an effect on employment, though not a major one, since these firms are usually not the main drivers of the economy.

One of the results of redirecting state-run economies has been the redefinition of the roles of the different actors.[32] In the state-run system, the roles of the government, employers and trade unions were blurred, leading to numerous irregularities. Now the head of a firm is generally the owner or the owner's representative (and no longer the government), the trade union is a democratic organization devoted to defending employee interests and not the party organ, and labour administration no longer falls under the "authority" (proprietary or political) of either of the two other actors. This makes it possible to restore labour inspection services that fulfil their role in accordance with international standards.[33]

The fact that nearly all ex-communist, or so-called transition countries have opted for market economy systems has led to major changes in education and training structures. These must now respond to the needs of the market and no longer to the demands of mandatory-type plans that pursued other aims.

The decision to switch to a free-market economy entails major transformations, particularly in the organization of the market and methods of production, but also requires the ability to change behaviour quickly. This is no doubt the most difficult obstacle to surmount, but global integration depends on it. Finally, economic integration must be accompanied by social integration of which the States, and labour administrations in particular, will remain the guarantors. Otherwise, the risk of social break-up will become increasingly likely.

1.1.4 Towards a single model?

The preceding pages described major economic and political changes witnessed recently throughout the world. However, we must be cautious in interpreting these changes and refrain from conceiving them in a deterministic or a univocal fashion. Indeed, although the various elements mentioned (new distribution of the workforce, new products and services, the development of computer technology, rising levels of education) are general enough to be followed by all countries, this in no way implies uniformity or the existence of a single model. The paradox of globalization is that it will affect all countries, but that it will do so without robbing them of their identities. The forms of access to globalization will undoubtedly be varied, as well they must be, or people would be likely to reject a model that threatened to take away their very raison d'être and their definition of themselves.

This is where interpretations vary. According to some, we are moving towards a new model of domination that can be seen at work in the modes of corporate governance and new management techniques. In their view, the changes in management that have been observed in recent years suggest a restriction of the freedom of actors in their individual and collective actions. It is increasingly difficult to understand the operation of contemporary enterprises without considering global structures and the mechanisms of the global market, including financial markets. Within the firm, the revival of shareholder influence radically limits, when it does not completely suppress, the managers' room for manoeuvre. The number of actors, their diversity and degree of autonomy are all decreasing. All management techniques (total quality management, re-engineering, resource planning, project management, etc.) seem to point to the emergence of a model of organizational governance based on universal domination.

This point of view is controversial. Although the authors of the present study do not deny either the existence of these techniques or the power of shareholders, they reject this interpretation because of its radical character, considering that it strips firms (and hence local actors, too) of their autonomy. There is little doubt that control within organizations has changed, but this neither suppresses cultures nor forces them into the same mould. Most studies on managerial techniques and their normative aspect tend to show that these tools are not used in one way only and that their results vary across cultures and firms. These studies demonstrate that there is no exclusive reading of new constraints. The latter are quite widespread, but they do not lead to a convergence of behaviours and do not provide proof of the universality of the rational model underpinning these techniques. Universality and constraint are issues that are raised when they are held to be inevitable. Although they undoubtedly have a powerful cohesive and constraining effect, management tools do not prevent actors from interpreting them or from fashioning compromises that give each firm and each national model a specific form.

Guided by its definition and its relationship to economic and managerial constraints, we can see that culture is a symbolic construction of practice. For Marshall Sahlins, for example, the distinctive quality of human beings is the fact that they live according to a schema of meaning that they themselves have forged, and this makes them unique.[34] All constraints are interpreted on the basis of this schema, which is therefore variable. Particular symbolic schemata give meaning to constraints and transform their effects. Economic or management laws are not independent, natural laws; they will be applied in ways that depend on the meaning given to existence or to the world, which is the definition of culture.

According to Alain Touraine, a culture is defined as the combination of techniques for using natural resources, modes of integration into a collectivity, and references to a conception of the subject.[35] Actors therefore always respond to historical circumstances, in terms of production constraints, in relation to the human group, and at the same time with reference to the universe of symbols and values.

The thesis of uniformity should therefore be rejected. With regard to corporate modernization, there is nothing to indicate that globalization and changing models of management will lead to the disappearance of local interpretations which modify and adapt those techniques to particular societies. The techniques will be adjusted and will be accepted only if they do not pose a threat to the constitutive elements of particular cultures.

Cultures are forged within ethnic groups, and therefore within national cultures that are rooted in the world of symbols and myths. This is also the context for professionalization, crafts and industrial sectors. The human group that comprises the firm produces sense and meaning that are expressed through and interact with this universe of symbols. This universe structures the "practices" of actors, to borrow a concept used by Anthony Giddens,[36] in the sense that their actions are structured by constraints of a symbolic order. Action is always linked to this universe of myths and symbols. The only way to understand the interaction between globalization and corporate modernization is to take this universe into account and to acknowledge its place in the world of the firm.

Globalization therefore puts national identities and cultures into question, even though it will only be accepted in so far as the essential elements of those identities and cultures are safeguarded. This is undoubtedly the biggest challenge of globalization today. Is it possible to remain oneself and still take part in the global marketplace? In other words, the techniques of globalization are always adapted to local cultures, and this adaptation is the most daunting challenge of the twenty-first century. Countries should find a way to participate in the technical world while simultaneously affirming their unique cultural heritage and personality. This is the meaning that should be given to the protests being waged in the name of respect for identities and cultures and against the operation of major international corporations.

What appears particularly unsettling about globalization is the accelerated pace of change, what Giddens[37] calls the reflexivity of modern social life, the fact that social practices are being constantly scrutinized and overhauled. Social practices have always been subject to modification, but in recent years change has become more radical. This constant revision is undoubtedly the factor that best defines modernity. It is not a matter of embracing novelty for its own sake, but rather a presumption of systematic reflexivity. Corporate modernization and the place occupied by management techniques are products of this phenomenon. It is important to be aware of this before launching reforms, whether of States, enterprises, or labour administrations.

This book analyses the evolution of labour administrations and proposes orientations and possibilities for reform. These proposals can only be understood and are only meaningful in terms of the perspectives outlined above. A deterministic view of change must be rejected, for the general direction of change does not determine the particular changes that take place in each country and each culture. Change has to be introduced cautiously, taking national cultures into account and being attentive to the upheavals that globalization brings in its wake, even if it does not dictate behaviour.

Although we consider labour administration as a factor in development, we are aware that it is not the only one and that its role as an agent of development is frequently contested. Without wishing to stir up a controversy, our starting point will be the assertion that those involved in labour administrations must realize that their role is not simply to apply directives aimed at protecting workers, but that they must also be agents of economic and social development. The two roles go hand in hand.

1.2. New operating conditions for public administration

The major developments described above affect all sectors of human activity. Thus they also influence the way in which these sectors are structured by States. As a result, public administrations, including labour administrations, are confronted with new operating conditions leading to extensive changes. These are sometimes wanted, but are most often imposed, as for example in China, Poland and Hungary (see Part II).

1.2.1 A new framework

The framework of state activity has changed significantly in many countries. Wide disparities undoubtedly exist, precluding sweeping generalizations. Nevertheless, the last 20 years appear to have produced a common orientation towards a State that is closer to its people and is more useful, but is also less generous with public funds (a "leaner, trimmer" State).

As indicated by the World Bank in a 1997 report,[38] government officials have thus been forced to take account of new demands when defining their activities, at the same time as democracy was being strengthened.

This development has, however, also taken place in States where democratic institutions are wanting. Economic globalization makes it necessary to adapt political structures to the new world order, despite resistance by leaders. Its scale is nevertheless limited by the persistence or resurgence of regional or internal conflicts that prevent any improvement in the state civil system.

1.2.1.1 The revamped role of the State

Re-engineering the role of the State, a traditional question of political philosophy from the late nineteenth and early twentieth century, has once again come to the fore, although this time in somewhat different terms.

This long-standing and heated debate over the functions of the State and its place in economic thought reveals differing approaches taken by the State in social matters in Europe and the United States.

There are four conflicting points of view that can be summarily presented as follows:

(a) *Traditional thinking is built around the concept that the State must be neutral* and should serve general interests, as understood by Jean-Jacques Rousseau. This concept of neutrality is extended by neo-classical economists who assert market superiority. The State therefore plays a regulatory role and is limited to maintaining equal legal conditions for all.

(b) In contrast to this concept, which they describe as hypocritical, *Marxist political philosophers totally refute the concept of the neutrality of the State.* In their analysis, the State is a superstructure essentially marked by the domination of one social class over another; as such, it is not neutral and is incapable of being so. The State would therefore have to disappear for individuals to be able to flourish. Until this ideal is attained, however, the structure of the State must be transformed and placed at the service of the new, presumably dominant class, the proletariat. Given the resistance of the forces of the past, dictatorship is an inevitable, but in principle transitory stage, the individual freedoms inherited from the capitalist state superstructure being merely "formal" freedoms.

This political theory certainly appears to be largely outdated today, but it has unfortunately affected the living and working conditions of millions of individuals for almost a century. Its effects on the organization of society and individual freedoms are still felt, even though its underlying economic tenets are disappearing.

(c) *The re-examination of the role of the State as developed by Keynes,*[39] widely disseminated and used since the inter-war period, concluded that it was necessary for politicians to know how to use the State's planning role so as to actively regulate the economy. However, Keynesian theory did not explicitly address the question of the democratic character of the State posed by the interventionist economic policies of totalitarian States during this period.

(d) Since the end of the 1970s, the questions of the legitimacy and advisability of state intervention in the economy have been the subject of much reflection among democratic and industrially advanced countries. This reaction to state control of the economy led to Western Europe and the United States (although in the latter the State has never played the same protectionist role as in Western Europe) calling into question most functions assumed or taken over by public administration in the economic sphere. This line of thought on the *need to reduce the role of the State in order to restore economic initiative* (in a way, a liberal version of the theory of the weakening of the State), initiated by the *ultra-liberal economists of Milton Friedman's "Chicago School",* has been supported especially by major international financial institutions and has given rise to some radical experiments, for example in Latin America. The economic precepts were not accompanied by a political moral standard that would have questioned, in the case of Chile and Peru, the non-democratic nature of their regimes; these radical experiments were thus carried out under military dictatorships or authoritarian regimes. Chile in the late 1970s was a textbook example of the attempt made by these economic theorists to disassociate the economic base, which was intended to be ultra-liberal, from the political superstructure in which democracy was not seen as being indispensable.

Going beyond these extreme cases, in which democracy was not viewed as a necessary condition for balanced development, *neo-classical economics challenged the quasi-institutionalized Keynesianism of the majority of industrial economies* because of the pernicious effects being felt: simultaneous hyperinflation and unemployment, as well as spiralling state debt. Deregulation in the United States, privatization in the United Kingdom and the experiments carried out in New Zealand,[40] where the dismantling of the public employment service was being envisaged at the end of 1998, or in Australia, illustrate this trend among democratic countries.

The debate continues today, but has evolved considerably and is now clearly directed towards giving a new legitimacy to the role of public administration within a democratic framework, as emphasized by the 1997 World Bank report[41] in which the restoration of conditions that favour "good governance" emerges as a major objective. A constant theme throughout this report is the need for a forceful and effective State to oversee and ensure the success of public economic policies through strengthened and revived public institutions. The report establishes a strong correlation between the effectiveness of public policies in the financial, social and employment fields and the existence of a structured State. Finally, it proposes strategies for improving public services.

1.2.1.2 The paradoxical scale of the role played by the State

Since the beginning of the twentieth century, we have witnessed the rapid increase in responsibilities entrusted to the State with the approval of the people, not only in the legal sphere, where it was established that only a monopoly on the enactment of laws would place everybody on an equal footing (the role of the State as arbiter), but also in social and economic matters.

The State has thus taken on a more pervasive role in both developed and less advanced countries. This can be seen from table 1.2 showing public expenditure as a proportion of GDP.

Among OECD member States, European and English-speaking countries have differed greatly from the United States by the gradual implementation, according to very different national models, of a framework of protection for citizens, particularly in the fields of social and labour protection. At the same time, the State has also taken responsibility in the economic sphere with the nationalization of whole sectors of the economy. This development was particularly acute after the Second World War.

In 1994 public administration expenditure accounted for 36 per cent of GDP in the United States and Japan, compared with 56 to 65 per cent in European countries; the highest rate, 70 per cent, was found in Sweden.[42]

The importance of the State in countries in which the economic system remains founded on free enterprise has been strongly contested for both theoretical and factual reasons.

Theoretical explanations have been put forward simultaneously, even complementarily, by economists and politicians. They found that the State was taking the place of individual initiative and contractual agreement between the parties in economic and social relations. Moreover, the existence of a social sphere administered by the State alongside the economic sphere, in which it would not intervene, has also been called into question, in that the social assistance provided is seen as anchoring the unemployed more firmly in that situation.

The practical contention regarding the importance and extent of the State's role in the economy results in particular from the observation that, in the industrialized countries of Western Europe, a growing proportion of GDP is absorbed by public activities. The rate of compulsory deductions has reached a significant level, almost half of the resources produced in industrialized countries, particularly by in Western Europe: in individual countries of the European Union and Scandinavia the State retains (and redistributes) 43 per cent of GDP, compared with only 23 per cent in the United States. Data on developing countries are insufficient, but it appears that during the 1990s the share of GDP taken by the State has declined.

Table 1.2. Public expenditure as a proportion of GDP

	Total public expenditure as a percentage of GDP					
OECD countries	1913	1937	1960	1980	1990	1995
	9	20	18	43	46	49

	Central administration expenditure as a percentage of GDP			
Developing countries	1960	1980	1985	1990
	15	25	30	25

Note: In so far as existing data are available and comparable, the above aggregates, as presented by the World Bank, show persistent growth in the proportion of GDP made up by public expenditure in OECD member countries, leading to the conclusion that policies aimed at reducing the role of the State have not achieved their intended goals; paradoxically, at the same time public expenditure in developing countries, although much lower in comparison, has stagnated or declined simultaneously with structural adjustment plans imposed on many of these countries over the last 15 years.
Source: World Bank: *World Development Report 1997: The State in a changing world* (Washington, DC, 1998). Elaborated by the ILO.

Under the theory of economic liberalism, this rate of redistribution greatly inhibits the initiative of economic agents, leading governments to attempt, with varying degrees of success, to level off the growth curve in the proportion of GDP redistributed by the State. This has a direct effect on public administrations, asked to "slim down", and consequently on their labour administrations. This reasoning may be justified in the case of highly developed countries, but transposing it to developing countries without prior adaptation does not improve the operation of these States, whose administrations lack sufficient resources to satisfy the needs of their citizens. Models cannot be transposed wholesale, as will be discussed later.

1.2.1.3 Budgetary constraints

In situations where public companies face difficulties, the State as entrepreneur has frequently demonstrated scant efficiency, while private entrepreneurs have shown increasing hostility towards the mobilization of considerable budgetary resources for public companies that are apparently exempt from market constraints.

Certainly, the imbalance in public finances has been considered, since Keynes, as a worthy means of stimulating economic activity. However, what was once a positive, active and energetic economic policy has over the decades become an annual exercise. In 1980,[43] public deficits were evaluated at an average of 4.3 per cent of GDP in industrialized countries. Little noticed in a period of regular – even limited – inflation, since it allowed the system to be supplied without disproportionately aggravating public debt (global inflation was at an average of 28.6 per cent between 1985 and 1995), the policy of constant revival clashed with the effects of the deflationary policies implemented after the oil crises.

The policy of reducing public deficits having become a priority, governments have had to re-examine the different components generating public costs; the issue of higher public debt servicing implies calling into question the habitual financing of the government's rate of expenditure and, therefore, questioning significant public expenditure items. The financing of public firm deficits, social welfare costs and the cost of state structures have been disputed at the same time as theoretical reflections were being made about the legitimacy of state intervention in areas far removed from its initial tasks. World Bank figures show a sharp drop in both public deficits and inflation, despite wide regional differences. In 1995, the public deficit in industrialized countries had fallen to –2.5 per cent of GDP. In developing countries the rate was only 1.8 per cent, while it reached –4.8 per cent in the European Union. The global rate of inflation fell to 12.1 per cent in 1995 (but remained at 215 per cent in countries with average human development levels, essentially Eastern Europe and the former Soviet republics). In free-market economy countries the wave of privatization of state companies – justified by the disengagement of the State from unprofitable activities – has also been significant and has had a marked effect on employment in particular.

The shift in priorities from economic activity towards deflation has had serious economic and social consequences. However, independently of the social problems generated by the disappearance of several large public companies in Europe since the early 1980s as a result of the gradual reduction in the financing of public groups, at first glance the effects of this change in priority seemed to be limited to the structure of labour administration. Logically, this decline in financial intervention by the State was followed by the more or less abrupt privatization of the sectors closest to non-subsidized economic activity.

It was later that all activities that by nature cannot be privatized came under scrutiny; everything relating to the State's social intervention budgets has been re-examined.

At the same time the organization of the State underwent similar changes, but different countries went about it in different ways. This is shown by devolution and especially decentralization measures in various countries: decentralization in France and Argentina, agency management in the United Kingdom, regionalization in Belgium and Spain. This trend is characterized by the desire to give jurisdiction over matters that affect the daily lives of people to the level closest to them so that they are better able to influence the choices made by those actually responsible for implementing policies.

The desire to loosen the grip of the central State has direct consequences on its ability to intervene in the field of labour and employment relations. The State finds such consequences a burden when its operating means do not allow it to respond as legislator or arbiter; it clearly welcomes them when the reforms and transfers lead to the disappearance of the ministry in charge of labour, employment and vocational training; finally, these consequences are perhaps badly evaluated when decentralization procedures result in a notable differentiation of the standards applicable to labour relations within one country, as this regionalization of labour standards clearly creates difficulties for employees.

In this regard, it should be noted that transition countries, which have changed from a regime in which the State left no room for social and economic partners to one where political institutions are in the process of democratization, have perhaps not had the opportunity to take these different considerations fully into account; transition is an active process that is not prepared in advance and over the course of which any external aid is a priori welcome, even if the implicit or explicit "conditions" it brings lead to new difficulties in the long term.

In fact, the financial institutions that provide considerable aid have been able, in almost all cases, to firmly guide their wards towards the forms of organization that they believe suitable.

The external reasons given for questioning the role of the State include the measures applied by international financial institutions, which have decided that service-oriented policies are characteristic of good government and have implemented them when implementing structural adjustment programmes (SAPs) in numerous developing countries. The SAPs impose the introduction of major administrative reforms which often affect labour administration as severely as other public administrations through radical cuts in its human and financial resources, but do not consider it to be as high a priority as the financial, health and education administrations.

Nevertheless, it is labour administration that is responsible for finding prompt solutions to the social problems connected with the redeployment of thousands of workers made redundant following the privatization of firms or their transfer abroad, or even ensuring the training and development of personnel for the newly constituted private sector.

Today, however, international financial institutions are recognizing that, despite the theoretical financial advantage of a much lighter structure, underestimating the role of a structured State compounds difficulties. For example, the result in terms of efficacy of decentralizing tax collection in countries as different from each other as Argentina and the Russian Federation turned out to be the reverse of what was expected.

1.2.1.4 The need to evaluate results

In order to justify the adaptation of government structures to the constraints of global costs, it is necessary to produce evaluation instruments so as to weigh the different priorities of public intervention.

In some States this became possible only when, under pressure from taxpayers, governments changed their attitude with regard to the aims sought by evaluation; there has thus been a gradual change from a political appraisal to an apparently more technical one, but the object of the appraisal is clearly to measure the gap between objectives and results.

The basic difficulty with regard to public service is to define criteria that take account of all contributions, and not only those that fall in line with a strategy for cutting financial costs (see Chapters 2 and 3).

The evaluation of public sector results has therefore followed two not always complementary paths:

— on the one hand, administration performance can be measured only according to criteria that are difficult to standardize and relate to user satisfaction, or to the number of actions carried out within a master programme: this type of evaluation is often based on internal state inspections of the administration, where they exist (see Part II, France: "The General Inspectorate of Social Affairs (IGAS)");

— on the other hand, the taking into consideration of essentially financial ratios has resulted in the search for profit centres in the same manner as in the private sector: this is the concept which lies behind the creation of paragovernmental agencies in some English-speaking countries.

However, the effectiveness of a public service cannot be judged on financial criteria alone; public service originated from the need to carry out tasks that were in the general interest but which the private sector did not find profitable, in exchange for a contribution enabling the State to carry them out.

This is why there was an attempt (and these efforts should continue) to systematically take into consideration the global cost–benefit ratio by evaluating all the effects involved. This means that the evaluation of the costs of implementing a public measure should not be limited to financial elements, but should also include social costs. The theory of social costs has, however, been barely taken into consideration, since it remains difficult to quantify.

Efforts have been made to show that strategic planning produces positive results. The national experiences that will be analysed will provide examples of these efforts.

1.2.1.5 The shift towards user satisfaction[a]

The user, now significantly referred to as the "client", in the terminology often used in relation to the modernization of public services,[44] has benefited from the redirecting of public actions over the last 20 years; the main role of the government is to satisfy the users, the electorate, which has become a major criterion in evaluating public policies, previously assessed on their public contribution towards economic objectives.

The concept of the citizen is by nature indivisible. Moreover, its primary significance is political. By contrast, the concept of the user is more "functional" because it makes it possible to define user profiles and services that are adapted to each such profile. It is therefore possible to better concentrate public activity on targeted categories and to offer improved service that is more precisely defined and therefore more effective.

The use of the word "client" often shocks advocates of the public service who fear that user-fee public services will become more widespread. When applied to the relationship between the user and public service agents, how-

---

[a] See also Chapter 2.

ever, it reveals the desire to better satisfy the user's expectations; in this sense, the term "client" introduces a constraint that weighs on the official, who has an obligation to render a service to that person, whereas the concept of "user" does not appear to include this constraint.

Nevertheless, resorting to the concept of "client" implies that the provider of a public service seeks to better identify (or "target") the beneficiaries so as to adapt supply to demand.

The risk inherent in this methodology is that it may over-fragment the public and move public services away from the overall vision based on equal access to public services. Moreover, measures that are too targeted may prove to be unsuitable, with the succession of specific public policy measures resulting in their "cannibalization" (this is the situation where, faced with the succession of targeted measures that are indicated by the political authorities as having priority, public agents direct users to avail themselves of the latest aid mechanisms, to the detriment of less recent measures that are still in force and which might be better suited to the users' particular situation).

1.2.2 New actors and new needs

Since becoming structured within a national framework, social relations in Europe's major industrialized countries have been based on the institutionalization of tripartism; the foundations of the ILO, which was set up after the First World War, reflect this trend at an international level.

However, the developments that have taken place in these countries over the last 30 years or so, together with the social realities in emerging or developing countries, have called this simple and practical typology into question.

Indeed, economic actors are becoming extremely diversified, and this fragmentation has made it increasingly difficult for governments to find suitable and effective solutions to the ensuing social difficulties.

1.2.2.1 New categories of workers in new forms of employment

Economic development in industrialized countries has led to the emergence of new fields of activity for salaried workers; the manufacturing sector has been gradually replaced by the services sector, and consumer demand has switched from the satisfaction of material needs to the consumption of services that were unimaginable only a few decades ago (see section 1.1 above).

New categories of salaried workers have also appeared in less developed countries. As much as the field of activity, however, it is the form of work relations that has changed, creating new forms of employment and career paths, including professional and geographical mobility.

The legal nature of work relations has become extremely diversified; this process can be regarded as a counterbalance to the desire of labour representatives, often aided by the State, to standardize, regulate and homogenize labour relations.

It may be suggested that countries where this legal relationship has remained the most basic had no need to seek different legal formats to cover the widespread precariousness in work relations. On the other hand, in European countries where the prevalent model is that of contractual employment on a monthly basis and of unlimited duration, myriad forms of work relations deviating from this principle have appeared, at the same time as entrepreneurship became highly valued once again.

The result today is a basic transformation in the career profiles of individuals. People no longer occupy a salaried position in the same firm until they retire: instead, at the start of their careers they know that their first occupation is probably very different from those that will follow for the duration of their working lives.

Furthermore, although salaried employment remains the most common form of employer/employee relationship, arrangements vary widely and seem to have increased in developed countries over the last couple of decades. The traditional full-time employment contract of unlimited duration has given way to, among others, salaried contracts of a limited duration or on a part-time basis, intermittent contracts of unlimited duration, contracts obtained through temporary work agencies, and subcontracting (in which the relationship between the salaried worker and the employer is replaced by a commercial contract between a "client" and a supplier or service provider). In addition, monthly remuneration is not the most common form of payment: payments can be daily, weekly, or by the piece, thus increasing the precariousness of the worker's status.

Available statistics highlight the growing importance of part-time work, showing that this form of activity is carried out mostly by women, but there is no proof that this is done by choice. According to statistics compiled for OECD countries,[45] 25 to 45 per cent (the highest rates being recorded in Australia, Turkey, Mexico and the United Kingdom) of women who work do so on a part-time basis; the proportion for working men ranges from 3 to 15 per cent.[46]

The recent expansion of home work should also be noted. This form of employment developed in Europe in the nineteenth century, essentially in the textile industry. Owing to the increase in production structures that required ever-greater investments, it had all but disappeared. Today it is expanding once again: in developed countries (although there it represents a relatively minor proportion of work), where computer networks make it possible for work to be carried out independently; and in developing countries, where the relocation of production has been accompanied by the rediscovery of this method of work organization, which involves a very uncertain economic relationship, the worker buys the material, transforms it and then resells it to the "client" for a non-guaranteed price.

One of the effects of such work organization is that it disassociates workers contributing to the same production process by denying them any opportunity to organize themselves vis-à-vis their employers.

Furthermore, professional and statutory mobility, sometimes coupled with geographical mobility itself prompted by workers having to seek employment well outside the area in which they live, creates sizeable migration flows both towards developed countries lacking sufficient manpower and towards neighbouring countries in which the quality of life was higher before the current economic crisis. These migratory movements, above all economically motivated, are generally kept in check by the immigration laws in destination countries wishing to protect the jobs of their nationals. The free circulation of workers existing within the EU is a long way from being implemented worldwide.

Finally, in transition countries in Europe, South-East Asia, Africa, Latin America and, to a lesser degree, within the EU, the phenomenon of undocumented labour has grown in the twentieth century on an unequalled scale, and governments have been unable to find sufficiently convincing arguments to induce economic actors to abandon such practices (see section 1.3.2.2 below). In the United States, nine million illegal immigrants actively participate in economic life without any social guarantees. In the southern hemisphere and East Asia, the expansion of the capitalist economy has taken place without being accompanied by any structuring of social protection in its broadest sense (contractual conditions, remuneration, security, hygiene, etc.) which should be afforded to workers. The same path is currently being taken in transition countries in the area in question, especially China. It should be borne in mind that the greatest concentration of the world's workers is to be found in this geographical area.

What we are witnessing today is a fragmentation of the active population on a previously unimaginable scale.

1.2.2.2 New enterprises

There have been large-scale transformations on the employer side, too; this group has become considerably more diverse as a result of the development of new forms of entrepreneurial activity. The organization of both private and public companies into extremely large economic entities, inherited from the industrial period, is giving way to the idea that "small is beautiful": small firms appear to be more "practical" and more efficient than large ones.

Here a parallel can be drawn with the search for "profit centres" on the part of large firms which prefer to split into smaller but homogeneous, legally independent entities. The links and consistency between them are then ensured by a "holding" company which implements the strategy of the whole mechanism. Another facet of enterprise destructuring is the growing outsourcing of activities that are not directly related to the core objective of the firm, for instance finance and personnel matters. This naturally has repercussions on labour relations within the firm. For example, when an individual labour dispute arises, it is difficult for the arbitrator to determine who is the actual employer. When part of the contract is carried out abroad, which labour regulations should apply? These questions have been addressed by regional economic forums, particularly by the Member States of the EU, where the freedom of a firm to operate in a different State presupposes its freedom to post its staff abroad. However, the working and compensation conditions of such staff do not have to be brought into line with the national law of the State in which the service is carried out if the latter is less favourable.[a]

Changes in work organization have been particularly far-reaching in the OECD Member States. During the 1990s, a third of European firms implemented labour reorganization procedures, while in the United States in 1997 the implementation of new methods such as quality circles, job rotation, teamwork and the concept of "total quality" affected two-thirds of firms and salaried workers, that is to say, twice as many as in 1992.[47]

Elsewhere, the apparent destructuring of the organization of the economy is evidenced by the fact that entire sectors find themselves a part of the informal economy; this concerns mainly small companies and the self-employed. Many of these economic actors come from sectors (generally the public sector) in which privatization has led to workforce reductions that bear no relation to the absorption capacity of the labour market.

1.2.2.3 Rising levels of education and information

The current rise in the levels of education and information (see section 1.1.1.4 above) within the population of the most developed countries may have serious consequences for the labour market, with people who have reached a high level of training refusing out of hand tasks that would deskill them and which workers who are less well trained or who originate from disadvantaged countries would readily accept.

Although less marked, this trend is growing in less developed countries as well, leading often to the exodus of the elite who are discouraged by unfavourable pay conditions or the lack of civil peace from assuming the responsibilities for which they have been trained.

1.2.2.4 The changing nature of the social partners

Two contradictory phenomena currently noted are falling union membership throughout the world and the strengthening of democratic organizations involving workers and employers. The recent disappearance of a number of regimes that were highly interventionist in the social sphere partly explains the fall in union membership, since the previously high levels of membership were essentially the result of the obligation to join and the existence of certain benefits for members. While workers' organizations were being radically reformed,[48] employers' organizations adapted to the new economic trends have appeared on the scene. Consequently, the data supplied in this regard by the ILO *World Labour Report 1997-98*[49] should be examined with care; although the overall rate of union membership is falling,[50] this is primarily

---

[a] Ruling by the European Court of Justice, of 27 March 1990 (*Rush Portuguesa Lda*).

because in certain parts of the world, in particular in the transition countries of Eastern Europe (a loss of 36 per cent of workers unionized over the last ten years), compulsory membership granting access to numerous social benefits elsewhere provided by the State has given way to new circumstances. It is not only the rise in unemployment but also rediscovered freedom that allow people, on the one hand, not to become members, and, on the other, to participate in the creation of a representative organization. The rate of union membership in Belarus in 1995 (95 per cent) compared with that of Estonia (25 per cent) clearly shows the path currently being taken: less unionization, no doubt, but also representation by one or more trade unions independent of the State. In the 1985-95 period, the rate of union membership rose by between 4.8 and 10 per cent in South-East Asia, while in the United States it fell by 22 per cent and in France by 37 per cent.

1.2.2.5 Greater demands on governments by public administration users

Democratically elected governments better reflect and are more interested in the opinions of their constituents; their electorate has made known its demands for greater efficiency, transparency and the provision of better services by administration services, in particular labour administration.

Users, for their part, are more demanding when it comes to the services provided by the labour administration. As taxpayers, they are increasingly behaving as well-informed consumers and expect a return on the investment of their taxes. With the help of consumer defence groups or trade unions and other employee advice groups, they are making more and more claims and demanding greater transparency regarding the use of public funds by requiring that accounts be made public.

Moreover, the reality of the labour market, characterized by the rise in unemployment during the 1980s in industrialized countries, is exerting an unprecedented pressure on labour administrations to ensure sound management of public affairs within the framework of an economy that creates few jobs (qualified by some as "management of the decline"[51]), and to be innovative and competitive in relation to private employment agencies.

The higher demands made by the government on its administrations lead to the reorientation of existing internal inspection authorities. The latter can no longer simply produce occasional reports on the activities of services; instead, they must define and apply evaluation criteria which render their conclusions at the end of the inspection more relevant and less subject to opportunist disputes. Any dysfunction noted during assessments carried out by internal or external evaluation bodies brings on the decision to take the opportunity to improve the situation.

The modernization of labour administration or the improvement of its services in this context is essentially the consequence of the interest in achieving results in terms of the profitability, effectiveness and quality of services. The various components of labour administration place greater importance on the effectiveness of services offered directly to users, notably by introducing productivity targets and developing public agents' corporate spirit and competitive behaviour. A more systematic examination of the users' complaints and claims, the analysis of needs and expectations through surveys and opinion polls, and the increasing awareness of the existence of specific problems when settling individual or collective labour disputes are further evidence of the additional demands being made.

There is also the attraction of "new public management",[52] a system which advocates replacing highly centralized and hierarchical organizational structures by a decentralized management environment where decisions on the allocation of resources and the supply of services are closer to the target groups, thus making it possible to receive feedback from users and other interest groups. These reforms are also aimed at strengthening, at the central level, the strategic abilities needed to guide the development of labour administration and enable it to react to external changes immediately, in a flexible manner and at a lower cost.

More profitable alternatives, in terms of cost performance, to direct public supply and regulation, such as the subcontracting of certain services or benefits to private agencies, are also being explored.

This development can be illustrated by the implementation of a quality assurance system leading to accreditation according to ISO 9000[a] standards, the acquisition of information technologies, the opinions given by the social partners and the management's decision to compete for the Speyer Prize.[b] It is possible to make new comparisons with experience in other countries or private firms. The rapid development of data transmission between States and the closer links between several States within a region have clearly facilitated exchanges of information about measures aimed at modernizing public activities. This encourages beneficiaries to study the outcome of these efforts.

In order to improve the services offered by public administration, including labour administrations, the training of public agents clearly needs to be adapted to these new demands. This involves a number of different considerations, which are discussed below.

---

[a] "The standards of the ISO 9000 family are the result of international agreement concerning good management practice. Their aim is to assure that an organization can regularly supply products or services which meet customer demands in terms of quality. These good practices have been grouped together into a set of standardized requirements for a quality management system, irrespective of the nature of the organization, its size, and whether it belongs to the public or private sector." ISO 9000 for businesses, Internet site of the International Organization for Standardization (http://www.iso.ch/9000/affaires.html).

[b] The Speyer competition is a result of the initiative of Hermann Hill and Helmut Klages, professors at the Hochschule für Verwaltungswissenschaften in Speyer (Germany). This competition seeks to encourage public administrations to intensify their innovative efforts by centring their activities more on performance, quality and clients. Participants are offered the chance to "test their products" on the basis of recognized criteria and to compare them with others. This step enables them to show the advantages as well as the shortcomings of their activities and to enable other candidates to benefit from their strong points.

1.2.3 New officials

Employment conditions and the profiles of recently recruited officials also reflect the development of the public service, the aims and resources of which have changed radically since the 1960s.

1.2.3.1 Changes in public administration since the 1960s

The operational means and organizational methods of public administration in the strictest sense (services supplied by the State and not public companies) have been seriously called into question by the search for new criteria with which to measure its effectiveness. As shown by an ILO report on the evaluation of human resources in the public sector,[53] both its structure and status are being transformed.

As regards the status of agents in public posts, it has been acknowledged that the statutory system imported into certain countries with a French administrative tradition often leads to inflexibility; in the view of international financial institutions in countries under supervision or of governments mandated by their public opinion in developed countries, the existence of too many officials has led administrations to try to ease statutory constraints in order to improve human resources management and the effectiveness of public activities.

The statutory system of lifelong employment with salary increases irrespective of performance now coexists with an increasingly widespread contract-based system under which qualified agents are hired for a limited duration and for a set task. It was a reform of this type, implemented in Burkina Faso in 1998, that generated problems in the country's public service. The trend is also affecting Switzerland, which appears to be replacing the recruitment of civil servants by the widespread use of contracts, even for the highest positions, as well as France, where the public service intermittently debates the issue of the growing recruitment of contractual agents who do not enjoy the regular *fonctionnaire* status.

Structural changes are an ongoing process: on the one hand, changeovers of political power inevitably lead to changes in organizational structures, even if these are most often purely symbolic; on the other, the drive since the late 1970s to make public services accountable has led to reorganizations centred around the administrative and possibly financial autonomy of sectors previously comprised by state administration.

Finally, the discharge of certain labour administration activities by the social partners has also contributed to the "dismembering" of public administration.

1.2.3.2 Rising levels of education

The higher levels of education of public officials mirror those of the population as a whole (see section 1.2.2.3 above), although in most cases qualification requirements have not been revised upward. This has a negative effect in the most developed countries, with recruitment benefiting officials whose qualifications are much higher than those required by the post for which they are applying; this can lead to a certain degree of demotivation. There is no easy solution to this problem, since it is not easy to control access to a competition by barring over-qualified candidates (see section 1.1.2.2 above).

The recruitment of officials in developing countries is an involuntary victim of this trend. The relative scarcity of elite groups able to ensure the smooth operation of the state apparatus and the scant consideration accorded to their position (lack of or insufficient remuneration) generally lead senior staff to leave the public service when an opportunity arises.

From this point of view, Labour Ministry senior officials are highly appreciated by the private sector because of their professional expertise. For example, only a small minority of labour inspectors trained by the ILO or the African Regional Labour Administration Centre (ARLAC) in French-speaking Africa over the last 20 years still occupy a position in the field under their original administration; they are either in central administration, on temporary assignments or on leave of absence, or else they have resigned so as to become human resources managers in public or privatized companies in which their expertise in social matters is highly valued. Given the extremely low number of labour inspectorate employees, this significantly weakens the activities of the labour ministries vis-à-vis their users.

1.2.3.3 Seeking higher abilities and level of responsibility

Labour administration systems in developed countries are characterized by the increasing complexity of labour relations, whether these are based on a developed system of collective agreements in addition to legislation, or else form part of a highly legalized environment. This implies that the tasks carried out by officials require a high level of qualifications, which should make it necessary to adapt job profiles accordingly. In particular, the overlapping legal structures of the various parties involved – contractors, suppliers and subcontractors – make it difficult to assign responsibilities in individual and collective labour disputes.

Finally, when 90 per cent of a country's active population is employed in the informal sector, the usual tools and methods of intervention used by labour administrations appear outdated, notably because they are only relevant within the context in which they were developed, i.e. one in which registered employment is the norm. It must therefore be emphasized that in such countries the training of Labour and Employment Ministry officials should take these phenomena fully into account.

1.3. New challenges for labour administration

The role and activities of labour administrations within a country are influenced by numerous factors. The ILO constituents, notably the worker and employer members, listed a few of these global considerations during the examination of the Overview Study of Labour Administration by the Committee on the Application of Standards of the International Labour Conference of June 1997.[54]

In the opinion of the *worker members*, it was essential to provide labour administration with the budgetary resources and political support it needed in order to effectively achieve its aims at a time when the economic and social changes resulting from globalization and structural adjustment required it to adapt and modernize:

> Labour administrations in many countries still occupied secondary places in the hierarchy of priorities, even if it was generally recognized that the proper functioning of the labour market was a decisive factor in economic success. (…) These conclusions should be borne in mind when the Committee of Experts noted the relatively low level of resources allocated to labour administrations in industrialized countries, or when it observed that this was one of the lowest budgetary priorities in the developing countries, because under-financing had a direct consequence on the services provided, and therefore on living and working conditions.

Furthermore, "while democratic progress supported collective bargaining and tripartite cooperation, their institutional framework was being weakened by economic difficulties". It was therefore essential to improve the conditions and mechanisms required for social dialogue, especially in countries where employers' and workers' organizations were beginning to become organized, by providing them with advice and technical aid likely to help them achieve autonomy and develop their negotiating abilities so as to be able to take an active part in defining national labour policy and to contribute to economic development and social progress.

For the *employer members*, "[e]mployment laws and regulations would be worthless if there were no system of labour administration to assess and enforce compliance. (…) The development of an effective system of labour administration was a difficult proposition which varied widely due to the broad diversity of national conditions, including their historical and economic development, culture, government structures, country size and financial resources". An effective system of coordination was therefore necessary, operating with the collaboration of employers' and workers' organizations.

Finally, given the numerous and important changes in the global economic and social context, "[a]lthough there were no simple strategies for labour administration, approaches adopting management techniques and treating users as customers who needed information and advice were yielding better results than the traditional and more expensive adversarial enforcement systems. Other approaches, including mediation and arbitration were providing swifter and more effective labour administration". States should make more sustained efforts to improve their labour administrations by using more flexible structures and methods of resolving problems, such as direct negotiation between the social partners, conciliation, mediation and arbitration.

Indeed, labour administration can no longer confine itself to its traditional roles, the main one being to act as a safety net. It has an obligation to contribute actively to national economic and social development through dynamic attitude and action, to promote development and tackle problems that might hamper it. Its flexible conceptual framework enables it to respond to all situations, to take initiatives and, above all, to enhance its own image by carefully selecting its priorities for action in collaboration with the social partners.

1.3.1 Being an actor in national development

The first challenge facing labour administration is to secure the means by which to stimulate progress while fulfilling its role of promoting social justice.

Being an actor in national development means taking an active role in the democratic life, economic growth and social progress of the country. Some of the factors that can influence labour administration are social climate, promoting active methods of intervention in the fields of employment and vocational training, making available the tools and resources necessary for decision-making, and elaborating economic strategies and the participation of actors within the community.

Within the governmental structure, this "interventionist" role is more readily attributed to economic or financial ministries or bodies. As we will see below, a labour administration that occupies the whole field of its activity can be counted among the actors in national development.

Regarding the ILO's role in this field, the Director-General's report to the Twelfth Asian Regional Meeting, held in Bangkok in 1997, suggested a number of discussion points, including: "How can ministries of labour and employers' and workers' organizations [the main components of labour administration systems] exert more influence on fundamental policy decisions that influence growth, employment, trade, investment and poverty alleviation?"[55]

To do this, labour administrations must take advantage of the fact that they are active in areas which give them the possibility to acquire a high degree of legitimacy and credibility with citizens, users and national decision-makers when it comes to the elaboration of government policies and orientation and decision-making by individuals and economic actors. Since the world of work allows labour administration to cooperate with partners having different sensitivities and can provide access to original data which are then processed and disseminated for information purposes and possibly used in decision-making by social and economic actors, labour administration can reach a large majority of people by offering products and services, some of which may prove essential.

Here we find the principal characteristics of organizations that respond to the criteria of good governance, which can be defined as "the manner in which power is exercised in the management of a country's economic and social resources for development";[a] these include *participation and account-ability* (often associated with the accountability of leaders, because they involve the social partners in the consultation and/or management of activities), justice (because it can adopt equitable rules for both citizens and firms, and can exercise control on their application), and *transparency* (offering vast quantities of information that is accessible to everybody).

Labour administrations that fulfil their role by profiting fully from these comparative advantages will be able to participate actively in national development and will themselves become actors that cannot be ignored. Their place in the hierarchy of ministries or governmental organizations will therefore depend on the services they are able to offer to users and clients, but also on the government's political will regarding the emphasis to be placed on social relations. Labour administration should occupy a high-ranking place, but this will be the case only if the government recognizes its importance.

In certain developing countries where labour administrations hit by large budgetary restrictions have lost their influence, or in transition countries where they have found it difficult to assume their role in the new dynamics of the market, it should be possible to refocus activities on the priorities. Adequate services should be provided to users in the sectors retained and depending on the resources available, as well as instruments (for instance, a system providing labour market information) which support development measures undertaken by the government or the social partners. Labour administration may therefore become a "promoter of development", as shown by specific examples given during a seminar[56] on the transition countries of Eastern Europe. Its role is all the more important since it influences the still fragile foundations of these new societies: individual freedoms, freedom of association and enterprise, democracy and market economy.

In developed countries, the traditional role of labour administration as a safety net – which often gives it a negative image, since it mainly takes the form of sanctions or the application of regulations – can be carried out constructively by simply modifying approaches and intervention techniques.[57] However, in these countries labour administration should profit from its comparative advantages to promote new methods of intervention, and in particular to initiate new activities and supply new products and services (see Chapter 2). These will provide it with the visibility and credibility it needs if it is to obtain more easily the resources required in order to provide a better response to needs.

Labour administration fully plays its role as an actor in development if:

— it contributes to the maintenance of a healthy social climate that promotes development in all fields;

— the services that it offers are effective and correspond to the needs of users in terms of active measures;

---

[a] *Webster's New Universal Unabridged Dictionary* (London, Dorset & Baber, 1979).

— the services and products contribute to the drafting of development strategies or to the development of growth and (political and economic) decision-making;

— the partners participate and can be identified in its policies and practices.

1.3.1.1 Social climate

As a result of the fragile state of our societies when faced with all the aforementioned changes, labour administrations have a major role to play as a societal monitor in the broadest sense: a system for observing the life of a working community (here it is the entire community), developed with the aim of detecting the existence of potential problems or actual industrial disputes and re(adjusting) social policy decisions.[58]

It is worth noting that a constructive social climate can contribute to a country's development, in particular its economic development. According to UNCTAD, some of the main factors determining the investment choices of transnational firms in a country are its economic, political and social stability.[59] From this point of view, labour administration can offer its clients – the government, enterprises and trade unions – and its users a series of measures which help to organize relations and avoid damage to the social climate.

Labour administration contributes to a healthy social climate by carrying out its traditional functions of protecting human rights and promoting social justice by making services and products available to everyone, by implementing policies, laws and regulations and by applying them without discrimination. On the other hand, it has the potential and the tools necessary for analysing social realities and their evolution, thanks to its constant interaction with the social partners and integrated processing of information at its disposal, enabling it to anticipate developments, to react and to propose its own measures for maintaining a favourable social climate; these tools include early-warning mechanisms (see Part II, Austria).

Consequently, when it promotes the introduction of new tools and new methods and approaches for settling disputes by offering the partners advice or support services (conciliation, mediation, arbitration, ombudsperson, a neutral third party), labour administration plays a positive role. This is further enhanced when in the field of professional relations it promotes greater autonomy of the social partners by encouraging collaboration and cooperation, while continuing to guarantee the rights of all. Its role as a key actor in development does not necessarily entail direct involvement in the activities undertaken. As A.M. Zack observed, parallel to the traditional procedures implemented by the State "Alternative Dispute Resolution (ADR) offers a means of bringing workplace justice to more people, at lower cost and with greater speed than do conventional government channels".[60] Where dispute prevention is concerned, by providing information on new negotiating techniques or relations between the partners, labour administration may also promote their complete autonomy, thereby leaving the responsibility for negotiation up to them.[61] The State will lower its costs by reducing the degree of its involvement, but it must make the partners more responsible, while continuing to strive for social peace and "a climate conducive to economic stability and efficiency with equity".[62]

In this regard, the participation of labour administrations within regional groupings' regulatory bodies helps to promote social tranquillity through the observation, comparison and harmonization of the different legislations of the member States. In each country, this role of observer can also be developed and systematized through labour administration through improving the methods used in evaluating policies and analysing relevant social factors.

1.3.1.2 Active measures

The role as a key actor in development is more tangible when it takes the form of active measures offered by labour administration to its users and clients.

In the field of employment, particularly in developed countries, labour administration may be able to improve the operation of the labour market by introducing measures that promote its transparency and fluidity, thereby helping to find the right balance between supply and demand. The response time and the quality of the information provided by labour administrations are often a decisive factor in the competition between firms to invest, since the availability of human resources that respond to urgent needs is a major asset. On the other hand, the possibility for jobseekers to shorten the period of time spent out of the labour force is useful on many counts.

Labour administration can play a crucial role in economic recovery programmes and conversions of entire sectors of activity when it is able to offer products and services such as labour market analyses and means of adapting, training and placing personnel. It may also be involved in promoting new activities, by helping to set up SMEs and develop self-employment, as well as by offering customized training programmes. In particular, it is often involved in programmes aimed at softening the impact of the restructuring, relocation and closure of enterprises.

In developing countries, especially in countries emerging from armed conflict, reintegration and reconstruction projects are essentially concerned with action linked to labour administration. Ranging from surveys of the size of the working population, the reintegration of former soldiers into active life, guidance and training for displaced people and the creation of SMEs to highly labour-intensive work, all these activities are part of the means used in restructuring a society. In countries grappling with structural adjustment programmes, labour administrations guarantee the balance needed between the economic and social measures that these countries must adopt under pressure from organizations such as the World Bank.

In the field of occupational health and safety, prevention campaigns to improve health and safety and working conditions should contribute not only to improving the quality of life at the workplace, but also the quality of products and services provided by firms, and therefore the latter's productivity as well (see Part II, Norway).

Finally, labour administration can actively contribute to national development by becoming involved in programmes combating poverty and social exclusion.

With regard to the promotion of labour equality, labour administration occupies a privileged position on account of both its legitimacy with the social actors and its strategic situation at the crossroads of public standards, the administrative network and economic and social realities.[63]

Where child labour is concerned, collaboration with other ministries and the social partners enables labour administration to draw up policies that seek to suppress this form of labour and to protect minors, as well as to ensure that regulations are circulated and applied in the workplace.

1.3.1.3 Decision-making tools

Trade globalization (see section 1.1.2 above) means that important and often urgent decisions have to be taken regarding the creation, mergers, relocation and even closure of firms. Countries that offer significant comparative benefits (e.g. availability of suitable resources) have an advantage over their competitors, provided that the decisions they take are based on a sound knowledge of their resources. As stated by the World Bank, the credibility of a State directly influences economic growth and investment.[64] In this regard, labour administrations are at a distinct advantage. They are able to furnish governments with original data on available resources, in particular human resources. This type of information is vital for drawing up a national economic development policy.

An effective system of information on labour market conditions is an asset to economic development, especially for reconstruction projects of industrial sectors. Together with other means, it enables ministries in charge of economic affairs to target their policies and national and foreign firms to make rapid decisions concerning their future.

In transition and developing countries, where inadequate information systems hinder development, labour administrations are at the origin of integrated structures that answer decision-makers' needs; this is the case, for example, with employment and training monitoring agencies which provide expertise that helps the decision process and is part of a network of partners that are linked by joint action and cooperation facilities.[65]

In countries emerging from a period of armed conflict, labour administrations can participate in development or reconstruction projects that require funds from international institutions or foreign governments. Projects are accepted and implemented more easily and more quickly if they are firmly rooted in a local structure that the conflict will certainly not have completely destroyed and that can furnish some of the data and basic resources needed for the project to get under way and then continue managing it independently.

1.3.1.4 Strategy tools

The decision-makers' ability to devise strategies, rather than intervening as and when needs arise, offers a definite advantage in terms of development. Individuals and firms need to know how the market is evolving. Governments, in particular ministries of education, need to know the future needs of firms so as to create appropriate educational, training and, where necessary, vocational training courses.

In this regard, the role of labour administration is not limited simply to recording or reporting on the situation of the labour market by means of regular statistical bulletins. It includes forecast studies and providing the tools needed in taking decisions to prepare a response to anticipated needs. Responses to the future needs of firms take shape in current training programmes. In certain countries vocational training depends not on the ministry that covers basic labour administration activities but on a different one, such as the Ministry of Education. It is up to the former to take the necessary steps to ensure that the needs of its users are taken into account by the body in charge. However, when labour administration itself is responsible for vocational training, it takes on the task of forecasting needs and creating appropriate training procedures.

Comparative data on the development of labour relations also enable partners to prepare negotiations based on reliable figures and to plan investments accordingly.

Generally, labour administration may be an actor, coordinator and support provider to ensure the consistency of the government's social and economic policies. By including measures relative to training, employment and working conditions, and by bringing in the social partners, labour administration can present integrated strategies on economic orientations, on policies and programmes, or participate in their elaboration. It can also assess the impact of these strategies when it "controls" both ends of the policy chain covering the use of human resources (projections, training, jobs).

1.3.1.5 Democratic life

One of the main potential strengths of labour administration lies in its ability to grasp the movements, reactions and needs of the creative forces of society, thanks to its large and diversified contact base. By promoting the organization of the social partners and by involving them in the definition of its policies and action programmes through the creation and regular operation of consultation and collaboration bodies in which other recognized actors also participate, labour administration can acquire a high degree of credibility that will provide a solid foundation for any action it may take. By ensuring respect for the right of association, by promoting dialogue and social debate and by providing information, it can promote democracy. In some cases it can help mentalities to evolve, for example in transition countries that have chosen the free-market economy system, by associating the social partners in discussion forums on new issues in society. In this way it can show that it is an agent of change and a promoter of development.

On the other hand, its constant contact with a varied clientele, recognition of different groups of users and presence throughout the national territory by means of public employment services and labour inspectorates, for example, heighten its awareness of changes in society and enable it to take them fully into account.

This position of strength should pave the way to its active participation in important decisions taken by the government to support development and tackle problems that stand in its way.

1.3.2 Tackling obstacles to development

Labour administration has the means needed to meet the challenges posed by the evolution of society. In some developed countries it is the main tool that the government uses to carry out activities in behalf of the active population, and it should take on a similar role in all the countries currently undergoing structural economic crises, from which workers and their families are the first to suffer. In its summary report, the ILO's Working Party on the Social Dimensions of the Liberalization of International Trade stated that:

> … globalization means new business opportunities and therefore better economic prospects, but it can also entail significant adjustment costs. More generally, there is concern about employment stability at a time when firms adjust to the pressures arising from greater international competition. Some are well placed to gain from this process, while others may be worse off in either relative or absolute terms. However, none of the countries under study has considered protectionist measures with respect to trade and foreign direct investment as a solution to these problems. Instead, the challenge lies in selecting the appropriate mix of measures (by governments and social partners) to improve the returns from globalization while reducing the social costs. The country studies show that, in contrast to the view that national governments are powerless in the face of globalization, domestic policies can have a strong bearing on the relationship between globalization and social progress. There is indeed scope for improving the domestic competition environment and, in so doing, taking advantage of the business opportunities arising from globalization. More importantly, the four 'social pillars' can provide a meaningful contribution to a successful globalization process:
>
> — equality of access to education and training;
> — a well-functioning social safety net;
> — labour regulations that combine the need for adaptability with that of protection;
> — the observance of core labour standards.[66]

There is still a long way to go to attain this objective; it is measured in particular by the position of the ministry in charge of labour matters in the government's organizational chart, and by the size of the budgetary resources allocated to it.

1.3.2.1 Combating unemployment

The recent economic crisis in South-East Asia has renewed and made more specific the questioning of the role and legitimacy of labour administration in the field of employment. Its weakness in this respect has been seen as one of the social factors aggravating the economic crisis.

The legitimacy of the fight against unemployment appears undisputed. The positioning of labour administrations in the fight against unemployment is a crucial factor; government response generally confirms their pivotal role in this regard. All ILO constituents, including the most liberal ones, have an administration in charge of employment. These services are generally important, even predominant components in labour administration systems, and this has become even more apparent with the rise in unemployment over the last 20 years.

Their method of organization varies little and is based on two major basic principles:

— a network for welcoming users;
— an administrative structure that is independent of the Ministry of Employment.

The means by which employment services intervene vary widely. Their organization and the scope of their jurisdiction vary widely and depend largely on the resources they are given by governments in order to combat unemployment.[67]

The functions fulfilled by the network of employment offices may be more or less comprehensive. They traditionally consist in receiving and registering users with a view to providing them with benefits depending on the means available in the country (this is the classical context within which employment services fulfil their role), but may also extend to providing advice to job seekers, for example giving information on the labour market and on job search techniques (see Part II, Germany; United States, "Information and self-information of workers").

When a so-called "active" policy for combating unemployment is put into practice, it is complemented by vocational training programmes or even by programmes promoting job creation in various "target" sectors (the most vulnerable groups, sectors with the greatest needs). An example of this type of action is the Informal Sector Support Fund (FASI) in Burkina Faso (see Part II, Burkina Faso, "The role of FASI"; Senegal).

A globally small but variable budgetary effort. Policies for combating unemployment mobilize a large share of state budgets, which is all the greater with benefits having to be paid to workers where employer and worker contributions are insufficient. When this proportion is considered to be too large, governments have no choice but to "activate" expenditure so as to make their intervention more operational.

Available data are scarce and extremely diverse, making analysis difficult, but studies that have been carried out show that OECD countries devote 1.4 per cent of GDP on average to combating unemployment.[68] There are large disparities within the area, since the figure ranges from 2.9 per cent of GDP in the EU to 4.7 per cent in Nordic countries, while in the United States it amounts to only 0.5 per cent. What little data are available show that share to be less than 1 per cent in most developing countries, in which unemployment benefit generally does not exist.

A more or less institutionalized partnership. Tripartite,[69] or even bipartite (i.e. by the social partners only) management of institutions that contribute directly or indirectly to the fight against unemployment may be more or less widespread:

— in certain cases, governments are tempted to believe that the introduction of government employment policies cannot be delegated or negotiated: the social partners are thus either ignored or relegated to playing a more or less consensual minor role;

— elsewhere, as in many OECD countries, governments and the social partners may have got into the habit of maintaining a close dialogue, the governments having realized the advantages of an equal division of responsibility with regard to unpopular measures taken in respect of benefits. In this case, many social institutions will be managed by a tripartite or bipartite administrative council (see Chapter 2, section 2.6).

In this regard, it will be recalled that a large number of social security institutions in industrialized countries were established despite the will of governments and management, who believed them to be simply a disguised form of workers' organization that had been seen both as illegal, by virtue of the principle of an individual's contractual freedom, and prejudicial to the same principle.

The extent to which employees are covered by collective agreements is not proportional to the level of development: in Cuba 90 per cent of employees are covered; many Western European countries come close, although their circumstances differ greatly, while in the United States the figure amounts to only 11 per cent of employees.[70]

Today, however, it should be noted that

> [t]wo important factors have changed the basis of tripartite or bipartite consultation and cooperation bodies. The first of these is the fact that these bodies operate in countries with unfavourable economic conditions where it is the equilibrium, rather than the development, of certain social systems that is open to question (...) The second factor affecting the development of tripartite participation is the change that has occurred in the interplay of the actors (...); over the past ten years in Europe, collective bargaining at national level has lost its importance with the globalization of trade.[71]

1.3.2.2 Combating clandestine labour and integrating the informal sector

The above notions are two facets of the same challenge facing labour administrations.

The awareness that some production and trade activities take place for the most part outside traditional commercial channels has given rise to statistical research which is far from complete but reveals the scale of the phenomenon:[72] the proportion of the active population working in the "informal" sector is estimated at 34 per cent in Indonesia, 46 per cent in Thailand and 57 per cent in Bolivia. The figure is somewhere between 20 and 30 per cent in Bulgaria[73] and should be about the same in other transition countries (for example, in the Baltic States), where clandestine labour is accompanied by systematic under-reporting of wage levels and complicity between the employer and the employee. Approximately 15 per cent of workers in the EU are thought to be in the same situation, sometimes aided by the gaps in legislation (in most Member States there is no obligation to declare certain tasks or amounts below certain thresholds). In developing countries (see section 1.1.1.1 above) the transfer of the rural population to industrialized occupations is accompanied by the growth of the "informal sector".

Combating clandestine labour

Industrialized countries have long been frictionally and marginally confronted with clandestine labour; this method of employing undeclared workers, that is, those whose social security contributions are not paid, is often confused with the employment of illegal immigrants, not only because of the lack of contributions, but also because they lack residence and work permits in the host country.

Clandestine labour often results from the encounter of a worker's preoccupation with finding a job at any cost and the employer's desire to reduce labour costs. However, it should not be forgotten that, despite this apparent collusion, one of the two contracting parties has no possibility to discuss the terms of the implicit work contract imposed by the other.

However, it is not simply humanitarian considerations that justify the fight against clandestine labour. It is of course immoral to employ people without respecting their basic social rights, in particular the right to social protection against occupational risks (accidents at work and illness) and to retirement benefits. However, business costs depend mainly on the level of competition, and using workers who are not reported to the social agencies distorts competition, which is particularly sensitive in highly labour-intensive sectors; this is why employers' organizations in developed countries generally condemn the use of undeclared workers and cooperate with governments in setting up prevention mechanisms so as to eliminate the effect of this distortion on the supply of services and reduce the losses incurred by the social protection systems to which they have to contribute.

Despite the repression mechanisms put in place by the labour administration to combat clandestine labour, in major industrialized countries some economic actors are trying to evade the growing burden of social deductions and their effect of adding to labour costs. Employers might wish to reduce the amount not paid directly to employees, and the latter sometimes find it advantageous to receive directly a higher amount than the one that would be forthcoming if they were declared. This is more and more often the case with employment of short duration: indeed, employees feel that they are receiving immediately what would be a contingent (sickness or unemployment benefit) or deferred (retirement) income, especially if they know that they could benefit from the social welfare system only above a certain level of contributions or after a certain length of time.

Labour administration is therefore tempted to develop repressive means, but these cannot be totally effective, especially when the application of sanctions jeopardizes the jobs of the employees concerned.

Since the 1970s, governments in industrialized countries have had to face a new development in clandestine labour which increasingly concerns national workers.

This development is also particularly marked in transition countries that have suddenly passed from a system in which social costs and benefits are allocated collectively to one in which contributions and benefits derive from the existence of an individualized, contractual working relationship.

Then there is decentralization, which often makes it more difficult for labour administrations to combat clandestine labour. Despite the positive effects of the closer links between users and the means of intervention of the ministry responsible for ensuring compliance with labour laws, decentralization often adds to the complexity of the levels of jurisdiction in labour law matters; this is what labour administration services in Argentina are trying to counter by reinstating coordination between national and federal institutions combating clandestine labour (see Part II, "The campaign against clandestine labour: The case of Argentina").

No miracle solution has been found.[74] The methods frequently employed, though in very different ways, include the suppression or reduction of social security contributions on very low salaries or on part-time jobs, as in the United Kingdom (no contributions below a certain number of hours worked per week), France (reduction of contributions on low salaries), Germany, Switzerland and many other Western European countries. The administrative complexity limits the effectiveness of these measures, as in France, even prompting the legalization of undeclared labour and not providing the employees concerned with any social protection.

Labour administrations should try, together with the social partners, to develop specific proposals that simplify and streamline these measures.

The priority should be to simplify social welfare systems, standardize them nationally and make them more manageable. Since a large number of States are nowadays grouped in regional economic areas, seeking convergence between policies dealing with labour and employment protection should become a major objective, especially so as to reduce distortions in competition resulting from social legislations that are geographically close but opposed in substance. Given the new and often precarious forms of employment that are difficult to fit into the traditional worker-employer relationship, perhaps social welfare can no longer be supported merely by the social contributions made by workers and employers. Once again, labour administrations should propose national legislative measures or supranational regulations aiming to fulfil these objectives.

Development of the informal sector

While industrialized countries are facing an increase in illegal labour, in developing countries this phenomenon has taken on a totally different dimension; there it is habitually referred to as "informal", though this is just a different way of describing the same reality: employers hire workers who enjoy no social protection at all, and domestic standards are not applied because the State is unable to ensure that they are respected.

As pointed out in the *World Employment Report 1998-99*, "the lack of jobs in the formal sector of the economy and the lack of qualifications of the general workforce have led to the growth of an informal sector in which the majority of workers occupy a badly paid position in mediocre and unsupervised working conditions"[75] and do not benefit from social protection.

The growth of this phenomenon, which affects almost 90 per cent of the active population in many developing countries (in Burkina Faso, for example, 95 per cent of the workforce in rural areas and 50 per cent of the active population in urban areas work in the informal sector),[76] challenges the foundations of social relations and the role of the State as a guarantor of balanced relations; moreover, no social welfare system based on the principle of distribution (the contributions of the active population pay the retirement benefits of the previous generation) is able to guarantee deferred benefits to its members if the premium base is not sufficient.

Furthermore, workers' and employers' organizations, which are the traditional actors in social relations, represent only a fraction of the active population. As for the State, it does not inspire any confidence in workers placed in this situation.

For countries with an administrative structure that is weak and has little credibility, this is therefore a particularly difficult challenge to overcome. Nevertheless, pragmatic solutions can be implemented, provided the State wishes to play an effective role once again.[77]

Knowledge of the actual context of the business environment, which can easily be improved by cooperating with the ministerial department responsible for tax collection, is vital to the new involvement of labour administration. To achieve this it is pointless to ask labour services to carry out a survey of employers before considering the data collected by the Ministry of Finance in countries undergoing structural adjustment; in the latter, the tax administration had to begin by updating its files on businesses so as to be able to reconstruct the taxation system; it would therefore be pointless for the labour services to carry out this survey a second time.

Next, awareness of the social reality – clandestine or "informal" or "irregular" work is not a deliberate choice but a means of survival for a relatively large proportion of the active population – should help promote the emergence of structures which, like the "labour exchanges" established in Europe in the nineteenth century, manage the social welfare of groups of workers and employers with very limited contribution rates. This process would make it possible to gradually reintegrate these people into a situation providing them with minimum social rights. Such a step can lead to definite results, as shown by Senegal's recent experience (see Part II, "Social security/informal sector: The case of Senegal").

It is only by demonstrating in this manner its ability to offer real services that labour administration can regain a certain amount of the credibility that for various reasons it has often been unable to preserve.

1.3.2.3 Involvement in dispute resolution

Acting as mediator is one of labour administration's main raisons d'être: it either attempts to prevent conflicts by promoting negotiation between the social partners, or it helps to resolve disputes within a formal or informal arbitration procedure.

It is often beneficial for negotiation between the social partners to be organized or at least promoted by the State; labour administration must be able to create the conditions for effective social dialogue. Its greatest success would be for the social partners to no longer need its mediation services in order to meet and negotiate. This is actually the case in some European countries. However, the social partners may also be convened by the public authorities. The periodic negotiation of collective agreements may provide an opportunity for regular meetings, thus making it possible for the representatives to get to know each other and facilitating future contact should social tension arise.

Should a conflict occur, the competent labour administration representative at the site of the dispute should have the personal ability to promote the search for a negotiated settlement that satisfies both parties. This ability is often required in less-developed countries, as in Africa, for example, where the economic context has led a number of governments to agree to the privatization of state companies.

Mediation has definitely proved its worth: implemented in a more or less institutionalized form, it enables the parties concerned to find a balanced solution and to possibly avert disputes through periodic collective negotiations. There are numerous elaborate examples of such procedures in industrialized countries. It is interesting, however, to see how such mechanisms are being gradually implemented in certain transition countries. In Hungary, for example, the National Interest Conciliation Council (ICC) has played such a role over the last ten years (see Part II), and a national arbitration body has recently been set up with a view to cutting down the number of disputes referred to the courts.

1.3.2.4 Maintaining the strength of the social partners

The success of all the activities undertaken by labour administration is greatly enhanced by the support it receives from the social partners; the latter oversee several activities of the labour administration system, either independently or as part of a tripartite procedure. However, recent developments[78] show a global weakening of the social partners. And when they have a particularly low representational profile, consultations with them lack proper legitimacy or become downright impossible or meaningless.

It is therefore vital that labour administrations encourage the strengthening of workers' and employers' organizations, while respecting their autonomy, so as to involve them effectively in defining labour policy.[79] This requires ensuring that the regulations governing the establishment of such bodies are applied, and helping the organizations to assume their responsibilities by promoting the decentralization of labour administration. In this respect, the study of economic liberalization procedures in the transition countries of Eastern Europe has shown just how necessary the role of the State was; labour administration has had to try to establish workers' and employers' organizations in countries in which trade union activities were based on strong ties with the socialist State, in the absence of any managerial structures, and even where the administrative tradition went against the recognition of the role of the social partners (see section 1.2.2.4 above). In Hungary, the re-establishment over the last ten years of an independent trade union structure, involving both workers and employers, in which the participation of the ICC was institutionalized very early on (see Part II) provides an example of this process.[80]

This is why interpretation of the decline in unionization throughout the world must be nuanced. It could be described as a quantitative fall in terms of membership of workers in trade union organizations mirrored by a notable advance in quality. Indeed, it is the trade union organizations re-established according to the principle of free membership that have become more widespread. As for employers' organizations, in many parts of the world they had to be recreated practically from scratch as privatization measures were implemented and despite the reluctance of new entrepreneurs to become involved in cooperation procedures with the State.[81]

Labour administrations can promote national development by tackling the obstacles that stand in its way. For this purpose, they have at their disposal a globally accepted conceptual framework drawn up by the ILO constituents.

1.3.3 A universally accepted conceptual framework

Labour administration activities, whose purpose was described above and whose operation will be described in the following chapters, fall fully into line with the regulatory policies defined by governments between two extremes – "total state control" and the "laissez-faire approach" – and within the framework of voluntary development policies in which, as we have just seen, labour administrations can play a significant role. This requires taking into account not only the economic and financial aspects but also all the other dimensions of the life of a society, in particular the active and democratic participation of economic and social actors and the establishment of balanced and respected rules.

The importance of the subject explains why it is periodically a major concern for States, why a conceptual framework should be defined and why the choices that promote the consistency of economic, social and democratic development should be enhanced and given added credibility.

However, certain conditions must be met for a beneficial dialogue to take place. These range from the choice of participants to the terms used so as to refer in an identical way to the realities being discussed. At first glance, the differences noted in the organization of ministries responsible for labour administration, in their activities, in their importance and in their relations with the environment in which they operate suggest that comparison is impossible and that the terms used just to describe them will mean different things to different people, thereby preventing real dialogue.

If we add the fact that the social partners themselves play very different roles from one country to another and that decentralization and even federalism make the situations observed even more diverse, one might be tempted to abandon the idea of discussing labour administration in general or global terms.

This would be all the more regrettable given the current weakness of this public administration in many countries, particularly in the least developed of them, and the need to show, through specific examples, the value and necessity of an effective labour administration in devising lasting development policies.

1.3.3.1 The role of the ILO

The ILO has proved to be the obvious forum for this debate, a place where the confrontation of different interests and opinions can produce agreement not only between governments, but also with employers' and workers' organizations.

From its foundation in 1919, the International Labour Organization has been interested in the role of labour administration, notably based on the consideration and drafting of texts relating to labour inspection. It has also been concerned with defining the role of the overall system of labour administration. Debates have regularly taken place since the 1950s, culminating, in 1978, with the drafting of a Convention and a Recommendation[82] adopted unanimously by governments and by workers' and employers' representatives; this universal recognition confers a high degree of credibility on the concepts contained in the two instruments.

It should be noted that at the time several standards already defined rules applicable to both labour inspection and employment services. The new instruments were innovative in that they addressed not only the most operational aspects of labour administration but the overall concept as well, providing a much broader view of the subject and no doubt new meaning to each of the components. This approach took into account the existence and the diversity of public structures in numerous countries, already grouping together labour administration's essential activities.

This framework was re-examined at the end of 1996 by the ILO Committee of Experts on the Application of Conventions and Recommendations and, in 1997, by the 85th Session of the International Labour Conference. The validity of Convention No. 150 and Recommendation No. 158 was confirmed and their appropriateness especially acknowledged. The international community considered that the two texts should be publicized and promoted in ILO member States so as to encourage their ratification.

1.3.3.2 The content of the common conceptual framework

One of the fundamental elements of Convention No. 150 is contained in Article 1 which, in addition to defining "labour administration", has conceptualized the notion of a "national system of labour administration".

The term "labour administration" refers to public administration activities, in the narrowest sense of the term, in the field of national labour policy. The "system of labour administration", for its part, is defined as covering all public administration bodies (including parastatal and regional or local agencies or any other form of decentralized administration) and any institutional framework for the coordination of the activities of such bodies and for consultation with and participation by employers and workers and their organizations.

This systematic conception enhances the complementary roles of the different actors. Therefore, there are national systems of labour administration in which the role of the social partners is extremely important, while in others, States or regions play a predominant role. The distribution of responsibilities varies widely from one country to another in all the different sectors covered (vocational training, employment or labour).

Even when it is possible to cite a significant field of activity in which, over the last few years, the responsibility of the State has become more common throughout the world, such as that of labour inspection, the way it is organized varies widely. In the majority of cases, this service comes under the Ministry of Labour, but often with decentralized management in a number of federal countries, or sometimes even under the responsibility of the Parliament or the Prime Minister.

The Convention therefore addresses the problem based on the functions that labour administration should carry out by giving special weight to the result of the operation of the system and not prescribing a rigid structure. The organization of the system can therefore have infinite combinations (excepting certain elements which will be discussed later) linked to the history of each country, to the strength and tradition of negotiation between the social partners, to the historical role of the State and to the political conceptions of the government. The extent of these differences is revealed by an examination of three very different systems of labour administration, each one of which conforms to the requirements of Convention No. 150 (see Annex, pp. 157-160).

This strong vision, concerned with obtaining concrete results and respectful of differences, is undoubtedly the main reason why these instruments are just as topical today as when they were adopted, over 20 years ago.

This great flexibility is complemented by the affirmation of a few important principles on which the system of labour administration is based.

Convention No. 150 and Recommendation No. 158 (1978) stress *the participation of the social partners* by means of consultation, cooperation and negotiation with the public authorities, at national, regional and local levels (Art. 5 of the Convention), as well as through the delegation of activities (Art. 2) and, finally, through resolving, by virtue of national legislation or practice, a certain number of issues through direct negotiations (Art. 3). Moreover, in its Article 5(1) the Recommendation calls for the active participation of employers' and workers' organizations in the preparation, development, adoption, application and re-examination of labour standards. It thus promotes a tripartite concept of the system's operation.

In addition, the Convention defines the phases for preparing, implementing, coordinating, checking and reviewing *national labour policy* (Art. 6) and the essential activities that the competent bodies of the system of labour administration should carry out in accordance with employment policies, professional relations and the technical advice to be offered to the social partners.

Finally, the Convention provides that the *functions and responsibilities* assigned to the system should be properly *coordinated* (Art. 4). For this purpose, its Article 9 specifies that the Ministry of Labour (or another comparable body) should have the means to ascertain, in particular, whether any parastatal agencies responsible for particular labour administration activities are adhering to the objectives assigned to them, thereby ensuring that the functions and responsibilities have been properly assumed.

To ensure the efficient operation of the whole system, the Convention recalls the need for suitably qualified *staff* with access to the necessary training, free from undue outside influence and enjoying the status and material and *financial resources* necessary for the performance of their duties (Art. 10).

Beyond these aspects concerning the make-up of the system, the Convention promotes the extension of the functions of the labour administration system to include categories of workers who are not, in law, employed persons, such as agricultural workers and self-employed workers who do not engage outside help, and so on. (Art. 7).

1.3.3.3 Beyond labour administration, a concept of public administration

This brief presentation of the content of Convention No. 150 and Recommendation No. 158 shows that, in addition to the importance attached to labour administration in accordance with the duties that it should carry out, a certain concept of the role and the operation of the State and of public administration has been defined.

It is an administration that is primarily concerned with the duties that it should carry out so as to serve the community and users. For this purpose, it constantly surrounds itself with the opinions of representatives of the social groups concerned and provides them with the information at its disposal so that they can themselves be involved in this dialogue. However, public administration does not claim to be the sole actor in areas where others can just as well (or better) supply the services expected, notably with regard to structures in which the economic or social partners may become involved.

At the same time, public administration should be able to have an overall view and ensure that the division of roles within its jurisdiction is consistent. Competition, compartmentalization and jurisdictional disputes between ministries and government agencies often create parallel operations that are detrimental to the quality and efficiency of services. Over and above the possible conflicts with federal jurisdictions, collaboration between the sectors of education, health, income security and employment is far from optimal. Indeed, it often appears that partnership with employers or workers is easier than that between agencies within the same government. This constitutes a major challenge for labour administration.

Finally, labour administration should have the resources to be able to meet the expectations of governments and citizens, both in quantitative and qualitative terms.

This concept brings us back to the heart of the current debate about the State, mentioned earlier in this chapter, and *calls for labour administrations in all countries to be modernized.*

This primarily concerns countries that have undergone profound transformations, bringing to an end non-pluralist political and social regimes or economic systems devoid of private enterprise and free markets. This need to modernize, however, also concerns all countries which have let their administrations become ossified by not supplying them with the necessary resources and impetus. As a result, they are unable to respond to the needs of firms and workers in numerous areas, notably as regards the labour market, vocational training and the improvement of working conditions.

Finally, it concerns other countries, that is, those with a competent and dynamic labour administration that operates in compliance with the requirements of Convention No. 150, but which are faced with a changing environment, as described in this chapter. The extent of these developments is such that adapting to the new needs, audiences and policies is an absolute necessity.

The following chapters describe examples of practices which we found to be making the necessary adjustments, *in their specific context.* They represent only a small sample of the good practices developed by labour administrations throughout the world. Many others could have been used, but, given limited space, it was necessary to concentrate on countries at very different stages of development and to cover the majority of fields of labour administration activity, providing concrete examples that would enrich the information at the disposal of decision-makers and encourage discussion and debate.

This information should be added to constantly and every effort will be made to do so. It also needs to be used with care; nothing is perfect, and nothing can be transposed out of context without being considerably adapted.

Notes

[1] M. Wallin: "Labour administration: Origins and development", in *International Labour Review* (Geneva, ILO), July 1969, p. 53.

[2] OECD: *Societal cohesion and the globalising economy: What does the future hold?* (Paris, 1997), p. 3.

[3] W. Sengenberger, G.W. Loveman and M.J. Piore (eds.): *The re-emergence of small enterprises: Industrial restructuring in industrialised countries* (Geneva, International Institute for Labour Studies, 1990), p. 53.

[4] OECD: *Science, Technology and Industry Outlook* (Paris, 1998), p. 52.

[5] C. Maldonado et al.: *Le secteur informel en Afrique face aux contraintes légales et institutionnelles* (Geneva, ILO, 1999).

[6] ILO: *World Employment Report 1998-99. Employability in the global economy – How training matters* (Geneva, 1998), p. 167.

[7] idem: "1997 labour overview. Latin America and the Caribbean", in *ILO News* (Lima, 1997).

[8] OECD: *Science, Technology and Industry Outlook*, op. cit., p. 37.

[9] ILO: *World Employment Report 1998-99. Employability in the global economy – How training matters*, op. cit., p. 38.

[10] OECD: *Science, Technology and Industry Outlook*, op. cit., p. 181.

[11] idem: *Science, Technology and Industry Outlook* (Paris, 1997), editorial, p. 16.

[12] ILO: *World Employment Report 1998-99. Employability in the global economy – How training matters*, op. cit., Ch. 6 ("Women and training in the global economy"), pp. 139-142.

[13] OECD: *Information Technology Outlook* (Paris, 1997), editorial, p. 1.

[14] ibid., Ch. 5 and Ch. 8.

[15] UNESCO: *World Education Report: Teachers and teaching in a changing world* (Paris, 1998), p. 91.

[16] OECD: *Information Technology Outlook*, op. cit., p. 3.

[17] ILO: *World Employment Report 1998-99. Employability in the global economy – How training matters*, op. cit., Ch. 2 ("Globalization, technological change and demand for skilled labour"), pp. 33-55.

[18] ibid., p. 34 (fig. 2.1).

[19] OECD: *Education at a Glance 1997: OECD Indicators* (Paris, 1997), p. 69.

[20] ibid., p. 60.

[21] idem: *Education at a Glance: Analysis* (Paris, 1996), p. 14.

[22] idem: *The world in 2020: Towards a new global age* (Paris, 1997), p. 110.

[23] idem: *Education Policy Analysis* (Paris, 1998), Ch. 1.

[24] idem: *Science, Technology and Industry Outlook* (Paris, 1998), p. 29.

[25] ibid., p. 31.

[26] IMF: *World Economic Outlook* (Washington, DC, May 1998).

[27] UNCTAD: *World Investment Report 1998: Trends and determinants – Overview* (Geneva, 1998).

[28] R. Kyloh (ed.): *Mastering the challenge of globalization: Towards a trade union agenda*, Bureau of Workers' Activities, working paper (Geneva, ILO, 1998), p. 2.

[29] OECD: *Information Technology Outlook*, op. cit., p. 142.

[30] UNCTAD: *World Investment Report 1998: Trends and determinants – Overview*, op. cit.

[31] OECD: *Information Technology Outlook*, op. cit., p. 10.

[32] ILO: *Les systèmes d'administration du travail en Europe centrale et dans les pays baltes: la renaissance, 1988-1997*, ADMITRA publ. No. 54 (Geneva, 1999).

[33] idem: *The role of labour inspection in transition economies*, ADMITRA publ. No. 48 (Geneva, 1996).

[34] M. Sahlins: *Culture and practical reason* (Chicago, Ill., University of Chicago Press, 1976).

[35] A. Touraine: *Pourrons-nous vivre ensemble? Egaux et différents* (Paris, Le Livre de poche, Biblio essais, 1999).

[36] A. Giddens: *The constitution of society* (Oxford, Basil Blackwell, 1984).

[37] idem: *The consequences of modernity* (Oxford, Polity and Basil Blackwell, 1990).

[38] World Bank: *World Development Report 1997: The state in a changing world* (Washington, DC, 1998), p. 112, fig. 7.1.

[39] J.M. Keynes: *The general theory of employment, interest and money* (London, Macmillan, 1936).

[40] S. Trosa: *Moderniser l'administration: comment font les autres? Approche comparative des stratégies de modernisation des administrations en France, au Royaume-Uni et en Australie* (Paris, Editions d'Organisation, 1997).

[41] World Bank: *World Development Report 1997: The state in a changing world*, op. cit.

[42] OECD: "National Accounts", in *Trends in Public Sector Pay in OECD Countries* (Paris, PUMA Edition, 1997).

[43] ibid.

[44] B. de Quatrebarbes: *Usagers ou clients? Marketing et qualité dans les services publics* (Paris, Editions de l'Organisation, 1996).

[45] OECD: "National Accounts", op. cit.

[46] ILO: *World Employment Report 1998-99. Employability in the global economy – How training matters*, op. cit., p. 141.

[47] ibid., p. 43.

[48] idem: *Les systèmes d'administration du travail en Europe centrale et dans les pays baltes: la renaissance, 1988-1997*, op. cit.

[49] idem: *World Labour Report 1997-98: Industrial relations, democracy and social stability* (Geneva, 1998).

[50] ibid.

[51] A.B.L. Cheung: "Understanding public sector reforms: Global trends and diverse agendas", in *International Review of Administrative Sciences* (Brussels, International Institute of Administrative Sciences), Dec. 1997, pp. 435-537.

[52] C. Hood: "Beyond the public bureaucracy State? Public administration in the 1990s", Inaugural lecture, London School of Economics, 16 Jan. 1990, cited in Cheung, op. cit.

[53] ILO: *Human resource development in the public service in the context of structural adjustment and transition* (Geneva, 1998).

[54] idem: *Record of Proceedings*, International Labour Conference, Provisional Record No. 19. Report of the Committee on the Application of Standards, 85th Session, Geneva, 19 June 1997, pp. 36-50.

[55] idem: *Report of the Director-General*, Twelfth Asian Regional Conference, Bangkok, Dec. 1997, p. 122.

[56] idem: Centre for European Studies in Strasbourg. *Labour administration as a vehicle for development*, Proceedings of the European symposium, 27-28 November 1997 (Geneva, 1998), p. 260.

[57] ILO: *Productivity in labour administration*, ADMITRA pub. No. 35 (Geneva, 1993), pp. 3-15.

[58] D. Picard: *Veille sociale: prévoir et gérer la conflictualité* (Paris, Vuibert Gestion), p. 1.

[59] UNCTAD: *World Investment Report 1998: Trends and determinants – Overview*, op. cit., p. 30.

[60] A.M. Zack: "Can Alternative Dispute Resolution help resolve employment disputes?", in *International Labour Review*, Vol. 136, No. 1, Spring 1997, p. 95.

[61] ILO: Governing Body doc. GB.271/4/1, 271st Session, Geneva, Mar. 1998, pp. 24-25.

[62] ibid., p. 22.

[63] idem: *Labour administration – A powerful agent of a policy of gender equality in employment and occupation: Guide to good administrative practices*, ADMITRA publ. No. 55 (Geneva, 1999).

[64] World Bank: *World Development Report 1997: The state in a changing world,* op. cit.

[65] ILO/Equipe multidisciplinaire d'Afrique nord-ouest (EMANO): *Observatoires de l'emploi et de la formation en Afrique du Nord-Ouest: des outils d'aide à la décision* (Geneva, 1996), p. 16.

[66] ILO: Governing Body, Working Party on the Social Dimensions of the Liberalization of International Trade. *Progress report on the country studies of the social impact of globalization* (GB.274/WP/SDL/2), 274th Session, Geneva, Mar. 1999, p. 13.

[67] Phan Thuy, Ellen Hansen and David Price: *The public employment service in a changing labour market* (Geneva, ILO, 2001).

[68] UNDP: *Human Development Report 1998* (New York, 1998).

[69] ILO: *Cooperative and consultative bodies in labour administration,* ADMITRA publ. No. 52 (Geneva, 1997).

[70] idem: *World Labour Report 1997-98: Industrial relations, democracy and social stability,* op. cit., p. 248.

[71] idem: *Cooperative and consultative bodies in labour administration,* op. cit., pp. 13-14.

[72] idem: *World Labour Report 1997-98: Industrial relations, democracy and social stability,* op. cit., p. 175.

[73] I. Beleva: *Le système bulgare d'administration du travail 1996,* unpublished study conducted for ILO: *Les systèmes d'administration du travail en Europe centrale et dans les pays baltes,* op. cit.

[74] Maldonado et al., op. cit.

[75] ILO: *World Employment Report 1998-99. Employability in the global economy – How training matters,* op. cit., p. 164.

[76] idem: *Mémorandum technique au gouvernement du Burkina Faso sur le fonctionnement du Ministère burkinabé de l'Emploi, du Travail et de la Sécurité sociale* (Geneva, 1998), p. 1.

[77] Maldonado et al., op. cit.

[78] ibid.

[79] ILO: *Cooperative and consultative bodies in labour administration,* op. cit .

[80] idem: *Les systèmes d'administration du travail en Europe centrale et dans les pays baltes: la renaissance, 1988-1997,* op. cit.

[81] idem: *World Labour Report 1997-98: Industrial relations, democracy and social stability,* op. cit., p. 57.

[82] Wallin, op. cit.

Trends in modernization

2

The aim of this chapter is to highlight general trends relating to labour administration activities in different countries. The discussion is based on selective observations whose long-term impact has not been determined; they were assembled by national specialists and form the basis of the case studies presented in Part II.

The information distilled from the case studies will be broken down into sections dealing with the following themes: historical background; institutional framework; policy implementation; active human resources management; information technology; partnership; funding; and evaluation.

Each section will include, in addition to a theoretical introduction, a presentation of typical national situations, an analysis of the practices observed and an examination of contemporary trends as portrayed in the many works, articles and studies surveyed. The various practices and analyses must be placed in the context of the theoretical discussion which gives them their meaning.

2.1 Historical background

2.1.1 The importance of historical context

In a reference work on the organization and management of labour administration, beginning the chapter that relates to specific studies with a historical summary reflects the authors' belief that the construction or development of a labour administration cannot be understood without a proper historical context. Providing as it does an insight into the way in which individuals and groups – we will call them actors – who have (or who wish to) set up institutions perceive society, history is an essential tool for understanding situations in general, and the establishment of a labour administration in particular. Society must always be seen as the result of a human construct that is based not directly on present, past and future constraints, but on the actors' specific interpretation of these constraints, be they political, sociological, economic, technical or financial. Past actors have constructed the place of work and the law governing work from a representation of what can and should be society's best method of operation, and of the role it assigns to labour and to its administration. Only by evoking the past can the present be reconstituted within the richness of the actors' experience.

Institutions – labour administration among them – are not a given; instead, they are the result of a social construct that is expressed in terms of laws, regulations, organization, administration and so on, and which may only be understood in the light of the past. This construct responds to real problems posed by the close or remote events which it is supposed to solve. The events may be recent and can be recalled in order to understand the significance attached to them by the actors, or they may be remote, in which case reference will be made to the culture of a country rather than to precise events. In most situations we find a combination of both.

In their account of the French Revolution, François Furet and Mona Ozouf[1] divide their work into four parts: the movement of ideas; events; actors; and institutions. Any description of reforms in a political and administrative system must necessarily recall that they are the result of these variables, which must initially be isolated even though they are in constant interaction. Of course, the changes that we are studying are infinitely smaller than those wrought by the French Revolution. However, even on our modest scale the understanding of an event and of its result requires that these variables be borne in mind, even where they are not explicitly referred to in the course of our analysis.

The creation or modification of a labour administration is an act by a political, legislative or administrative authority aimed at introducing voluntary change. The term "voluntary" is here used deliberately instead of the expression "social change", the latter being a slow transformation of society subject to the effect of uncontrolled movements, that is, an involuntary, unforeseeable, lasting and collective change whose occurrence can be perceived over time. Voluntary or organizational change is actively sought, desired, clearly identified and decided by an individual or a group. The consequences of a higher level of knowledge on the organization of labour are an example of the former type of change, whereas measures taken by a labour administration in health and safety matters correspond to the latter. However, each one is – or should be – based on the other. The saying that "society cannot be changed by decree" is a popular one, but it masks an important reality: decrees are necessary if society is to change, if not in its entirety at least in certain sectors. Therefore, what we should be saying is: "Society cannot be changed by decree alone". Decrees are a necessary though insufficient condition of change promoted by a political authority. Their scope is entirely dependent on the will of political actors.

Taking into account the difference between these two types of change is important for the evaluation of the foreseeable results of the actions undertaken. Voluntary change can succeed only if it is based on deep-seated feelings within society. It needs social legitimacy which – in the case of labour administration – could lie in a tripartite approach. Any description and analysis of a decision taken for or by a labour administration must be based on the clearly stated reasons for them, and on what is known of the legitimacy that will be recognized by those called upon to implement the decision.

In order to emphasize the significance of a historical approach, we will begin with a description of a number of typical situations illustrating the importance of past events and of their interpretation by the actors concerned.

2.1.2 Typical situations

2.1.2.1 China

It is impossible to understand the reform of the management of redundancies in Chinese public enterprises without taking into account the country's social, economic and political context, and in particular the fact that the vast majority, or almost all firms of any importance, were publicly owned. Considering it essential to undertake structural reform, the Government decided to privatize public enterprises, to encourage the search for profit and the setting up of joint-stock companies, to accept their going bankrupt, to reduce staff numbers and therefore to lay off workers. This reform drive caused massive disruption to the production mechanisms of the previous period and brought onto the labour market a considerable number of workers; at the end of 1997, 6.3 million employees of public enterprises (about 8.8 per cent of the total number of workers employed by such enterprises) were made redundant while continuing to be paid by them for a three-year period.

The weight of the past and the situation specific to Chinese reform are clearly visible here. Faced with huge numbers of redundant workers, the Government could not allow free-market rules to come into play, even though it was seeking to establish such laws. The solution it found consisted in having the firms take care of the workers for a further three-year period, during which they had to look for work or accept jobs offered to them by official bodies. The new labour regulations and the guidelines given to the labour administration would be incomprehensible without knowledge of these events and of the difficulties experienced by current government actors.

2.1.2.2 Fiji

In Fiji, the spirit and letter of the reform undertaken are in total contradiction with health and safety legislation and organization previously in force. The legislation, drawn up and imposed by the Government without consulting the parties concerned and applied by inspectors considered as industrial police officers, was more concerned with examining industrial accidents once they occurred than with preventing them.

Both the spirit of the law and its implementation have changed. Future legislation must be passed in consultation with the parties concerned, and self-regulation by the actors must be introduced, including employers, workers, machine designers, suppliers, installation engineers, and so on. There is an explicit drive to create a culture of preventing industrial accidents.

Labour organizations being set up will have the duty to facilitate consultation between interested parties. The decision-makers' stated aim is to do away completely with earlier, non-consultative methods, deemed to be ineffective, and to opt instead for a more participatory approach. They are therefore placing their bets on the future, based on what they believe to be the causes of past mistakes.

2.1.3 Types of normative practices observed

As stated, the various practices adopted are the result of historical and contingent features (they could have been different and no form of determinism explains their current state). Labour administration activities belong to one of the following types.

2.1.3.1 Law based

Most labour administration activities studied have a legislative basis, usually a law or a set of regulations adopted by the authorities, a flexible regulatory framework or standards adopted at the government's initiative and followed up by different methods of application. This is what was observed notably in the case of Austria, Belgium, Canada (Province of Quebec), Fiji, France, Hungary, Norway, Peru, Poland, Spain and the United Kingdom.

2.1.3.2 Generated and supported by supranational organizations

This scenario may be complemented by measures inspired or imposed by directives issued by supranational organizations in the field of labour law. ILO Conventions must then be incorporated into national law, with the ILO's technical support, or European Union Directives into the law of European Union Member States (or applicant countries during the accession process, as in the case of Norway); these different supranational normative sources must be combined. This is the case observed in Argentina, Austria, Norway, Philippines, Poland and Spain.

2.1.3.3 Result of negotiations with the social partners

In several cases, labour policies are established and implemented following negotiations between the social partners and/or between these partners and the authorities, be they central or decentralized. As in Argentina and the United States, this may be in the form of negotiations and agreements between various government bodies at different levels (federal State and federal provinces or other public entities such as municipalities or subregional groupings, whether governmental or not). There may also be negotiations between the social partners, then between them and the Government, followed by implementation through a law or regulations, which are sometimes incorporated in the Labour Code (Austria, Burkina Faso, Fiji, France, Hungary and the United States). In countries where federal or provincial bodies traditionally have extended powers, such bodies may also have broad decision-making powers, provided that general rules are observed.

2.1.3.4 Other grounds

Other reasons may also be at the origin of internal standards in the field of labour administration, such as constraints resulting from the social and political environment, for instance (Austria, China, Fiji, France, Hungary, Poland and the United States); however, this statement should be treated with caution since no constraint determines a particular type of decision.

In other cases, decisions were taken under pressure from public opinion or for reasons of internal economic policy, as a result of budgetary cuts necessitating a different allocation of resources, or else were simply a reorganization based on the lessons learnt from experience (Austria, Burkina Faso, Fiji, France, Hungary and the United States).

Decisions may also have been made following the first oil crisis (Austria, France), in anticipation of changes or as a result of comparison with what was being done elsewhere.

2.1.4 Current trends: Deregulation differentiated according to its aim

Studies on labour administration conducted in the 1990s appear to show that the trend is that of social deregulation. Our studies, for their part, reveal an increase in the number of laws and regulations in the sphere of labour administration. Is this an effect similar to those revealed by Karl Polanyi,[2] that is, a phase of resocialization following a period of liberalism? If liberalism was or had been in fashion, then States, nations and social partners would in fact be moving away from introducing regulations.

An apparently general effect is that of opening up to the experiences of others. We may consider that this is a consequence of globalization, in the sense that advances in the means of communication have provided access to the experiences of others, but also that globalization leads to an opening up to the experiences of others. We have seen that many practices are influenced, if not directly inspired, by supranational or international organizations. The ILO plays an important role in this field, which has a direct effect on labour administrations.

It could be said that the general theme of labour administration (the creation or development of its services and organization) lends itself to the establishment of regulations and laws. By contrast, as soon as it proves necessary to enter into the details of actual management (the administration of human resources, information techniques, partnership, funding and evaluation), the trend towards deregulation will remain significant and will be accompanied by an approach involving closer contact with users, according to various methods that will be examined below. In order to deal with employment situations, for example, to which public opinion is particularly sensitive, governments have made choices that differ widely between different countries, or even successively in the same country. In the field of labour law, deregulation policies or strong encouragement towards an active employment search as a condition for receiving unemployment benefit require that the public employment services (PES) give absolute priority to jobseekers. Many active employment policies of all kinds have been adopted and are generally managed by the PES for the benefit of certain categories of jobseekers, in most cases young people and the long-term unemployed. These active policies are one of the principles of the new employment strategy adopted in 1997 by the European Union, and they are also one of the principles of the welfare reform adopted in the United States in 1996. [a]

2.2 Changes in the institutional framework

2.2.1 The institution and organization of labour administration functions

Any reference to an institutional framework combines two levels of analysis, those of an institution and of an organization. An institution may be defined as a body which, in society, carries out the function of orientation and overall social regulation. The commonly recognized institutions are the family, school and, in broader terms, the education system, churches, the army, the courts, and the state apparatus. An institution is a framework constructed in and by society. In order to understand it, reference must be made to the cultures and traditions particular to each type of society. The organizational framework is a different body, which stems from the first, and acts as a specific and transitory means of structuring the institution, in other words its inner workings. Such a framework is translated into organization charts, a hierarchy, formal and informal accounting rules, workforce management and funding, but also into decision-making processes whose form and reality rarely coincide.

Labour administration is therefore an institution of the state apparatus through which society expresses its willingness to submit human labour to rules, in that it cannot be an object left to arbitrary treatment and must be submitted not to individual decisions but to a will common to the whole of society. Inspired by the experience of the past and, in this case, the importance of the social problems generated by the development of industrial society dur-

---

[a] Public Law 104-193 of 1996, Personal Responsibility and Work Opportunity Reconciliation Act (*United States Code Congressional & Administrative News*, October 1996, No. 8, pp. 2105-2355).

ing the eighteenth and nineteenth centuries in industrialized countries, this administration is the visible trace of society's will to regulate what one may generally refer to as working conditions. For example, by means of a system of laws or agreements, society will delegate to a labour administration, thus considered to be an organization, the task of controlling working hours throughout life (excluding of child labour and work by the elderly) or daily working hours, together with wage levels and working conditions, including accident prevention or even the conditions in which hierarchical relations can be exercised, and so on.

Institutions and organizations become part of national cultures. Presenting the framework in which labour administration developed in different countries is tantamount to the dual use of the culture that has structured institutions and organizations. These bodies are not dependent only on the objectives specified for the structures concerned, but on the manner in which actors consider that they must embody their values, either through a system of laws, or through negotiations. Both form an integral part of these cultures.

2.2.2 Typical situations

It would be easy to believe that the activities of labour administration departments form part of the remit of the Ministry of Labour and Employment, on which such administrations generally depend. This is the case in the majority of countries, but there are other situations that differ from the traditional scenario. Paradoxically, such situations occur when new activities are introduced, and rather than establishing new bodies with jurisdiction over the activities, they are assigned to other departments or networks already in existence, in particular outside the field of the government administration of labour. Based on the existing momentum, it is often local networks, nongovernmental departments or even independent networks that are responsible for this. This trend is strengthened by a concern with not overburdening the state apparatus, given the context in favour of the reduction of administrative structures, which was discussed in Chapter 1. The following two examples show that the situations generated by history or culture vary, but are also influenced by recent developments.

2.2.2.1 Canada (Province of Quebec)

Quebec presents an interesting case in the sense that it is a federal State and also that it has a long-standing negotiating tradition. The labour administration there is very fragmented and decisions which are be taken only by administrative authorities often become enmeshed with negotiated decisions. Furthermore, responsibility for applying the laws relating to labour and employment is shared between about a dozen bodies which in 1998 came under either the Department of Labour or the Department of Employment and Solidarity in addition to the role played by the Executive Council in planning-related matters and the Office of the Auditor General of Quebec for assessment purposes.

Each of these bodies has a specific vocation. The majority, under the supervision of the Department of Labour, are generally grouped together in two large categories depending on their method of funding; firstly, those referred to as budgetary organizations, that is, whose funding comes from the portfolio of the Department of Labour itself; and secondly, so-called non-budgetary organizations which receive independent funding. The Joint Committees, an institution specific to Quebec and not to Canada, should also be added; they are independent bodies to which the legislator has delegated the role of supervising and monitoring the application of the collective agreements extended by decree.

The Canadian Constitution Act of 1867 did not make provision, in labour-related matters, for power sharing between the federal and provincial levels. Following the onset of industrialization and the development of trade union organizations, among others, it was the Federal Parliament that initially undertook to legislate on these matters, so as to follow up on certain Conventions adopted by the ILO. Those first federal initiatives subsequently gave rise to debates during which guidelines for power sharing were laid down, assigning the major role to the provinces in labour-related matters.

The situation is complicated by the fact that Canadian federal labour law applies to what are commonly called "federal enterprises," a term that covers "sites, works, enterprises or sectors of activity falling under the legislative competence of Parliament". This includes activities relating to navigation and water transport, railway installations or projects, telegraph channels or connections, in fact to all such installations whenever they go beyond the borders of a province or involve two or more provinces. Each of the two levels of government, federal and provincial, therefore has its own field of competence for all labour-related issues. In practice, however, the vast majority of Canadian workers are under the authority of provincial legislatures, while about 10 per cent of wage earners are subject to federal legislation and regulations.

Canada therefore has a system which, on account of the historical and cultural features peculiar to the country, combines different levels of responsibility in labour administration.

In Quebec, responsibility for labour and employment-related issues is shared by two ministries: the Department of Labour is responsible for issues relating to working conditions, standards and the organization of labour, labour markets, industrial relations, and occupational health and safety; the Department of Employment and Solidarity, for its part, is in charge of matters relating to vocational training, employment and active measures designed to facilitate the return to employment or employment maintenance.

The Department of Labour is assisted by different councils, commissions and committees. The first of these is the Advisory Council on Labour and Manpower, a study and consultative body whose mandate is to issue opinions to the Minister of Labour on all subjects submitted to it in relation to the subjects within its remit; it can also study any labour- and workforce-related issues. The Pay Equity Commission is entrusted with establishing pay-equity programmes and ensuring their maintenance in Quebec. The Quebec Construction Commission ensures that coherent labour relations are maintained and manages the workforce in this branch of industry; it also establishes an integrated system of training and vocational qualifications.

The Occupational Health and Safety Commission is responsible for developing, proposing and implementing policies relating to the health and safety of workers so as to ensure that better working conditions are provided. It administers the occupational health and safety system.

The Labour Standards Commission has the task of supervising the implementation and application of labour standards in Quebec, that is, the rules governing minimum working conditions.

The Essential Services Council is primarily an administrative tribunal responsible for ensuring that citizens continue to benefit at all times from the services considered to be essential and to which they are entitled during a strike, in certain public services and establishments of the health and social services network.

Joint committees are set up by parties to a collective agreement extended by decree; their task is to supervise and ensure compliance with the decree.

The Department of Employment and Solidarity has the task of assisting the development of the workforce and employment, and of combating poverty. Its mandate is to promote economic and social integration. For that purpose, it administers all activities relating to the labour market (employment, active measures, vocational guidance, skills acquisition) both for the unemployed and for employed persons wishing to change jobs; it also manages social assistance activities and pays benefits to those receiving such assistance.

"Employment-Quebec" is an independent unit within the Department of Employment and Solidarity. Its aim is to provide the conditions to increase effectiveness and improve the quality of services. Its task is to generate employment for the workforce available, to improve labour supply and influence the demand for workers so as to promote the balance between the two on the labour market.

The Commission of Labour Market Partners helps to devise government policies and measures in the fields of manpower and employment, in particular by promoting the development of training, and contributes to decision-making related to the implementation and management of measures and programmes forming part of the Department's remit in these fields.

2.2.2.2 Hungary

In 1998, the old centralized command system was abandoned in favour of a new institutional framework, established within a specific cultural and historical context. The new institutions are qualified by observers as truly innovative, given the mechanisms that prevailed under the old command system. We will refer here only to the field of collective bargaining, as the Hungarian Government introduced original structures intended to develop negotiations between the social partners and to provide services to users in this field.

The National Interest Conciliation Council (ICC), set up in 1988, is a tripartite body operating as a forum for exchange and negotiation, which was and is of great importance at a time when the social partners were/are in the midst of restructuring. Although funded by the Ministry, it appears to enjoy a certain autonomy and is jointly managed by the social partners. In addition to this institution, collective negotiating practices have begun to develop in certain occupational branches. An arbitration and mediation body was set up in 1996.

These processes are still in their infancy. They have not spread to all parts of the country, nor can they be found in all occupational sectors; instead, they remain confined to the national level and to certain branches. They do, however, illustrate the capacity of the labour administration to devise certain previously unknown types of procedures.

The current institutional framework is embodied in the renamed Interest Conciliation council (ICC). The council comprises a secretariat, funded by the labour administration department within the Ministry of Labour, and several standing and specialized committees dependent on other ministerial departments. The ICC holds monthly plenary sessions, as well as restricted sessions. In 1997, the former labour market committee was transformed into the Labour Market Steering Committee, which became a tripartite body independent of the Government. Its main task is to manage the allocation of funding for the employment policy, by means of an independent agency. The ICC cooperates closely with the social partners and government, while employers and workers are represented by their national organizations.

Collective agreements come into force after being signed by the parties concerned and following a request made by an employers' organization and other organizations representing workers. They are extended by the department of social relations, a specialized department of the Ministry of Labour, which registers collective branch agreements and verifies their formal validity.

The Labour Mediation and Arbitration Service is a specialized department within the Ministry of Labour. Although it is intended to settle disputes before strikes are called, it was not set up because of the number of labour disputes, which was particularly low during the transition period, but as a form of recognition, at the political level, of the need to establish a professional conciliation and arbitration body.

Finally, it should be pointed out that the powers of the ICC do not cover individual legal disputes, which fall within the jurisdiction of labour tribunals. Since the tribunals have rapidly been inundated with work, the possibility of voluntary mediation in the disputes prior to recourse to the courts has been opened. The social partners are closely involved in the ICC's activity, but not with its day-to-day functioning.

These two examples show that on an institutional level the activities of the labour administration can be very fragmented (entrusted to a large number of organizations and shared between different levels of government) or else much more centralized within a single organization and under the remit of a single political authority. It is also clear that in many countries this institutional framework is evolving towards a greater involvement of actors in bipartite or tripartite arrangements. Finally, the bodies responsible for labour administration activities can be organized in several very different ways, depending on their degree of independence from the political authorities.

2.2.3 Practices: Different types of structures

Broadly speaking, there are four major models for implementing the activities conducted by labour administrations; they are not mutually exclusive, even within the same country.

2.2.3.1 Direct management: most activities are under the remit of the Ministry of Labour and its departments

In this model, activities are managed by the Ministry of Labour, which can establish consultation bodies that are generally tripartite in nature; the role and independence of these bodies are undeveloped and variable. This is the case in particular in Austria, Burkina Faso, Chile, China, Fiji, France, Hong Kong (China), Japan, Norway, Peru, Philippines and Spain. Most of the bodies comprise government representatives, employers and workers who have equal standing within the same authority.

In this scenario, the most frequently encountered organization is that in which a department of the Ministry of Labour sets the objectives, supervises their implementation and manages the funding of activities, and where the department itself is assisted by a consultative committee that, within the confines of the policy set by the Ministry, may put forward opinions on the implementation of these guidelines. In most cases, a director of the administration is in charge of the department in question.

In the case of significant intervention, for example when an administrative employment department receives a complaint regarding the threat of numerous redundancies on an industrial site, the Ministry of Labour intervenes directly in cooperation with the Ministry of Finance and the Ministry of Economic Affairs (if one exists), and in consultation with the social partners and the other institutions concerned, but it retains sole responsibility for operations. Such situations may be generated by a country's particular history (the case of China where the Government wished to privatize public enterprises is noted above), or be the result of the malfunctioning of an independent body. The Government thus considers it necessary, frequently for a limited period, to retake control of the body by using only the labour administration services.

There may be cases where the action taken requires unilateral intervention by a labour administration. In Belgium, for example, the labour inspection services may paradoxically be obliged to decide for themselves to summon the parties to a mediation procedure so as to reach a consensus between them and to achieve conciliation in individual labour disputes.

2.2.3.2 Recourse to existing independent bodies under the remit of the Ministry of Labour

In a number of situations there may be organizations which, although they are financed by the Ministry, retain their independence, often by means of their bipartite or tripartite composition, but this independence is never really complete. Examples include Belgium, Canada (Province of Quebec), Hungary, Spain and the United Kingdom.

Labour policy procedures or related aspects may be managed by such bodies, which remain under the supervision of the Ministry of Labour, chaired by an official appointed by the State and subject to the authority of the Ministry; they do, however, have a certain degree of freedom to take decisions and enjoy organizational independence to a greater or lesser extent.

This is generally the case with regard to the employment services, which form independent agencies managed by a tripartite administrative council. Partners may make their voices heard and are therefore jointly responsible for the decisions taken, even when these organizations are funded mainly by the State.

2.2.3.3 Activities entrusted to decentralized departments

In many cases, when a new labour administration activity is introduced, a new organization is not set up to take responsibility for it. Alternatively, as was the case in Argentina, France and Poland, an existing organization is used and its mandate is broadened to ensure that the activity is implemented as close as possible to the beneficiaries. This leads to a re-evaluation of the role of decentralized bodies, either as a result of a federalist tradition or because local bodies appear to be more effective. They are supposed to extend government activities so as to complement, continue and adapt them. Situations of this kind are to be found in Argentina, Burkina Faso, China, France, Japan, Poland and the United States.

Furthermore, decentralized authorities have assumed sole responsibility for defining and implementing certain aspects of labour policy. They must provide the necessary funding, where required through the reimbursement by the State of a portion of the tax collected; the State does not supervise this activity.

2.2.3.4 Management by ad hoc or independent bodies

In a number of countries, we are witnessing the development of mutual protection organizations for workers, to which the State does not contribute or in whose management it does not participate; management duties may be assumed jointly by workers' and employers' representatives.

One extension that should be mentioned is the transfer to private bodies of the management of certain sectors of labour administration. This is the case with regard to protection against the risk of illness or industrial accidents, or retirement, according to very variable methods: voluntary or compulsory contributions paid by salaried employees, participation (or non-participation) of employers, basic or additional system and so on. Such diversity may bring into question the existence of basic protection for all.

Mention should also be made in this category of the services that are coordinated or are dependent on different bodies. This type of structure is probably the most innovative and one that will be widely used in the future. When countries put in place new structures following a change of system or after major developments, the State rarely assumes sole responsibility for the actions undertaken.

Finally, there are situations (as in the United States, for instance) where ad hoc structures uniting state and federal agencies have been created; the Federal Government finances only the setting up of these structures and provides the different states concerned with the opportunity to participate in the work done to devise and launch operations, in particular in the area of employment. In certain cases, as in France, a number of activities are entrusted to independent bodies, and this seems to allow them to develop more fully. In other situations where a very developed informal sector does not offer any social coverage, such coverage is envisaged through the use of existing institutions.

2.2.4 Current trends: Independent bodies and development of networks

Situations where all departments are exclusively under the remit of a ministry are less and less common and, as we have seen, departments always retain a degree of independence. The most common trend is to reduce the number of structures, to level out hierarchies and to develop synergy, with the common denominator being a concern with bringing activities closer to beneficiaries. This arrangement is similar to that encountered in the business world: the end of major conglomerates, monopolies and integrated enterprises carrying out all the functions that generate the final product. The trend is towards developing independent but interlinked bodies, which may be referred to as networks, even though the term has not been formally adopted.

In the United Kingdom, labour administration services are equally complex, but for different reasons from those found in Quebec; they are largely the result of the different government policies adopted in succession since the end of the Second World War. National labour administration is shared mainly between two ministries: the Department for Education and Employment (DfEE) and the Department of Trade and Industry (DTI). Agencies located in various departments are responsible for providing a variety of services. There is a whole series of non-governmental departments that are responsible for regulating the various aspects of the labour market and the provision of services. The number, composition and functions of the institutions comprising the national labour administration system have been gradually modified and their responsibilities have been reassigned at regular intervals. At the initiative of the Labour Government, the functions of the different non-governmental departments are currently being restructured in the field of industrial relations, education and training.

The explanation of these changes lies in recent history. From the point of view of industrial relations, the period following the Second World War was often characterized by the term "voluntarism". The decisions relating to wages and other working conditions were taken by employers or were defined in agreements between employers and trade unions. The State's role in the regulation of labour relations was minimal. From the end of the 1960s onwards, the importance of the authorities in the regulation of these relations began to increase, a change brought about by the developments at the European level. This has frequently been referred to as a period of corporatism. Subsequently, after the Conservative Government of Margaret Thatcher came to power in 1979, changes were implemented, the most notorious of which was the marginalization of the unions, coinciding with legislation which redefined the relations between employers, workers and trade unions in the workplace. The Labour Government, elected in May 1997, and re-elected in June 2001, is more favourably inclined towards union participation and partnership, and encourages negotiations between unions and employers. These relations are characterized by a very large degree of informality and piecemeal negotiations. They play a major role in the overall functioning of the national labour administration through their involvement in a multitude of non-governmental bodies and institutions in the field of industrial relations, employment, education and training.

The evolution of the institutional framework of each country depends on these policy changes. An illustration of this, however, may be found in the case of the United Kingdom. In more general terms, the 1990s saw a withdrawal of the State comparable to that observed in the United Kingdom, especially in a number of English-speaking countries (Australia, Canada and New Zealand). A period during which the State was strong was followed by one where Conservative governments reduced the role of the social actors and of the structures for social dialogue. We are now witnessing a return, albeit a cautious one, to active labour relations and the setting up of institutions that sustain them.

2.3 Policy implementation

2.3.1 The role of the actors

Although the theoretical elements allowing us to understand what is meant by the method of application of an institutional framework are the same as those used to understand history and the creation of institutions, in the first case – the method of application – the role of the participants is, if not more important, at least more visible than in the second case. In both cases, the participants have a completely separate role. History is not characterized merely by the events by which it is marked; the participants play a significant role, on an equal footing with the other elements of the action. We have chosen, however, in the previous paragraph to perceive an institution as a construct and not as a process, that is, to view its history in terms of the past, the culture in which institutions have emerged, the social and economic system in a greater or lesser state of flux of which the institutions form part, and so on. Although an institution is a whole unit responsible for providing guidance and overall social regulation, it can be perceived as a cultural product. That product will be defined here as an established system of rules accepted by a social corpus, an element present at a given moment in a society, without looking back further at the reasons that have produced it. Of course, the establishment of institutions can also be understood by means of the participants involved. In our analysis, however, we have considered such institutions to be an accomplished fact. An account of their formation in terms of the participants involved is not therefore essential in any consideration of it.

If, by contrast, an observer chooses the current development of this institution as his or her subject, the actors involved assume major importance. The institutional framework in the process of development cannot be understood merely by listing the relevant constitutions, laws, regulations and decrees. If we have not gone back to the actors in order to understand the establishment of the institutional framework, its method of application requires in contrast the intervention of the actors who, under our gaze, implement this institutional framework. This is a method, or rather a point in time when the actors turn to the framework and the rules, and begin to implement them. In a clearer sense than in building the framework, the role of the actors and the strategies which, in their minds, are intended to amend the rules and regulations for the better must be taken into account. This is particularly true of national labour administration systems that are organized around institutionally independent actors.

The theoretical tools to be used correspond to the subject under observation. These are essentially strategic analysis and the interaction of the actors in the broad sense of the term. We are not looking at a more or less complete construct – the institutional framework – but at the manner in which this framework develops and is amended. Knowledge of the actors, their roles and strategies will become the focus of our observation. Since these roles are uncertain or incomplete, they are modified in the course of interaction. To understand how an institution develops, knowledge of the actors and the manner in which they will govern their interaction prove to be essential.

A method of application is characterized by a political vision in the broad sense of the term, that is, by measures that reflect, in a coordinated manner, the trend desired by a labour administration, or even directly by a political authority itself.

The general trend is towards bringing a beneficiary closer to an activity and making the actors at all levels aware of their responsibilities. This will be demonstrated firstly by a number of applications, prior to summing up the practices observed.

2.3.2 Typical situations

We have chosen two typical situations where the roles of the actors – in most cases the Ministry of Labour itself, or even the Minister, but also the labour administration – lead to changes in the institutional framework, in new directions that initially do not appear obvious.

2.3.2.1 Senegal

In Senegal, the decision to extend the social security system to the informal sector was taken in 1996 at the explicit request of the Minister of Labour and Employment. The aim was to enable informal sector workers to benefit from the social coverage managed by the Senegal Old-Age Pension Insurance Institution and by the social security authorities. For the time being, only the component relating to family allowances and protection against industrial accidents is operational. The system implemented is currently being evaluated.

The informal sector in Senegal is considered by all the social actors to be the main provider of employment, together with the State. It is estimated that this sector comprises about 60 per cent of the economically active urban population and that it is expanding more rapidly than the salaried employee sector. For the time being, the members and institutions representing this informal sector, on the one hand, and the social security authorities, on the other hand, ignore each other. This situation is firstly the result of feelings of mistrust towards administrative authority among the actors in the informal system. Secondly, the social security authorities are apprehensive about the inflexibility of the legal arsenal and probably of the functioning of the administration, which make it difficult to integrate the actors of the informal system. However, the two spheres appear to have the means to join forces; firstly, the informal sector operates through an organization which, although informal, is remarkably dynamic; and, secondly, the social security authorities have the legal and material means to take account of that sector.

As stated, the question was raised during a speech given by the Head of State of Senegal on 1 May 1996. He presented the extension of the protection offered by the social security system to informal sector workers as an important objective, thus legitimizing a long-standing demand made by local craftspeople, who were aware of the precarious situation of those who have left the formal sector as a result of the closure of enterprises, and who therefore have no social protection. From the very beginning, this initiative therefore involved a major political actor, the minister, taking up an important demand made by another social actor. This activity involves membership of part of the social and economic corpus, the aim being for the new service to be managed jointly by two bodies.

Under the auspices of the Ministry of Labour and Employment, with the support of the labour administration department, the social security services, the ILO Regional Office for Africa and the Friedrich–Ebert Foundation, a joint working group was therefore set up to deal with this subject. Their work led to the signing of a draft agreement between the professional organizations of craftspeople and the Social Security Fund proclaiming freedom of choice of affiliation and defining the documents necessary for membership. The agreement will relate to membership, by means of voluntary insurance, for voluntary workers in the informal sector, in a fund covering industrial accidents and occupational diseases. Membership of a welfare retirement fund is also made possible. Any individual whose activity is registered in the Chamber of Trade Directory may become a member.

An advisory council on occupational risks and a medical insurance consultation body have been set up and are both joint bodies. On their recommendation, a discussion of the introduction of a medical insurance scheme has begun and a complex system of contributions is envisaged.

Benefits paid should already include prenatal and maternity allowances, daily allowances for maternity leave, family allowances, insurance covering industrial accidents and occupational diseases, and so on.

Information and awareness campaigns for craftspeople are planned, the aim being to encourage each informal sector participant to join the insurance scheme by means of individual contributions.

We are therefore witnessing an original method that can be called joint, in the sense that it offers partly public social protection to informal sector workers by means of individual membership. A particular series of actors are involved, under the influence of the State.

2.3.2.2 Peru

In Peru, a recent law[a] provided for the implementation of the "Production Retraining Programmes for Enterprises in the Urban Informal Sector". This is designed to set up SMEs in a sector close to that of craftspeople but better structured. This is part of the extension of the Programme for the Promotion of Self-Employment and Microbusiness (PRODAME), initially implemented at the end of 1990, and the decrees made since then.[b] Although it has just been implemented, the description of its structure and of the actors involved give an idea of its possible future development and a framework for action to consider for similar situations.

---

[a] Title VI (articles 107-112) of Supreme Decree No. 003-97, 27 March 1997 on Labour Productivity and Competitiveness (http://www.asesor.com.pe).

[b] See in particular Legislative Decree No. 705, 5 November 1991 on the Promotion of Small and Microenterprises (*El Peruano*, 8 November 1991).

The scheme in question has been launched by the National Directorate of Employment and Vocational Training of the Ministry of Labour and Social Promotion. The programme essentially consists in providing simplified procedures, together with technical and legal advice for establishing, formalizing and strengthening SMEs. The services provided are free of charge and the assistance provided by the programme enables members to significantly reduce several costs incurred when setting up.

The legal advice services dealing with the formalization and registration of SMEs appear to have obtained the most satisfactory results. By means of these services and advice, users are able to draw up and approve the formal instrument establishing an enterprise within a very reduced time frame of a maximum of 48 hours. This can be as little as half an hour in the case of individual businesses with limited liability. Furthermore, the programme provides training in the form of informal talks, seminars, workshops, conferences, etc., often in consultation with other training organizations.

The implementation process appears to be enhanced by the internal organization of the labour administration, which has entrusted the management, implementation and assessment of the programme exclusively to the National Directorate of Employment and Vocational Training. This body has great flexibility of adaptation and an ability to adopt corrective measures quickly. Non-governmental organizations (NGOs) and SME employers' organizations appear to have difficulties participating in the programme.

This scheme, launched by a directorate of the Ministry of Labour, is obviously economic in nature. Its originality stems from the fact that it acts by means of advice and encouragement rather than by direct funding. It appears to have been mildly successful, despite the difficulties with other organizations able to act in the same sector (NGOs and professional bodies). This success is undoubtedly due to the advice and encouragement which characterize it.

2.3.3 Methods: From a logic of compulsion to a logic of encouragement

The methods revealed by the analysis of the cases studied fall into three broad types.

First there are methods explicitly based on support, advice and belief, and provided by ministry or labour administration departments, replacing policies decried as being outdated and which were founded on control and coercion. Although, in both cases, powers of sanction exist, the process and attitude vary profoundly.

These new attitudes are to be found in Senegal and Peru, as well as in many other countries where labour administration is a key element of a policy of introducing inter-enterprise advice and assistance services for SMEs which do not have the necessary resources.

Elsewhere, as in Austria, Belgium, Chile, China, Hong Kong (China) and the Philippines, administrations seek to establish a dynamic of cooperation, information and conciliation with employers, trade unions and non-unionized workers, or rather emphasize a strategy designed to persuade parties to a dispute to find negotiated solutions to their differences of opinion. In other situations, for example in France, where the State displays a willingness to develop partnerships with actors from the new occupational sectors, what has changed is that the definition of training priorities in branches of industry is assigned to the social partners and no longer to the administration; similarly, the joint committees are entrusted with a new consultation role. In certain cases, training programmes are introduced to improve understanding and awareness of the actions undertaken to promote the development of industrial relations. The situation may be described as the transition from a centralized and coercive model to a decentralized and incentive-based system where the role of the social actors is highly valued in all fields pertaining to industrial relations.

The general trend is to seek recourse to all kinds of means designed to encourage the partners to become members, and to provide information through information and awareness campaigns. In certain cases, material benefits are even provided (financial assistance by the authorities) for enterprises participating in the programmes. In most cases, coercive measures establishing obligations or constraints are rejected.

The second strategy – identical in terms of the desired aims but different in relation to the means used – consists in using private sector resources within the framework of public sector rules. This is the case in federal States such as the United States, where the central administration delegates the task of tool development to the states, while controlling the application of those tools. Management is entrusted in certain cases to non-profit-making organizations or also, as is the case in France, to particular operators following a call to tender.

These strategies are generally conducted in conjunction with a large-scale decentralization of the services concerned.

Finally, in most of these cases the organizational actors are frequently involved from the very outset, even when the situation can be a delicate one for them. This was the case in China, for instance, where the trade unions have participated in workers' assistance programmes from the very beginning of a redundancy procedure.

2.3.4 Current trends: Changing the function of labour administration

Specialist literature indicates that the dominant contemporary trends may be grouped under four headings.

2.3.4.1 New roles

While assuming in overall terms their "original" functions (see Chapter 1, section 1.3.3 above) in order to meet new needs, provide new benefits and operate in a more efficient manner, labour administrations attempt to play or adopt, according to the field of activity, a different role in support of users' activities, which is more constructive, incentive based and makes matters easier.

Their role in the field of labour standards, in particular that of inspection, will relate firstly to advice rather than to control and suppression. In terms of employment, their first activity as an intermediary between employment supply and demand has developed, inter alia, towards the promotion of active measures, making users independent, and à la carte services. In the field of vocational training, they assume a specially important role in the training of adults in cooperation with local governments. Finally, and this is one of their most significant new roles, they are becoming one of the best-placed suppliers of information (source, diversity and means of dissemination) for decision-making by individuals, government institutions or enterprises; general information on labour market realities, processed and made available to decision-makers while being widely disseminated, enables situations to be assessed more effectively so as to define economic policies, enhance collective negotiations or take enlightened decisions on possible industrial investments. More relevant information on the probable development of enterprise needs in terms of employment and qualifications in the years to come and on the training organizations and services of use in finding a job makes jobseekers more employable.

2.3.4.2 Decentralization, deconcentration, subcontracting and service purchasing

The difference between these concepts is well known.

Decentralization is the transfer of responsibilities, together with the related state powers and budgetary management to a politically independent level. For example, central administrations were themselves responsible for distributing subsidies to social actors. Since they consider themselves to be too remote from the specific situations experienced by these actors, they entrust independent organizations with this responsibility, for example locally elected entities such as regions, communes, and so on, which are not accountable to the central administration with regard to the policy that they define and implement in the field of competence transferred to them.

Deconcentration consists in actions being carried out by a state body or department, without in any way changing the political responsibility involved. The desired aim is often to carry out the actions in a different place, for example in a region rather than in the capital, so as to provide a service that is closer to its users.

Subcontracting involves entrusting certain projects to a different organization under commercial contract, be it a non-profit-making body or private firm.

Finally, *service purchasing* establishes a client/supplier relationship in which the organization responsible for a labour administration activity purchases a service, such as a skill assessment sheet in the case of France, from another public organization or private enterprise.

The trend observed in each country is at least towards deconcentration, but more and more towards decentralization and even beyond, whereby the State has activities carried out by organizations, including private enterprises (for example, training activities).

In the case of decentralization, for example, the responsibilities of local agencies are increased and those agencies are requested to improve their knowledge and understand the area that they cover in order to assess its needs and be able to adapt the application of the programmes and policies to the real situation existing in each area. This is a strong trend, often supported by funding methods enabling these local authorities to choose from the programmes available by applying them according to their users' needs.

With regard to subcontracting, this trend obviously raises the question of defining the public service and of devolving some if its activities to private bodies. In the case of assistance services for the economic sector, in particular private enterprises, the implementation of this type of activity is underpinned by the question of the effectiveness of public actions. The more or less explicit justification for these decentralization activities is their effectiveness. Responsibilities are transferred to the private sector since it is considered that private bodies will be more effective; this is as much a social representation as it is a reality that can be evaluated. This gives rise to the question of the monitoring and evaluation of these activities. In the examples mentioned in Part II of this book, it will be seen how certain countries have attempted to respond to this problem in the field of labour administration.

In the same perspective, a strong trend observed is that the public sector does not do everything itself, but uses the private sector to carry out certain activities.

2.3.4.3 Service beneficiaries

Traditionally, those using public services have been referred to as "users". However, the term "client" now appears frequently in specialist literature. Language therefore conveys a change in the conception of a relationship. That relationship was previously based on a model whereby a service was provided to which the beneficiaries were entitled as a result of their status. A market-based model now exists whereby a service is provided as effectively as possible and for which a client should probably pay, even if this payment is not explicitly stated. The idea is that the beneficiaries will be better served if they are considered as clients rather than users, in other words, the market-based model introduces a service-related dimension that would have been neglected if reference had been made only to a user. (It will be recalled that the French administration traditionally preferred the term *"administrés"*, that is, administered subjects.)

This idea contains a more or less explicit criticism of bureaucracy, which is understood to be a situation where an institution tends to see users' interests primarily through its own interest. In keeping with this new idea, the client reigns supreme. This shift in meaning leads to specific organizational consequences: the simplification of formalities, greater accessibility for the public by all possible means, in particular technical ones, and even, in certain cases, a remodelling of the whole organizational structure.

An ILO-commissioned study on labour administration in Finland pointed out that the Ministry of Labour would henceforth be divided into two parts, each of which follows a different direction depending on the clients served:

— a ministry or department responsible for policy under the authority of a Minister, which serves parliament; its responsibilities cover policies, strategies, legislation, funding and the evaluation of the labour administration system; and

— an administrative department under the authority of a management council, which serves partners and users; its responsibilities include the management of economic development and local employment centres.

These two different but functionally related bodies have a secretary-general and a centre director.

By contrast, there is no uniform implementation of the financial equivalent of the shift towards the client concept. Examples in which beneficiaries pay the real price for a service are rare, since they have generally already paid for it in the form of taxation. Systems of direct payment by insurers will preferably be established, in which the department providing a service is actually paid for it, but payment is made by a different body whose "client" is the beneficiary.

This new relationship is characterized by a reduction in standardized services to the benefit of services adapted to individuals and the granting of independence through a simplification of procedures and direct access to the required information.

2.3.4.4 Consultation with social and economic partners

The latest trend observed in this process is the emphasis given to consultation with social and economic partners. In accordance with methods which often appear to differ but are actually related, all the practices observed highlight the idea of consultation with the social partners. It is difficult to ascertain whether this consultation is carried out with the pragmatic and utilitarian aim of improving the operation of services (there is less risk of mistakes being made if people's opinions are sought; there is less risk of disputes if the social partners are consulted), or to achieve the ideal of a human being who must participate for the purpose of self-fulfilment, based on the democratic political model whereby the largest possible number of people are consulted.

Whatever the case may be, most of the practices are implemented with a view to consulting partners or establishing direct partnerships. Irrespective of whether this involves employers, trade unions, non-unionized workers or actors in the new occupational sectors, the new policies conducted under the authority of the labour administration highlight consultation and persuasion strategies. In other situations, the State displays a willingness to form partnerships through its administration. In such cases, the partners will not simply receive information and be consulted. Negotiations will be conducted with them by considering them, if not as equals, at least as actors whose opinion is not only worth seeking but essential to the implementation of a reform.

The analysis of new practices thus reveals a comprehensive change in the function of labour administration. This comes in the form of a transition from a logic of compulsion to a logic of encouragement, from a centralized authoritarian model to very decentralized practices, and in partnership, from a user-type relationship to one that is market based. The transformation is comprehensive. It is in complete compliance with the principles on which the ILO's activity is based, for which the relationship of the state labour administration services to the representatives of employers and workers is the basis of stable and constructive industrial relations.

2.4 Active human resources management

2.4.1 The bureaucratic model

In a public administration, human resources management (HRM) traditionally follows the Weberian bureaucratic model.[3] This model, linked to a form of legitimacy that Weber calls "rational-legal", is characterized by the following main features: it functions according to impersonal rules, resulting from the refusal to consider personal criteria, the definition of posts corresponding to specialized functions, and the hierarchical principle of structuring, the function of which is to monitor operations; the regular nature of the operations is a condition for their being reproduced and the recruitment of officials, who are full-time career specialists, thus ensures the continuity of the organization.

The advantages of this model are obvious: continuity in the performance of tasks, equality of treatment between citizens and the security of officials who protect the model from external pressures. The shortcomings that may lead to serious malfunctioning have been noted by Weber himself, and also by authors critical of bureaucracy. These include a trend towards the levelling of capacities and impersonality (devoid of hatred or passion, as Weber noted, and therefore of love and passion), as well as the formalism that can lead to ritualism (the interiorization of the rules means that these acquire an intrinsic value and become independent of the organization's aims); the whole process results in a mechanical construct of human behaviour. The logic of control is opposed to that of innovation and the search for alternative solutions, while departmentalization induces the primary group to focus on its own problems and lose sight of the overall aims.

It will be seen in the following section that the practices observed appear to take account of the criticism levelled at the model formed by Weber. They apply in particular to HRM for labour administration staff; this management can be defined as the entire means used for the individual and collective management of employees of labour administration departments. The field of HRM therefore includes the organization of work – including the description of tasks – recruitment, career management, remuneration, evaluation, training, development, and hierarchical and collective relations. HRM now also includes management of and by senior managers, whose management style is considerably re-evaluated in the light of the new requirements of making staff aware of their responsibilities and motivating them.

2.4.2 Typical situations

2.4.2.1 Fiji

The action of the labour administration in Fiji is designed to make employers and workers aware of their responsibilities in relation to occupational health and safety. This involves a radical change in the philosophy of intervention of the Ministry of Labour. It implies a transition from a repressive approach to one that provides enterprises and workers with advice and information so that they can, in a concerted manner, assume responsibility for occupational health and safety in their working environment.

In specific terms, the action begins with a simplification of procedures by adopting a framework legislation that can be complemented by regulatory measures and codes of practice. This law aims to promote and support self-regulation on the part of key actors. It recognizes that occupational health and safety is the responsibility of all those who are involved: employers, workers and government.

With regard to the HRM of the labour inspection department responsible for this activity, a relatively bureaucratic hierarchical structure groups together all the staff working in the department: a chief inspector, a deputy chief inspector and two divisions directed by a manager, each of which comprises three units wherein inspectors work in direct relation to firms. All these employees have civil servant status. The framework law makes specific provision for post descriptions, the required qualifications, duties and obligations, and the method of appointment of the inspectors.

In order to implement the new philosophy, the operational structure of the labour inspectorate must be made less cumbersome and coordination more flexible. For this purpose, it is essential that staff contribute and cooperate. Inspectors must move from the role of police officers to that of partners, who operate as close as possible to everyday reality. They must act as mediators and advisers, education specialists and trainers, while nevertheless remaining responsible for implementing occupational health and safety legislation, prohibiting situations which may endanger the health and safety of workers, and sanctioning violations. This radical change of role implies that inspectors must develop new skills. Further training enables them to do so.

The Minister of Labour is highly involved as an agent of change in this reform, in particular by identifying his or her "vision" in a yearly plan. Several values are firmly expressed in the plan, such as professionalism, competence and expertise, a client focus, ethical practices, accountability and respect for others. The plan also gives specific form to the shift in focus to the client, by adopting a service payment policy whereby users pay for a number of services provided by a labour inspectorate (training, consultation services, etc.).

The priorities of the service are subsequently established on the basis of strict strategic planning. All employees are involved at different levels in the preparation of this planning. Objectives, both quantitative and qualitative, are set in a three-year plan. They relate to seven key sectors of results, including the reduction of industrial accidents, data collection, the improvement of the quality of the services provided, the improvement of relations between employers and workers so as to increase productivity in the professional environment, and so on. Finally, there is an obligation to respect the service efficiency criteria corresponding to the ISO 9000 quality standards.

In order to follow up this planning, monthly reports are submitted to the chief inspector by those in charge of all the units and divisions. They describe the results obtained and identify the sectors where difficulties are encountered. By analysing these reports, decisions can be taken about the measures to be adopted. Specific expectations are indicated to each manager. Output is evaluated in relation to the aims set in the three-year plan, which has been broken down into a work plan for each unit.

In order to initiate this change, although it is still difficult to release new resources in a developing economy where funds are limited, the State has agreed to increase the resources of the labour inspection service, which has had a very positive impact on staff morale. These resources of course include additional inspectors, but also more equipment (cars, computers, etc.). A large number of resources are also made available to labour inspectors enabling them to be very rapidly informed of industrial accidents, cases of occupational diseases, and so on, wherever they might occur. Codes of practice are drawn up for that purpose and offer guidance to labour inspectors, thereby granting them a great deal of independence in the performance of their duties, in accordance with the plan of action.

This change has been well received by the inspectors, whose level of satisfaction has increased due to the enhancement of their role and the fact that most of the targets set by the programme have been reached.

2.4.2.2 The Philippines

Approximately 90 per cent of enterprises in the Philippines are small or medium-sized, and working conditions are rather poor. Based on the methodology put forward by the ILO,[4] the Ministry of Labour has introduced a programme to assist SMEs in increasing their productivity by improving employees' working conditions. This programme is based above all on a comprehensive transformation of the procedure and action of the labour inspection system. The methods of participation and the culture of the profession of labour inspector must therefore be radically transformed. A heavy-handed approach must give way to advice and promotion.

These changes are taking place in a fairly difficult context and will quickly give rise to the question of priorities. Although the task of inspectors has become very onerous owing to the number of enterprises to be visited, the aspects to be verified and the time devoted to giving advice, the number of inspectors has not increased. Moreover, inspectors are asked to involve partners in their work and to respect different local practices in the course of their duties.

In this context, the success of these changes is considered to depend on investing in HRM. Emphasis is placed on the development of participatory management in order to generate a driving force. The positive repercussions of the new programme are valued at the different hierarchical levels. Intensive training specifically linked to these changes is offered to those who so desire. A client-centred approach is promoted, which gives priority to user satisfaction. Labour inspectors develop a much more satisfying relationship with SMEs, one based on cooperation rather than confrontation, which was previously the case.

Even though the basic requirements of recruitment have remained substantially the same, emphasis is placed on certain personal qualities based on the new role played by inspectors. Components linked to the success of the programme are also added in the performance evaluation system. In this forward-moving context, staff have achieved fixed objectives. The necessary changes have been fully achieved and the programme is a real success, as shown by the very thorough assessment conducted.

These two cases show, in an eloquent manner, the importance that must be attached to HRM in a context in which new programmes or comprehensive changes are introduced in the way that labour administration policies are applied. Clear objectives, suitable recruitment, appropriate training, advanced management practices, the availability of appropriate tools and an assessment suited to the aims to be achieved are all areas in which the enlightened participation of both politicians and administrative officials is required so that staff can achieve everything that is expected of them.

2.4.3 Practices: Expansion of the bureaucratic model

The practices undertaken will be grouped together by theme and will focus on particular points that correspond to the Weberian model described above.

2.4.3.1 Recruitment

Labour administrations now recruit few employees. When they do, for example in Fiji, such recruitment may obviously follow the usual practices for recruiting civil servants, which are not very innovative. However, in many cases, for example in Argentina, Austria and China, recruitment is external to this body and the situation is very different, reflecting what is increasingly encountered in the private market-based sector. Hiring is based on contracts which may be for temporary employment. In certain cases, the contract states explicitly that employees are not covered by the regulations protecting civil servants. Registered as working in an institution, that is, the administration, such employees are entrusted with the tasks usually performed by civil servants and, in this case, are not always instructed by such officials, just as the duration of their employment is not always specified. Recruitment under contract thus tends to complement the statutory recruitment of civil servants, or to replace it, in countries where it is not the norm.

In some cases, for example in Argentina, teams are formed from the different bodies involved in a particular programme, to which are added contract workers for the duration of the programme. For particular tasks, civil servants may be assisted by a number of contract workers whose contracts end when the task is completed.

2.4.3.2 Training

Training is clearly an important concern for human resources management, as shown by the case studies in Part II (Austria, China, Japan, Norway, the Philippines, Poland and the United States). In the traditional model, training was particularly limited or even non-existent. While theoretically focusing on aligning an employee's skills with the requirements of the task to be completed, training did not actually correspond to a conscious and organized procedure. In the practices surveyed, vocational training has been renewed for public administration officials, including those in the labour administration services who are being offered (or obliged to undertake) training essential to their adaptation to new expectations and likely to enhance their professional mobility. This means that an expansion of their skills beyond their strict job description is envisaged in the form of further training in a classroom situation or on the job.

The reason for this expansion is undoubtedly related to the trend towards decentralization noted above, which limits specialization and requires multiskilling. One of the features of the old Weberian bureaucratic model was the recruitment of technical specialists for each function alongside "generalists" responsible for administrative duties. As soon as the transfer to smaller, closely related administrative units prevents an official or employee from devoting himself or herself to a particular task, a certain degree of multiple skills is required of the person in charge of the tasks in question. Thus, the new arrangement partly contradicts bureaucratic specialization.

The emphasis placed on training is probably also due to the current social phenomenon of the rapid development and specialization of knowledge. This is evident in the introduction of different forms of technology such as computers. It is also encountered in the field of labour administration where laws, regulations and circulars, resulting from the intrinsic complexity of the law and of the environment, as well as of globalization, which means that national rules are interlinked and international rules are increased, make further training necessary so as to ensure that the knowledge acquired is updated.

In another scenario – that of training in the workplace – in Japan there are trainers responsible for particular activities such as health promotion. For this programme, experts have been gathered together (i.e. doctors, trainers, advisers, nutritionists and "health leaders") and made responsible for an overall health project at work, in professional life or on an extracurricular basis.

In certain cases, for example in China, the importance of training is emphasized by the fact that it is linked to promotion, or in any case, to career progress.

Training in areas such as new technologies, in particular computer tools, can be done through networks, so that the administration does not necessarily need to have buildings specifically for that purpose. However, labour administration activities also involve specialized vocational training in the labour law, business and employment sectors, for which the number and complexity of the measures designed to promote a return to employment require the constant updating of the officials' knowledge.

2.4.3.3 Evaluation

Staff evaluation is a concern noted in some of the case studies featured in Part II, notably in Belgium, China, Fiji, France, the Philippines, Quebec (Canada) and the United Kingdom. It reflects a growing preoccupation on the part of administration representatives as regards the effectiveness and mobilization of their officials.

The range of bodies responsible for evaluation include: a council set up by a ministry, that is, a very centralized body (dependent on a programme piloted by the ministry and comprising evaluation procedures); self-evaluation in China (individual and/or in groups); the immediate hierarchy in Fiji, Peru and Quebec (results evaluated on the basis of the aims set); or in the Philippines, systems of evaluation mentioned without further specification. The evaluations are conducted periodically, in most cases on an annual basis.

The whole difficulty of staff evaluation procedures lies in the definition of the aims in relation to which an evaluation is conducted: if no measurable and realistic objective has been fixed beforehand, the evaluation of individual performance remains a formalistic ritual.

2.4.3.4 Description of tasks

The situation where there is usually no job description, frequently the case in the statutory public service in which recruitment is not carried out for a particular task but for a type of post, is giving way to a situation in which a job description is clearly attached to the offer of a post, which is generally the case for contract-based recruitment.

Provision may be made for job descriptions in legislation, as is the case in Belgium or Fiji, or such descriptions may be mentioned in a procedural handbook or in regulations emanating from different levels, often regional, such as in Austria or Chile.

2.4.3.5 Staff mobilization

A variety of measures are taken for the explicit or incidental purpose of staff mobilization. These include participatory management, special training, definition and specification of objectives, task force, redefinition of roles, job enrichment, and so on.

In certain cases, explicit mention is made of a system of bonuses comprising output premiums, more flexible working hours and the application of the principle of merit in promotion or wage increases. One experiment refers to management on a case-by-case basis.

2.4.4 Current trends: Going beyond the bureaucratic model

In overall terms, all the indications are that in HRM the Weberian model discussed above appears to be on the way out, without it being possible, however, to signal the emergence of another clearly defined model.

In any case, it will be noted that the development of techniques provides significant opportunities for modernizing administration activities in many areas. A number of major features of this development can be extracted from the reports on adopted practices but also from the knowledge of the practices of firms, which may make for an ideal proposal for change in HRM methods.

The decentralization noted above, together with deconcentration and flexibility, appear to be the major features of such change. They can be categorized under the following headings: in general terms, responsibility for HRM is now more frequently devolved to departments and agencies, which have a certain amount of budgetary independence for that purpose. The aims are set within a general framework, emphasis is placed on the general rules and less interest is attached to detailed monitoring.

These features are also found in the labour organization sector. This is intended to be more flexible and make possible the initiatives taken by the lower ranks on the basis of the aims set for them. This organization encourages a certain degree of power sharing through greater independence, if not in the design at least in the performance of tasks. The brand new idea is introduced, in relation to the previous model of task division, that in even the most routine tasks there are great uncertainties and unpredictable factors which mean that they must be defined more flexibly and that the person performing the tasks must be given the opportunity to develop his or her initiative. In extreme cases, room is even given for interpreting the aims set by the powers that be.

In this new organization of labour, the status of officials undergoes major change. In some countries they are recruited on a fixed-term contract basis, on the grounds that job insecurity means that individuals attach greater importance to carrying out their tasks as well as possible, which would not be the case if they had a job for life protected by the law, as was previously the case. Switzerland (by abolishing the traditional way of recruitment for public servants), United Kingdom (by transferring public servants to agencies governed by private law) and Burkina Faso (by amending the conditions for recruiting public servants) are countries which, in broad terms, have systematized this trend, by applying it not only to managerial ranks but, in principle, to all public administration posts. It should be stressed that the mention of these cases does not constitute a value judgement on the resulting changes, whose effect will have to be evaluated in precise terms after a period of several years. It will be recalled, however, that recruitment governed by statute guarantees loyalty and impartiality in the exercise of an official's duties owing to his or her independence from political contingencies, and that certain systems of public service manage to combine the two methods of recruitment without difficulty, for example in France or Germany.

The evaluation of public employees appears in our surveys to be a relatively new activity. Nowadays, the trend in enterprises is for employees to participate in their own evaluation and for activities to be assessed jointly by supervisors and their immediate subordinates. More important still, careers appear to be evaluated more according to whether the aims set are achieved than respect for rules, and more according to the initiative shown to achieve these objectives than ritualization. Evaluation is used in career management whereby public employees are encouraged to manage their careers themselves and the organization facilitates this management, for example, by opening up an internal labour market and giving bonuses for mobility, or at least rewarding it, by giving a degree of transparency to staff movements. These trends can also be observed in the case of labour administration, since the situation is different and more stable than in the case of private firms, where these programmes are generated in an environment that is not very favourable to long-term projects owing to corporate (mergers, acquisitions) or commercial (market trends) movements, which may lead to redundancies.

Finally, the majority of labour administration practices surveyed devote significant attention to the training of administrative staff, in particular owing to the changes in the duties of civil servants. These changes have taken place along three main lines:

— their role is gradually being transformed from one of monitoring to one of providing advice;
— their attitude to the public is changing: there is a transition from a relationship in which users are above all "administered subjects" to one based on partnership, where users are "clients" for whom a service must be provided;
— their methods are being transformed: the transition from a "paper jungle," which often accompanies the picture of a typical public servant, to computer technology involves a change in the way cases are handled and therefore how tasks are organized.

In overall terms, the content of the new HRM practices is, however, relatively modest, if it is compared to the fundamental changes which call into question the practices of both private and public sector enterprises. It must be emphasized that personnel managers working in public administrations have a major advantage over the private sector: whatever happens, they keep their jobs. Even if it is necessary and desirable for economic reasons to reduce staff numbers in the public services, it is nevertheless true that the State retains a hard core of skills. This is particularly true in the labour administration sector, which is probably the least numerous of all ministerial departments, and whose slimming down does not appear to be desirable in countries concerned with the development of an active employment and labour policy. Such continuity provides these managers with the opportunity to reflect on the medium term, and therefore to establish future-oriented staff, job and skill management policies.

The trend towards a new model has clearly been set in motion. Truly innovative features sometimes appear to deal with specific problems to which the old formulae could not provide a response. However, they are still in the formative stages and are not yet fully implemented by administrations.

2.5 The contribution made by information technology

2.5.1 The role of technology

The authors of the case studies have all dealt with technologies, essentially computer-related, which comprise computer hardware as well as what may be referred to as the networks set up by means of hardware, such as databanks, exchange of information, and so on. It might be specified that these are usually social networks, that is, a series of more or less specific relationships (information, advice, etc.), between actors who in most cases, but not all, are defined.

These apparently commonplace descriptions conceal, however, the fact that information technology is considered to be an element for extending or arranging policies or data. It is not a compulsory tool, but is an obvious feature of a contemporary approach.[5] Since the 1980s there has been a constant reassertion of the urgent need to use information technology in order to deal with the different upheavals affecting economic structures. It is seen as an instrument able to help us through crises and restore economic growth.

The new technologies (databanks, networks, Internet, etc.) have unquestionably facilitated communications and helped to eliminate borders. They are praised for reducing costs, improving services and increasing flexibility in response to citizens' needs. Information technology also helps to reduce the physical effort required on the part of manual workers. This has led some people to decry its rapid development for exacerbating unemployment, whereas others say that short-term unemployment affecting less well-trained workers will be largely offset in the long term by the creation of new jobs requiring greater expertise and offering better pay.

It can therefore be seen that technology is always tied to non-technological aims. Technology is not introduced in an abstract sense, nor is it an adjunct to an organization's internal environment. It reflects the cultural values and environment in which it is introduced. It is therefore clear that the acquisition of technology is not sufficient to benefit from these advantages. Its compatibility with the environment at the time of introduction, its success and its appropriate use by employees are all conditions that must be met if its full potential is to be realized.

2.5.2 Typical situations

2.5.2.1 China

China's economy has undergone profound changes. State enterprises have had to lay off large numbers of workers. Central and local governments have important decisions to take with regard to the labour market. The same is true of employers and trade unions. In order to do this, they need precise and accurate information on the employment market. However, the Ministry of Labour has only a traditional system for processing information manually.

Within the Ministry of Labour and Social Security, and directly attached to the Ministry, the Information Centre has been set up to take charge of the labour and social security management system. The aim is to provide the Ministry with the means to take general policy decisions based on reliable data, and to provide central and local governments, employers, trade unions and workers with information corresponding to their specific needs. The objective is therefore to move from a manual to a computerized information-processing system in the field of management.

The developments are taking place in the form of projects. The system functions on a supplier–client basis with the different administrative units using the Information Centre's services. These units may or may not accept the products offered to them. Of great interest is the fact that the establishment of each project is evaluated by a group comprising specialists, clients and users.

The data processed are grouped into four major categories relating to general policy decisions, programme management, support for local units and ministry management information. The information available on computer makes it possible to offer a better service to employers who wish to recruit staff (demand) and to workers trying to find a job (supply). The information is freely accessible on computers set up in local employment offices. It is emphasized, however, that in fact the assisted services (assisted self-service) offered are used much more frequently.

The systems have been developed in a network, thereby allowing long-distance communications, facilitating the exchange of documents between the central and local offices, and enabling information resources to be shared and the workforce to be more mobile. The latter advantage is quite important, given the mass redundancies made by Chinese state enterprises.

The measures taken therefore involve the use of technology, which, according to the actors, has been a factor in the development of society.

2.5.2.2 United States

In the United States, the use of technology has transformed employment services as they used to be and as they still operate in most of the countries in the world.

The marked reduction in the operating budgets of the employment services since the 1980s and the obligation to maintain a level of service acceptable to the general public have justified the use of new technologies. The aim has also been to make information on the employment market accessible to as many people as possible. For more than 15 years, several projects involving the use of computer technologies have seen the light of day, with the effect that there is now a complete and integrated range of information directly accessible in relation to employment vacancies, job offers (workers' curriculum vitae), available training and so on.

Technological choices have been made on the basis of technological monitoring activity which aims to identify and analyse all the initiatives taken by different States regarding employment market information systems. The members of Congress had insisted on the use of the latest technology. It is interesting to note the guidelines that have been given for monitoring these numerous projects, which must:

— be based on users' needs and take into account the systems already in place;
— stay within the legislative framework and funding available;
— plan the organization, coordination and management of the system, including the role of different States;
— respect the capacity of States and local employment services to use these systems;
— take into account the impact on central government funding; and
— observe pre-existing rules of integrity and confidentiality.

The systems were designed by different ad hoc groups bringing together state agencies and the federal government, which bore the cost of development. At the local level, advisory groups comprising employers, trade unions, workers, educational establishments, social groups, and so on, were consulted on the setting-up of this system.

Very elaborate employment market databanks now exist, which are grouped together and accessible on the Internet, throughout the United States and all over the world. Users – employers or workers – and institutions are now able to consult a single integrated data system, from the place where they have access to a computer.

As regards the impact created, this has enabled users to become more responsible and has probably helped to compensate partially for the closure or relocation of numerous local employment offices. It is emphasized, however, that it is now much more difficult to evaluate the performance of the employment services. It is impossible to estimate the number of people finding work as a result of this self-service system or the Internet. A decision has therefore been taken to evaluate this service on the basis of a user satisfaction survey.

2.5.2.3 Germany

The aim is to make available to users the enormous amount of information now available from the existing documentation on professions, training and employment: for this purpose, information offices for the workforce have been set up, with major investment in new information technologies. This provision of technology includes all modern means of access (media library, Internet access, employment databases, local documentation centre, etc.) to professional documentation, job offers and applications, and possible training courses. Users seeking employment or wishing to make a career move are encouraged to undertake their job search by themselves, with the technical assistance of the staff working in the employment information centre. Employers have also been targeted by these centres, which are designed as a meeting point between employment supply and demand. The network covers the whole country and is strengthened where needed by mobile information stations. This is becoming a more generalized phenomenon since an assessment of users' attitudes has shown a high degree of satisfaction.

In conclusion, we have considered three very different countries that have used information technologies to improve their labour administration activities and, above all, to provide better services for employers and workers, as well as for managers and politicians in charge of devising and managing labour administration policies. The impact of these technologies can be significant, but they require changes in the organization of work and services. They need to be implemented carefully if the re-engineering is to succeed and the expected benefits are to be attained.

2.5.3 Practices: Technologies and efficiency of activities

Most of the case studies refer to the existence of computer resources and their increased use: "Each employee has a network computer link". In certain cases, it is specified that computer tools are not essential to the development of an activity or that departments use them where necessary. By contrast, some countries such as Burkina Faso complain openly that they do not have sufficient means to invest in computers, which limits programme development and hampers reliable processing of data and reduction of project study periods. The negative effects of the lack of computers therefore demonstrate the latter's usefulness.

In certain cases, the use of these means is specified in terms of particular subjects: in Austria, Chile, Hong Kong (China) and Spain, there is a connection between central departments and decentralized administrations; in Argentina, Austria, Belgium, Hong Kong (China), the Philippines, Poland and the United States, databases are used to provide access to practical examples or cases; in Hong Kong (China), the Philippines and the United States, users are given free access to data so as to ensure that collective agreements are recorded; in Poland, there is cooperation with the World Bank or other international organizations such as the ILO. In Hong Kong (China), the Philippines and the United States, for example, the use of the Internet is sometimes specified for the broader use of data, in employment departments, so that they may be consulted at the national level. These tools allow activities to be conducted more efficiently, or should do so in the future.

In certain cases, such as France, Peru, the Philippines, Senegal and the United States, it is stated that new tools will enable specific practices to be implemented (France, for example, has a new system of knowledge evaluation). In addition, the grouping of several databases will improve employment forecasting, thus providing a service which could not have existed without the aid of computers, but which presupposes that the whole of the population concerned is able to use them. The programme has been put on the Internet, thus providing access to everyone who is connected and knows how to use it. This presupposes a highly developed computer culture among the population, the availability of the required tools and the establishment of employment services so that all citizens may benefit from such information. The large increase in the use of computers in labour administration services is linked to the dissemination of these tools among the public. As we saw in Chapter 1, this dissemination has been rapid in industrialized countries.

We are therefore faced with several different kinds of situation. In addition to the observation of the simple development of computers beyond the specification of their different uses, there are cases where certain activities would have been impossible to achieve without computers and where the use of these tools is linked to the diffusion of knowledge about them among the general public. Consequently, the role of labour administration officials has been changed profoundly: *instead of providing information, of which they can no longer have exhaustive knowledge, they teach users to look for and find this information.*

2.5.4 *Current trends: Technological progress*

In brief, everybody is moving towards a wider use of modern technology but, as we saw in Chapter 1 regarding developing countries, progress is slow and quite uneven, depending on the case. Everything hinges, however, on how these tools are used. Firstly, this use may be specified, which in the long term can limit the influence of computers. They are in fact linked to the average and diffuse knowledge of the population groups targeted by such activities. An administration can only implement a programme based on modern technologies if the potential users of these activities are able to use the technologies in question. However, it is also true that these activities can be a means of disseminating the use of these technologies, provided, however, that they are not the only means used. There is a high level of interaction between designers and users in the application of information technologies.

In the field of communication, this rapid progress opens up perspectives relating in particular to employment services, a major portion of whose activities are based on communication or information processing. New methods of intervention are now made possible and new relationships can be formed between the actors on the labour market through the opportunities created. For example, in Zimbabwe the public employment services have set up a pilot office in Harare. This office is well equipped with computers and aims, without making innovations in its traditional operations, to use the computers in a dynamic and "proactive" manner, and to change the image of the employment services in the eyes of all public groups, in particular firms and public authorities. Although information-processing technologies are now everywhere in the form of computers, interactive terminals or other devices, they have also become part of staff culture; when accompanied by a suitably trained staff member, they are a way of improving relations with the public. They are also an important internal management tool.

2.6. Partnership

2.6.1 Current status and definition of partnership

The term "partnership" has become a buzzword. It can be defined as the fact of creating or developing particular links between different institutions or organizations which previously had been external to each other and had no ongoing relationship. Partnership implies that they combine their efforts, on a voluntary and regular basis, while retaining their own identity.

Partnership may be institutional (between the social partners) or functional (among the main economic actors). It may also involve the necessary collaboration between central public administrations with a view to providing an integrated service organized on the basis of an overall vision of clients' needs rather than on an administrative logic. Almost all the practices observed refer to the existence or creation of partnerships, a phenomenon that is developing to an even greater extent in the field under study since it is indivisible from industrial relations, which by nature involve actors who to a large degree are independent.

The concept of partnership is not limited simply to institutionalized social relations. It is also used to describe the operational changes in relations in the world of enterprise. Partnership is often described as the transition from a model of relations based on the market to the so-called partnership model, which brings out the ideas of proximity, duration and exchange between independent units. It involves the voluntary development of close links between two or more actors which had hitherto been *external* to each other. In fields that are clearly defined and cannot be extended, at least not without an explicit redefinition of the contract concerned, these actors will pool their efforts beyond simple contractual links, in relation to each other and in a context of competition.

This partnership is linked to the phenomenon of contracting out certain duties, whereby numerous firms entrust services in which they do not specialize to external enterprises. The traditional example is that of upkeep – maintenance services. For a long time it was considered essential that these services be carried out by the firms themselves. However, the political will to reduce internal operating costs (transaction costs) and to establish special relations with the enterprises responsible for these services, together with the sophisticated nature of the machinery used, forced firms to turn over these services to external enterprises. This process of externalization is carried out in most cases in relations of proximity, which are called partnership relations. The use of this concept conveys a semantic shift. Such relations have often been referred to as subcontracting, a concept that implies a relationship based on subordination between two bodies. Even if economic reality does not change, particularly when an enterprise providing a service has only one client, the notion of partnership seeks to re-establish a balance.

These relations, which are referred to as partnerships, have therefore developed in our societies, independently of the trend observed in labour administrations. In the latter, partnership is often mentioned in relation to the administrations themselves. This may be a relationship between national authorities and partners at local level, whether or not they belong to the same institution. Two different administrations may form a partnership, that is, decide to work together, exchange information at their disposal currently or in the future, combine their efforts for a specific period in order to achieve a particular objective, and so on. Territorialization is a good example of this, since managing problems locally appears to be more effective than doing it at the national level.

Partnership and participation should not be confused. On the one hand, in terms of the theory on which they are founded, participation is based on the idea that by nature people at work need to understand the task they are carrying out and to take part in the decision-making process that relates to it. This natural and universal need is expressed in the context of the traditional hierarchical relationship. Partnership, on the other hand, involves actors who are not linked in hierarchical terms and come together of their own free will. Participation is designed to create a sense of belonging in employees and to mobilize them, without clearly linking them to the structures of authority. An attempt is made to replace the traditional top-down relationship with one where the lower ranks have their say. By contrast, partnership forms part of relations based on equality, at least in formal terms, since the two independent actors rarely enjoy equivalent positions.

It may be added that the emergence of the idea of partnership is linked to that of the development of the role of the State. If it is accepted that this development takes place by moving away from the idea of the welfare state towards that of the regulatory state, which plays a less interventionist role but rather arbitrates or more simply is responsible for making sure that the rules of society and the economy – those of the market and of labour in the case of enterprises, and gradually introduced in other non-market based institutions – are respected, the idea of partnership is more easily assimilated. There is a new distribution of powers. The State abandons part of the powers that it held in the welfare state to the other authorities, and considers these authorities (regional or local, as well as the social actors, either individually or in groups such as committees) to be partners with real powers.

Finally, it should be noted that joint management, be it on a bipartite or tripartite basis, is not the same as partnership. The former is a method of operation in which the social actors are consulted or recognized as parties to negotiations but which, unlike the latter, does not necessarily entail an egalitarian relationship in formal terms. By contrast, cooperation between workers' and employers' organizations in different fields of labour administration is, or must become, a major method of operation for such administrations.

2.6.2 Typical situations

2.6.2.1 Poland

At the beginning of the 1990s, following the restructuring and privatization of the state sector, Poland experienced a very rapid increase in the number of unemployed. This situation led the Government to consider that the creation of jobs by the unemployed should be strongly encouraged. The Ministry of Labour therefore adopted a policy to establish SMEs. This policy was designed in particular to provide start-up loans for SMEs or to increase staff numbers in existing enterprises.

From the beginning, the introduction of the programme was accompanied by the firm willingness to involve the social partners and, in addition, the different actors, whether institutions or not, in the economic life of the country. These actors were therefore consulted on the development of the programme. Subsequently, a partnership was established between the Ministry and numerous local bodies in order to introduce the programme. The Ministry promotes the programme through its network of decentralized labour offices. The local bodies then continue and complement the activities undertaken, thereby literally creating a "snowball" effect in relation to the promotion. Business incubators, vocational training centres, business people's clubs, guarantee funds, non-governmental employment promotion agencies, and so on, are being set up. The local communities also sign cooperation agreements with several other private or public institutions in their area.

The interesting thing is that the social partners help to monitor the implementation of the policy in question, as part of local or regional employment councils. These consultative bodies have the particular feature of involving four partners: the State, local communities, employers and trade unions. Local councils are also involved in loan-allocation mechanisms. Since the Government wanted the legislative framework establishing this programme to evolve, in order to give due consideration to the results of the changes in its application by these councils, its impact has been considerable.

The end result is synergy, meaning that the Ministry of Labour is no longer the only body providing enterprise start-up loans. Local communities are also devising similar programmes, and regional governments, banks and various non-profit-making funds are following suit.

This programme, based on an intensive partnership, appears to have generated positive results. For the Government, the aims set with regard to the increase in the number of jobs created by unemployed wage earners have been fully achieved.

2.6.2.2 Spain

The Spanish Government has set up a Wage Guarantee Fund to ensure the payment of wages, financed by contributions from public and private enterprises, and compensation for workers made redundant by bankrupt enterprises. This type of measure is common to many national labour legislations and is in conformity with European Directives and international labour standards.

The innovative contribution of the Spanish programme is that it extends the Fund's terms of reference to situations of partial crisis or insolvency affecting enterprises so as to clean up their finances. This avoids any liquidation of assets and enterprise closures, as well as safeguarding part, if not all, of the jobs at stake.

As soon as the programme was established, the Spanish labour administration made clear its desire to enter into a partnership arrangement. The regulations governing this new function of the Wage Guarantee Fund were prepared in close consultation and cooperation with the social partners.

The Fund is administered by an independent public entity headed by a tripartite administrative council (employers, trade unions and the State). The participatory structure of this organization is decentralized. Also of interest is the fact that a provincial committee for monitoring the Fund is responsible for evaluating its activities and operations. It comprises three state representatives, three representatives of workers' organizations and three representatives of employers' organizations.

In addition to the partnership found in the management and evaluation of the Fund, there is close interaction between the fund administration, the Labour Inspectorate, the Social Security Treasury and the National Employment Institute in order to develop concerted action to assist enterprises in difficulty to recover and to help workers made redundant following a closure to find new employment as soon as possible.

The intensive use of several forms of partnership is probably the main reason for the success of this programme.

The examples dealt with here demonstrate that partnership can be a determining factor in relation to the impact that a labour administration activity may have. Partnership can take several forms, operate at different levels and involve all kinds of participants. The result remains the same, however, since partnership enables the resources and the efforts invested by labour administrations to be greatly increased.

2.6.3 Practices: Several forms of partnership

These relate primarily to two areas: partnerships between public institutions having similar labour objectives, and institutionalized partnerships between the social partners.

Partnerships between a central administration and regional, local or municipal administrations, or between different administrations, concern among others certain activities studied in Argentina, China, France, Hong Kong (China), Japan and Poland. These activities may be jointly coordinated and planned by the central administration and the states or provinces. For example, as in the case of Spain discussed above, both the national and local administrations are authorized to provide loans to SMEs and negotiate with each other regarding the more difficult cases. In such situations, the municipalities may be considered more relevant to the decision-making process than the ministry, since they are closer to the realities of the SMEs. However, the central administration, which does not relinquish all power in the settlement of these cases, considers itself to be in partnership with these local bodies. Local communities, which are independent of the labour administration, cooperate actively with it in order to establish structures that continue and expand its activity to assist business incubators, vocational training centres, guarantee funds and non-governmental employment promotion agencies. The activities in question give rise to cooperation agreements between the institutions concerned and local employment offices.

The designation of responsibilities at the local or regional level depends on the need for independence and administrative capacities particular to each level. This situation is typical of countries with a tradition of decentralization. In this case, there is no uniform regionalization; in general, it is asymmetrical and gradual. In other countries, the trend is towards a uniform independence. In either of these situations, the trend is towards an increased role for the social partners at the different levels of decision-making and therefore towards an expansion of partnership-based activities.

Certain countries operate according to the principle of developing a social consensus and promoting consultation at the stage when measures are applied, whereas others aim to achieve consensus at the time such measures are devised and applied.

The partnership activities between the different services, as in the case of China, Fiji, Poland and Spain, have a significance linked to the number and diversity of the administrative services dealing with the problems. As was seen above, there is a great variety of institutions, as a result of the variety of tasks assigned to them. The institutional framework is therefore complex.

The presence of other local organizations undertaking social and economic activities is becoming increasingly common. In several countries, municipalities play a leading role in the organization and provision of services (social assistance, unemployment benefits and family allowances) on their territory, in liaison with the decentralized ministerial departments.

The cooperation between these different bodies can be analysed effectively through the concept of partnership, which does not remove their particular features but encourages them to work together while respecting their individual identities. There are at least four or five departments whose tasks coincide with particular aims. Rather than abolishing these departments, a solution to work in partnership that does not reintroduce hierarchical relations between them may appear preferable.

The second area covered by the concept of partnership is that of relations between administrations and social actors, primarily employers' and workers' groups, but also consumers' organizations and non-governmental agencies. In this area, practices appear to be linked to the different national traditions of labour relations. Thus, certain countries have long engaged in consultation (e.g. Austria), some have a tradition of centralized decision-making (e.g. Chile), while in others federalism has introduced compulsory negotiating practices based on partnerships. The three situations are quite different. Nevertheless, examination of current practices reveals that the trend in most countries is towards the introduction of partnership, regardless of national culture.

Thus, in Austria, France, Hong Kong (China), the Philippines and Senegal, situations are encountered where consultation in the form of partnership between administrations and social partners, and not only consultation between decision-makers and users, is systematic and often instituted legally. This may be in the form of management committees involving labour administrations, together with associations representing workers and employers. There are also situations where partnership becomes official as soon as laws and regulations are drafted, while other situations are closer to joint management in which the administration attempts to involve actors in certain activities.

Finally, the existence of unofficial consultations should be noted. These are designed to solve difficult problems by sidestepping official consultation mechanisms, which appear to be too lengthy and likely to give rise to complications.

2.6.4 Current trends: A notable increase in partnerships

The practices observed point to a clear trend towards activities that can be qualified as partnerships. They show that administrations in most countries are aware of the need for change in this regard and that they are beginning to introduce various kinds of partnership-based activities, for example in the form of interaction between different activities, levels of government and social partners. As has been noted, this trend is common to other social and economic institutions.

In general, national authorities are developing more and more partnerships with local administrations. This form is the most frequently mentioned. It is motivated by the fact that this is where users can be met, either directly or through organizations representing them, and this proximity enables the most appropriate solutions to be found. However, as has been said, other forms of partnership exist between administrations and other actors. These forms are relatively new and appear to be developing.

Entering into partnership with an entity, or forming a partnership between two organizations, is a question of making a transition from external relations to closer relations, or from a market-oriented existence to one of sharing, at a time when economic relations appear to be the most important.

All this is based on an apparently dominant philosophy, that is, a quite radical change in the presence and role of the State in the social and economic sphere, but a change whose major trends are not completely clear. There is surely a rejection of the welfare state, of a State responsible for the general well-being of its users. Many of the facts observed indicate that the State acts as a simple guarantor of the established rules. In accordance with this trend, in overall terms the State should continually reduce the level of its participation. Between the roles of architect, participant, partner or police officer the exponents of this trend support the fourth role, provided that the aim is only to prosecute those who infringe the rules, and wishing also for fewer and fewer rules. In the countries advocating a liberal model and with an active labour relations field, it is the State's regulatory role that is recognized.

At the same time, however, the number of areas in which labour administrations operate is on the increase not only in order to ensure that the rules are observed, but also because, owing to the economic difficulties experienced by most countries and whose consequences lead to unemployment, governments and their administrations are requested to intervene to assist those out of work and social groups in difficulty, or to participate in assistance mechanisms for the creation of jobs. The introduction of some of these mechanisms was noted above, focusing directly on employment by means of assistance for the unemployed in the form of training, personal assessment, enterprise establishment grants and so on.

We are therefore faced with contradictory trends. The State is less important but there are more and more requests for its intervention. Are any of the trends linked to the level of economic development, whereby the industrialized countries favour a more implicit role and developing countries are more supportive of an interventionist philosophy? The trend established is probably true of the first group, but this is not the case for developing countries where both trends are observed. By contrast, the traditions of social dialogue, in particular through structured industrial relations, play a role in support of partnership activities, whereas more centralized national cultures tip the balance in favour of activities where state intervention is more significant. It is therefore not only the level of economic development but equally the negotiating traditions that play the major role.

It is more or less certain that in all countries preference is given, firstly, to partnership through management methods uniting the actors concerned and, secondly, to local management generating activities based on close links and which are supposed to be more effective.

2.7 Methods of funding

Since funding generally reveals – but is not the driving force behind – social and political trends, as the dominant economic discourse would have us believe, such trends emerge through the methods of funding the activities undertaken by labour administrations.

2.7.1 A variety of principles

The sphere of funding methods covers the manner in which public administrations finance activities and their management costs. It is necessary to ascertain whether this funding is provided from general public receipts and, if so, whether the services used are paid for by the users or by all taxpayers, or indeed whether the funding is based on contributions. The first system corresponds to the centrally based model described above. It appears to offer the advantage of a faster decision-making process, and is egalitarian but probably less relevant to the adjustments made to decisions based on local requirements. The system of contributions appears to meet criteria of fairness more than it satisfies egalitarian principles; it allows greater foreseeability in so far as it is based on individual approaches.

Here too, funding methods correspond to the general principles of philosophy regarding the role of the State. According to whether these principles enhance the State in its capacity as an architect, participant, partner or police officer, the methods will be many and varied, as the following practical examples show.

2.7.2 Typical situations

2.7.2.1 Fiji

The country's labour administration activities aim to make employers and workers more aware of their responsibilities in relation to occupational health and safety. As regards the funding of this activity, it is interesting to note that the law provides for the establishment of a fund for occupational health, training, safety and the prevention of accidents at the workplace.

The funding comes from several sources. First and foremost, there is the State's annual contribution and the contributions paid by employers, on the basis of their wage bill. To these should be added the amounts received yearly for the registration of enterprises with more than 20 employees. There is also the income from the fees paid for services provided by the occupational health and safety department, relating in particular to training, technical advice and so on. Receipts from the sale of publications and the fees charged for using the training centres of the occupational health and safety department are also paid into the fund.

2.7.2.2 Poland

The case study on Poland looks at the action of the labour administration in support of the creation of SMEs. This concerns the introduction of a system of start-up loans for the establishment of SMEs or to assist existing enterprises wishing to increase their staff numbers. This scheme involves both the Ministry of Labour, through the activities of its field offices, and numerous local bodies.

The network of local offices of the Ministry of Labour is financed by the Employment Fund, whose resources come, firstly, from state contributions and, secondly, from employers' contributions. It should, however, be emphasized that the state share is being greatly reduced, falling from 61 per cent in 1996 to 48 per cent in 1997. This Fund is responsible for paying benefits to the unemployed, but also for financing employment policies. The expenditure that it may finance is determined by the Law on Employment. A share of this Fund is devoted to loans for enterprises creating new jobs.

Another point of interest in relation to the funding of this activity is that the rate of recovery of the loans paid varies between 70 and 90 per cent according to different regions of the country. Such a performance therefore enables the monies reimbursed to be reinvested in new job-creation projects.

Finally, one of the criteria for assessing the performance of the programme is the rate at which loans are reimbursed. Two other criteria are the analysis of cases of business failure and the cost of creating a new job. Concern with the financial viability of the programme is therefore very much present.

2.7.2.3 Austria

The activity conducted by the Austrian labour administration relates to the introduction, as part of a preventive employment policy, of an emergency mechanism in the case of a reduction in staff numbers in an enterprise. These regulations, the application of which is entrusted to the Employment Department of the Federal Ministry of Labour, do not make the prior notification of all employment terminations compulsory, but only those exceeding a certain threshold established as a proportion of the total workforce of an enterprise. This activity is designed to help enterprises develop the means to preserve the same level of employment, or to provide timely information to workers threatened with redundancy and to help them find a new job; it also helps to extend the payment of unemployment benefit provided for by the Law on Unemployment Insurance.

The funding comes mainly from employers and workers, in equal shares, through unemployment insurance contributions, which currently stand at 6 per cent of the gross wage. Furthermore, in accordance with the employment responsibilities of the Federal Government, an annual subsidy is also paid, but it represents only a minimal share of the funding.

Another feature of interest in the case of Austria is that the State has granted additional credits to the Employment Department for financing the establishment of the new emergency scheme. This special budget covered both the costs linked to additional staff expenditure and those needed for the necessary equipment, including computers.

As for all the expenditure incurred within the country's employment policy, permanent monitoring of the budget enables the financial management of the scheme to be monitored. A complex system of monitoring by the Employment Department and the Federal Ministry of Labour, Health and Social Affairs exists for this purpose. Finally, an independent public body, the Court of Auditors, carries out an annual audit of the financial position of the Employment Department.

The three situations described above are typical in that they show that several different sources of funding may be used to ensure that labour administration activities are properly conducted. However, even in cases where employers and workers are involved to a significant degree the State continues to participate, albeit to a limited extent, in the funding of the labour administration activities it introduces.

2.7.3 Practices: An even greater variety of methods

The practices undertaken cover more or less all the possible scenarios, as described below.

2.7.3.1 State funding

Firstly, there are activities that are funded entirely by the authorities. This is the case in Belgium, Burkina Faso, Chile, China, France, Hong Kong (China), Hungary, Peru, the Philippines and Senegal.

The funding consists of two main features: the wages paid to state officials, when labour administration is the responsibility of a body of public officials or employees who are either specialized, or seconded for a particular activity, are paid out of the general civil service budget, and the sums intended to finance the labour policies conducted. There are numerous situations in which this occurs. In certain cases, it is stated that the programme activities are the responsibility of labour administration officials, who receive financial assistance from a private foundation, without it being made clear exactly what this foundation subsidizes.

2.7.3.2 Mixed funding

In many cases, for example Argentina and the United States, costs are shared between different levels, that is, national and local. This is the situation encountered in federal States where traditionally responsibilities are shared, as is funding between the different levels. A distinction between wages, operating funds and intervention funds is rarely made.

A number of practices refer to the sharing of costs between the authorities and employers. This is the case for a particular activity in China, as mentioned above, where the workers dismissed from public enterprises remain the responsibility of their employers for three years, while the State covers the cost of training, retraining assistance and so on. This is the case of certain employment funds (which provide unemployment benefits and fund employment policies) financed by the State, as well as of employers' contributions, for example in Fiji and Poland.

2.7.3.3 Funding by employers

In other cases, for example in Austria, Norway and Spain, employers have sole responsibility for the funding of activities. This funding may be charged directly to enterprises, or taken from the interest generated by employer contributions to a special fund. These contributions can be broken down into a workers' portion and an employers' portion, both of which are paid by the latter.

Funding can also be provided, as in the case of Fiji illustrated above, by the sale of services provided by different bodies. This system often complements financing from public funds; organizations responsible for managing a programme receive an operating budget from the State and finance their expenses by selling the services offered by the programme.

Finally, in a number of temporary situations the State issues a call to tender for organizations or private enterprises with a view to contracting out certain public services. Those that are successfully awarded the service contracts will be responsible for financing these services, it being understood, however, that they have put forward their tender on the assumption that the services will be profitable. In principle, the State no longer bears any responsibility whatsoever for financing such services. Such a situation can be found in France in the specific field of the provision of vocational training.

2.7.4 Current trends: Diversification of funding sources

A number of trends may be discerned from the practices studied. Firstly, since public receipts are generally decreasing, there is a trend towards funding through employers' and employees' contributions, although the State also continues to pay contributions. This leads to a system of joint funding, which may involve different social actors or decentralized authorities. More and more, charging for services is becoming a means by which the State may fund the activities in question.

The concept of a financially independent body is being strengthened, thereby enabling such bodies to manage surpluses – which are not profits – as they see fit. This is the case for the organizations established by the social partners (this is how the first social protection funds for workers were established in Europe in the nineteenth century). The State should not intervene in such situations. It appears, however, that the financial difficulties of some of these organizations lead to state intervention in their management, since the State helps to keep them afloat. The idea of project financing, linked to that of partnership, is also developing whereby for a particular project the logic of the parties concerned differs and those parties agree on a method of funding enabling public financing to be combined with external resources, and the funds to be managed independently.

The underlying idea is that a call to tender is the most appropriate method for managing services with the maximum efficiency and leading to gains in productivity. Whether or not this idea is based on strict observations is not certain and the majority of scholars are divided on the subject. It appears to be just as much an ideological type, that of ambient liberalism, which is currently dominant in industrialized countries and leads to this type of solution. For most activities, funding that is entirely the responsibility of the State appears to be a thing of the past, although this depends on a particular service. The ideal, however, would be to exclude any kind of dogmatism in the search for solutions.

2.8 Evaluation: A growing concern

Most States and administrations have established evaluation systems, or at least the reports on the practices adopted refer to such systems. This seems to be – although it is difficult to verify in the documents supplied – an innovation or at least a serious re-evaluation and reorientation of the function of labour inspection, specific to the majority of public and labour administrations, which frequently appeared to be merely a formality. The variety of formulas used bears witness to this, although they do not appear to have proved their worth over the long term.

2.8.1 The multiple dimensions of evaluation

It is difficult to give a general definition of evaluation, since it has various aims. There may be a desire to evaluate the theoretical quality of activities, the results achieved, a necessarily retrospective measure in relation to the objectives set, and the more or less expected impacts on other activities or in other fields – sometimes referred to as secondary effects; administrations may emphasize the observance of procedures and so on. Since the resources devoted to evaluation are limited, the sole aim may be to monitor activities; the measures taken can be quantitative (number of enterprises visited) or also qualitative, where monitoring is more limited in number but often more heuristic. A systemic approach can also be used, since it does not exclude fields that may or should be affected, or else a comparative approach. The evaluations conducted may be comprehensive (of a whole ministry) or partial (focusing on a department or programme). They may also focus on social impacts, which is a more complex but increasingly frequent process that requires that the necessary integration of various ministries and agencies be taken into account. A targeted social impact such as decreasing unemployment will be evaluated based on the combined action of several factors: increase in education level; increase in economic activity; quality of job matching mechanisms; and improvement in the quality of working conditions.

Also of importance is the source of evaluation. It may be *internal* to the departments concerned, in which case it will most often be self-evaluation. It may also be *external*, often provided in the form of ad hoc services or by external enterprises such as audit offices. In some cases it is the users themselves who conduct the evaluation by completing questionnaires or by other means.

2.8.2 Typical situations

2.8.2.1 Hong Kong (China)

The labour administration of the Hong Kong Special Administrative Region of China is permanently "under surveillance". This surveillance is based on regular or ad hoc measures and is conducted by the State, the Legislative Assembly and the public itself. For this purpose, there are several mechanisms designed to assess the efficiency of the operations conducted.

Agencies and departments within the government apparatus must submit performance statistics on a regular basis. This measure applies to all labour administration activities in Hong Kong (China). The statistics relate in particular to management, since this central government initiative aims to ensure that the resources allocated to the different programmes are used efficiently. As soon as performance does not meet the required standards, the people responsible are notified accordingly and requested to take the necessary corrective measures.

External audits are also provided for. All government agencies are required to establish, on an annual basis and at the same time as their budgetary forecasts, performance targets and the indicators used to assess them. For example, for the Employment Department these indicators include the number of registered jobseekers, the number of positions filled and the number of young people participating in the career activities conducted by the department. These performance targets are conveyed, along with the budget, to members of the legislature. Before the beginning of the each financial year, a legislative council will examine budgetary requests and performance targets of each government agency.

In addition to the statistical measures, there are also mechanisms for evaluating the quality of the services provided by government agencies. The legislator requires each agency to set service-quality objectives and to guarantee that they will be met. In addition, an agency is required to inform its clients accordingly so that each one is able to evaluate the quality of the service obtained. For the Employment Department, these service-quality objectives include the following: information on available posts should be displayed within 24 hours of receipt of the information, the waiting time for jobseekers wishing to register should be less than 30 minutes, a written guide should be supplied to all newly registered jobseekers, and so on. Each year, the Ministry of Labour publishes a list of the results obtained by each government agency under its supervision. A client liaison group has also been set up, comprising members selected from among the users of the Ministry's different agencies. This group's mandate requires it to give its point of view on the quality of the services provided and on the public's expectations in this area.

In addition to the regular mechanisms described above, government agencies may at any time be subject to an examination by a committee of the Legislative Assembly. This committee has full powers to question, investigate and make judgements, and recommend changes in relation to all the features affecting the performance of the government agency being examined.

2.8.2.2 United Kingdom

The introduction of a system of management by objectives based on an ad hoc administrative structure has resulted in the United Kingdom in the establishment of agencies responsible for implementing government policies. Labour administration has also been affected by this reform.

This development has been accompanied by rhetoric referring to delegation and assignation of responsibility. The establishment of agencies has also been accompanied by the granting of gradually increased autonomy to agency heads in relation to their finances and human resources management. In return, performance evaluation has again come to the fore. The results obtained by the agencies are directly linked to the remuneration of the employees working for them. Instead of an index-based progression relating to seniority, gradual increases in remuneration are granted in accordance with the extent to which individual objectives set on an annual and contractual basis have been realized.

As regards internal evaluation mechanisms, the Department for Education and Employment (DfEE), which is responsible for all labour administration policies, has set up an executive group responsible for such evaluation. This group devises evaluation programmes, taking into consideration the effectiveness of new policies or changes that have been made to existing ones. Twelve evaluation specialists work within this group in order to carry out audits and to ensure that internal monitoring mechanisms exist in each labour administration agency. Their examination relates to the results of internal evaluation and client satisfaction surveys conducted by each agency, which verify the extent to which the shortcomings underlined have been rectified.

This evaluation programme set up by the central organization is combined with a research programme designed to provide information of use in the development of policies and the evaluation of the effectiveness of existing programmes. This unit conducts surveys notably on the quality of services but also on the levels of satisfaction among staff working in the different agencies.

The Government obliges agencies to identify performance objectives and targets comparable to those in the private sector. The principle of market testing has thus been introduced, obliging agencies and ministries to select activities that could potentially be provided by the private sector. Subsequently, it becomes possible to ascertain whether it is more expensive to conduct such activities through public organizations.

The principle of accounting for the resources used is also taken into account. This obliges agencies and ministries to conduct an annual analysis of their expenditure based on the results achieved and the financial objectives set.

The Government has also adopted a Citizen's Charter, in which standards are established for the provision of services to the public. This Charter, which is universally applied, identifies performance principles in six areas and sets six standards that are central to client-based services, such as that of providing a clear response to all letters received within 15 working days. Each agency must produce an evaluation of its performance measured against each of these standards. It must publish the results through various media, including a website.

The British Government has an executive evaluation agency charged with applying the framework establishing the responsibilities of ministers and senior officials, as well as the system of financial rules and responsibilities in the field of staff management. This agency is responsible for administering the "prior options test", that is, considering whether the services provided by agencies are still required and, if so, whether it is more efficient for the Government to take charge of them or to privatize them. The results of the review of the performance of agencies are published on an annual basis. This document includes the performance results obtained by each agency, during the past three years, in relation to the key elements targeted in measuring performance.

2.8.2.3 Canada (Province of Quebec)

All ministries and public organizations in Quebec have methods of internal evaluation of their activities and performance. The mechanisms used, however, vary between organizations. Evaluations are frequently based on the quality of services provided to users, the reduction of programme costs and the improvement of productivity of resources.

A number of labour administration laws contain so-called "sunset clauses" by virtue of which the Department of Labour must conduct an evaluation at a given time. In most cases, the strategic plans for the implementation of these laws provide for the obligation to carry out an annual or a one-off evaluation. The Department also conducts enquiries and user satisfaction surveys on a systematic basis.

All departments and organizations are subject to two types of external evaluation. The type that is common to all government departments and organizations is carried out by the Auditor General of Quebec, who is directly answerable to the National Assembly, which grants him or her a great deal of authority and independence. The Auditor General's mandate goes beyond the task of auditing the national accounts. He or she evaluates how best to use the resources available and sheds light on the mechanisms put in place to manage those resources efficiently. In addition to verifying all departments and organizations, the Auditor General may evaluate the use of any subsidy granted by the Government to an establishment, institution, association or enterprise. He or she submits an annual report to the National Assembly and adds recommendations designed to generate improvements in management.

In addition, a number of organizations sometimes use various external agencies for the purposes of either providing expert opinions or auditing accounts. This is the case, for example, with regard to the joint committees that do not come under the remit of the Auditor General, but that must submit an annual report to the Department of Labour containing the financial statements audited by a recognized firm of accountants.

These are three cases that clearly demonstrate the concern of political leaders with achieving higher and higher standards of public management. For this purpose, they attach major importance to the function of evaluating the efficiency of government organizations, in particular those in the field of labour administration. This helps us to understand the breadth of the resources that can be implemented so as to be able to measure and improve the efficiency in question.

2.8.3 Practices: Four major categories

We have classified the different practices in four major categories, corresponding to the results given in the reports.

2.8.3.1 Self-evaluation devised simultaneously with the measures taken

The established practice is for the different components of evaluation to be put in place before activities are carried out. This is the case in Canada (Quebec), China, Hungary, the United Kingdom and the United States. The principle of evaluation is therefore laid down before the event and such evaluation is carefully prepared. The indicators are put in place at the same time as the programme itself. In certain cases, there is a whole mechanism of performance indicators, the collection and processing of which are planned and organized at the time the programme is devised. These indicators can take into account the impact of the programme on users. In other situations, mention is made of evaluations that are either external, conducted for the Government or the social partners, or internal, in some cases through precise indicators such as the rate of interest on loan repayments.

The results of an activity may give rise to a dual evaluation, both internal and external. Internally, the measures taken may be quantitative, that is, they relate to the number of activities carried out as part of a programme, the sectors where the activities have taken place, and the amounts of money involved and paid to the actors concerned. The evaluation is carried out by the administration concerned. Externally, the measures taken will generally be different, for example an assessment may be conducted by an independent audit office, either based on its own measures or by questioning participants, users or beneficiaries. In some cases, when two administrations participate jointly in activities, both their opinions may be requested separately.

The source of this type of evaluation can be found in legislative provisions containing an obligation to carry out an evaluation, for example in laws on government performance in the United States, parliamentary committees legally responsible for conducting inquiries in the United Kingdom, Auditors General in Quebec and so on. These may also relate to joint bodies, for example in Spain, which are responsible for evaluating the activities conducted. In some cases, for instance in China, Quebec and the United States, a ministry may conduct inquiries and satisfaction surveys among users or through subscribers to magazines linked in one way or the other to the ministry. Such inquiries can also be conducted among employees, in order to assess the working environment, or even to request them to estimate the productivity of their departments.

Although it might be expected that a prior evaluation is the most common form of assessment, such a situation is rarely encountered. This fact calls into question the strategy adopted for implementing activities and ministerial decisions. A decision or programme that is not accompanied by an evaluation of its effects is part of a bureaucratic model in the most traditional sense of the term, that is, a model where administrative decision-making is sufficient in itself. It therefore appears to be incongruous to try and assess the effects of such a process.

2.8.3.2 Retrospective evaluation

The second type of practice most frequently encountered is that where evaluation is carried out retrospectively and there is no evidence or mention of a previously established programme. In such cases, an evaluation of the results of a programme or the activity of an administrative department is envisaged after the event. Such an evaluation may be internal, as in Argentina, Fiji, France, Peru, the Philippines and Poland, or external, for example in Chile, France, Hong Kong (China), Hungary, the Philippines, Poland, Quebec (Canada) and Spain, and use methods which scarcely differ from the previous model. By contrast, its objective may be different, such as an assessment of the impact of the programme on other activities, an impact that was not envisaged at the beginning of the activities since they could not have been anticipated. This is the case in Argentina, for example. In other cases, such as Austria, the results achieved by the public administration are evaluated in that they are monitored and observations are made by politicians (government and parliament) during budgetary discussions.

2.8.3.3 The temptation of comparative evaluation

A third type of practice consists in using, as in the United Kingdom, sophisticated tools that have served other purposes, usually in non-public enterprises. In such cases, it may appear possible to formulate comparisons with the results achieved in the public services. For example, ISO accreditation may be requested for an administration, a department, or even a programme, as is the case in Quebec. In addition, the procedure of market testing may be used, consisting in comparing the results of the public sector with equivalent services – as far as possible – with those of the private sector. Finally, "benchmarking" is being introduced, which is a more refined method and consists in comparing things in their context and then benchmarking performances. Attempts can be made to establish benchmarks within an individual department, or between different departments or organizations, while ensuring that the processes involved are similar. One shortcoming of "benchmarking" can be that attention is focused on a limited number of advances and narrow perspectives rather than on an overall view of the situation.

2.8.3.4 Conditional evaluation

The last type of practice, which can be found notably in France, relates more to the effect of the results achieved and can be referred to as a consequence of evaluation. The practice in question links the performance for a given period to the allowances for subsequent periods. This type of practice is common in administrations and is systematized in certain countries.

As we have seen, different types of evaluation are encountered without it being possible to cite common variables. It can be said, however, that these methods are related to those used in the same country but in other sectors, which is the case, for example, for the use of sophisticated tools. It is obvious that the practices adopted by society, enterprises or other sectors have an effect on public administrations and state departments. It therefore appears probable that we will witness the emergence of tools such as quality measurement through ISO standards, market testing or benchmarking in the countries where these tools are already used. Experience with these tools means that they can then be applied successfully to public activities or administrations.

We can, however, confirm that labour administrations are increasingly concerned with casting a critical eye over the different features of their activities. For this purpose, they use various methods, all with the same aim: to strengthen or correct the processes implemented.

2.8.4 Current trends: Towards systematic evaluation

For several years, administrations have been more and more concerned with assessing the effectiveness of activities through the development of indicators enabling performance to be measured. The practices of evaluating the activities and results of labour administrations are gaining ground in all countries. According to the state of development of the management process particular to each one, evaluation will be one of the steps of a programme planning process, will allow better targeting of the activity sectors likely to undergo reductions in resources, or will provide a framework for assigning responsibility to political and administrative officials; this management trend has been observed during the past few years. In none of the situations observed has evaluation failed to generate comment. A review of the literature on the subject also strengthens this trend.

The indicators of this evaluation are very diverse, in relation to the stage at which they are prepared. In many situations, they are envisaged and considered only once activities have been launched, thereby considerably weakening their scope. In order to be effective, an evaluation must be devised at the same time as the programme to which it relates. Many administrations are aware of that fact. The current trend is to devise and prepare such evaluations prior to the implementation of activities, or to organize them a long time before a decision is taken to apply them.

According to an OECD document, the preliminary findings of an ongoing cross-national study suggest that developments in new public management have many implications for the function and practice of evaluation: evaluation is substituted (new internal markets are intended as intrinsic evaluators), complemented (the regulation of privatized monopolies is creating a huge demand for evaluation) and offered new subjects (evaluating new tools, for example internal contracts).[6]

A number of general trends prevail in the way the tools developed are used. There is a comparison of activities, as well as between different administrations and with external bodies. Despite the difficulties of this type of comparison (the subjects are never the same, the projects never identical), it is gaining ground. Subsequently, activities and administrations are called to tender against each other or with comparable bodies (always in a difficult and uncertain manner) in the private sector. Despite the difficulties encountered in making comparisons, the idea of a call to tender is gaining popularity.

A large number and a wide variety of evaluation tools are used. The introduction of a single measure appears to be insufficient for evaluating programme performance, given the interrelation between the different elements in question. A programme may appear to be effective and to achieve its aims, but prove to be expensive, that is, not to perform well from a broader perspective. Similarly, the definitions of results are not the same between different countries. This may relate to final results or to parts of activities, as well as limited or broader objectives. The result of a programme may be qualitative, while the results anticipated are quantitative. How must a programme be judged that seeks to reduce the number of unemployed by means of a training policy? The criteria used could be a reduction in the actual number of unemployed and the quality of the training provided, even though unemployment is contingent on a large number of variables.

2.9 What conclusions can be drawn from the trends described?

This chapter has presented different trends, in relation to eight specific subjects or rather practices common in the management of labour administration activities in different countries. What conclusions should be drawn from the information presented?

Firstly, the practices vary enormously across countries and even between different activities within the same country. It is difficult to identify, at least from the information contained in the case studies, the causes of these variations. Notwithstanding, certain trends do emerge. They correspond to the provisions of the ILO's Labour Administration Convention No. 150 and confirm the relevance of the important principles it puts forward for the sound operation of labour administration systems, namely:

— participation by the social partners;
— definition of the phases of preparation, coordination, monitoring and evaluation of national labour policy;
— coordination of tasks and functions assigned to the system;
— importance attached to human and financial resources.

As regards the historical justification for labour administration activities, it is clear that consultation between the social partners is an important concern for those responsible for devising labour administration policies. Great efforts are made to achieve a social consensus that will be formulated as a law serving as a basis for the establishment of labour administration activities.

Partnership operations, which can take several forms, are a very important concern for most of the labour administrations studied. An understanding appears to have been reached whereby partnership is the most effective way in which to obtain the voluntary participation of those directly involved in the activities conducted by a labour administration. Furthermore, it is an excellent way to ensure that these activities develop continuously in accordance with the needs of the participants.

With regard to the method of application, it is clear that a logic of obligation has given way to one of promotion and encouragement to apply the measures introduced through labour administration activities. The trend established is one of generating the voluntary participation of partners by all sorts of means.

As regards the definition of the phases of implementing national labour policy, the only factor to be retained is the importance attached to evaluation, since the practices examined did not concern the policies themselves.

The evaluation of labour administration activities is undergoing significant developments. Never has such progress been made in the assessment and comparison of the performances of public organizations. There is a wide range of resources to assess the efficiency of labour administration activities. It should be emphasized that those means include client satisfaction, on which judgments about the performance of organizations is increasingly based.

As to the institutional framework or the coordination of labour administration responsibilities, different bodies are used to implement the activities conducted. These may take the form of a department of the Ministry of Labour, a decentralized body, a consortium or a completely independent organization such as an agency. In short, it is not so much the body that makes the difference as the human resources used to staff it.

Finally, as regards resources:

— an analysis of the HRM aspect leads us to observe a certain expansion of, but not yet a complete break with, the bureaucratic model. The increasing importance attached to staff training and mobilization is a tangible sign of this trend;

— as regards technology, in particular information technology, it is clear that this is used as a means to improve activities and above all to provide better services to employers and workers. Information technology is also a form of support for managers and leaders who have to devise and manage labour administration policies. Furthermore, it may be observed that the impact of such technology is often considerable, since it requires changes in the organization of labour and its services, if its potential benefits are to be enjoyed;

— with regard to methods of funding, the State is scaling down its involvement in the financing of most labour administration activities. It must, however, be borne in mind that governments, in response to the pressures of public opinion, are called upon to intervene in an ever-increasing number of activities.

If an attempt is made to sum up these observations, it can be said that as regards the features of labour administration activities, partnership, joint management and decentralization are playing an ever-increasing role. The State is gradually withdrawing from the funding of each activity, but this is compensated by its direct participation in an growing number of activities. Finally, growing importance is attached to the evaluation of the efficiency of the activities conducted by labour administrations and, more specifically, the assessment of client satisfaction plays a central role in this evaluation.

All the case studies analysed show how active governments are in relation to labour administration. It is easy to deduce the willingness and desire to contribute to social and economic development that guide both politicians and public managers in this field. However, there is still room for improvement, and specific and straightforward methods of application exist, all the more so since in a large number of States labour administrations are not yet able to provide services that are comparable, all things being equal, to the processes presented in this work.

In the current context of economic globalization, more than ever it is the effectiveness of the management of labour administration policies that will make the difference between countries that will benefit from this globalization and those whose populations will suffer its often disastrous consequences. Labour administrations that are responsible for the preparation, promotion, implementation and evaluation of these policies can and must strengthen themselves and carry out their tasks, in effect by becoming development actors and agents of change.

In Chapter 3 we will consider what the concept of change implies in general terms and by what more elaborate means it is possible to conduct an assessment of an administration and propose positive change, while bearing in mind two additional features:

— bringing about change in labour administration bodies follows the same rules as in all other public or private organizations; we will therefore not be proposing a revolutionary method that would apply specifically to such bodies;

— it should be borne in mind that, more than in other fields of public activity, the bodies responsible for labour administration are noted for the principle of partnership on which their labour relations are based; the conduct of change in such bodies will therefore have to give greater consideration to the actual or potential role of the social partners, and workers' and employers' representatives, who are the labour administrations' main points of contact.

Notes

[1] F. Furet and M. Ozouf: *A critical dictionary of the French revolution*, translated by A. Goldhammer (Cambridge, Mass., Belknap Press, 1989).

[2] K. Polanyi: *The great transformation: The political and economic origins of our time* (Boston, Mass., Beacon Press, 1957).

[3] M. Weber: *From Max Weber: Essays in sociology* (New York, Oxford University Press, 1958).

[4] J.E. Thurman, A.E. Louzine and K. Kogi: *Higher productivity and a better place to work: Practical ideas for owners and managers of small and medium-sized industrial enterprises, Action manual and trainers' manual* (Geneva, ILO, 1988).

[5] G. Larochelle: *La communauté comme figure de l'Etat* (Chicoutimi, Québec, Les éditions JCL, 1998), p. 173.

[6] OECD: *Improving evaluation practices: Best practice guidelines for evaluation and background paper*, Public Management Service, PUMA/PAC (99)1 (Paris, 1999), p. 16.

Making improvements

3

The changes taking place in society continually force labour administrations to question their own role, functions and organization, ultimately bringing about change within the administrations themselves. As shown by the experiences described in the present study, getting the process under way under optimal conditions necessitates a more theoretical review of some of the parameters of change. It is also useful to recall that, like other administrative apparatuses, labour administrations are affected by major modernization trends. Finally, since the question is not one of creating new entities from scratch, but rather of adapting existing ones to the reality of the day, it is necessary to start by making an accurate definition of that reality.

3.1 The parameters of change

3.1.1 Introducing change

The issue of change is a recurrent and complicated one. Both its theoretical and its practical aspects have been studied extensively, and although the resulting works have not brought any solutions, they have made it possible to identify a number of parameters and define some frames of reference. The most important of these are presented below: first, misconceptions about change; second, the two main reference theories (strategic analysis and the theory of collective learning); and, finally, some practical advice on implementing change.

It is important to remember the distinction between social and organizational change. The former has extremely wide implications (for a society or a part of it, the borders of which are often indistinct), it is not wanted (at least not explicitly), it is unforeseen, lasting, collective and identifiable over time (a higher level of knowledge in a society, for example). Organizational change – the only type being examined here – is desired, identified, and is the subject of a more or less idealized representation or image; it stems from a known and rejected state, and is decided by an easily identifiable individual or group, at least initially.

3.1.1.1 Common misconceptions about change

This section is meant to put into perspective what everyone says or does instinctively when faced with the need for change.

The first misconception is the hierarchical illusion, that of the order and the leader. When holders of official authority – the hierarchy – decide on a course of action, they believe that it should happen because they have decided that it should do so. In this mechanistic vision the organization operates like a cogwheel: once the order is given, the first cog is set in motion and the others follow. If they do not, then the leader is at fault. Anyone who has held a minimum position of power knows that this reasoning is incorrect; subordinates unwilling to follow orders can resist them in a number of ways, the first and simplest of these being passivity: dragging one's feet, waiting for the counter-order, and so on. An order may not be sufficient, but it is still useful, if not vital. In an administration, orders are a necessary (although insufficient) precondition.

The second misconception concerns structure. It consists of the belief that changing the organizational arrangements of a service is enough to bring about real change and that any change should therefore begin with the transformation of the existing structure. Once again, experience has shown that this type of change is effective only if it is preceded by a very thorough and detailed analysis of the reasons why certain activities that need to be remedied are not functioning properly, and this requires a reliable analytical tool. The reasons may include the need for reorganization, but changing the structure is meaningless if it does not correspond to the needs of the service. For example, trying to make a person more compliant by subordinating him or her to a colleague who has hitherto occupied a similar hierarchical rank can lead to disaster, especially if the subordinate contrives to obstruct the orders received and to mobilize other staff members against the promotion of the new hierarchical superior. If two services are in frequent conflict, the reasons must be sought primarily by looking at their respective tasks, rather than putting it down to personal differences.

Another misguided concept, relating to the human factor, holds that in order to change an organization it is enough to change staff, either by dismissing or relocating those who appear to be least competent, by taking on new staff, by providing training aimed at introducing factors (such as new technologies) that would bring about change, or through a combination of the above. The underlying assumption is that people are self-sufficient and that their interaction with others and with structures is a negligible variable. It is true that in any firm or administration there are people who are more or less well suited to their posts. The more strategically important the post, the more fundamental is the choice of the person occupying it; the solution lies in redefining the functions involved.

However, pointing a finger at people without questioning their position within the organization is a futile exercise. There are no people who are totally useless, there are only situations that do not suit them. This last principle, expressed here in simplistic terms, is of great heuristic value. Before asking whether a person is unsuitable, one must ask whether or not he or she is suited to a particular post. The firm or administration is responsible for finding a post suited to the person's powers and capabilities.

Another false belief, still widespread, is that of "the fear of change". Human beings are said to be "naturally" afraid of change. Proposing or imposing a change on someone clearly means changing that person's social, material and relational position. The only question that needs asking, therefore, is on what conditions people are prepared to accept and to commit themselves to change. What is important is not the nature or the fact of the change, but the conditions in which it is to take place. If these are satisfactory and have been mastered (notably by eliminating the unknown), the person concerned will be willing to accept change and committed to it. The greater the degree to which the individual dominates the situation, the easier it is for the change to be accepted.

The last misconception about change holds that it is sufficient to have the necessary resources in order to bring about change. This comes close to the discourse on the power of money. Must it be pointed out that numerous firms and administrations have instituted change using enormous resources and have failed? Although material resources certainly help, they do not guarantee success. Many large industrial projects or administrative reforms have fallen through despite being backed by huge resources. There are more computer projects gathering dust on their inventors' desks than those that are actually in operation. Resources are a variable which, although important, is not enough to ensure the success of a new organization or change.

3.1.1.2 Theories of change

To understand the theories of change, it is necessary to abandon certain paradigms, such as determinism and evolutionism. The determinism of change is either a sweeping statement ("everything changes"), or is too vague to describe change in a given situation. As for evolutionism, in its pursuit of the great laws of evolution it does not allow the relevant consequences to be drawn, except by using very broad determining factors (technical progress, the environment) which offer little explanation and are therefore not very helpful in decision-making, either.

Where the operation of organizations (both administrations and firms) is concerned, it is more interesting to look at the theories surrounding regulation, in the sociological sense of the term. Two of these will be discussed: *strategic analysis* and the *theory of collective learning*. How do they explain organizational change?

According to the proponents of *strategic analysis*,[1] the only change is in the rules between actors that make up the organization, actors whose autonomy is postulated. If external or hierarchical constraints press for change, the latter will take place only if the actors decide to go along with it (although they could also refuse).

Change can be understood only by acknowledging the autonomy of the organizational phenomenon. Any form of organization is contingent (it could have been different from what it is) and based on the conduct of actors who are themselves autonomous, thereby forming an overall system of conduct. The survival of the organization, which functionalists see as a biological near-necessity, is considered here to be one hypothesis among many. This principle puts the organization beyond any exogenous constraint. New technologies and more participatory forms of work organization are choices that are not imposed from the outside. The organization should be regarded as a structure, an instrument that the social actors have designed to govern their relations in order to obtain the minimum cooperation needed to pursue collective aims while maintaining their relatively independent status. There is therefore scope for obtaining either minimum or maximum cooperation. All the actors are aware of the need for cooperation, albeit to varying degrees, while retaining their autonomy. Production constraints are known to all, but may be hidden by diversions such as red tape, when the internal strategies of groups some-times conceal the aims of the organization and the importance of the tasks to be completed. The bureaucrat is concerned only with the internal problems of his or her group.

Operational rules are not mechanical responses to constraints, even if they are conditioned by them, but are instead the expression of the relational abilities of the group. This means that each group is capable of inventing new solutions, even if it may temporarily feel unable to do so. The example often given is that of semi-skilled workers or implementation officials who for years carry out the same repetitive tasks and who appear not to be able to invent solutions when faced with problems that are presented differently. For change to take place, the group must retain its reorganizational capacities so that it can face up to new situations by inventing new relations. It should remain an open structure that is ready to accept new associations. A closed structure is a poor structure that has problems dealing with change. Being part of an organization today requires greater relational abilities than the former Taylorist model. It is much more difficult to invent new relational models than it is to buy a new machine. It could be added that this invention also entails a symbolic type of work, an appeal to the imagination to come up with new solutions.

Any type of change presupposes a break with the past, which is always difficult and is expressed in the form of a greater or lesser crisis, but is viewed in a more positive light if there is room for manoeuvre. This is why organiza-tions with an established culture and a strong identity find it so hard to change. Culture and identity conjure up the ideas of permanence, and dura-tion, of the influence of society, its values and its rules on the behaviour of the organization's members. They have a conservative and determinist aspect. Culture should be considered as an ability. What creates a system of relations is not a cultural model, but an action strategy.

The concepts of strategic analysis are based on very specific surveys that highlight the existence of actors who exploit the uncertainties present in all organizations. This is the exact opposite of a mechanistic view of human behaviour. In this perspective, it is clear that it is not possible to codify actors' behaviour, nor to plan change using procedures or even computerized programmes.

Strategic analysis has been replaced by *the theory of collective learning*,[2] whose central tenet is that of learning focused not only on individuals, but also on groups and the organization as a whole. Basing itself on educational discoveries made about knowledge, this theory further stipulates that individuals and groups can learn only through trial and error. A child does not learn by being shown models, but by discovering things by itself and then developing new cognitive systems that are linked to its relations and its effects. It is only in this way that new behaviour is acquired.

Theoreticians point out that individual action has a cognitive foundation. It is based on knowledge, which is not acquired by being transferred from one person to another, but by being built up, both individually and collectively. This building process is based on the standards, strategies and assumptions that individuals create or reformulate when interacting with other people. During this interaction process, each person tries to anticipate the behaviour of others, a priori based on his or her own experience. Learning therefore can be conceived not in terms of strengthening or eliminating models of behaviour, but as a process of building, testing and, ultimately, restructuring knowledge.

Learning is therefore:

— a building process: through experience and on the basis of their knowledge or ideas, subjects build up a new situation and a store of knowledge;
— a testing process: subjects test, evaluate and rectify their behaviour;
— a restructuring process: knowledge modified in the light of experience is reformulated until a clearly satisfactory or at least a less unsatisfactory solution is found.

Experts make a distinction between shared (or espoused) theory and theory in use; in other words, what is found in official documents is often different from conventional practices, which can be observed through actual behaviour. These conventional practices often exist by tacit agreement, with people knowing more than they are able or willing to reveal and being unaware of the shared theory. The practice of these tacit regulations forms the basis of the organizational identity and the continuity of the organization. Although shared theory may change along with management, theory in use has a permanent quality like that of culture. It evolves through employees' working practices which, once accepted, constitute knowledge.

Two learning methods exist side by side: individual and organizational learning. Individuals can learn things that an organization does not know. For instance, informal behaviour limited to the interaction between individuals (e.g. people come to agreements concerning certain adjustments to machines or the interpretation of a procedure, which the hierarchy ignores or does not wish to know about) is an example of specific practices that the organization is unaware of. If individuals are relocated, the organization will have retained nothing, since it has not taken these practices on board. It is therefore vital for the organization to retain these practices and understand their significance, while refraining from ascribing them to human nature.

There are therefore two types of change. The first may aim at a simple reconversion so as to restore equilibrium within a service. The second type goes further: it is aimed at transforming the system in respect of its operating rules and methods, even in respect of the implementation of change. Single-loop learning corresponds to the first type of change, which consists in detecting errors, and correcting and maintaining traditional practice. If, for example, a large number of errors are noted in the issuance of unemployment insurance cheques or the production of statistics on accidents at work, the data capture forms used by labour inspectors or career guidance officers could be revised or the data entry process to be done by them could even be computerized. An analysis is carried out, the causes are understood by means of deductive reasoning and changes are made, possibly by developing a new strategy.

In this case, the organization remains stable within a changing context. The standards remain the same. The necessary adjustments are carried out while maintaining stability, meaning that the members of the organization have nonetheless learnt how to communicate with each other. However, if one of the services does not pass on information, the person who noticed the mistake will have learnt something, but not the organization. Individual learning is therefore a necessary, although insufficient, condition for organizational learning.

Double-loop learning is true organizational learning. If there is great pressure for change and the actors agree to change conventional standards (e.g. new work rules are instituted by promoting a different approach to the user, favouring advice over supervision in the case of labour inspectors, or offering specialization for career guidance officers following the introduction of self-service facilities), it is no longer enough simply to adjust old rules and make them more precise. They need to be amended or changed, and new ones established. The first step consists in recognizing that the rules must be changed, rather than managing better with the old ones. Establishing new rules inevitably sparks conflict. Consequently, what needs to be done is to create situations prompting individuals and groups to invent solutions, such as fine-tuning for which the operators must be trained and the appropriate testing carried out, so that the operators develop new rules within this situation of mutual dependence.

Change is essential when the actors are aware of their inability to solve a problem within the framework of old rules. They need to invent new ones, and this can be done only by allowing individuals – faced with a new situation and therefore a different set of relations – to assess these new rules through trial and error. Furthermore, it must be ensured, on the one hand, that these new rules are assimilated by the different groups within the organization, which presupposes that they have provided a sufficient response to the requirements of the actors and the demands of the situation, and, on the other hand, that all the actors, and not only those directly involved, have used these rules enough times to have memorized them.

These two theoretical concepts, strategic analysis and organizational learning, are the most recent tools used to handle changes within organizations. How can they be put into practice?

3.1.1.3 Change in practice

The following practical advice on how to implement change has been drawn up empirically, on the basis of experiences that have been analysed specifically according to the theories presented above.

Legitimacy

Change is *accepted* in organizations only when the actors are *convinced of the need* for change and then of the type of change that should take place, either by being persuaded by management or by their own situation. Employees of job placement offices, for example, know that for budgetary reasons their office would disappear if its efficiency and relevance were not demonstrated. To accept the idea of change and to commit themselves to it, actors need to have grasped the fact that change is inevitable.

This brings us to the idea of *legitimacy*. Being convinced means acknowledging that change is right, therefore accepting that it is necessary. An actor who wishes to introduce a particular change must always consider the way in which it will be regarded by those responsible for implementing it.

When management wishes to introduce change, it must demonstrate the need for it and ensure that this need is acknowledged. To do this, it may be sufficient to provide sound information through demonstrations and discussions. This should, however, be based on specific evidence that could be furnished by a reliable assessment tool. However, this does not apply to the *type of change*. In companies or organizations, the type of change and the means by which it is implemented should be negotiated, otherwise the legitimacy of change could be questioned. The project should therefore be specific enough to be a real project, sufficiently open for actors to be able to organize the part concerning them. Without this, the intended change runs the risk of being rejected.

Strategies

If employees or officials feel any hesitation on the part of management when change is initiated, if they feel that those responsible have a strategic intention that has little to do with the nature of the change (for example, the person in charge initiates the project so as to improve his or her image in the eyes of senior management), if they think that the desire for change and the direction to be taken will change along with those in charge, the project certainly has little chance of success. It is vital to ensure the *consistency* of those pressing for change, on the one hand, and *continuity over time* while change is being implemented, on the other, as well as having a good strategic awareness of the organization. It is a question of ascertaining a priori the foreseeable positions of the actors when faced with the project. Any implementation of change should be preceded by a strategic analysis. This is where the actors and their personal interests, foreseeable alliances in relation to change and shared viewpoints likely to create the strongest links should be studied. The person in charge should try to anticipate the interests and strategies of those he or she is guiding, as well as those of all the actors within the administration who may be called on to participate.

From the point of view of the actors directly affected by the intended change, it must be remembered that they will *accept* it only when they know roughly where the change will *lead* them. As already mentioned, there is no natural resistance, but only strategic resistance, to change.

In addition, change is *accepted* only if the actors understand why the new mode of operation *casts doubt on their working methods and mechanisms*, since these are the very reasons which, in their eyes, have enabled them to succeed or at least to be where they are.

Still in terms of strategy, any change, be it voluntary or evolving, entails the creation of a *network* linking actors who previously had little contact, with all the conditions and constraints of a network. The setting up of a network within an organization requires a *translator* or a *facilitator*. The correct way to go about this is to set up a project (not a firm or service project, but project-based operations) where management entrusts an ad hoc team with implementing change; the project team should consist of representatives from different services and be dissolved upon completion of the project. The various representatives will put forward their points of view and the positions of their departments. Reciprocally, once they return to their respective departments, they should try to make their colleagues understand the views and positions of the other services comprising the project team. Networking and the project are central to carrying out change. The project leader should be as independent as possible from management if it is the latter that has initiated the change, and have sufficient legitimacy vis-à-vis all the actors involved.

Putting actors in contact with each other and therefore introducing change means creating new actors. There is no change without the creation or emergence of *new actors*. Their strategic position and legitimacy are difficult to define beforehand (there are as many as there are changes), but they are vital, although they will disrupt the routine of *former actor*s and therefore provoke resistance. It must be remembered that any technical or organizational change has an effect on the system of relations. This is the principle behind the *interdependency of factors*, a phenomenon already discovered in the 1930s by American researchers in the human relations school. No change is neutral with regard to the system of relations formed by a group of people. Even a seemingly minimal technical change always leads to disruption within this system.

Finally, it must be remembered that all change requires time, and that its instigators must be persevering and patient. Public administrations, in particular labour administrations, cannot afford to ignore this practical advice on implementing change.

3.2 From the search for effectiveness to quality management

Although, in addition to providing services, labour administration also has a normative and regulatory responsibility, it has joined the general trend and undertaken to modernize its operating methods so as to make them more relevant, effective and efficient. Charged by the government with interpreting the general interest, bound by values of equality and social justice and entrusted with ensuring social cohesion, labour administration is the guarantor of equal treatment and equal opportunity, of social welfare and of compliance with basic labour rights. Its push for more comprehensive, diversified and specialized state operating methods as a means of tackling increasingly prevalent and complex social problems (poverty, exclusion, long-term unemployment, major work accidents, child labour, gender inequality, precarious employment, to mention but a few) has been regularly checked by public budget restrictions. These constraints were the first to bring labour administrations face to face with the problem of setting priorities and making optimal use of existing budgetary resources, and therefore with the need to implement change. Moreover, the democratization of administrative life and the participation of employers' or workers' organizations and users' associations in socio-economic development have naturally led these entities to regard themselves as *actor*s involved in change, with a legitimate right to judge whether public funds are being used properly.

The question of the effectiveness of labour administration activities is not new in itself. It has long been one of the main preoccupations of the heads of this administration responsible for finding solutions to the ever more complex problems in the field of labour. The spate of public administration reforms, which began in the mid-1970s following cuts in public spending, has affected ministries of labour and other public bodies involved in the labour and employment fields. The question of their effectiveness was at the heart of the debate held by the international community in 1976 when the ILO felt the time had come to set up, by means of an international standard (Convention No. 150 and Recommendation No. 158 concerning labour administration: role, functions and organization, 1978), an institutional framework for the preparation, administration, coordination, checking and review of national employment policy.

The turning point came in the early 1980s with the spectacular reforms adopted in several English-speaking countries (Australia, New Zealand, United Kingdom, United States)[3] whose governments had decided to scale down the presence of the State and to disengage it from the direct production of services, on the grounds that it did not need to provide services that the private sector could supply more effectively and at a lower cost. The large-scale movement to improve working methods and streamline public service resources gathered further pace at the beginning of the 1990s. This period saw the disappearance in several sectors of the preferential position of certain public entities, the authorities having decided to force them to confront competition from private operators by subjecting the services they provided to a competitive bidding system of a commercial type. The 1990s were also marked by the implementation of citizens' charters, management contracts, progress contracts and finally, today, of quality assurance systems leading to certification of conformity with ISO 9000 quality standards. The basic principle behind such measures is that if it wishes to strengthen the legitimacy of its activities, public administration should no longer be anonymous and removed from the user. The application of the principle is justified by both the desire to reduce the public deficit and the changing attitude of users and citizens who are increasingly sensitive to questions of public spending.

The pursuit of productivity and effectiveness in public administration has now given way to the pursuit of quality thanks to quality-management techniques perfected by private companies. The former involved changes aimed at a simple readjustment within the organization, while the latter deals with a transformation of the system by introducing new concepts such as new public management and good governance. New public management has begun to be introduced no longer only in industrialized countries, but also in a number of developing countries (e.g. Brazil, Malaysia, Poland,[4] Zimbabwe), with the support of international financial institutions.

The issues of effectiveness (understood as the realization of the expected effects on the intended targets), efficiency (realization of maximum results for each financial unit committed) and relevance (the correct response to user expectations) have become extremely important for the public heads of labour administration in developed countries, and in some developing countries concerned with the well-being of their workers.

Several labour administrations have drawn up practical guides on mediation and conciliation, largely inspired by the approach used by companies and consisting of first making a critical analysis of the situation, identifying the different actions to be taken, grouping them together within phases or stages of a process, each with its own objective, and finally proposing one or more approaches that are most likely to lead to the desired result. Internal organization of information is another activity where labour administration has used management techniques to gather the required information and pass it on to the internal managing bodies that need it to make their decisions. The same applies to the decentralization of Labour Ministry structures throughout national territory. Rather than passively accepting existing administrative divisions, some labour administrations have used the methods applied by the initiators of industrial projects when searching for an optimal location for their firm, the location being planned in accordance with, in particular, "employment needs". Marketing and sales techniques have also been used by labour administration when devising communication and publicity policies. There are many examples of training institutions, social security funds, public employment services, career counselling services and the like, which have used these techniques to explain or simply to make their purpose and their services known to the public, to improve the quality of the reception given to users, to make information easily accessible or to make their premises more attractive and more comfortable.

Today, spurred on by their governments, certain labour administrations no longer seek simply to offer effective service, but aim at total quality. According to several authors who have studied the major reforms linked to the process of economic liberalism in English-speaking countries, classifying them under new public management, this development took on a more tangible form during the 1990s.

A number of these authors emphasize that the concept of public management is much broader than the commercial interpretation of management in terms of the internal operation of government affairs. During a symposium devoted to administrative reform at central government level[5] it was pointed out that public management is not simply internal, but also and primarily external, in a complex socio-political context, and that one should rather speak of *public governance*. Although the two fields of study (public and private management) had much in common and could learn much from each other, there were nevertheless fundamental differences both in context (the *Rechtsstaat* and political democracy) and organization (legality, bureaucratic legitimacy and rationality).

The reforms of the 1990s show that there is a desire to bring the service closer to the user. The publication of objectives and annual reports promotes transparency vis-à-vis the public. Systematic consultations, in the form of surveys and opinion polls, are regularly carried out to learn about public expectations. In the United Kingdom, for example, central directives require that quality standards assigned to agencies be defined in absolute numbers and not in percentages so that progress is more evident to users. The publication of quality standards acts as a support for promotional activities and is one of the instruments that have replaced traditional market forms. At the end of the process, certification of conformity that is concerned with user satisfaction also represents a reward for services which have shown that they have successfully implemented more effective management methods.

Since the concept of the client is central to it, quality certification is not evaluated in terms of general criteria determined by a competent authority, but according to the degree of user satisfaction. There are nine criteria used to evaluate quality: publication of measurable standards to be attained and respected in terms of the results achieved; means of information available; efforts made to establish a dialogue with users; taking account of the users' point of view and being able to offer them a choice; officials' politeness and helpfulness in their dealings with users; attention paid to complaints and claims made by users; the quality/cost ratio of the service provided; proof of a satisfied clientele; and, finally, the improvements made during the years preceding the request for certification of conformity with quality standards.[6]

Quality commitment often takes the form of "management contracts", as in the Netherlands and Austria, or "progress contracts", as in France, between the Labour Minister and the implementing agencies or bodies. These contracts fix, for a specific period extending over several years, the entity's production (tasks, results, aims) and resources (financial, material, personnel, equipment), and set out contractual conditions (legal and political). Other possibilities are quality charters, which are published (e.g. Zimbabwe), or service contracts (Quebec, Ontario, Alberta and other Canadian provinces). In all cases, bodies that have adopted a quality assurance system indicate that they have obtained positive results.

All the examples studied show that it is essential to analyse the current situation before introducing change. It is only by assessing the existing structure that it is possible to decide what to change and where, and how to proceed to improve the quality of labour administration services. We have seen that public authorities have used various approaches and techniques to identify the processes involved and the manner in which the weaknesses detected should be corrected. This helps to pinpoint the real problem facing labour administrations in developing and transition countries, on which international financial institutions impose drastic public administration reforms.

The effectiveness of public policy in labour and employment matters necessitates the adoption of coherent, integrated and coordinated policies that draw on resources through a series of services and activities aimed at satisfying the needs and expectations of users, clients or beneficiaries in accordance with the required level of intervention.

Introducing and managing improvements in labour administration implies addressing the question on at least two levels. The first relates to services: the aim is to discover to what extent the services supplied in response to demands from users, and therefore target groups, reach the desired quality standard. These services include those which provide a direct response to users and are furnished by each branch of labour administration, such as labour inspection, counselling and placement of job seekers, vocational training, collection and processing of data, provision of technical advice and opinions to workers' and employers' organizations, and so on. At the second, policy level, the aim is to discover to what extent administrative policies,[a] resource allocation and regulatory frameworks allow needs to be satisfied in an effective and equitable manner, and to what extent the participation of the social partners is facilitated and the necessary degree of coordination between the appropriate bodies is achieved.[7]

---

[a] UNDP publications refer to "administrative governance".

In other words, one should analyse the manner in which central administration is able to develop the public[a] labour administration system – that is, all the public or parapublic bodies and agencies with authority within the field of activity of this administration – and achieve quality. These two levels of analysis refer to what Pollitt and Bouckaert call "meso-quality" for the first level and "macro-quality" for the second level, "micro-quality" in their analytical framework relating to the performance of a given agency. [8]

It is important to study the status, operating rules, aims and results of the Ministry, which is the focal point of administrative policy, and of all the satellite agencies within labour administration, in order to see whether the system is built correctly and structured to respond to needs at all levels; and to assess the possibilities for institutional and organizational change so as to improve the entire labour administration, rather than analyse or study only the services provided. In this respect, the analysis of institutional structures and of the roles and aims of the agencies with regard to user expectations is one way of generating a policy debate concerning the continued improvement of the whole labour administration. Continued improvement is also helped by the drafting of terms, rules and conditions for establishing a partnership involving delegation of services under certain conditions, or even the option of subcontracting activities to the partners, with precise specifications that take into account the definitions of the services expected and the constraints related to their realization and monitoring.

However, an improvement strategy cannot be improvised; it must be planned in minute detail, especially so as to be able to deal with any resistance. It goes without saying that it is necessary to know in advance what changes need to be made and at what level. Here too a number of administrations have for some time been using tools borrowed from private enterprise, such as "benchmarking" (standardization through comparison) and "re-engineering" (reorganization), and others which allow the reasons for the dysfunction or insufficient performance of an agency, service or functional unit to be identified. This is the aim of the assessment tool described below. It is designed to respond to the specific problems facing labour administrations and is an example of the expertise and advice that the ILO can offer to its member States.

3.3 Assessment in the labour administration system

The profound changes facing contemporary societies reassert in a new way the need to envisage changes within the administrative structure responsible for

---

[a] This concept is used to distinguish between public bodies and joint or tripartite consultation and coordination bodies, as well as private bodies that play a part in the national labour administration system.

developing and implementing labour policies. The evolution of labour admin-istration is more a question of improving existing structures in order to best meet current challenges (effectiveness and equality) than one of creating new administrations.

When contemplating changes to labour administration structures, it is necessary to clearly define the issues and challenges at stake and to identify as well as possible their resources and potential. Establishing an objective view of the existing system is vital to the introduction of change. How should an objective analysis of the existing system be made? What strict procedure should be followed? What indicators can help to objectively determine the relevance of the organization and operation of a particular body and to iden-tify more easily existing problems and the elements that need modifying?

It should also be recalled that labour administrations enjoy specific charac-teristics which distinguish them from other administrations. These characteris-tics may affect their organization and operation. They include, for example, the continuous "integrated" relationship with the administrations' main partners, in particular trade union and employers' organization representatives (tripartism), relations with users or clients, often involving a third party (administration/worker/employer, administration/job-seeker/future employer) or a third-party institution (public, parapublic or private social welfare body, employment fund, vocational training, etc.) and their quasi-judicial role (control, sanction, conci-liation, etc.).

The ILO's Labour Administration Convention No. 150, and Recommen-dation No. 158 (1978), are the only international instruments providing for the establishment of an institutional framework within which national labour policy is developed, implemented, coordinated, monitored and reviewed.

The Convention defines labour administration and the concepts covered: a coherent national labour policy, a coordinated system, an institutional structure integrating the active participation of employers, workers and their respective organizations, and adequate human, financial and material resources for the provision of effective and efficient services. In this sense, a labour administra-tion system covers the following fields of activity:

(a) labour standards (working conditions, wages, employment conditions, occupational health and safety, working environment, social security, labour inspection, etc.);

(b) research in the labour field (data collection, studies, forecast analyses, dissemination of information, etc.);

(c) employment (national employment policy, employment insurance schemes, vocational guidance, vocational training programmes, employ-ment services, etc.);

(d) industrial relations (services provided to employers and to workers, col-lective bargaining, settlement of labour disputes, etc.).

All these areas, often grouped under one administration, make up the labour administration system. Each of them may also be entrusted, depend-ing on existing social relations practices, to non-governmental organizations, in particular employers' organizations, trade unions, organizations with equal labour/management representation or tripartite bodies. The quality of the system therefore depends as much on the quality of each component of the system as on the quality of the relations between the different components.

Consequently, Convention No. 150 provides a reference framework for objectively monitoring the operation of the labour administration system. For this purpose, it sets the following requirements in particular:

(a) the labour administration system should be regarded as a whole. It concerns all structures (whatever their status) that contribute to its effective operation;

(b) all tasks and responsibilities should be organized and coordinated effectively;

(c) the labour administration system rests on its ability to bring about agreement and negotiation between public authorities and employers' and workers' representatives;

(d) the quality of the system depends as much on the planning, implementation, coordination and monitoring as on the evaluation of policies;

(e) the relevance of the system depends on its ability to reach the participants of all spheres of economic activity (including farmers, sharecroppers, self-employed workers, people working in structures established by custom or community traditions, etc.);

(f) the quality of the system depends on the means available to the administration for ensuring that directives are applied correctly throughout national territory and within all structures making up the system;

(g) the quality of the system also depends on its ability to monitor the training and professionalization of its agents and of private sector agents made available to ensure the operation of the system.

Convention No. 150 thus proposes a certain number of points of reference which should enable countries to analyse their own system of labour administration and set improvement goals, taking into account their own local context and concerns, and to envisage how best to reach those goals.

An assessment process facilitates a proper analysis of labour administration systems. Unlike an audit procedure, which aims to reduce deviations from the norm and standardize structures by seeking to make them fit a predetermined framework, the assessment process helps governments set attainable goals by furnishing information on the current operation of their labour administration system. It is thus primarily a decision-making aid.

For the benefit of governments, the following sections of this chapter illustrate the various characteristics of the assessment process, the rigorous methodology it requires and the optimal way of putting it to use in developing national labour administration systems.

3.3.1 *What is an assessment?*

In 1997, the ILO Committee of Experts on the Application of Conventions and Recommendations and the Governing Body emphasized the importance of labour administrations, the modernity of Convention No. 150, and Recommendation No. 158 (1978), and the need to strengthen labour administration at a time of great economic and social upheaval. The widespread reform of the role and operation of the State throughout the world is an additional reason for providing these public services with the means needed to reflect on the issues involved and take decisions accordingly. No national labour policy can be effective and efficient without sustainable means of implementation and renewal. The best plans resulting from the best policies will come to nothing without sufficient managerial know-how for a lasting implementation of the plan. To this end, the proposed assessment process is aimed at re-examining these means to produce more effective public policies in the fields of labour, employment, vocational training and social welfare.

For this purpose, when assisting labour administrations ILO experts use a strictly defined method and common means in order to meet as closely as possible the needs of these public administrations in taking stock of their situation and practices, and finding a balance between what they would like to be, what is expected of them and what they actually are.

3.3.1.1 Definition

Assessment is intended to be a systemic and functional analysis process of the organization and management of a labour administration (for example of a Ministry of Labour, or part of it) considered as a coherent unit with a specific mandate.

The aim of the assessment process is to identify:
— the challenges and issues at stake,
— all available resources,
— the potential for change,
within a system in order to be better prepared for the decisions that may be made subsequently.

The assessment process involves taking a step back so as to be able to question and examine the relevance of the organization and management practices with a view to identifying not only operational problems, but also the margins that can be exploited in order to promote development of the administration. This exercise, proposed by ILO labour administration experts, is carried out using a structured interpretative grid based on the common principles of labour administrations, making it possible to appreciate both local distinctions peculiar to each country and the room for manoeuvre that can be utilized to plan the transformation and development of a labour administration system.

This short process (of two weeks' duration) cannot provide an exact assessment of the services supplied to clients/users and, therefore, of the resources needed to provide these services. However, it makes it possible to ascertain whether the services offered are effective and whether they correspond to the aims and priorities of the organization, and to support possible recommendations to be made.

A process based on action and change

Assessment is not an end in itself, but forms the basis for an action plan and any desired change. It is thus distinguished from inventories of fixtures or studies (which provide essentially descriptive, static views of reality) in so far as it is intended to initiate and actively accompany the development and modernization of labour administrations. It does not and cannot provide an immediate solution to noted problems. It is not a substitute for a policy-maker, but aids decision-making and guides any action taken.

A process rooted in local potential

Assessment is not aimed at imposing external business models on administrations. Its role is not to judge or monitor "satisfactory operation" and "good practices". Unlike an audit procedure, which aims to identify and reduce deviations from a pre-existing standard, it seeks to draw on local resources and potential so as to envisage new modes of operation relevant to the specific context.

A strategic process

Assessment is not a miracle tool that will immediately solve all problems. It is simply a stage in a continuous development process, allowing those in charge to take some distance from daily realities in order to define existing challenges and available room for manoeuvre that are likely to guide the modernization of the administration. It is a step that will lead to other, more decisive steps being taken.

A forward-looking process

Assessment is a process that is decidedly oriented towards the future. It is therefore different from evaluation procedures which provide a retrospective analysis of whether a certain number of objectives have been achieved. The assessment process aims to create favourable conditions for the development of labour administration systems and to identify room for improvement (and not only existing problems) on which those involved may focus in order to bring about change.

A global and systemic process

Assessment seeks to obtain an overall view of the complex structure and multiple interactions of the labour administration, and thus differs from "problem resolution" procedures which are aimed at solving specific problems independently of the system in which they occur. It also differs from internal or external user satisfaction surveys, which allow only partial and biased representations of the situation. In contrast, it tries to analyse the complexity of the whole system and the various interactions within it. Within this broad scope, the assessment may concern only one specific and targeted sector of labour administration (the public employment service (PES); labour inspectorates (LI) or central administration, for example); nevertheless, the particular sector will be analysed in relation to the entire system to which it belongs with a view to understanding its role, specific nature and the challenges with which it is confronted, to avoid creating imbalances within the system.

A process that relies on findings and multiple points of view

In order to grasp the complexity of the situation, an assessment draws on a large number of different sources of information and points of view. In the final analysis, it will involve all the people concerned by the project in all their various functions (civil servants as well as social and institutional partners, users, etc.) so as to have the most objective representation of reality possible.

An educational process

The assessment process mobilizes and establishes accountability among the different actors within labour administration systems. It differs from a "study" approach, which is carried out in isolation by an external intervening party in the form of a subcontract, and establishes continuous and close interaction. It is designed to aid decision-making and provides an ideal occasion for all of the system's actors to identify, understand, analyse and master the various problems, challenges and openings, applying educational logic from the earliest stages and throughout the procedure. Particular attention should be paid to any "resistance to change", discussed at the beginning of this chapter, and the fears of certain actors should be taken into account as much as possible in order to overcome that resistance.

A professional process

Finally, an assessment of a labour administration system cannot be carried out without prior preparation. If it is to be reliable, the process requires methodological rigour of the highest order and the use of a number of specific skills.

3.3.1.2 Assessment and self-assessment

Two types of procedure can be envisaged, each corresponding to a distinct logic:

— assessment, which explicitly requires the services of an external third party, is alone capable of producing a distanced and objective analysis of the situation. The ILO puts teams of competent experts at the disposal of administrations wishing to carry out such a procedure;

— self-assessment, which can result from internal work carried out by the government, without the help of an external expert. However, this course of action constitutes an inventory rather than an assessment process.

The choice of one or the other approach depends on the nature of the project and on the context. Proceeding from the definition of the concept of assessment, it is possible to describe the good practice and limits of either approach.

Assessment is justified when the following requirements must be satisfied:

— pooling available information, thereby enabling those in charge of the system not to have to judge a situation in which they are directly involved;
— ensuring objectivity by resorting to an external third party whose analysis is imposed on all parties;
— producing a feasibility study in order to assess the resistance and possible obstacles to the intended project;
— mobilizing all parts of the system.

In contrast, self-assessment is justified in the following cases:

— mapping out an entirely new situation (a new government taking office, etc.);
— establishing a status report for information purposes and not necessarily to examine the feasibility of a still unstructured political project;
— the impossibility of using an external third party because of the local social situation;
— the need to carry out an internal assessment so as to gather all pertinent information before turning to an external third party.

It is difficult to define a model framework for self-assessment. The main aim of this type of procedure is to accumulate information that can be used as points of reference by government teams in charge of devising strategies for improving their labour administration system. In this sense, self-assessment is not a procedure additional to the assessment process, but rather a preliminary stage. Indeed, the assessment can validate or invalidate the hypotheses made during self-assessment. The latter is therefore an accumulation of disparate information (studies, statistics, expert points of view, etc.) making it possible, in a second phase, to outline both the aims of change and the ways of bringing it about.

The basic purpose of the discussion that follows is to grasp the meaning of an assessment process, while specifying the skills brought in by teams of external experts and the methodological elements relative to the request for assessment.

3.3.2 Initiating an assessment process

The first step in an assessment process consists in clarifying what needs to be observed and to objectivize and anticipate the conditions in which the assessment should take place.

Thus, before starting the assessment proper, two types of questions must be addressed:

— the identification of responsibilities in carrying out the assessment;
— the clarification of the assessment plan.

They will help to define the actual conditions in which the assessment should take place and to draw up a reference document (terms of reference) specifying the framework, objectives and conditions for conducting the assessment.

3.3.2.1 Identifying responsibilities in the assessment process

First of all, it is necessary to identify the team that will be responsible for carrying out the assessment. For this purpose, two types of responsibility must be clearly distinguished:

(a) the responsibility of the requesting party, who represents the contractor in the procedure. This is the person who initiates and controls the assessment and is usually the minister in charge or, if there is no ministry involved, the highest authority responsible for entrusting the operating agent with the task of carrying out the assessment according to his or her requirements. The conclusions of the assessment will be submitted to the contractor, who will then use the material resulting from the assessment to refine his or her decision and to initiate a modernization process best suited to the circumstances that have been analysed and objectivized;

(b) the responsibility of the team in charge of actually carrying out the assessment, which represents the operating agent.

The operating agent, made up of a team of experts, provides short-term support to the labour administration, helping it to identify and make use of the possibilities to modernize the system. The operating agent has the following tasks:

— to collect all information likely to enhance and strengthen a project to develop the labour administration system;
— to mobilize those involved in the improvement and implementation of a project to develop the system (or a clearly identified sector within it).

In this sense, as an objective observer, the operating agent ensures (by re-examining the facts and questioning – in the true sense of the term – the system) that the difficulties and potential of the labour administration system are brought to light and that the relevant actors are involved, through issues of common concern, in the developments and changes that take place.

This team must be made up of skilled external professionals who have the distance from the labour administration system in question, in order to avoid any confusion or substitution between the contractor and operating agent or between the operating agent and the system actors. It is clear that in this type of exercise the team conducting the assessment cannot be both "judge and judged".

The "contractor/operating agent" relationship is therefore richer than a simple client/supplier relationship. It is more like "co-contracting" than "sub-contracting" and will bear fruit if the operating agent possesses the following professional abilities:

(a) putting itself at the disposal of the entire labour administration system (as defined by Convention No. 150 and Recommendation No. 158) and its development, and not of any particular actor;

(b) keeping its distance and providing a global, systemic and objective analysis of the situation. The former rests not only on the agent's knowledge of labour administration systems, but also on its ability to examine and "question" local realities. Its analysis will therefore make it possible to determine how local concerns fit into more global ones, and to cut across the different dimensions (institutional, strategic, organizational, social, operational, etc.);

(c) establishing a close partnership with the local actors (and not supplanting them by treating them as subcontractors or by stripping them of responsibility) so as to identify possible room for manoeuvre and to enhance the development project, while respecting the role and responsibilities of each party. The operating agent should therefore not be involved in either the decision-making or the implementation process, but should instead confine itself to assisting in the preparation of both;

(d) making use of relevant information that will enhance the intended development project; to this end, it should examine all the different aspects of the labour administration system using various (objective et subjective) sources of information;

(e) initiating this phase of the project by adhering to a strict methodology, by helping to make headway, in particular by clarifying the role and aims of an assessment (so as not to generate frustration) or by setting on paper the material prepared in the course of that work.

It is these abilities that the ILO's team of labour administration experts bring to labour administrations when carrying out an assessment.

A team of experts charged with carrying out an assessment should have a counterpart, an official representative who will facilitate the relationship between the contractor and the operating agent throughout the assessment. This official representative is appointed by the minister; his or her role is to accompany the team of experts throughout the assessment procedure in order to:

(a) provide a constant link with the requesting party by enabling the latter to participate in the process and to be informed of the progress of the assessment. The representative's close relationship with the Minister will help create an atmosphere conducive to a smooth running of the operation (thanks to continuous interaction);

(b) facilitate the working conditions of the team of experts carrying out the assessment, by:

— giving official status to and institutionalizing the various stages of the process;

— facilitating contact both within the Ministry and between actors within the labour administration system (in particular the social partners) or the other actors involved (the different institutions approached);

— enabling the operating agent to access relevant information;

— helping the operating agent to understand the specific context (cultural interpretation of situations);

— facilitating communication (notably by providing translation, although in his or her absence an additional interpreter may be necessary);

— finally, creating the conditions necessary for the continuation of the process.

Indeed, the counterpart is a vital intermediary as regards the continuity of work, providing links and ensuring consistency between the assessment and the implementation of reform. The implementation may, for instance, be entrusted to a project team, as suggested earlier in this chapter (see "Strategies", pp. 127-129 above).

This high-level official will be closely involved from the very beginning of the assessment and throughout the process (either during investigations or during systematic and regular meetings).

3.3.2.2 Clarification of the assessment project

The assessment process must always be guided by a number of questions that should be clarified before any investigation is undertaken:

— What is being assessed and why?

— To what end?

— What information is it hoped will be produced?

— What is expected of the external third party (or of the internal team in charge of conducting the assessment)?

When the process is initiated, one of the first tasks of the team of experts will be to assist the requesting party to set out in detail its assessment request, the objectives of the assessment and the conditions in which it is to be carried out: these questions may at first seem complex, but the primary role of the external third party is precisely to bring them to the fore and thus clarify the process. As a result, information may be solicited before the definitive, official request for assessment is formulated. Assistance in formulating the request thus forms part of the assessment. Within this framework, the operating agent can help the contractor to specify the nature of the intended project, the "ideal" or the "minimum acceptable level" to be attained, and to define reasonable medium-term objectives and evaluation criteria.

The co-contracting relationship between the contractor and the operating agent referred to above obliges the parties to carry out a formal exercise to clarify the request. This request, as formulated, will constitute a reference throughout the assessment, providing a coherent, rigorous framework for the process. It will in particular allow the actors involved at a later stage to understand why the assessment is taking place. The formal document attesting to the request is called the "Terms of reference" and should set out a number of points (see box 3.1).

3.3.3 Carrying out the assessment

Once the terms of reference have been established, the investigation can get under way. Its aim is twofold:
— to garner all the information that may help the assessment team to make an objective analysis of reality;
— to involve all the actors in formulating proposals and participating in the process of change.

However, before this stage, it is important to enable those who will meet the assessment team to have access to information on the purpose of the process and the role of the team. The terms of reference help to formalize communication with the various services and social partners. This preliminary step helps the actors to get ready to provide useful information.

The aim of the on-site investigation should be to allow a more in-depth assessment based on the following factors:
— the current situation of the labour administration (as it is perceived), its structure, role, functions, tasks, decision-making practices, procedures, the way in which its services operate and are interlinked, the flow of information, hierarchical structure, the composition of staff, etc.;
— what the administration would like to be (in light of its projects and ambitions);
— what is expected of it (as a public administration, but also from the point of view of its partners and users, etc.).

Where the challenges faced by labour administration and its specific nature are concerned, the on-site investigation should in particular make it possible to:
— verify the consistency between the Ministry's tasks, intentions and practices;
— identify the services provided (quantity, quality, meeting the needs) to different sectors of the public and public satisfaction with these services;

Box 3.1   Terms of reference

The "Terms of reference" document should specify the following:

1. The aims and nature of the document itself

2. Details of the instruction, its nature and scope

- the drafted request and its aims;
- certain elements relating to the background to the request (current situation of the labour administration, political, economic and social context, etc.);
- certain hypotheses relating to the requesting party's project (general intentions, ambitions, reasons for the request, etc.).

3. Details concerning presentation of the process

- the aims of the assessment (attainable aims so that the activity is realistic and does not pursue vague aims), its limits and scope;
- the nature of the process initiated;
- a brief introduction of the team in charge of the assessment (composition of the team, etc.), its institutional authority and role;
- detailed timetable for the process;
- the boundaries of the process (clear identification of sectors, services and actors concerned and, where relevant, explicit designation of fields to be excluded from the process);
- the nature of the results expected (notably the fact that the proposals and recommendations resulting from the assessment are primarily decision-making tools);
- means for internal control of the process (intermediary meetings, liaising with people responsible for following the process internally, etc.);
- identification of the "official representative" and his or her role in the process;
- the logistics of the process, in particular:
  - preliminary information concerning the initiation of the process with the actors likely to be encountered (what form the information should take and what areas it should cover);
  - scheduling interviews, in particular within the administration;
  - use of an interpreter;
  - means of travel.

4. Methodological factors

Concerning the investigation:

- the different methodological stages envisaged, their nature and aims;
- the sources of information mobilized for the purpose of the assessment (ILO, institutional actors within the labour administration system, actors at grass-roots level, labour administration users, partners, etc.);
- the actors to be approached as part of the process (those contacted during interviews, the negotiation stages, etc., including, where relevant, the involvement of a national consultant or a local expert on a particular subject, for instance on national legislation) and the aims of these approaches.

Concerning the presentation of results:

- the nature of the final presentation, its aims and the forms it will take (one or more presentations, made to whom?);
- the nature of the assessment document, identification of the recipient and the forms in which it will be transmitted (channels for submission of the report, means of circulation among other actors, conditions of confidentiality, etc.).

Concerning follow-up to the assessment:

- possible follow-up to the assessment process;
- deadline for reactions from the recipient;
- the possibility of turning to the ILO in the follow-up stage;
- the possibility of undertaking an evaluation – within a specified period (with or without the expert);
- bringing in other persons of authority within the labour administration system (the social partners, for example, depending on local conditions, or other labour administration actors directly affected by the reform process).

— gain an understanding of internal "cultures" and climate;
— understand the relations with the social and other partners (other ministries, regional or local authorities, etc.);
— assess existing obstacles;
— evaluate possible support for changing the system;
— compare the system's organization and mode of operation with the organizational principles proposed by Convention No. 150 and Recommendation No. 158.

In particular, sources of information should be diversified (while remaining within the limits of the instruction and the remit received) in order to obtain a global representation of the labour administration in its entirety. For this purpose, "objective" information should be assembled (both quantitative indicators such as the number of visits and formal information such as organizational charts and institutional data), but particular attention should also be paid to more "subjective" information, including remarks made by the actors during formal or informal meetings and interviews. This "subjective" information could throw light on the actual operation of the administration or service concerned (role of the local actors, professional practices, etc.).

To fulfil this mission and meet its aims, the team of experts charged with carrying out the assessment will conduct its work according to three methodological phases:

3.3.3.1 Analysis of documents

The team of experts will mobilize and analyse all the documents produced not only by the administration but also by the actors in the environment. This information must be closely linked to the contractor's request and the aim of the assessment, so that it can be used in the analysis. It is to the requesting party's advantage to facilitate the team's access to the information that it considers useful for the assessment.

3.3.3.2 Interviews

With the aim of gathering information and involving the actors in the change process, the experts will conduct individual and group interviews with the various actors.

To facilitate the interviews, to reduce the time needed for the presentation and thus have more time to devote to analysing the situation and its development prospects, a briefing note setting out the terms of reference and presenting the team in charge of the assessment should be given to the various contacts beforehand.

For this purpose, investigations may be carried out on several levels.

With those responsible for labour administration, in particular:

— the Labour Minister, or ministers in charge of the labour administration;

— the executive managers in charge of the intermediary levels of the central administration;
— the executive managers in charge of devolved or external services.

These interviews are aimed at collecting critical analyses of the current operation of the labour administration, the context in which it operates, the challenges confronting it and its prospects for development.

With actors at the grass-roots level of labour administration

This category covers civil servants in contact with the users. The interviews, which take place in a real situation (usually by accompanying civil servants in their work – visits to firms, or processing a file from beginning to end), at the level closest to the users, will allow an on-site examination of practices and investigation of management resources available (classifications, records, schedules, statistics, liaison tools, etc.). The team should note the conditions in which requests from different sectors of the public are received and taken on board (in respect of existing services, as well as those whose lack seems to be most acutely felt). It is at this stage that a significant part of the actual operation and impact of the labour administration will be revealed. This is therefore a crucial stage and should be conducted rigorously, in particular by restating the scope and aims of the assessment to the actors encountered and seeking to establish a relationship of trust so that the process is not perceived as an inspection.

With actors involved in the labour administration system, in particular:

— social partners;
— civil servants working within tripartite consultative and cooperation bodies and cooperative structures.

These interviews are aimed at analysing the labour administration in a more global manner, such as it is perceived by its main partners, and its potential for development within the labour administration system.

With actors in the labour administration's immediate environment, in particular:

— other public administrations, depending on the circumstances, such as the Ministries of Planning, Economics, Development, Administrative Reform/Public Service, etc., with a view to gaining a better understanding of the labour administration and its development prospects within the public administration system in general;
— users (certain enterprises, for example), with a view to gaining an insight into their critical perception and expectations of labour administration: even if a visit cannot be considered representative of the situation in the country, it may reveal all sorts of important information, in particular concerning the relations between the firm (employers' and workers' representatives) and labour administration.

— potential partners likely to cooperate in the process of developing the labour administration, depending on the context and nature of the project (the representative of the United Nations Development Programme (UNDP), donors' representatives, potential sponsors, the World Bank, other institutions, and so on).

The interviews will provide the various national actors with the opportunity to state their difficulties, expectations and proposals: the experts' ability to listen and to ask pertinent questions will lend further credibility to their findings. In particular, they need to create conditions in which the different actors can express themselves freely. Therefore, when the terms of reference are being drawn up, the team of experts should be able to decide whether the presence of the counterpart is desirable or not (especially when it comes to interviews with employers' and workers' representatives).

3.3.3.3 Analysis of material by the team of experts

Throughout the assessment process, the team in charge will have the task of analysing the material gathered as it relates to the objectives defined in the terms of reference, so as to:

— help formalize an objective presentation of reality;
— identify possible means of leverage and potential of the situation;
— formulate working hypotheses with regard to change.

This analytical capacity depends of course on the skills of the experts. Their global knowledge of labour administration systems enables them to produce a reasoned analysis of the room for manoeuvre and the system's potential, while being mindful of the specific local context.

3.3.4 Intermediary presentations

During the investigation, intermediary meetings between the contractor and operating agent are indispensable. They will be used not only to review the nature of the material collected but also to test certain possible hypotheses already likely to form part of the final presentation.

Intermediary presentations can also be made to actors within the labour administration. This helps to create conditions conducive to change by involving the different actors affected by the project, and allows the experts in charge of the assessment to test the recommendations envisaged and thus to refine their analysis.

3.3.5 Final presentation

The final presentation, made during a meeting between the team of experts and the requesting party, provides an opportunity to:

— give an oral presentation of the analysis carried out by the experts in charge of the assessment;

Box 3.2   What is the team looking for?

The overall analysis will focus on:

The degree of implementation, in particular:

- Labour administration's spheres of activity (role and functions as opposed to legislation and labour context):
    - Employment
    - Industrial relations
    - Vocational training
    - Information (on the job market)
- Management and administration functions
    - Organization of the labour administration system (tripartism, other organizations)
    - Organization of labour administration (the administrative unit being assessed):
        - structure
        - management (principles and management process, communication)
        - resources:
            - human
            - financial
            - material
            - informational
    - activities
    - results and performance (evaluation)

Causes of dysfunction, with a view to proposing possible changes

---

— test and improve the recommended hypotheses;

— exchange and confront different points of view with the requesting party so as to envisage the future of the labour administration and specific ways of implementing change;

— validate the presentation and the ensuing recommendations.

It is worth recalling here that the basic aim of an assessment is to find possible room for reform of the labour administration system. However, the persons in charge of modernizing the system may at first perceive this as a denunciation of dysfunctions. It should therefore be remembered that the role of the team in charge of carrying out the assessment is not to make value judgements about the operation of the system, but to provide the requesting party with material that can then be used to construct the system's future.

The aim of the oral presentation to the requesting party is to consider together the challenges, difficulties, constraints, means of exerting pressure and the room for manoeuvre, and operational prospects of the reform process. The team of experts will seek the endorsement and possibly enhancement of the assessment by the requesting party. At the end of the meeting, the team should ensure that any points resulting from the discussion and likely to improve the assessment are validated by the requesting party.

After the interview and within a restricted time limit, a short round-up paper will be given to the requesting party so as to keep a written record of the main points of the presentation and the subsequent discussion.

3.4 Assessment report and recommendations

Following the presentation and within the time limit set by the terms of reference, a single final document, drafted by the experts in the form of a confidential technical memorandum, will be submitted to the requesting party (contractor). The experts will see to it that it is transmitted no later than one month after completion of the assignment so as to ensure that the assessment information is not dated and the impetus generated during the procedure has not slackened.

The document should contain the elements presented orally by the team, as well as the improvements resulting from the debate, and marks the end of the assessment process.

This technical memorandum is sent to the Labour Minister, who must officially approve it.

In accordance with official instructions, the memorandum will be transmitted through one of the following channels:

— when the ILO has an Area Office in the country concerned, the director of the office sends the memorandum to the Labour Minister. A copy of the report is addressed to the UNDP Resident Representative (whether or not the UNDP has financed the assessment) for information purposes. The director of the Area Office will follow up the report with the national authorities to ensure that it is approved;

— when the ILO is not represented in the country concerned, the UNDP Resident Representative sends the report to the Labour Minister, and a copy of the report is addressed to the director of the Area Office responsible for the country in question.

The experts in charge of the assessment will pay particular attention to the drafting of the report, which should be clear, legible and concise. It will not provide descriptions from which conclusions cannot be drawn. Each part of the report will highlight strengths or weaknesses as well as proposals, and will not provide an academic description. The analysis made in the report will contain only information necessary for understanding the recommendations. Each report will be adapted to the specific nature of the situations encountered; there can be no single format to fit all assessments. However, it is necessary to follow a certain pattern of thinking and a consistent and coherent framework. For this purpose, the assessment should consist of an introduction outlining the aims of the assignment, terms of reference and a brief summary of the course of the assignment. The other parts of the report should follow the outline presented in box 3.3, although the importance given to each section part will depend on the national situation, the strengths and weaknesses recorded, and the recommendations made. If some topics are not of direct use, they could be mentioned "for the record". The assessment document could later be used as a reference against which to measure developments and their progress.

Box 3.3   Assessment report plan

Introduction

1. Background

1.1 General survey of the economic and social context
  - Government policy in the fields covered by labour administration
  - Wide-ranging socio-economic reforms in progress or planned, including public administration reforms
  - Legislative reforms under way

1.2 State of ratification of international labour standards relating to labour administration

2. Description of institutional and management capacities

2.1 Brief presentation of the labour administration system
  - Global structure
  - Social partners

2.2 Tasks/functions of the labour administration
  - Role and rules of law
  - Aims of the ministry/ministries in charge of labour administration

2.3 Organization and operation of the Labour Ministry (or other ministries in charge of labour administration matters)
  - Structure
  - Human, financial, material and informational resources
  - Management of services provided by the Ministry
  - Management of benefits and services provided by subcontractors, by delegation or through partnership
  - Methods of internal and external evaluation of results

3. Analysis of problems/needs
  - Assessment (see section 3.3.3.3 above)
  - Degree of implementation of the role and functions, and analysis of the causes of dysfunction

4. Conclusion

The conclusion should put forward a global synthesis of the assessment, revealing the constraints, possible means of action and room for manoeuvre in effecting change.

5. Recommendations
  - Responses to the requesting party's priority concerns
  - Restating the relevant recommendations made during earlier visits
  - Measures proposed depending on the analysis framework (see section 3.3.3.3 above)

6. Feasibility of recommendations (with or without external support)

7. Plan of action

8. Annexes

The experts will ensure that the recommendations set out in the report are clear, not too numerous and that they concern operational and practical matters. These recommendations should be presented in a coherent manner (grouped around major issues such as organization, decision-making, activities, resources, operational development, etc.) They should take account of the specific nature of the context and feasibility (the time limits and stages of which could be envisaged). Rather than proposing recommendations that require excessive investment (for instance financial), it would be better to formulate suggestions that can be easily put into practice (by specifying the conditions for their implementation).

The recommendations should use the skills of the experts and the information gathered to explore the different possibilities of structuring a reform project. For this purpose, it appears important to point out the advantages of these recommendations, but also their effect on the labour administration system (possibly also their limits and disadvantages).

3.5 Assessment follow-up

Assessment is merely a tool for introducing change. Its usefulness will be demonstrated only as a result of its use, and the use will depend on the choices made by the Minister and the latter's willingness to implement them.

For this purpose, ILO experts will monitor the assessment follow-up, not only in order to evaluate the effects of the process, but also with a view to providing support (the methods of which must be specified), where necessary, in implementing the reform project.

Under the Regulations, if the ILO receives no reaction from the Minister within six months, the report is "declassified", that is, it is no longer considered confidential. This rule should be made clear to the requesting party in the terms of reference. The experts reserve the right to contact the requesting party before the deadline expires in order to review the project and the Ministry's intentions.

Several forms of follow-up and assistance can be envisaged; the possible role of the ILO in the different initiatives is negotiated on a case-by-case basis:

— participation in a tripartite national meeting. This offers the opportunity to make the social partners understand the meaning of the recommendations and their implications, while facilitating the drawing up of an action plan and partners' support for its implementation;

— participation in a meeting to present the assessment (analysis and/or recommendations) to other actors within the labour administration (in particular those encountered during on-site investigations) or other institutional actors;

— meetings to present the recommendations (according to a format to be agreed with the requesting party) to potential partners (in particular UNDP representatives) with a view to examining their possible involvement in the project.

The drawing up of an action plan will be one of the first positive elements in the post-assessment stage; the plan will state what action will first be taken by the Ministry itself, the areas in which the ILO may be of help, and projects to generate donor support.

* * *

These different stages of the procedure should help to assemble quality information and to envisage implementation scenarios that might open up new possibilities for the requesting party in its decision-making.

Notes

[1] J.G. March, H.A. Simon and H. Guetzkow: *Organizations* (New York, John Wiley, 1966); M. Crozier: *Strategies for change: The future of French society*, translated by W.R. Beer (Cambridge, Mass., MIT Press, 1982).

[2] C. Argyris and D.A. Schoen: *Organizational learning: A theory of action perspective* (London, Addison-Wesley, 1978).

[3] S. Trosa: *Moderniser l'administration: comment font les autres? Approche comparative des stratégies de modernisation des administrations en France, au Royaume-Uni et en Australie* (Paris, Editions d'Organisation, 1997).

[4] C.J. O'Leary: "Performance indicators: A management tool for active labour programmes in Hungary and Poland", in *International Labour Review*, Vol. 134, No. 6, 1995, pp. 729-751. The author of this study shows how labour administration in Poland, where public policy is now focused on results, implemented a system of evaluation and planning to manage active labour programmes.

[5] W.J.M. Kickert and T.B. Jorgensen: "Introduction: Managerial reform trends in Western Europe", in *International Review of Administrative Sciences* (Brussels, International Institute of Administrative Sciences), Vol. 61, No. 4, 1995, pp. 499-510.

[6] Y. Emery: *La démarche qualité totale dans l'administration*. Séminaire "Le manager public" (Lausanne, Institut des hautes études en administration publique, 1997).

[7] I. Sanderson: "Evaluation, learning and the effectiveness of public services: Towards a quality of public service model", in *International Journal of Public Sector Management* (Bradford, MCB University Press), Vol. 9, Nos. 5/6, 1996, pp. 90-108.

[8] C. Pollitt and G. Bouckaert: *Quality improvement in European public services: Concepts, cases and commentary* (London, Sage, 1995).

Conclusion

The operation of contemporary labour administrations rests on a paradox that we have sought to bring out in this volume: it is when their services are most needed that their weaknesses are most pronounced. In general, enterprises look for skills, established or new, that they need if they are to move forward. In almost all developing countries, labour markets and occupational training systems function inadequately, often to the detriment of the needs of workers and firms. All economic actors should have access to the social information enabling them to make choices in respect of pay, recruitment, jobseeking, and so on. Without wishing to go into the issues of industrial conflict, workers' status, legal developments, working conditions, or health and safety problems, it must be said that, in the face of ever-growing needs in each of these areas, labour administrations – with no alternatives other than admitting defeat or finding new strengths – are displaying increasingly obvious weaknesses.

Renouncement is sometimes political in origin and therefore outside the scope of this discussion, but it is also frequently a matter of strategic choices (or non-choices) on the part of labour administrations themselves, of their lack of creativity in response to the problems facing them. What we have sought to stress is revitalization, and it is in this perspective that the present work was conceived.

First, we set out to show that labour administrations are able to offer significant services that can help workers, firms, and political, economic and social decision-makers to tackle today's complex problems and to anticipate tomorrow's challenges. We cannot expect markets (including labour markets) to do everything, and so government action (adapted to national, and even regional and local circumstances) is very often necessary. Government involvement is needed in order to gain the most benefit from globalization and technological change, while at the same time avoiding their inherent dangers.

At a time when the social and economic context is undergoing such profound and rapid change, it is crucial to avert or to contain the most painful and destructive situations through proactive, supportive and regulatory policies, especially since such policies also encourage initiatives that enable individuals and firms to participate in development more fully. This approach is amply demonstrated in the real-life examples provided in the numerous case studies in this volume.

Second, we have tried to demonstrate that these policies have to be promoted and implemented by efficient actors or they will remain simple declarations of intent that will only disappoint the population. Labour administrations cannot be just virtual instruments; they must also be modern organizations, concerned with the quality of the services they provide and with the appropriate internal processes needed to achieve that quality. Clear strategic choices and the targeting of means (even limited ones) to respond to well-defined priorities can help convince government leaders and reticent finance ministers of the potential contribution of labour administration.

However, once this potential has been demonstrated, it is imperative that the public organizations concerned have at their disposal resources commensurate with the tasks that have been assigned to them. Very often this entails reversing the spiral of impoverishment that a number of these administrations around the world are caught up in. Indeed, fewer resources imply fewer results; fewer results then lead to a reduction in resources, a loss of influence, and marginalization.

Some will regret seeing labour administrations weaken, but this is less important than the decline, if not the disappearance, of their capacity to influence economic and social policies so as to ensure that the problems of labour and employment are taken more fully into account. Also of importance is the disappearance of support for development and/or for the fight against unemployment, inequality and poverty in the interests of those who most need that support.

The third issue highlighted by the present study is the need for direct involvement of the parties directly concerned and permanent dialogue with their representatives. This makes possible, first of all, a better understanding of their expectations, of the requirements and of the most viable solutions. However, what is also at stake is a particular mode of State–society relations. Whether through the drafting of legislation, the design of policies, or policy implementation, the involvement of the social partners in the decision-making processes of the State, the definition of the fields over which they have authority, the distribution of management responsibilities, and so on, are all elements that define a modern conception of the State and foster democracy.

As pointed out in Chapter 1, there is an international legal instrument that can be used, if needed, to reinforce this kind of approach: the ILO's Labour Administration Convention, 1978 (No. 150). Armed with the mandate that the Organization has given it to increase the number of countries ratifying this Convention, the International Labour Office is pursuing its efforts to establish a support mechanism for these public structures within the framework of the principles set out above.

Our decision to focus on the sphere of labour administration and not to deal with the overall reform of the State and the modernization of the public service as a whole was deliberate. However, it goes without saying that, although it does not take very long to rethink and improve the functioning of labour administrations, no significant action can be taken without an overall reform of the public sector. Many of the problems we have identified, such as the status of civil servants and their remuneration, cannot be satisfactorily resolved within the individual ministries concerned.

It is also necessary to take into account conceptions of the role of the State, its field of jurisdiction, and its methods of intervention, as well as of its relationships with the various representatives of civil society.

These issues are of crucial importance. The creation in 1999 of a Department of Government and Labour Law and Administration responsible, in particular, for strengthening the expertise of the International Labour Office in these matters should soon make it possible to put forward proposals, both practical and theoretical, that will encompass state reform and the modernization of public service.

Annexes

ORGANIZATIONAL CHART OF THE NATIONAL LABOUR ADMINISTRATION SYSTEM (A)

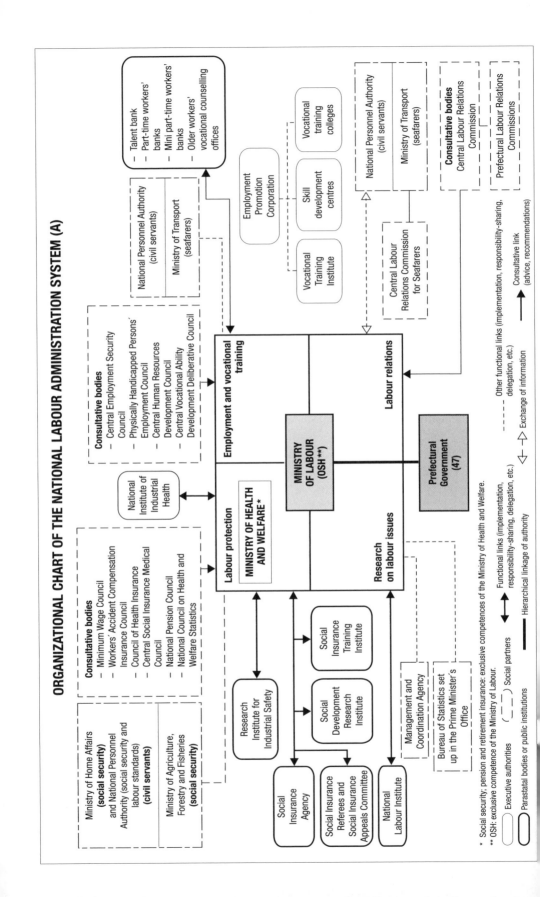

Consultative bodies
- Minimum Wage Council
- Workers' Accident Compensation Insurance Council
- Council of Health Insurance
- Central Social Insurance Medical Council
- National Pension Council
- National Council on Health and Welfare Statistics

Ministry of Home Affairs **(social security)** and National Personnel Authority (social security and labour standards) **(civil servants)**

Ministry of Agriculture, Forestry and Fisheries **(social security)**

National Institute of Industrial Health

Labour protection

MINISTRY OF HEALTH AND WELFARE*

Research on labour issues

Research Institute for Industrial Safety

Social Development Research Institute

Social Insurance Training Institute

Social Insurance Agency

Social Insurance Referees and Social Insurance Appeals Committee

National Labour Institute

Management and Coordination Agency

Bureau of Statistics set up in the Prime Minister's Office

Consultative bodies
- Central Employment Security Council
- Physically Handicapped Persons' Employment Council
- Central Human Resources Development Council
- Central Vocational Ability Development Deliberative Council

- Talent bank
- Part-time workers' banks
- Mini part-time workers' banks
- Older workers' vocational counselling offices

National Personnel Authority (civil servants)

Ministry of Transport (seafarers)

Employment and vocational training

MINISTRY OF LABOUR (OSH **)

Labour relations

Employment Promotion Corporation

Vocational Training Institute

Skill development centres

Vocational training colleges

National Personnel Authority (civil servants)

Ministry of Transport (seafarers)

Central Labour Relations Commission for Seafarers

Consultative bodies
Central Labour Relations Commission

Prefectural Labour Relations Commissions

Prefectural Government (47)

---

* Social security; pension and retirement insurance: exclusive competences of the Ministry of Health and Welfare.

** OSH: exclusive competence of the Ministry of Labour.

Executive authorities   (– – –) Social partners

⬭ Parastatal bodies or public institutions

— Hierarchical linkage of authority

⟷ Functional links (implementation, responsibility-sharing, delegation, etc.)

- - - Other functional links (implementation, responsibility-sharing, delegation, etc.)

⟽⟾ Consultative link (advice, recommendations)

⟽⟾ Exchange of information

ORGANIZATIONAL CHART OF THE NATIONAL LABOUR ADMINISTRATION SYSTEM (B)

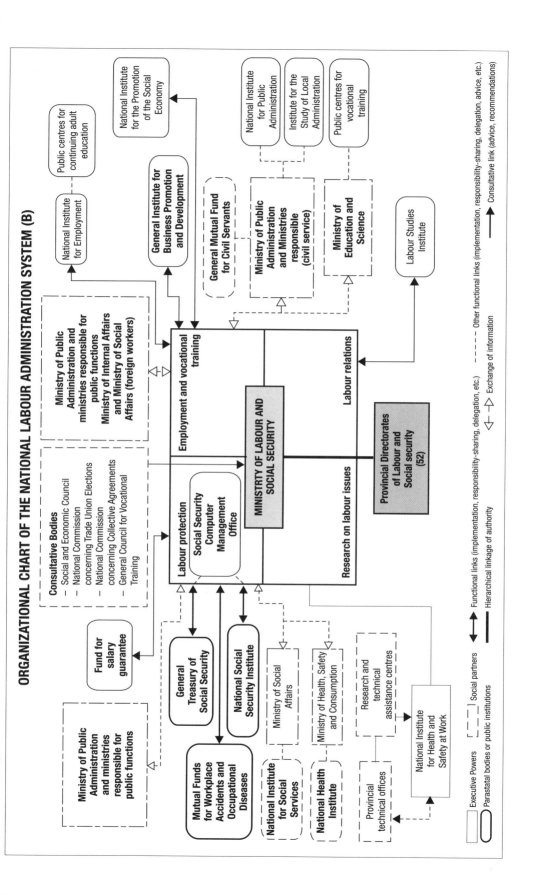

ORGANIZATIONAL CHART OF THE NATIONAL LABOUR ADMINISTRATION SYSTEM (C)

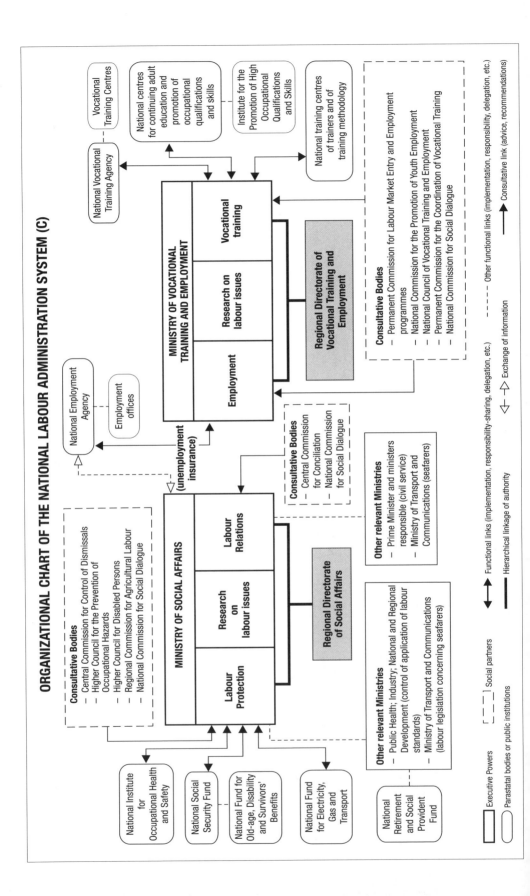

Part II

*This section contains 27 case studies
analysing labour administration practices
in the fields of labour, employment
and vocational training,
industrial relations, and evaluation.*

Introduction

The practices and innovations that make up the second part of this volume have been grouped under four sections: labour, employment and vocational training, industrial relations, and evaluation.

The list of countries where these innovative practices have been put in place was drawn up using specific criteria as follows:

— the principal fields of activity in which labour administration is involved;

— balanced representation according to geographical region, stage of economic development, etc.; and

— the principal forms of government (centralized or decentralized, etc.).

Each practice or innovation was first studied in Part I of this volume from the following viewpoints: historical background; institutional framework; policy implementation; active human resources management; information technology; partnership; funding, and evaluation. They are described below, taking into account three dimensions specific to labour administration, namely:

— the fields of activity in which they are implemented;

— the various users to whom the services are made available; and

— the different levels at which these practices are implemented.

To provide readers with the tool to analyse the case studies, a methodological framework of analysis, which sums up the principal components of a service or activity related to labour administration, is presented below.

1. The mode of functioning of the various legislative, political and administrative authorities

Before describing a particular country's socio-economic situation, an overview of the normal mode of functioning of the legislative, political and administrative authorities, that is, the traditions and culture in these matters, is necessary. Does the country have an oral or a written tradition, a tradition of negotiation between the various social partners or of decision imposed by political authorities, a tradition of social conflict or workers' participation, and so on? To the greatest extent possible, the characteristics of the country's administrative functioning will be specified, indicating which national bodies (Parliament, Prime Minister, Ministry of Labour, etc.) are usually responsible for the measures being dealt with in the study. Important events which may have an impact on these characteristics are also taken into account.

The historical stages of implementing the administrative system are sometimes noted in so far as they help gain a better understanding of the action undertaken and the goal pursued. This is followed by a synopsis of the situation in the field on which the decision impacts. This situation can be political, economic, social and sociological. If the measure in question is concerned with the retraining of workers made redundant – as in the case of

China – then the background situation on the one hand, and the level of commitment of the government and popular perception of and support for the changes on the other are both considered, in order to understand the significance of the measure. What problems are being addressed and by what means (regulation, laws, decrees, etc.)?

2. The origin of the action

The origin or origins of the action are provided with a date. A law, decree or regulation may have been planned at a specific moment, drafted then revised, reviewed, amended, etc. It is then necessary to determine the actors who initiated the action. Was it the Parliament, the Prime Minister, the Minister of Labour, the labour administration, or a special committee? What are the relationships between these actors? A theoretical factor comes into play. The organizational analysis conducted here is based on the theory of strategic analysis, according to which all organizational and socio-economic systems depend on the power relationships that structure the relations between actors.[a] Thus, understanding a system implies knowing the actors and their interests; this is known as contextualization. In the case being examined, can the actors, their interests and the strategies that they have used be understood?

3. Objectives of the action

Next, the official, publicly stated objectives are described, keeping in mind their political context and strategic value. The success or failure of a measure can depend on the manner in which it sets in motion, assists, promotes, obstructs or constrains an actor. For example, an initiative to protect the health of workers, the aim of which is humanitarian and may appear neutral and above partisan conflict, can still only be understood if we take into account the interests of the actors involved, especially those of the workers' and employers' organizations, regardless of whether they have a tradition of antagonism or negotiation.

This simple methodological and analytical framework should guide the actors in describing their situation and the actions they commit to. Those who implement activities that are part of the remit of labour administration have elements at their disposal to frame the action to be initiated.

Note

It should be kept in mind that these examples were examined primarily in 1998 and 1999 and that the information given therefore refers to that period. In some instances the political and legislative contexts and the measures themselves may have evolved considerably since then.

---

[a] J.G. March; H.A. Simon: *Les organisations*, op. cit., p. 172; M. Crozier; E. Friedberg: *L'acteur et le système* (Paris, Seuil, 1977).

Labour

Programme for the Promotion of Self-employment and Micro-enterprises (PRODAME)

The case of Peru

The labour administration in Peru has introduced a scheme to create employment by encouraging the establishment of enterprises or the registration of small and micro-enterprises in the informal urban sector.[a] This scheme was implemented by the National Directorate of Employment and Vocational Training of the Ministry of Labour and Social Promotion, which entrusted the task to a small team of promoters who were given a wide remit with a view to achieving the quantitative goals recommended by the Directorate. Since 1995, this body has offered users various services, including technical and legal assistance, the organization of business management training courses, and various information and management tools for business leaders.

In the early 1990s, statistics pointed to an increasing concentration of employment in the small and microbusiness sector, which covered more than 40 per cent of the active wage-earning population. Small and medium-sized enterprises (SMEs), which represent a high percentage of existing businesses, generate approximately 75 per cent of national productive employment and 42 per cent of gross domestic product. Since small and micro-enterprises play a major role in job creation, the Ministry of Labour and Social Promotion decided to adopt various programmes aimed at the labour market in order to promote employment, including the Programme for the Promotion of Self-employment and Micro-enterprises (PRODAME), in operation since November 1990 in the metropolitan area of Lima and, since October 1994, in all regions of the country.

PRODAME activities, which are aimed in particular at workers in the informal urban sector, are based on the provisions of two decrees[b] adopted in 1991 and 1997 respectively.

PRODAME's aim is to promote the creation of job opportunities by encouraging the establishment of small and micro-enterprises. It places the situation of such firms active in the country on a formal footing by allowing them to register in accordance with the law; PRODAME substantially reduces the length of the formalities involved in and the cost of setting up businesses by offering fast-track procedures free of charge, and also provides the opportunity to conclude interinstitutional cooperation agreements.

---

[a] In 1997, the working population employed in the Peruvian informal sector represented approximately 50 per cent of national employment.

[b] Legislative Decree No. 705 of 5 November 1991 respecting the promotion of small and micro-enterprises (*El Peruano*, No. 4126, 8 November 1991, pp. 101517-101519); and Supreme Decree No. 002-97-TR of 21 March 1997 respecting the approval of law on labour training and promotion (ibid., No. 6116, 27 March 1997, pp. 147989-147994).

All private individuals wishing to set up or to obtain legal recognition for a small or medium-sized enterprise, whose capital is less than or equal to 5,000 US dollars and, in the case of companies, whose maximum number of members is six, may participate in the programme; there is no upper limit on the capital for individual enterprises with limited liability.

The following services are offered as part of the programme:

1. Technical assistance relating to the legal aspects and management of a business.
2. Free preparation and registration of formal instruments of establishment of small and micro-enterprises.
3. A 50 per cent reduction in notary fees, pursuant to the Agreement signed with the Lima Chamber of Notaries.
4. Talks and seminars on vocational training and retraining, information days relating to social security, fiscal obligations and business management, organized by relevant specialists.
5. Provision of information on:
   — the institutions offering funding, vocational training, technical assistance and other services to the small and microbusiness sector;
   — the investment alternatives for small and micro-enterprises, grouped by economic sector; and
   — the conditions and procedures for obtaining operating licences from municipal authorities, as well as special authorizations and permits from public institutions.

The management, implementation and evaluation of PRODAME have been entrusted to the National Directorate of Employment and Vocational Training (NDEVT), a technical standard-setting department of the Ministry of Labour and Social Promotion; the Sub-Directorate of Employment Promotion manages the implementation of PRODAME through a team of seven specialists in the field, four lawyers, an economist, a business administrator and a systems analyst in charge of developing appropriate software. This software, known as the "System for devising formal documents of incorporation (SEM)", automatically establishes such instruments; the required details are entered and the document is ready within about 20 minutes.

At the national level, the implementation of PRODAME has been entrusted to the Regional Directorates of Labour and Social Promotion; the staff in charge of programme implementation at regional level consist of three officials appointed by each headquarters; only one of these officials works exclusively on PRODAME, the others carrying out various activities within the purview of the Directorate of Employment and Vocational Training.

PRODAME services are promoted using various media – brochures, leaflets and other means of communication – either directly through the promoters of PRODAME, or at the request of third parties and as part of informal talks on vocational training, workshops, seminars, conferences, and participation in festivals and exhibitions.

The activities undertaken and the results obtained by PRODAME, both in the metropolitan areas of Lima and Callao and at national level, are assessed on a permanent basis and published in the monthly statistical report issued by the Ministry of Labour and Social Promotion. These statistics are calculated monthly, on the basis of information forwarded by the Regional Directorates of Labour and Social Promotion; the statistics are compared with the objectives assigned to the Ministry and allow the implementation of the programme to be monitored in a satisfactory manner. For example, the aim for 1998 was to establish 3,500 small and micro-enterprises at national level, while in fact 3,689 were set up, i.e., the results obtained exceeded target by 5.4 per cent. In 1998, 530 informal talks were held on vocational training, in which 28,572 people took part; furthermore, 19,682 users requested the services provided by PRODAME. In the first quarter of 1999, 119 informal talks were held on vocational training at national level, in which 6,799 people participated.

PRODAME not only makes it easier to set up businesses, it also takes the lead in improving vocational training and distributing useful information to business leaders, both in Lima and through the Regional Directorates of Labour and Social Promotion. In this context, the "Annual Vocational Training Scheme for 1999" was designed; the scheme provided for the organization of 12 different events in the course of the year in the metropolitan area of Lima; to this end, it sought to combine all possible efforts to offer better information to users as regards business management and the labour-related provisions in force, with the support of the National Directorate of Fiscal Administration (SUNAT), the Social Sickness Insurance Programme (ESSALUD), a non-governmental organization, and officials of the Ministry of Labour and Social Promotion.

In addition to the measures taken in line with the Programme's main aim, a first follow-up and evaluation study was carried out in 1997 on the businesses set up under PRODAME. A survey was designed and conducted on a sample of 872 businesses in the metropolitan area of Lima in order to assess the degree of effectiveness, productivity, growth and job creation in these economic units, and also to obtain information that would help identify the needs of these units in terms of vocational training or technical assistance.

This study collected basic information to assess the state of micro-enterprises in this sector. The results showed that half the businesses had continued to conduct their activities since the day they were set up and that the main problems affecting the sector were primarily a lack of access to funding, excessive taxation, too limited a market and inadequate vocational training.

The productivity levels achieved by PRODAME staff testify to their commitment to the successful operation of the programme. The fact that the staff members, who are young experts, are directly responsible for their results helps to make the internal operations of the work team very dynamic, and thus contributes to the effectiveness and efficiency of the services provided.

In 1999, the aim was to set up 5,000 small and micro-enterprises countrywide. During the first quarter, PRODAME in particular managed to establish and obtain legal recognition for 1,109 such units at national level, with an efficiency rate[a] of 83.4 per cent of existing demand. A comparison of the results shows that, during the reference period, the increase was 22.5 per cent over the corresponding period of 1998, a phenomenon explained partly by the fact that during January 1998 no businesses were set up because of the amendment to the General Law on Companies. The results obtained were essentially due to the measures continuously taken by national promoters with regard to guidance and market communications. In addition, PRODAME's presence at various events – such as informal talks and seminars organized at the request of corporate associations of microbusinesses and various other institutions – also played an important role.

Furthermore, it was planned that the monitoring and assessment of the businesses set up through PRODAME in the metropolitan area of Lima would coincide with the beginning of validation of the sample so that the pilot scheme could then be surveyed. Similarly, a promotional campaign was to be organized by distributing posters and leaflets in the areas where the concentration of unregistered businesses is highest.

The implementation of the Specific Development Project (*Fronteras vivas* = Living Frontiers) in the border region with Ecuador in the northeastern sector of Condorcanqui was planned for the month of May. The Programme for the Promotion of Self-employment and Micro-enterprises was to be defined and implemented taking this new project into account, and two promoters were put in charge of promoting the Programme in coordination with the Bagua Regional Directorate of Labour and Social Promotion and the National Directorate of Employment and Vocational Training.

In the same way as people who are unemployed and wish to set up their own businesses, small and micro-enterprises in the informal sector benefit from this free and decentralized service. It not only enables them to set up businesses and considerably reduce the administrative procedures necessary and the attendant costs, but also to make a 50 per cent saving on notary fees thanks to the Agreement signed with the Chamber of Notaries of Lima and Callao. Consequently, the service provided offers considerable assistance, meaning that an ever-increasing number of businesses in the informal sector will move to the formal sector of the economy, without being obliged to do so.

The scheme in question was originally set up without any legal basis, but the results it has produced have surpassed all hopes, thanks to the services provided, which meet the needs of the labour market and the national economy.

---

[a] Efficiency rate = formal instruments established/formal instruments established + those still to be approved.

Social security/informal sector

The case of Senegal

This practice concerns a project in which the labour administration is extending social security programmes to the informal sector. At the explicit request of the Minister of Labour and Employment in 1996, that ministry worked in conjunction with the Senegal Old-Age Pension Insurance Institution and the Social Security Fund to set up, after consultation, the necessary elements for the social coverage of workers in the informal sector. Only the "Family Allowances and Protection against Industrial Accidents" section is currently operational and its implementation is being assessed. The "Old Age Pension Insurance" and "Sickness Insurance" sections are still undergoing a feasibility study.

The existence of the informal sector in a country essentially means that, depending on the circumstances, a large proportion of workers do not contribute to tax revenues and social insurance contributions, and consequently do not receive any social benefits in return. It is thus advisable to design a suitable voluntary scheme which enables as many workers as possible to be integrated into a system of social insurance contributions and benefits. In Senegal, the informal sector and the State are the two main providers of jobs and incomes. In 1991, the sector accounted for 58.7 per cent of the working urban population with, from 1986 to 1991, a growth rate that was 1.8 times as rapid as that of the modern sector. The importance gained by this sector was compounded by a major change in the characteristics of its population as a result of the various structural adjustment programmes, implemented in the country since the early 1980s.

The development of the informal sector was a response to the economic crisis and the macroeconomic adjustment context (adaptation to the low incomes of households). The shock felt by households which had lost or had suffered a drop in state income contributed to the "informalization" of the modern sector, since people sought new jobs in the informal sector and/or changed their consumption patterns, i.e., there was an increase in the demand by these households for less expensive goods and services from the informal sector.

Although the informal sector in Senegal is remarkably well organized and the social security system has the legal and financial means to cover it, both until recently completely ignored each other. Statistics revealed a situation which was worrying to say the least because, compared to the total population, only 14 per cent of the working population enjoyed social protection.

This situation was due to several factors including attitudes, feelings of mistrust towards any administrative system among the actors in the informal sector, and/or the inflexibility of the body of laws, which made it difficult to integrate this sector into the social security system. It must be added that instead of having a legally organized social security system, society had a system peculiar to itself, which was based on people's and family solidarity. But that system is now dying out, due mainly to the phenomenon of urbanization.

At the traditional May Day festivities 1996, the Senegalese Head of State made the following statement in his address to the trade union and employer organizations:

> Another challenge which we must take up is that of extending social protection to what is known as the informal sector. The contacts which have already been established are very encouraging, and I call on the Minister of Labour and Employment (MTE) and on the Senegal Old-Age Pension Insurance Institution (IPRES) and the Social Insurance Fund (CSS) to take all of the necessary initiatives to meet the challenge of integration in this field.

> Of course, the objective is not to impose the rules governing the structured sector on this sector but to apply rules which take account of its specific nature and of the aspirations of those who operate in it.

This statement was the response to a long quest by the craftspeople's organizations, which were aware of their members' social insecurity and of the urgency required to put the situation right. It was a realization which came about primarily through those who had left the structured sector for the informal sector as the result of staff cutbacks and closures of enterprises, mainly in the wake of structural adjustment programmes.

Concerted measures

On 8 May 1996, the Social Security Fund set up a working group to prepare a one-day conference on this issue, in which the deliberations were to focus mainly on:

— the target group;
— the reference wage;
— the benefits to be provided;
— the contribution rates and dates of payment; and
— the methods of benefit payment.

The one-day conference on the extension of social protection to the informal sector was held as scheduled on 22 May 1996 under the auspices of the Ministry of Labour and Employment, the Labour Administration Support Project, the ILO Regional Office for Africa and the Friedrich Ebert Foundation, in the presence of the Austrian Ambassador.

It was attended by 146 participants from the crafts sector. The Ministry of Labour and Employment, the IPRES and the Social Security Fund provided technical assistance, each conducting a workshop.

(a) The Social Security Fund (CSS), which is a joint body made up of worker and employer representatives (the State participates as an employer), conducted the workshop on voluntary insurance against industrial accidents and occupational diseases. The discussion led to an agreement on freedom of choice for workers to join a social security branch run by the CSS and on certain technical aspects such as adding a certified photocopy of the person's ID card to the membership documents.

(b) The Senegal Old-Age Pension Insurance Institution (IPRES), which is also a joint body, broached the topic of old-age pension insurance. The resolutions adopted concerned:

— the definition of the persons affected, i.e., any individual whose activity is registered in a Chamber of Trade directory;

— the methods for calculating and collecting contributions; contributions were to be calculated for each individual trade and possibly also for each income bracket; and

— the age at which the payment of retirement pension begins (this age is set at 60).

(c) The Ministry of Labour and Employment chaired the workshop on sickness insurance.

It should be noted that this ministry has an "Advisory Council on Occupational Risks", in which the social partners take part. The recommendations adopted by the workshop participants concerned mainly:

— the establishment of a sickness insurance scheme;

— the introduction of a test phase for the creation of a sickness insurance institution (IPM);

— the introduction of a ticket-based contribution system taking into account the fluctuation in incomes;

— coverage by the scheme of workers and their families as well as their apprentices;

— the establishment of an information and awareness-raising system to encourage craftspeople to join the scheme;

— public authority support for the creation, implementation and operation of an IPM for craftspeople; and

— uniformity of contributions for the three schemes.

And finally, the one-day conference led to the official signing of a Draft Agreement between the craftspeople's organizations and the CSS on the freedom of choice of affiliation and the documents necessary for membership.

The role of the main actors

Craftspeople

Craftspeople are organized at three levels:

— grassroots groups;

— regional groups; and

— national groups.

A recent census shows that there are some 78,000 crafts enterprises employing around 400,000 persons, the permanent labour force being estimated at 158,000.

The institutions

The Ministry of Labour and Employment is the body which supervises the IPRES and the CSS, which are run by managing boards "comprising representatives of all the participating members concerned, at least half of each board being made up of representatives of the participating members appointed in accordance with the statutes of the institution".[a]

— The IPRES and the Ministry of Labour and Employment have not yet launched their programmes under the project. The IPRES will be conducting a feasibility study after obtaining the necessary information from the craftspeople's organizations. The Ministry, on the other hand, will be instigating a test phase to create a sickness insurance institution (IPM). The pension system, which seems to be of particular interest to the craftspeople, is encountering a technical problem in that it seems to be rather difficult to obtain a true picture of the crafts population's status. The age distribution of that population is not clearly known, and the feasibility study would help solve this problem. These two components of the project could be launched rapidly, taking advantage of the current mobilization of experts and technicians and of the work carried out by the CSS.

— The CSS has managed to launch its activities more rapidly. In concrete terms, it is Article 36 of the Social Security Code which stipulates that "voluntary contributors" shall receive the benefits of the industrial accidents and occupational diseases section, which allows the Social Security Fund to open up to the informal sector.

The main features of the special social protection scheme for workers in the informal sector are as follows:

1. The target group

— Self-employed workers, who are traditionally defined on the basis of the following factors:

  – personal exercising of the activity concerned; and
  – independence with regard to other persons;

are the main target group of the special scheme, as well as workers who operate in the fields of agriculture, fishery, stock-breeding, handicrafts, and wholesale and retail trade.

2. The benefits offered are:

— prenatal allowances;
— maternity allowances;
— family allowances;
— daily maternity leave allowances;

---

[a] Article 5 of Act 75-50 of 3 April 1975 respecting social insurance institutions (*Journal officiel de la République du Sénégal*, 28 April 1975, No. 4419, pp. 557-560).

— benefits in kind for mother and child in the mother-and-child protection centres;

— coverage of industrial accidents and occupational diseases;

— coverage of medical and surgical care, pharmaceutical and incidental expenses, hospital costs, and the supply, repair and renewal of prostheses and orthopaedic appliances; and

— the annuity paid to dependants of the victim in the event of a fatal accident.

3. The administrative procedures concern:

— membership: submission of an application for voluntary insurance accompanied by a national identity card;

— the option on the risks covered: the voluntary contributor is free to choose coverage for one or several risks covered by the CSS;

— the periodicity of payment: on a monthly basis with the obligation to pay within eight days of the date of payment; and

— the suspension and termination of entitlements which occur whenever the monthly contributions have not been paid after two successive dates of payment. Entitlement ceases definitively at the end of a six-month suspension period.

The partners

The National Union of Chambers of Trade and the Friedrich Ebert Foundation are involved in the project. All the chambers of trade thus participate in the awareness-raising action and in the various seminars which are organized jointly for workers in the informal sector. The Dakar Chamber of Trade has seconded an official exclusively for the management of the "social protection file" of its craftspeople.

The social partners are also involved through their participation in the decision-making bodies of the Ministry, the CSS and the IPRES.

Implementation

The CSS is thus the only institution which has actually launched its activities. To do so, it carried out a twofold action: promoting the scheme; and implementing the scheme.

Promotion

An information and awareness-raising campaign was first launched from 22 July 1996 to 30 September 1998, the objectives being to encourage actors in the informal sector to seek protection and to induce them to join the scheme. The expected outcome was a consolidation of the results already achieved and more craftspeople joining the scheme. The main targets were the densely populated areas which will subsequently be used as pilot cities

(Dakar, Touba). In these areas, the CSS focused primarily on the chambers of trade and groups operating on a national basis. The main promotional media were the national radio and television channels, leaflets and printed T-shirts.

The CSS is now planning to set up a popularization programme in collaboration with the Senegalese Radio and Television Corporation to integrate the institution's products. The CSS's Directorate for Decentralized Surveys and Services is to set up a committee (which will meet on a monthly basis) to pilot this project.

The project is set to be extended to other regions of the country in the near future, and a joint campaign in this regard was recently launched in several regions by the CSS and the Directorate for Handicrafts.

Organization

The project has been integrated into the activities of the CSS, which already had qualified staff available. Special training did not prove necessary, since it is a complementary activity concerning products of a similar nature.

The CSS plans to decentralize and set up agencies (kiosks) in craftspeople's villages in Soumbedioune, Colobane and Touba, through which it should be possible to overcome certain difficulties, since all the craftspeople will consequently have easier access and will thus understand the scheme better and contribute to it normally.

A computer application has been developed to manage this scheme; it is run by the various persons in charge of the six agencies and eight regional establishments that have been set up throughout the country.

The project activities are supported by the CSS with the assistance of the Friedrich Ebert Foundation. A common budget was drawn up for the 1998 financial year.

Impact

Approximately 1,000 craftspeople have been registered by the CSS to date in the Dakar region alone. The number is considered insufficient but this was not unexpected in view of the complexity of the issue. Numerous craftspeople (500 in the Tamba region) have apparently stated recently that they intend to join the scheme.

The craftspeople are interested in accident insurance and especially in family allowances. The first case where a craftsman benefited from family allowances was on 22 July 1998.

The project was to be evaluated at the end of 1998 in the context of a seminar attended by the supervisory authorities, all of the partners and occupational groups. The purpose was to ascertain the reaction of the target groups to the products offered and thereby evaluate the degree of satisfaction and make corrections or go further if necessary, that is to say, to offer the scheme to all groups throughout the country while maintaining its flexibility and voluntary basis.

Occupational safety and health

The case of Fiji

In Fiji, the activities of the labour administration in the field of Occupational Safety and Health (OSH) are based on the concept of "duty of care". The foremost objective is to establish a proactive OSH risk management culture with all potential risk creators in the labour market to ensure that those who create the risks in the workplace as well as those in their employ have the primary duty to take all necessary steps in order to avert those risks (rather than relying on government inspectors as stipulated in the former statutory and administrative arrangements).

The reformed Occupational Safety and Health Legislation simplifies and clarifies the administrative responsibilities of all social partners in OSH matters. The legislation is supplemented by regulations and codes of practice. Coordination is flexible and priorities are established on the basis of rigorous strategic planning. The distribution of responsibilities between the three partners (employers, workers and government), at both the policy and technical levels, is clearly defined and the Ministry of Labour and Industrial Relations is fully involved in the implementation of policies for change and improvement. Finally, all the partners at all levels are held to be responsible, thereby encouraging the autonomy of users.

In view of the consistently increasing number of workplace accidents up to 1989, the Ministry of Labour and Industrial Relations concluded that the former OSH labour administration system was neither effective nor efficient. The total national annual cost of workplace accidents and occupational diseases was estimated to be about 70 million Fijian dollars, or 2.7 per cent of the country's GDP. Further, the Ministry also realized that there were major shortcomings in Fiji's OSH legislation and administration systems, which contributed to the overall ineffectiveness of national OSH management activities. The three main shortcomings were: too many OSH laws, too many government departments involved in OSH administration, and legislation did not cover all workers, was out of date and poorly structured in its design, format and language. Further, it became apparent that there was an urgent need for public authorities and social partners to change their attitude to OSH and to attach as much importance to the health of workers as to the environment in which they work. This heightened awareness was the prime mover in the formulation in 1993 and the enactment in 1996 of Fiji's new Safety and health at Work Act.[a]

This awareness was instrumental in the initiative of the Minister for Labour and Industrial Relations to launch and encourage dialogue on the reform of OSH administration. This led the Ministry to facilitate thorough

---

[a] Act No. 4 of 28 June 1996 respecting health and safety at work (*Gazette*, Acts, pp. 19-62).

consultations with the social partners over a three-year period (1990-1992) to define the most urgent economic and social needs and to reform the current OSH administration. This resulted in the acceptance by the social partners and the Council of Ministers of the ILO's Pearse Report and its 23 recommendations in early 1993. The Report basically recommended the complete overhaul of both the OSH and Workers' Compensation legislation and its administration. From the outset, the Minister's personal commitment and political will was a determining factor. This, combined with the determination and patience of the Ministry's staff, led to the recognition by all the social partners of the need for change and facilitated the adoption of the Act by Parliament.

The process of change was based on the concept of "duty of care" in an overall philosophy designed to introduce a new culture in which employers and workers, rather than OSH inspectors, have the primary responsibility for OSH risk identification, evaluation and control in workplaces. In this context, OSH inspectors are no longer seen as "police officers", but agents for change who play a secondary facilitative role for the social partners as advisers, mediators, conciliators, educators and trainers. This strategy adopted by the Ministry of Labour and Industrial Relations strengthens the managerial know-how of OSH organizations to effectively minimize risks. It emphasizes the direct involvement of employers, workers and the Government (which is represented by the OSH Inspectorate of the Ministry) in determining the policy governing action related to OSH. Within this framework, OSH inspectors are obliged to achieve the following objectives:

— improving OSH management by encouraging and facilitating the development of OSH policies and programmes, and by supporting OSH management action plans in organizations;

— strengthening OSH self-regulation within an organization by establishing and training OSH committees and/or representatives, including the training of senior and line managers;

— prohibiting situations likely to endanger the health and safety of workers;

— penalizing violations of the legislation through penalty notices or prosecutions; and

— implementing other administrative provisions of the OSH legislation.

In order to achieve these objectives, inspectors have at their disposal a whole range of means enabling them to learn rapidly what they need to know about industrial accidents, occupational diseases and other occupational risks in various sectors. Inquiries are then conducted to identify more accurately the causes of occupational accidents and diseases so as to be able to avoid them in the future. The prerogative to penalize is based on in-depth study of each case.

The measures taken in the field of OSH are based on the balancing act between the elements of "grace" and "justice" entrenched in the provisions of the Act, supplemented by regulations and codes of practice. This is reflected in the OSH Service Enforcement Policy of initially demonstrating "grace" (providing advice, consultation, mediation, conciliation and training) in the implementation of the Act, before subsequently undertaking "justice-related" measures (such as the issuing of improvement notices, prohibition notices and warning, penalty notices, and as a last resort, prosecution). The Act clearly defines the objectives, responsibilities, functions and structures both within the Ministry and the enterprise.

Responsibility for OSH is entrusted to a Chief Health and Safety Inspector (administrative aspects are handled by the Permanent Secretary for Labour and Industrial Relations), who is also responsible for the entire Labour Inspectorate and for advising the Minister of Labour and Industrial Relations on national, regional and international policies on OSH and related subjects. A Deputy Chief Health and Safety Inspector, who fulfils the functions of Director of National OSH Service, assists the Chief Health and Safety Inspector in his or her everyday duties and manages the National OSH Service. Under the Act, both the Chief and the Deputy Chief Health and Safety Inspectors have the same powers. The National OSH Service has two divisions, one being responsible for OSH Policy and Administration, and the other for OSH Field Operations. Each Division is led by a Principal Labour Officer who supervises his or her respective three Strategic Business Units (SBUs). In total, the Service comprises six SBUs and each unit falls under the responsibility of a Senior Labour Officer who manages it.

The three SBUs which cover OSH Policy and Administration are mainly responsible for the administration of the OSH Education and Accident Prevention Fund, the National OSH Board, the delivery and supervision of OSH training courses for managers and workers, the consultation on the development of regulations and code of practice with the social partners, the management of the national chemical/hazardous substance control scheme, the delivery of occupational hygiene services, OSH management audit, chemical audit, risk management consultancy, engineering design vetting, non-destructive testing (NDT) services, OSH Research and Development, including the management of the OSH information/statistical service. The three SBUs covering OSH Field Operations are responsible for the effective application of the law and practices in all private and public sector enterprises. The main role of inspectors in these Units is to facilitate the setting-up of self-regulating OSH management systems within respective organizations as required under the Act. This approach is implemented through a well-defined six-point OSH Management Action Plan that includes workplace registrations, formulation of OSH policies, establishing OSH representatives and/or committees, training of managers/OSH representatives and committees/workers, establishing OSH risk identification/evaluation/control system and review/evaluation of the OSH management system. Moreover, they also undertake technical inspections of selected plants and machinery, investigations of workplace accidents and occupational diseases, and solution seeking to OSH disputes.

The Occupational Safety and Health Service establishes relations in partnership with all the agencies of the public administration, and with universities and non-governmental organizations whose activities are related, closely or not, with occupational safety and health matters, for example, the complementary link with the Department of Environment for the national management of hazardous substances/chemicals; with the National Health Promotion Council in implementing health promotion programmes in workplaces; with the Fiji National Training Council in improving productivity through better OSH risk management practices; with the Marine Department and Civil Aviation Authority for the improvement of OSH in locally registered or government-owned ships and aircraft; with the Transport Department in improving OSH for cranes and forklifts, and road transport; and with the Forestry Department in improving OSH practices in logging, wood transport and use of electric saws.

The National OSH Advisory Board was established in February 1997 as a national coordination mechanism. It is a tripartite body responsible for advising the Minister on OSH matters; inquiring into and reporting to the Minister on matters entrusted to it by the Minister; liaising with the OSH Inspectorate to facilitate the development of OSH regulations and approval of OSH codes of practice for the Minister's consideration; and such other functions imposed on it by the Act. This Board, which reflects the economic diversity of the country, is composed of the Permanent Secretary for Labour and Industrial Relations or his or her deputy, who acts as Chairperson of the Board, two deputy chairpersons one each nominated by employers and workers, and 15 members appointed by the Minister for Labour and Industrial Relations. The appointed members are composed of five members representing employers' organizations, five representing workers' organizations and five appointed by the Government from other government agencies, such as Health, Mining, Agriculture, Transport and Civil Aviation, Environment, etc. The members of the Board are appointed for a period of two years and their mandate is renewable.

The underlying concern in the action taken to improve OSH service quality to both internal and external customers is to ultimately reduce the incidents of industrial fatalities and injuries, while promoting progressive OSH management practices to improve industrial relations and productivity. This is achieved through a rigorous strategic planning process at each structural level of the OSH Service. Each year, the Ministry of Labour and Industrial Relations prepares a Corporate and Management Plan in consultation with all Ministry staff, with a strategic vision to promote excellence in the labour market. This Corporate vision is defined and reflected in the Management Plans of the various Services of the Ministry, which are approved and signed by the Permanent Secretary and respective Service managers. The requirement for the various Services to achieve concrete results is based on the values of professional competency and expertise, participatory management culture, the provision of appropriate resources to users, strategic human resources development, emphasis on continuous improvement, customer focus, attention to ethics and public interest, as well as respect for the individual and accountability.

The Director of the National OSH Service also prepares, in consultation with his or her collaborators, a National OSH Service Management Plan in which priorities and indicators of achievement are set out in detail for both revenue and non revenue services. Once this Management Plan is finalized, each of the six SBUs prepares, in consultation with its collaborators, a Business Plan which sets out in detail its weekly, monthly and annual work plans together with respective performance indicators for progress management by respective SBU managers. Once these SBU Business Plans are finalized, each officer within the unit prepares, in consultation with each other, their individual officer's Business Plan which sets out in detail the officer's weekly, monthly and annual work plans with respective performance indicators. The SBU and individual officer's Business Plans are then approved by the Director in consultation with respective managers and become the basis for the evaluation of the results achieved.

The Director of the National OSH Service also formulates a three-year programme with the objective of ensuring the effective implementation by the OSH Service of the relevant legislation and other standards relating to OSH and the promotion of the highest standard of safety and health in all workplaces. In particular, the following objectives must be achieved during the implementation of the three-year programme:

— increased awareness of OSH issues by employers, workers, students and the general public through OSH promotion and training programmes;

— improved overall standards of OSH within the private and public sectors;

— more effective control of OSH risks through the promotion of better OSH management practices in workplaces;

— improvement in the overall management of the newly commissioned National OSH Service;

— a reduction of between 5 and 10 per cent in industrial accidents nationally;

— the appointment and operation of OSH representatives and/or committees in 50 per cent of workplaces nationally;

— the establishment of a system to collect OSH data (fatalities and injuries) through which areas requiring greater attention can be identified;

— the improvement of the quality of services provided to clients through better training of OSH inspectors;

— the establishment and operation of an effective National Chemical Management System for assessing and controlling chemical and toxic products;

— the establishment, on a user-pay basis, of consultancy services on occupational hygiene, OSH management, risk management, and ISO 9000/14000 quality management;

— improvements in employer/worker relations on OSH and other work-related matters;

— increased productivity and improved product quality resulting from improvements in OSH; and

— effective implementation of all OSH legal and administrative reforms.

The procedures are adequate and flexible. They allow OSH inspectors to take any initiative or introduce any innovation to resolve OSH problems wherever they arise. However, the role of the inspectors is a facilitative secondary one to support the primary role played by OSH representatives and/or OSH committees in the workplace. Specifically, the Act calls for the appointment of persons responsible for OSH in enterprises and establishes the composition of OSH committees including the election of OSH representatives, as well as their roles and functions.

The following are a few examples of provisions applicable to this field:

— in workplaces where less than 20 workers are employed, a majority of workers at the workplace may appoint an OSH representative for that workplace;

— in workplaces where 20 or more workers are employed, it is compulsory for the employer to establish an OSH committee for that workplace with at least half the committee to be appointed by the workers;

— workers' representatives and the members of the committees must have sufficient experience with essential accredited OSH training provided for them by the employers to fulfil their functions. This obligation makes it possible to guarantee the optimal functioning of these bodies, which are not obliged to refer systematically to higher management levels to take the necessary decisions for the improvement of working conditions in the field of safety and health;

— enterprise managers are required to give OSH representatives and members of OSH committees time off so that they can fulfil their functions and attend approved training programmes without any reduction in their wages;

— safeguards are envisaged to prevent any abuse of their powers by members of OSH committees or OSH representatives in the exercise of their respective responsibilities; and

— guarantees are envisaged to prevent any act of discrimination against workers acting in their capacity as OSH representatives or members of OSH committees.

Action in the field of OSH is based on the several tools developed by the Service. OSH codes of practice, which are approved by the tripartite National OSH Board and gazetted by the Minister, are formulated by employers, workers and OSH inspectors. These codes of practice do not have legal substance and cannot in any event replace the Act. They are designed to guide the OSH inspectors, employers and workers in applying the Act and regulations. An OSH management audit guide developed by the Service for employers and workers, known as SMART (Safety Management Assessment and Review Tool), assists managers and workers in auditing their workplace OSH management system in order to identify more effectively the safety and health problems (management and operational) at the workplace which require immediate and long-term action. This emphasis on OSH management is essential since at least 80 per cent of the total causes of poor OSH performance or productivity or quality results from a poor OSH management system. The remaining 20 per cent is normally attributable to workers' personal factors which can be also reduced through effective OSH training. Furthermore, an explanatory guide has been prepared for small businesses to improve their understanding and hence the observance of the provisions of the Act. Similar advisory guides are currently being developed to specifically target employers (managers), workers, OSH representatives/committees, importers, suppliers, installers, schools and the self-employed. For effective OSH promotion and training, the Service has designed a series of targeted OSH training packages in accordance with the provisions of the Act used to train senior managers, line managers, workers and OSH representatives and committees. To improve the overall administration efficiency for OSH inspectors, the Service is currently developing a number of OSH management manuals with respect to inspectors' field services functions, investigations/prosecutions procedures, standards development, engineering inspections, financial procedures, consultancy services, enforcement policy, quality policy and OSH Service code of ethics.

To inform the public on the progress achieved in the field of OSH, the Service uses the traditional channels of communication such as the radio, daily newspapers, television and the Government information bulletins. For the targeted social partners' market both nationally and internationally, the Service established a quarterly OSH newsletter called the "Lali", launched in 1998. Furthermore, to improve its image and raise awareness of its activities, the OSH Service has developed and used its own slogan and logo.

The paradigm shift and pragmatic approach of the reformed OSH Legislation required change in OSH management culture, both within the Ministry and at the workplace. In the Ministry, this necessitated the initiation in 1997 of the development and transformation of the Service from the former Factories Inspectorate organization structure to the new National OSH Service organization structure and management system commissioned in 1998, as explained earlier. In order to introduce a participatory management culture within the Service compatible with the functions of the new Health and Safety Inspectors under the Act, the Ministry embarked on an aggressive and strategic human resources development (HRD) programme for both serving and newly recruited inspectors. Under Section 41 of the Act, the Health and Safety Inspector is required to be a "suitably qualified person," as defined under Section 5(1) as "a person deemed by the Public Service Commission to satisfy the requirements for relevant occupational safety and health training, education and experience". In view of this requirement, the Service embarked on an intensive HRD programme for its staff in 1990 in the form of formal tertiary education (at the certificate, diploma, degree and masters level), skills training, and through workshops, seminars and conferences on

OSH management, while developing the inspectors' experience under the OSH legislation in addition to the early OSH experience in their former workplaces or under the former Factories Inspectorate. In addition to the required qualifications, the Act also specifically covers job descriptions, duties and obligations and the manner of appointing inspectors who are responsible for protecting and promoting occupational safety and health. Strategic staff management is used as a change agent in the transformation of both the organization structure and the management culture of the new National OSH Service to implement the new Act. To facilitate this change, the Director of the National OSH Service demonstrated strong visionary leadership and commitment to participative management practices in order to improve the quality of service delivery. Consistent with this management culture is the empowerment of SBU managers using clearly structured SBU Business Plans. This systems approach through the SBUs is designed to facilitate the shift in the corporate culture of the OSH Service from its bureaucratic form to a market and customer-oriented management culture, thus preparing the way for the corporatization of the OSH Service in the near future. Enhancing this shift, the OSH Service started to align its management processes in 1998 to ISO 9000 quality standards. With regard to HRD, the continuous training of the inspectors is regarded as essential in order for them to keep their knowledge and practice up to date, particularly with regard to newly introduced OSH risks associated with imported or locally manufactured plant and substances, and toxic products. The inspectors enjoy very broad autonomy in accordance with their Business Plans which they have helped to formulate. Their work is evaluated and the results recorded on the basis of the objectives set out in the Management Plan and Business Plan for the unit. Managers responsible for the unit are also evaluated on the basis of the Management Plan.

National action in the field of OSH is financed by the annual OSH budget as approved by Parliament. For example, in 1998 Parliament approved a total budget of 1.184 million Fijian dollars, made up of 519,000 dollars as capital budget and 665,000 dollars as operating budget. The capital budget covers motor vehicles, computers, fax machines, photocopiers, office equipment and occupational hygiene equipment. The operating budget covers staff salaries, travel and communications, maintenance and operations, purchase of goods and services for effective OSH administration. However, the Act also sets up an Occupational Health and Safety Education and Accident Prevention Fund under the Government's Consolidated Trust Fund for the sole purposes of safety and health education, training, research and promotion at workplaces. Being a Trust Fund, it is directly managed by the Minister on the advice and under the supervision of the National OSH Advisory Board. This Fund is financed by:

— subsidies from Parliament;

— annual taxes for the registration of enterprises with 20 or more workers;

— payments for the services provided by the National OSH Service in terms of OSH training, statutory engineering inspections of plant and machinery, non-destructive testing (NDT), OSH risk management consultancies, occupational hygiene services, OSH management audit and OSH-related consultancy services;

— the sale of OSH publications developed by the OSH Service; and

— the use of the Ministry's training centre by the National OSH Service to train clients.

However, this Fund has to date not been established due to the current ruling by the Ministry of Finance to use all the revenue injected into the Fund in 1998 and 1999 in order to help the Government pay its debt. The total Fund revenue collected in 1998 amounted to 406,722 Fijian dollars, with the 1999 figure expected to reach at least 600,000 Fijian dollars. It is envisaged that the Government will finally establish the Fund as originally intended under the Act in order to improve the effectiveness of OSH administration nationally and at workplace level.

The results achieved by the National OSH Service are analysed and evaluated on the basis of several elements. First, the legislation authorizes the collection of data and any other information on OSH issues for statistical purposes. This is complemented by a separate set of statistical data on work-related accidents and fatalities reported to the Ministry on a regular basis. The compilation and analysis of OSH and workers' compensation data are an important element in determining the prevention strategies at the enterprise level and for all industries at the national level. For the adoption of preventive measures, it is important for the Director to have statistics on accident rates and the use of dangerous products and toxic substances. The compilation of statistics at the national level makes it possible to reorient prevention strategies at the workplace, in industries and, generally, at the national level. Second, monthly reports describing the results obtained and identifying sectors in which difficulties have been encountered are submitted to the Director by the managers responsible for the six SBUs. An analysis of these reports helps identify the measures that need to be taken to remedy these difficulties and ensure the quality of follow-up action. Finally, the impact on target groups of the measures taken is evaluated in relation to the objectives set out in the Management Plan. The primary performance indicator of an effective OSH legislation and administration is an increasing or a declining national rate of industrial accidents or occupational diseases, as intended in the OSH Reform currently undertaken by Fiji.

To conclude, the following are the vital success elements identified in Fiji's OSH Reform since its inception in 1989:

— strong conviction, commitment and initiative to undertake the OSH Reform agenda from the Factories Inspectorate and senior managers of the Ministry in 1989-90;

— strong commitment and initiative for the OSH Reform by the Minister for Labour and Industrial Relations, thus ensuring the essential political will of the Government of the day;

— timely response from the ILO at the request of the Government to provide consultancy in reviewing Fiji's OSH and workers' compensation legislation and administration systems;

— efficient and effective secretariat service provided by the Factories Inspectorate to promote and facilitate the OSH Reform agenda with the social partners along clearly defined OSH management reform and workers' compensation reform guidelines recommended by the consultants;

— endorsement of the vision and principle of the OSH Reform by the social partners which resulted in the Government's political will to undertake the reform;

— endorsement at the local level and ease in the implementation of the OSH legislation due to the first Health and Safety at Work Bill (1991) being undertaken at the local level and refined by Fiji's social partners after thorough consultations;

— to take advantage of the expertise of developed countries, Fiji's first Bill was developed with the kind assistance of Worksafe Australia and Workcover Authority in New South Wales, who had access to all national OSH information and data in Fiji to refine the legislative provisions for Fiji before the final amendments of the Bill by the social partners;

— complementing the adoption of the 1991 Act, a clear strategy was developed and applied based on a well-defined schedule to ensure the effective implementation of the OSH Reform after the Bill was enacted by Parliament. For example, in 1991 a strategic HRD plan for the Factories Inspectorate and the rest of the Ministry staff was set to be implemented throughout the following five to ten years to facilitate both the OSH and Workers' Compensation reforms. The first training course for all Ministry staff on the Bill and the OSH Reform was delivered in 1991 by Workcover Authority (NSW) trainers. Other donor and training organizations involved in the intensive HRD programme for Factories Inspectorate and Ministry staff included Worksafe Australia, AusAid, Ballarat University, Sydney University, Newcastle University, Safework Queensland, Brual and Kjaer, KKS Instruments, Japan International Cooperation Agency (JICA) and Queensland University of Technology;

— the early start of OSH promotion and training by the OSH Service for the private and public sector senior managers. This programme began in 1994 as the Bill was in its first reading in Parliament. Between 1994 and 1996 the Inspectorate launched an intensive OSH training programme based on the underlying philosophy of the Bill rather than on its contents which were finalized in its Act form later. The voluntary creation of OSH committees by proactive employers at this stage was also a significant contribution to the minimization of OSH risks in these organizations. During these early OSH promotion and training activities, copies of the Bill were circulated to participants to familiarize themselves with and master the paradigm shift and management culture required by the reformed legislation. After the Bill was passed in 1996, a second series of

OSH training was implemented by the Service focusing both on the philosophy and contents of the new Act so that managers and workers can apply it. The basic strategy in both series of training is to target first CEOs and managers before workers, including OSH representatives and committee members. The OSH management training also includes workshops on developing OSH policies and programmes, more particularly the implementation of OSH management systems within an organization.

— the timely commitment by the Government to supply adequate financial, staff and material resources in order to kick-start the new OSH administration through the commissioning of the new National OSH Service in 1998, after the intensive proactive HRD training of staff since 1991;

— the strong participatory and consultative leadership style of the Director and the accompanying corporate culture which facilitates the ongoing transformation of the National OSH Service from a bureaucratic to a customer-based organization;

— the rigorous strategic planning process at each structural level of the Ministry and the National OSH Service since 1996, after the Bill was enacted by Parliament, ensures better productivity through effective use of meagre resources by the Service;

— the provision of a one-year grace period in the enforcement of the new Act after it was passed by Parliament in order to give social partners adequate time to adjust to the new duties imposed upon them by the new Act. The OSH Service helps the social partners adjust to the new provisions, by providing OSH promotion and training activities, including advisory services;

— the proactive enforcement policy of the National OSH Service in first entertaining the "grace" element in its approach (i.e., advise, promote, train, consult, coach, mediate, conciliate) before using its "justice" element (i.e., improvement notices, prohibition notices, penalty notices, or prosecution as a last resort) creates a conducive and enabling environment for the much needed OSH management, attitude and culture change at the workplace, industry and national levels;

— strong commitment by the social partners in implementing their respective responsibilities under the Act, both at the enterprise and national levels, to ensure a safe and healthy workplace for everyone; and

— last but not least, all the social partners finally share the same belief that human beings are the most important resources in Fiji's social and economic development.

From statistical records, it was pleasing to note that there was a consistent and significant decline in Fiji's workplace accident rates between the years 1996, 1997, 1998 and the first quarter of 1999, after the high rates prior to 1996. This can only confirm the continuing improvement in the injuries/accident rate for Fiji's workforce since the new Act came into force. This is a clear testimony to the collective effectiveness of the key success elements in Fiji's

OSH Reform, as summarized in this case study. The drastic decline in the accident rates for the years after 1996 is significant because the Ministry was expecting an increase in accident reports as a result of the aggressive OSH promotion and training under the new Act. In conclusion, the significant reduction in industrial accidents recorded to date bears witness to the effective and efficient application of the measures which have been adopted by the Service in Fiji in the field of Occupational Health and Safety.

Development and implementation strategies for the national occupational safety and health policy

The case of Japan[a]

The Total Health Promotion Plan

In the face of an ageing population and in the light of statistical data showing that the rate of industrial accidents was still high in the 50-59 age group, as well as of a growing trend of overall health problems in the working population, the labour administration of Japan developed and implemented a new health policy for workers based on the promotion of a "total health" approach. This policy, called the Total Health Promotion plan (THP), aims at making workers recognize personal responsibility for their long-term health status and maintain a healthy physical and mental condition.

Accordingly, the policy required that total health promotion programmes be established at each workplace in order to introduce "health education" and "guided physical exercise" into the everyday life of workers so that these principles will become commonplace.

The administrative structure directly responsible for THP implementation is the Industrial Safety and Health Division of the Ministry of Labour. The implementation strategy of the THP relies on the Japan Industrial Safety and Health Association (JISHA) and its network of industrial experts and professionals on the one hand, and the direct involvement of all workplaces with the support of a national network of 343 Local Labour Standard Inspection Offices (LSIO), on the other. These two entities work under the overall supervision of the Ministry of Labour.

In 1979, the Ministry of Labour developed and implemented an occupational health policy called the Silver Health Plan (SHP) for middle-aged and older workers with the purpose of reducing the number of accidents. At that time, the total number of industrial accidents was over 1.1 million. Although the overall number had been decreasing over the last two decades, statistics showed that over 600,000 workers were still victims of work-related accidents each year. Among these accidents, the number of fatalities and injuries[b] exceeded 160,000, of which 2,000 were deaths.

An analysis of the statistics on industrial accidents rate by age group showed that although the 50-59 age group represented only 30 per cent of the total workforce, it had the highest number of accidents – twice as many as the 30-39 age group – and represented almost 50 per cent of all work-related deaths and injuries. Given the demographic structure of the population, the labour administration estimated that workers of this age group had a high risk of being victims of industrial accidents. Thus, the priority of the occupational safety and health administration was the implementation of practices such as the SHP.

Other factors considered as contributing to these statistical results were population ageing, lack of exercise, nutrition, and the increase in stress at the

---

[a] This case study has been drafted on the basis of a study prepared by Jun Kumamoto.

[b] Defined as requiring more than four days' leave.

workplace. Statistics showed that numerous workers fell ill because of the unstable pace of life and, on the basis of disease reporting rates, there was a growing trend in diseases such as diabetes and high blood pressure, detected during periodic health checks. The reporting rates increased from 23.6 per cent in 1990 to 38 per cent in 1996.

In view of these data, the labour administration decided to amend the Industrial Safety and Health Act (ISHA)[a] in October 1988 in order to develop policy measures aimed at improving the overall health of workers. The Silver Health Plan was revised and replaced by a new plan called the Total Health Promotion plan (THP). While the SHP focused primarily on maintaining and improving the health conditions for older workers, the THP promotes "total health" for all workers.

The THP is based on an approach according to which workers must recognize the importance of self-responsibility for their long-term health status and thus maintain a healthy physical and mental condition. Therefore, workers should establish a healthy lifestyle based on the active and dynamic principle of "self-care", interpreted as managing one's body. Total Health Promotion programmes should emphasize the principle of "self-care" in workers' everyday life. Hence these programmes should introduce "health education" and "guided physical exercise" into workers' everyday life so that these principles become commonplace, and a detailed health promotion programme for workers must be defined for each workplace.

According to the ISHA, the implementation of this new approach must take into consideration the following elements:

(a) development of the system needed for the structure to implement "health checks";

(b) training and education of industrial doctors;

(c) training and education of the leaders (corporate, administrative, and social) responsible for the promotion of total health; and

(d) preparation and establishment of the infrastructures or equipment needed for the promotion of total health.

THP implementation is governed by the guidelines stipulated in the ISHA (Article 70.2, relating to the maintenance and promotion of occupational health at the workplace).

The THP is administered by the Ministry of Labour which is responsible for the formulation and planning of the policies and procedures necessary to the promotion of occupational safety and health. The administrative structure responsible for THP implementation is the *Industrial Health Division* which is under the authority of the Industrial Safety and Health Department of the Labour Standards Bureau of the Ministry of Labour.

---

[a] Act No. 57 of 8 June 1972 respecting industrial safety and health. An updated version of the Act (11 November 1994) was published in *Labour Laws of Japan*, 7th edition, Ministry of Labour, Institute of Labour Administration, Tokyo, 1995, pp. 161-224.

This Division is responsible for drafting various policy measures and promotion programmes of the THP, as well as achieving the overall objectives set out in the guidelines established and enforced by the Ministry of Labour. This central body, which plays a leading role, devolved the management of THP promotion activities to two entities, to which it provides support and guidance. The first entity participating in the strategy for THP implementation is the Japan Industrial Safety and Health Association (JISHA) created pursuant to a 1964 Act.[a] Within JISHA, the division directly responsible for THP implementation is the Industrial Health Promotion Department. The second participating entity is the workplace (companies, offices, factories, warehouses, construction sites, etc.). As the main actors in THP implementation, workplaces establish detailed practices that are adapted to their specific situations with guidance and regulation from the Ministry of Labour, and are applied to improve workers' health conditions.

The Industrial Health Division works in close cooperation with the decentralized network of Prefectural Labour Standards Offices (PLSO) and their subordinate local agencies called Labour Standards Inspection Offices (LSIO). The latter are the main local authorities that promote occupational safety and health. Forty-seven PLSOs are established in each prefecture and supervise the work of 343 LSIOs operating on projects related to labour administration and providing direct services to companies and administrations throughout the country.

The Division also relies on its network of 347 Regional Occupational Health Centres (ROHCs). These centres, which started operating in 1993, have been established pursuant to an amendment made to the Industrial Safety and Health Act adopted in October 1996, in order to promote and provide industrial health services to workers and employers in enterprises employing fewer than 50 workers (ISHA; Article 19, Clause 3). The ROHCs are run by the local medical associations based on contracts with the central government. Hence, a centre is located in each office of the medical association.

Finally, the Industrial Health Division of the Ministry of Labour has jurisdiction over the services of the Prefectural Occupational Health Promotion Centres (POHPCs), established in the prefectures in order to provide support to the ROHCs, to industrial health professionals, and to firms employing more than 50 workers. The POHPCs work under the authority of a public institution, the Labour Welfare Corporation,[b] and in close cooperation with the medical association in each prefecture. These POHPCs started operating in 1993 and by the end of March 1999, there were 29 such centres in the country. The Ministry of Labour aims to have them established in each prefecture.

---

[a] Act No. 118 of 29 June 1964 respecting industrial accident preventive organizations (*Labour Laws of Japan*, 1980, pp. 247-261). An updated version of the Act (1 October 1990) was published in *Industrial Safety and Health Law and Related Legislation of Japan*, Japan Industrial Safety and Health Association, Tokyo, 1991, pp. 1013-1030.

[b] The Labour Welfare Corporation is under the authority of the Workers' Compensation Administration Division of the Labour Standards Bureau, Ministry of Labour.

The Industrial Health Division of the Ministry of Labour

The Industrial Health Division is in charge of the work related to industrial health standards, the registration and supervision of the health and working environment assessment institutions, the procedures concerning the registration of health consultants, and the administration and supervision of the Institute of Industrial Medical Science. An Industrial Environment Improvement Office was established within this Division to manage the work related to the improvement and development of the working environment.

JISHA

Means to promote and implement THP in workplaces as well as research and survey plans are discussed on a regular basis at the Meeting for the Maintenance and Promotion of Workers' Health [a] organized by JISHA in accordance with the Guideline for the Maintenance and Promotion of Workers' Health at the Workplace mentioned in Article 7 of the Act. The Health Promotion Department of JISHA carries out plans for THP promotion which are developed on the basis of the results of discussions and after further consultation with the Industrial Health Division at the Ministry of Labour.

JISHA's roles in THP promotion are:

— back-up health promotion activities in workplaces;
— training and education of health promotion personnel;
— back-up and registration of health promotion personnel;
— authorization and registration of institutions which offer THP-related services to workplaces; and
— THP promotion and research.

The categories and roles of health promotion personnel are defined below according to the Guideline for the Maintenance and Promotion of Workers' Health at the Workplace mentioned in Article 7.

Industrial physicians – Carry out health checks on workers, and on the basis of the results obtained, make an instruction sheet for each individual. They give instructions to the personnel in charge of health maintenance and promotion, based on the instruction sheets.

Exercise trainers – Based on results of the health check, set up a specific exercise programme for each worker and assist the person in carrying out the programme. Also provide support and instructions in person, or train an exercise leader to put the programme into practice.

Exercise leaders – In accordance with the exercise programmes and instructions from the exercise trainers, help each worker to carry out his or her individual exercise programme.

---

[a] Group of experts and officials of relevant government agencies in charge of THP promotion and implementation.

Psychiatric counsellor – Based on results of the health check and in accordance with instructions from the industrial physician, take care of workers' mental health when necessary or when requested by a worker during a medical consultation.

Industrial nutritionists – Give advice on nutrition, based on results of the health check.

Industrial health leader – Give health guidance to each worker according to the results of their health check.

Details of health promotion activities are defined below according to the "Guideline for the Maintenance and Promotion of Workers' Health at the Workplace" mentioned in Article 7.

Health check

In order to carry out measures for the maintenance and promotion of workers' health, workers must have accurate knowledge and information about their own physical condition and continue to control their health condition by following the instructions of the personnel directed by industrial physicians.

A "health check" includes various inspections of the lifestyle and physical condition of each worker to collect pertinent data in order to provide, based on its results, guidance in areas such as physical exercise, mental health, nutrition, and hygiene. It has a different purpose from that of a conventional medical check-up which is mainly for early detection of diseases. The health check at the workplace should, in principle, be done under the leadership of industrial physicians. Based on its results, instruction sheets are made for each worker according to his or her own physical condition, giving guidance about physical exercise, hygiene, and so on.

Practice and contents of the health check

Health checks will be given regularly to every worker so as to provide health guidance on a continuous and systematic basis. The health check consists of a medical consultation, a survey on the worker's lifestyle, a medical examination, a medical observation and physical tests.

Instruction sheets

Industrial physicians evaluate the results of the health check and medical examination, and make out an instruction sheet to provide health guidance such as physical exercise, and instruct other personnel in charge of health maintenance and promotion.

Physical exercise guidance

Based on results of the health check and the instruction sheet provided by the industrial physician, the exercise trainer develops an exercise programme for each individual and gives guidance on how to practise the programme.

The exercise trainer and exercise leader shall help workers practise these pro-grammes. Thus, it is recommended that the personnel in charge encourage each worker to act positively and spontaneously.

Programming of physical exercises
When developing a physical exercise programme, it is important to take into account the individual's lifestyle, favourite leisure activities, wishes and other personal factors to make the type and content of the exercises safe, enjoyable and effective.

Assistance for carrying out physical exercise programmes
When carrying out a physical exercise programme, it is important to pro-vide appropriate exercises for each worker and make it a constant activity at the workplace, thus establishing a healthy everyday habit.

Mental health care
When, based on the results of the health check, it is judged that mental health care is needed by an individual or if the individual requests it during a medical consultation, a psychiatric counsellor should provide mental health care in accordance with the industrial physician's instruction. The "mental health care" mentioned in this guidance is for workers who actively seek a healthy life, and consists in assistance to detect potential stress or the use of relaxation methods.

Nutrition guidance
When the results of the health check reveal problems in a worker's diet, the industrial nutritionist not only gives guidance on nutrition but also evalu-ates the worker's eating habits and diet in order to help the person improve them.

Health guidance
In order to solve health problems deriving from working conditions or lifestyle, the industrial health leader should give guidance and training in the workplace, based on the results of the health check and the industrial physi-cian's instructions. The guidance relates to healthy living including sleeping habits, smoking and drinking, oral hygiene, and so on.

The health promotion personnel operating in workplaces or institutions that offer THP services are required to have technical knowledge related to health and a healthy lifestyle. JISHA gives training courses to specialized per-sonnel such as industrial physicians, in a variety of areas such as physical exercise, mental health, nutrition and hygiene. JISHA is recognized as a train-ing institute authorized by the Ministry of Health. It also takes charge of THP promotion by registering trainees who have taken these courses and by sup-porting their activities.

There are two types of institutions that provide THP services:

— those authorized to conduct health checks and offer every kind of health guidance; and

— those authorized to conduct health checks only.

These institutions provide direct support to foster occupational health by sending health promotion staff to workplaces.

JISHA, in cooperation with the Industrial Health Division of the Ministry of Labour, provides assistance and instructions to institutions that offer THP services.

The local level

The 343 Labour Standards Inspection Offices – working under the authority of the 47 Prefectural Labour Standards Offices (PLSOs) – operate projects related to labour administration and provide direct services to companies and administrations throughout the country. Where the promotion of safety and health is concerned, with the help of Corporate Associations these offices provide guidance and support aimed at preventing industrial accidents.

The Corporate Associations, which are organized within a particular industry and operating area, also work independently to motivate their members to improve the level of safety and health at the workplace. They hold regular meetings, publish periodicals and information bulletins containing mainly articles on amendment of laws and regulations, on economic prospects and changes occurring within their sector and those of their members. These publications also provide several sets of statistical data including the number of industrial accidents.

In the Tokyo Metropolitan Area, for example, there seems to be a unique THP promotion practice. The Tokyo Prefectural Labour Standards Office has selected several companies or factories to become the future "excellent safety and health workplaces" – called "model workplaces". They are required to make every effort with the support provided by the 18 Labour Standards Inspection Offices in the Tokyo area to achieve safety and health conditions in line with THP. The Tokyo PLSO then evaluates their implementation arrangements and annual results. If the examination shows the improvements and achievements to have reached a satisfactory level, they are publicized as "model examples". In addition to financial subsidies, these companies are granted some advantages in the insurance system for industrial accidents.

The purpose of this programme is to promote these good practices and the results of THP implementation. The Tokyo PLSO expects other enterprises to follow suit and adopt the methods used in these model workplaces so as to expand them to other prefectures or regions.

The Regional Occupational Health Centres (ROHCs)

The ROHCs work in close cooperation with the Prefectural Labour Standards Offices and exchange information on a regular basis with the local Labour Standards Inspection Offices. Their main task is to promote workers' occupational health in companies employing fewer than 50 workers through the provision of: (a) an industrial health counselling service, (b) an individual industrial health guidance service at the workplace, and (c) information on occupational health. These services, which are free of charge, are funded by the Government. The ROHCs distribute to companies registered with them the lists of experts and organizations working in the field of industrial health. These lists contain the names of industrial physicians, industrial health consultants, hospitals and other medical institutions which agree to take part in the implementation of industrial health promotion programmes, such as regular health checks. Most industrial physicians are accredited by the Japan Medical Association and are members of local doctors' associations.

The Prefectural Occupational Health Promotion Centres (POHPCs)

The POHPCs help the ROHCs to gather information and give them advice on the technical skills and know-how that the ROHCs need in order to carry out smoothly their industrial health promotion activities at the workplace.

Workplaces

The second entity to which THP implementation has been devolved is the workplace (companies, factories, warehouses, construction sites). Detailed practices for improving workers' health conditions are established for the specific situation of each workplace on the basis of rules and regulations issued by the Ministry of Labour. Procedures at the workplace include a health check, which is the precondition to THP implementation, health guidance related to physical exercise, nutrition, and psychological counselling. These services are provided by external experts assigned to each workplace.

Small enterprises lacking the resources to employ experts can use the institutions authorized by the Ministry of Labour to provide services in accordance with established standards. These institutions are registered with JISHA. Besides providing THP-related services, they also provide advice on the procedures and documents needed to apply for subsidies. Companies are required to submit an application every year.

THP promotion at the workplace is implemented in five different stages: (a) health check; (b) physical exercise guidance; (c) mental health care; (d) nutrition guidance, and (e) general health advice.

Small firms that face difficulties in operating health promotion programmes are granted financial support by the administration. The criteria required for eligibility to financial subsidies are the number of full-time workers (fewer than 300), existing application for work-related accident insurance, and implementation of at least three of the five stages of THP operations (i.e., health check, physical exercise guidance and health advice).

Workplaces with more than 50 workers have the obligation to (a) establish a "health committee" in which detailed practices for health promotion and maintenance should be discussed, and (b) elect and appoint an industrial doctor. This enforcement is regulated by the ISHA (Articles 13 and 5). Moreover, it is recommended that an "expert committee on health promotion and maintenance" consisting of experts such as industrial doctors, be established at each workplace. More elaborate health guidance can then be provided to each worker.

The Industrial Health Division of the Ministry of Labour is comprised of 18 civil servants, including two for THP operation and five for the Industrial Environment Improvement Office. Human resources for the PLSOs are determined by the Total Staff Number Law, which specifies the number of civil servants in each public administrative body. The Tokyo PLSO, which is the largest in the country, has 755 officials. This number includes all staff of the Office itself and that of the 18 LSIOs in the Tokyo Metropolitan area. The number of staff at each LSIO in Tokyo may range from eight to 66.

The JISHA, whose Board includes several members who are former government officials, has around 310 employees. The Industrial Health Promotion Department of JISHA, which is directly responsible for THP implementation, is composed of 20 employees, including those who have been transferred from the Ministry of Labour. In addition, there are several agents who have experience and have attended technical training programmes and obtained professional degrees and/or licences necessary for THP promotion. They cooperate with outside experts and independent consultants.

The Ministry of Labour and the JISHA have developed their home pages on the World Wide Web. The contents consist mainly of the organizational structure and a summary of the main policies and operational services, including THP promotion. The Ministry's home page provides information on THP policy and structure, while JISHA's home page gives more practical information and allows direct registration for seminars and training programmes.

The Labour Welfare Corporation has also set up a home page on the Web. It presents the tasks and functions of ROHCs and POHPCs. It also lists the address and phone number of each Centre for the convenience of THP leaders and workplace managers. In addition, several POHPCs have installed audio-visual equipment in their waiting-rooms for visitors to learn about industrial safety and health implementation programmes. The industrial physicians in charge of the health condition of a large number of workers at the assigned workplace use a computer database in order to manage the results of consultations and diagnoses. As mentioned above, the Industrial Health Division of the Ministry of Labour has conducted the THP policy-making and operations in partnership with various organizations, including workers' and employers' organizations. As the local branches of the central Labour Standards Bureau of the Ministry, the PLSOs and LSIOs have a cooperative relationship with the Division in order to promote THP locally and enhance understanding of its importance.

As well as these central-local government partnerships, the Division provides guidance to the Labour Welfare Corporation to administer the POHPCs and to the medical associations to establish the ROHCs in order to help promote industrial health.

The Division cooperates with JISHA to put its policies into practice. JISHA is thus in charge of the actual promotion and support of THP implementation at the workplace, cooperating with private and public experts working in THP. Finally, the workplace is the real enforcer or operator of THP practices. The relationship between the Division and the workplace is based on a principal-agent mandate rather than partnership.

THP implementation relies on financial resources that come entirely from the Ministry of Labour. The structure of financial resources for the industrial safety and health measures including those for THP, is generally divided into two types of accounts: the general account and the special account. In the general account, the 1997 budget for the industrial safety and health measures was 292.5 million yen. In the special account of industrial accident compensation insurance, the budget for industrial health promotion was 6.826 billion yen, the budget for guidance for industrial accident prevention was 6.721 billion yen, and the budget for the subsidy/grant for industrial safety and health activities was 6.767 billion yen. The total amount of financial resources devoted to THP implementation therefore comes from these various resources. In addition, the 1997 budget for the PLSOs in the general account was approximately 10.61 billion yen, and the budget for the LSIOs was about 18 billion yen.

The JISHA, on the other hand, has a total annual budget of some 16 billion yen. Out of this total, approximately 10 to 20 per cent is used by the Industrial Health Promotion Department which is responsible for THP implementation.

There seem to be few evaluation standards or measurements of THP implementation at the workplace provided by the central Government. It is generally acknowledged that the work of public administration, in partnership with these related organizations, should be limited to a role of support and guidance rather than of inspection or supervision of THP operation and management.

Therefore, the central Government's evaluation and appraisal of THP implementation is limited to conducting a survey by means of a self-evaluation form in the workplace and then publishing a case study of model enterprises. This evaluation is not directly conducted by the Government but by the THP-related organizations. A survey conducted by JISHA entitled "Survey on Workers' State of Health", seems to be the only tool measuring the effectiveness of THP implementation in the workplace. In addition to the survey, the JISHA indirectly evaluates THP programmes by evaluating experts and trainers who work to improve industrial health.

Government officials seem to recognize that effective THP implementation and the improvement of industrial health are the responsibility of the company or enterprise which runs the workplace and that the Total Health Promotion plan itself is merely a "tool" to help the implementation.

The evaluation of the implementation of these practices was conducted by the Labour Welfare Corporation. It is based on the number of consultations at the centres and/or the number of participants in seminars and conferences. However, the goal of the practices involving these centres is not a decrease in the number of industrial accidents and/or workers affected by a disease. It is more a matter of improving the effectiveness of support and guidance given to industrial health experts such as industrial doctors, health leaders, and managers of the workplaces. After receiving the evaluation report from the Corporation, the central Government seems to have recognized the necessity and importance of these practices, and thus continues to provide the funds needed to continue setting up other such centres throughout the country.

The role of these centres may become even more important in the future since a great number of small companies and workplaces are making serious efforts to improve productivity in an economy seriously affected by recession. The THP review has brought to light the need for cooperation between the labour administration, enterprises, and workers in order to promote occupational safety and health, as well as the advantages of such cooperation. The THP and SHP have been applied and practised for almost 20 years. They have been successful and are now effectively implemented at each workplace where various partners are coordinating their efforts and cooperating in order to obtain suitable methods and procedures for carrying out THP.

Occupational safety and health (the WISE Programme)

The case of the Philippines

> This practice refers to the implementation in 1994 by the Department of Labour and Employ-
> ment (DOLE) in the Philippines of a policy of support for small and medium-sized enterprises (Work
> Improvements in Small Enterprises (WISE)) directed specifically at increasing productivity through
> the improvement of working conditions.

Given the notable shift towards a market economy and the importance of
SMEs (90 per cent of all firms) for the country's economic well-being, the
Philippine Government has in recent years adopted a series of specific measures to improve their performance and propel them into the twenty-first century. Since traditional approaches, such as opening up financing opportunities
and new markets, or access to new technologies, have been more or less
excluded by the uncertain economic climate, and since working conditions in
the SMEs tend on the whole to be rather poor, the State, in association with
private organizations, has looked for new avenues of support for SMEs. The
Department of Labour and Employment, main promoter of both labour standards and employment in SMEs, decided to concentrate on the improvement
of working conditions and participation at enterprise level, in the expectation
that this would then translate into productivity gains.

The WISE Programme implemented by the Department of Labour and
Employment necessitated an overhaul of the procedures and operation of the
country's labour inspection system. The methods of intervention and the very
culture of the profession of labour inspector had to be radically changed in
order to make the transition from a service conceived as a straightforward
labour-monitoring organization to a global advisory and promotional process
integrating improved working conditions into a shared vision of enterprise
development.

This Programme was adopted by the Government after a series of studies
carried out at both local and international levels had established the direct
relationship between working conditions and improved productivity. It also
represents the culmination of a gradual evolution of the conception of labour
inspection which got underway at the beginning of the decade. This was preceded by a growing awareness of the need to refocus the traditional labour
inspection approach to the enterprise, in particular on the safety and health of
the workforce.

In this process, the Department of Labour and Employment drew on the
ILO's "Higher Productivity and a Better Place to Work" methodology. Similar early experiments had already been undertaken between 1976 and 1985,
and they gave rise to the development of a completely new mechanism of

intervention in small and medium-sized enterprises (i.e., those employing fewer than 100 wage-earners), known as the Technical Assistant Visit (TAV). During such visits a full review is undertaken, in the presence of the labour inspector, of all health and safety-related information and an action plan emerges taking into account the enterprise's productivity problems.

However, despite an impressive training apparatus aimed at the labour inspectors, TAVs developed in a highly fragmented fashion. After several years of application, the methodology has yet to produce the appropriate documents for reporting the state of working conditions and improvements implemented. Nevertheless, the process – which involves 40 per cent of the enterprises affected by labour inspections – has paved the way to a more comprehensive approach which, by combining the pursuit of higher productivity with a transformation in the working environment, brings about a broadening of the Labour Inspectorate's mission.

With financial support from the UNDP and technical assistance from the ILO, the WISE Programme was tested in four pilot regions from 1994. Subsequently, it was extended to all the Department's 15 regional offices on the basis of internal funding from the Department's own budget. The funds were released in the light of the ambitious goals of the WISE Programme, namely its explicit strategy of bringing about fundamental changes in labour inspection and in its environment. The broadening of the Programme was made possible by training a large number of trainers based within the organizations involved, who then took the information back and spread the message within their institutions. Moreover, other government institutions also became involved, namely the National Wages and Productivity Commission, the Conciliation and Mediation Bureau, the Rural Workers' Bureau, the Department of Trade and Industry and the University of the Philippines Institute for Small Scale Industries.

Objectives

The WISE Programme forms part of the Labour Department's wider policy, which is to pursue with perseverance and determination three clear objectives:

— to develop its institutional capacity to better respond to the expectations of the general public and, given the scope of the tasks to be accomplished, to do so in association with other partners;
— to achieve continuous improvement of the workplace environment at low marginal cost; and
— to establish a databank of improvements in working conditions.

The achievement of these objectives depends on the implementation of six guiding principles:

— build on local practices;
— capitalize on positive outcomes, even when these are based on highly localized achievements;

201

— relate improvements in working conditions to other management objectives;
— make use of learning by doing;
— encourage people to share their experiences; and
— promote active participation by the workforce.

These new objectives reflect new challenges to the responsibilities and functions of the State in the labour sphere, and constitute in particular a response to:

— heightened expectations of worker involvement in enterprises;
— heightened awareness of the need to take greater account of safety and health issues, especially with regard to small and medium-sized enterprises in the industrial sector, where risks are considerably higher than elsewhere.

But they also constitute a call for the State to combine its ability to regulate and "police" labour situations and relations with a capacity to *advise and promote* desirable or necessary changes, which means including raising awareness and training as fully-fledged parts of the function of a Labour Inspector.

A further question relates to the Department's ability to *evaluate* situations encountered within enterprises so as to document opportunities for improvement and the level of *advice and assistance* required by the actors concerned.

This evaluation approach is fully integrated into the WISE Programme framework, since it has set up an entire mechanism of indicators and monitoring procedures. Apart from helping to evaluate the performance of the Labour Inspectors themselves, these indicators must also show:

— the number of establishments visited for the purpose of providing advice and assistance;
— the number of safety and health committees that do not necessarily represent the enterprises in the WISE Programme but are created to monitor the adoption of WISE procedures in enterprises;
— the participation of workers and managers in the process; and
— the number of improvements brought about and of persons benefiting from those improvements.

The information has been included in the Department's Statistical and Performance Reporting System, which produces numerous quantitative and qualitative parameters concerning worker protection and safety, as well as the state of employment and industrial relations.

Thus, a process is launched which, through its explicit directions, visible dynamism and the internal coherence of the instruments put in use, seems to respond to strategic planning.

The role of leading actors

The WISE Programme was originally conceived by the Department of Labour and Employment for its own internal use. The test bed is the Working Conditions Bureau, charged with drawing up and applying all standards relating to working conditions, especially where safety and health at work is concerned. The Bureau's theoretical and practical action framework has subsequently been applied in the 15 regional offices under the supervision of the regional directors. In every regional district, a Standard-Implementation Division is responsible for technical monitoring of the labour inspectors' on-site work in the field as they carry out their basic mission among workers and employers.

Begun as an experiment with UNDP funding over three years and ILO technical support, the Programme was then taken over, enlarged and made permanent with an earmarked allocation in the Department of Labour's annual budget. This covers both the awareness-raising and training activities for the labour inspectors to prepare them for the WISE Programme, and also the inspectors' subsequent actions to promote an appropriate culture within enterprises.

Between 20 and 50 per cent of the Regional Bureaus' budget is earmarked for inspection. This therefore is the standard structure of a state institution, in which the central body *formulates* the framework, objectives and strategy, while an implementing office carries out the consequent actions, using for this purpose the instruments and methodology devised by the central bodies. Between the policy-making level and the implementing level, a regional office plays an important role by conveying national strategy, adapting it to local conditions, and sustaining and stimulating its practical application.

The generalization of the Programme to the country as a whole was achieved through a network of partners (Government, enterprises, teaching institutions, working groups). On account of the weakness of the regional partners – especially trade unions – participation was opened up to other groups such as Rotary Clubs, and Industrial Associations such as PHILEX-PORT (the Philippine Exporters Federation), principally to raise awareness among their members and to extend the provision of training.

If the WISE Programme confers on the labour inspector a quite specific role in relation to the legal provisions, forcing him or her to abandon a purely subordinate position, it also confers on all the social actors involved the need to adopt an approach combining responsibility and active participation.

This combination of efforts and the acceptance by all the members of the social network of responsibility for the factors over which they have influence, are key determinants of the expected process of transformation.

However, although such synergy can be observed at the national level, and even more in those enterprises where it has become an essential tool for the achievement of the desired outcomes, much still remains to be done at the regional level, especially in view of the lack in institutional capacity of trade unions and employers' organizations to take on their assigned role as full participants in the process.

203

Implementation

The policy-making level – the Working Conditions Bureau – draws up guidelines for the Labour Inspectorate, but the linkage between this level and the implementing offices is conceived not merely on a "top-down" model, but also as a dynamic exchange of ideas: once the central body has drawn up the guidelines, the regional office is encouraged to take charge of its own objectives and to submit them to the central body, which in turn takes on a supportive and coordinating role. At a later stage, feedback based on information gathered on-site by the implementing level leads to further adjustment of the objectives.

The various stages in the definition of objectives and of their adoption, and the allocation of responsibility among the various actors, are laid down in a clear theoretical scheme which seems to improve efficiency.

The programme is operated on a voluntary principle. Almost half of the country's 250 labour inspectors are involved in it already, but the report does not conceal the strong resistance which arises from a conflict in priorities which lend themselves to contrasting interpretations. For example, the emphasis on quantitative targets, and on monthly visits of a purely monitoring kind, can easily undermine the desire that labour inspectors extend their involvement in enterprises beyond merely checking for deficient observance of legal or regulatory rules and prescriptions.

Overall, it is the value added at different levels of intervention to the positive fallout in terms of efficient results and the participatory management that strengthen this special move specific to this mechanism.

Respect for the actors' autonomy also contributes to achieving these outcomes, as seen in the positioning of regional services in such a way as to correctly link the vision of the central guidelines with the local reality as grasped through a good knowledge of local conditions.

Some officials have even expressed the view that there is a tension between their monitoring tasks and the tasks relating to support and advice to enterprises, but this resistance has been effectively dealt with, not by an imposition from above of the new procedures, but rather by a combination of intensive training for those requesting it and spreading the news of good results from the programme. In this way, emphasis is placed on client satisfaction and also on the more rewarding role for the inspector as a facilitator in the emergence of new patterns of relationships.

Nevertheless, the task ahead is highly challenging, on account of the ratio of inspectors to the enterprises to be visited (250 for 450,000 firms) and the number of inspection points which need to be "checked out". The budget does not provide for the recruitment of additional inspectors. The trend in terms of workplace improvement initiatives is to prefer self-regulation and self-evaluation. Furthermore it is hoped that quality will take precedence over quantity through a slight reduction of the number of visits to be made by each labour inspector.

The basic qualities required in the recruitment of inspectors remain unchanged, though there has been a slight change of emphasis in the light of the new role required from inspectors:

— knowledge of examples of practical and familiar solutions;
— ability to intervene in support of actions undertaken;
— ability to bring workers and employers together in a common task;
— ability to plan monitoring and supporting actions;
— ability to give sound advice and to help people overcome obstacles;
— ability to encourage worker participation; and
— ability to combine the improvement of working conditions with improvements in productivity.

The special kind of training offered in the framework of the WISE Programme is designed to bring about this change of attitude even if there is the usual resistance to change observed in such programmes.

The computerized Database Management System (DBMS) is used to evaluate the direct effects of the WISE Programme and the Programme's own database is a source for information on methodology and for practical case studies for small and medium-sized enterprises interested in joining.

The home page of the Working Conditions Bureau Website which will eventually be linked to the ILO Website is still being developed. All information on the component elements of WISE will become accessible. Training materials and successful cases of application of the Programme to small and medium-sized enterprises will also be included.

All these measures allow enterprises to see that the Government takes this Programme extremely seriously.

Impact

Following the implementation of the Programme, two external impact studies have been conducted. The first, which centred on productivity, was carried out in 1996 on 14 participating enterprises, and found that after measures to improve working conditions had been introduced, production capacity rose by 23.1 per cent in quantity and two per cent in quality, while absenteeism declined by 4.73 per cent. The second evaluation, which centred on working conditions, also showed that the Programme produced conclusive results.

The contributions and impact of the WISE Programme are subject to regular monitoring and evaluation based on the collection and processing of a series of performance indicators. These indicators are included in a statistical feedback process which is part of the nationwide statistical system (SPRS) managed by the Bureau of Labour and Employment Statistics. The system has been devised to process a set of parameters which enable the Department to assess the state of working conditions and the degree of protection provided to workers in the framework of the labour relations system.

The Productivity Performance Assessment System (PPAS) and the DBMS allow the direct effects of the Programme to be monitored and evaluated. In addition to a qualitative evaluation through checklists, automated quantitative formulae have been devised for labour productivity, the productivity of materials used in production, of equipment and of energy use. An evaluation before and after the implementation of low-cost measures is undertaken with these indicators over a period of weeks or months and the results are compared with those of a qualitative evaluation. The results give indications as to the impact of an improvement or else point to areas where further improvement is desirable. The more successful the use of this data collection and processing system, the more its maintenance is encouraged and the more users it attracts. At present a new project is under way to correct certain shortcomings and improve the evaluation system.

With regard to the role of evaluation in improving the efficacy of the structure, it can be said that by including specific indicators from the WISE Programme in its nationwide statistical database, the Department has added a new dimension to the evaluation of the effectiveness of the Labour Inspectorate in all its spheres of activity. These indicators, which show the allocation of the labour inspectors' time and effort result in the outlines of a type of "social accounting" which enables the inspectors themselves, through the results of their support and advisory activities, not only to have their efforts recognized, but also to defend the efficacy and impact of their initiatives.

Moreover, it enables the regional directors to guide the Programme with an accurate perception of where the Programme is heading, through a clearer picture of the use of human resources in the light of targeted priorities. As for the Department, the evaluation system is not only a useful guidance system for the Labour Inspectorate, but more fundamentally, it enables them to assess the quality of the response provided by its component parts to small enterprises. As far as these enterprises are concerned, the evaluation system gives them, through continuous, voluntary processes of change, an opportunity to take into account both the requirements of labour law with respect to working conditions, and the benefits of improved overall productivity. Hence the emphasis placed on indicators such as improvements achieved at low marginal cost, or the number of employee beneficiaries. Furthermore, it proved advisable to pay close attention to the number of training exercises undertaken at the instigation of the labour inspectors so as to raise awareness of their usefulness and support the early stages of their development. Finally, there was a need to keep a record of follow-up visits and "support-cum-advice" interventions. Taken together, all these measures should contribute to the creation of conditions favourable to the birth of a new enterprise culture based on the voluntary acceptance of continuous change.

Still, there remains the danger that this vision of a labour inspection system for the future could be undermined by the sheer pressure of contradictory priorities. In the case of the Philippines, the focus on ensuring that the labour inspectors fulfil their visit quotas makes it difficult, if not unfeasible, to implement the time-consuming qualitative changes called for by "support-cum-advice" visits. As in many other countries, we are faced here with the issue of properly allocating available human resources so as to achieve targeted objectives. An appropriately managed evaluation should help the labour administration, as would be the case with any other social group, to examine adequately and coherently its ordering of the priorities which society as a whole expects it to accomplish.

In conclusion, the WISE Programme can be credited with the following achievements: creating an extensive network of actors including the social partners, led by DOLE; producing a larger than expected group of trainers (including labour inspectors) – 246 instead of 64 as originally planned; providing the Department of Labour with the means of monitoring and evaluating the project's effectiveness; training people responsible for developing teaching materials; producing educational materials for all the interested parties; putting 720 owners and managers of small enterprises through complete training courses, and 1,400 managing directors and 720 workers through awareness-raising courses, at the end of which respectively 70 per cent and 30 per cent of participants have implemented measures to improve working conditions; and providing support and advice to more than 5,000 enterprises during regular inspection visits.

LABOUR

OCCUPATIONAL SAFETY AND HEALTH

Self-regulation by firms of occupational safety and health

The case of Norway

The Labour Inspectorate normally enjoys the right of access to all workplaces at all times to monitor the proper implementation of occupational safety and health (OSH) regulations. The employer carries full responsibility for any failure to comply with the regulations. Nevertheless, in practice, there are many places where, for purely material reasons, the Inspectorate cannot intervene, such as oil platforms and logging sites in the far north.

Since the late 1970s Norway has therefore developed a policy of transferring the obligation to undertake preventive measures in the field of Ocupational Safety and Health to the firms themselves. As a result, the Inspectorate has been in a better position to target and adapt its monitoring of firms according to their internal health and safety policies.

In Norway, a 1977 Act[a] stipulates that employers have the obligation to systematically seek to improve the working environment of each and every worker.

In 1992, a regulation was introduced concerning the internal monitoring of occupational safety and health by firms themselves. This new measure gives priority to a systematic approach to this issue, in contrast to the traditional approach based on monitoring visits by the Labour Inspectorate. The 1992 Law makes this approach obligatory for employers.

This regulation was revised on 1 January 1997 so as to facilitate the implementation of internal monitoring of small and medium-sized enterprises, which are less advanced in this field than the larger firms. These texts are harmonized with the standards of the European Free Trade Association (EFTA), which are themselves established with the framework of the Agreement on the European Economic Area, in line with the European Union's directives in the field of occupational safety and health.

The reasons behind the introduction of this new regulation were as follows:

— to emphasize the responsibility of employers; and
— the process calls for a democratic dialogue with employees.

The concept of self-regulation of occupational safety and health conditions by firms is grounded in the integration of these issues into the internal organization of the firm, converting it into a contribution to the firm's overall productivity and making it a management issue rather than a problem of additional costs.

---

[a] Act No. 4 of 4 February 1977 respecting workers' protection and the working environment (*Norsk Lovtidend*, Part I, 14 February 1977, No. 4, pp. 77-109).

Its basic objective is to encourage a shift away from a method of inspection led by the Labour Inspectorate which becomes increasingly detailed and burdensome as a result of the complexity of technology, and towards an assumption by the firm of responsibility for the establishment of a self-regulating occupational safety and health environment.

This implies, on the one hand, systematic and continuous action on the part of the firm, which must be described in its administrative procedures and, on the other hand, documentation comprising the following elements:

— a description of the aims of a firm's occupational safety and health policy;
— a description of roles and responsibilities in relation to occupational safety and health;
— safeguards to be set up on the basis of a risk assessment;
— routine procedures for an internal self-monitoring system; and
— routine procedures for taking corrective measures.

The action is set in motion by the Labour Inspectorate, but is implemented by the firms themselves.

In other words, the firms are obliged to produce results. They define their own means to achieve these results, but the means must be explicitly described in internal monitoring reference manuals. As a result, the relationship between the Labour Inspectorate and the firms undergoes a profound transformation: the Labour Inspectorate no longer checks machines, but monitors a firm's occupational safety and health policy instead.

From inspecting machines to monitoring firms' policies on occupational safety and health

The implementation of this concept brings about a significant change in the methods of labour inspection: specifically, the process of inspection begins with an examination of the documentation prepared by the firm. Thus, in the chemical industry for example, as in all sectors, the law on workplace environment makes the employer responsible for the organization of the firm's occupational safety and health policy. The employer must therefore make it possible to assess risk factors at every work station; assess risk and take the necessary technical preventive measures; inform staff and worker representatives of the risks they face and the preventive measures they are to take; restrict the amount of dangerous chemical products used at any one workplace; and provide occupational safety and health training specifically adapted to the workplace.

For the inspector's part, he or she will, by conducting a systematic audit, be able to ask questions concerning:

— the file of dangerous chemical products (is there a file in the firm? is the workers' safety representative aware of its existence?, etc.);
— the internal monitoring system:
  – has the firm set up such a system?

- is there an updating procedure?
- do the workers receive adequate risk training?

The Labour Inspectorate will therefore, as a matter of priority, examine the documentation on the organization's occupational safety and health policy as defined by the employers themselves.

A certain amount of time is needed to set up this newly established system of inspection, but firms have gradually been rallying to it.

New organization of the Labour Inspectorate's tasks

This process of change has had consequences for the planning of the monitoring activities of the Labour Inspectorate, which is now in a better position to target its interventions in accordance with the extent to which firms are committed to an internal safety and health policy.

Firms are classified into four groups according to the extent of their compliance with this new mechanism, and a specific approach to intervention is defined for each category:

— firms possessing the means and exhibiting effective compliance with the new guidelines are in principle no longer in need of technical monitoring;
— firms wishing to comply but – especially on account of their small size – lacking the resources to do so, receive advice and assistance in the establishment of inter-firm internal inspection services on occupational safety and health;
— firms having neither the desire nor the means to comply; and
— firms which possess the necessary resources but have yet to embark on the process.

Firms in this last category are the subject of extensive technical monitoring, and risk incurring penalties amounting to twice the estimated cost of establishing a self-monitoring system. The procedure followed by the Labour Inspectorate is described below.

If a visit to a firm shows that the internal health and safety monitoring system is not in place, or if a systematic audit reveals deficiencies in the existing system, the Labour Inspectorate notifies the firm that it must set up or remedy the system. After each monitoring visit, the firm receives a list of observations and must correct the situation within six months. The financial penalty for non-compliance is calculated at least at double the cost of establishing the self-monitoring system.

However, there has been no change in the structure of the Labour Inspectorate itself, although the training of inspectors has been adapted to enable them to modify their monitoring methods.

New organization within the firms themselves

Self-monitoring of health and safety has had organizational effects in the larger firms because they needed to make it an internal objective of each department. The opportunity to recruit inter-firm technicians in health and safety has been developed for the benefit of small and medium-sized enterprises. Appropriate information has been disseminated to firms.

Within firms, a condition for the successful self-monitoring of a safety and health policy is the active participation of the social actors: workers must be kept informed of the risks they are subject to, and of the procedures enabling them to avert or reduce those risks. They must adhere actively to these procedures since it is they who will, at least in part, have to put them into practice.

The firms themselves have had to release the resources needed to set up this policy, but it is believed that the savings arising from the internalization of monitoring procedures (especially through a reduction in work stoppages) are well in excess of the initial costs: in 1996, 69 per cent of firms who had set the system up reckoned that the implementation of the occupational safety and health policy could save them significant amounts, and most expected to achieve positive economic returns from a systematic approach to these issues.

Far-reaching results

The results of building this integrated monitoring methodology into enterprise activity can be evaluated on the basis of two principal indicators:

— The development of the risk monitoring methodology in the field of occupational safety and health and of working conditions within firms: thus, between 1993 and 1996 the number of firms that have implemented this methodology grew from 8 per cent to 45 per cent. In 1996, only 19 per cent of firms (versus 67 per cent in 1993) had not undertaken this procedure.

— The rate of workplace accidents seems to be closely correlated with the adoption of the new methodology: thus, in a firm which had established this procedure since 1988, the number of days lost annually through industrial accidents fell from an average of 80 in 1981-87 to less than 20 since 1991. The slight increase noted in recent years indicates that the policy has doubtless been less aggressively pursued.

The fact that the internal monitoring of occupational health and safety risks has been mainly applied by the larger firms has led the authorities to re-examine the mechanisms of application of the process: the changes introduced in January 1997 are based on the principle of adaptation of the methodology to the size of a firm, so that the efforts required of small and medium-sized enterprises are only those which are truly necessary and not the entire range more appropriate for larger concerns.

The existence of a hard core of refractory firms who have resisted the introduction of the self-monitoring mechanism has led the Labour Inspectorate to tighten up traditional monitoring procedures on them after an initial period of tolerance.

The approach described here is a particularly innovative one, based on sustained commitment on the part of employers and also on the ongoing involvement of the staff of the Labour Inspectorate.

Wage guarantees in the case of business insolvency

The case of Spain

The Wage Guarantee Fund

In order to guarantee the payment of wages and compensation owing to workers made redundant by failing or technically insolvent enterprises, the Spanish labour administration has introduced legislation and a specific measure for the setting up of a Wage Guarantee Fund consisting of the contributions made by all public and private enterprises employing workers. This Fund pays the amounts owing directly to the workers concerned and acts as a substitute to their rights in relation to the defaulting enterprises.

The Fund is administered by an independent body under the supervision of the Ministry of Labour, Social Security and Social Affairs. This body is managed by a Secretary General and a tripartite Administrative Council. The General Secretariat, which comprises a central headquarters and a peripheral administrative unit in each province, manages a large amount of financial capital which it uses to fund its own operations, and employs modern administrative practices.

According to the general principle of Spanish law relating to bankruptcies, creditors have equal status. This means that when a debtor's assets are insufficient, all creditors may assert their claims on an equal footing, with the effect that available funds must be distributed proportionally so that all parties may partially recover the money owed to them. The recognition of "privileges" in cases of bankruptcy, established by the civil law in the 1930s, was not sufficient to take into account the natural differences between workers and other creditors. The Labour Contract Law[a] of 16 October 1942 required the application of these privileges to workers. However, in most cases, bankruptcy procedures led to the closure of enterprises and job losses. In the 1970s, the State decided to intervene to provide a wage guarantee for workers in failing enterprises. Thus, it proved necessary to extend the period of special wage protection in relation to other creditors, and to establish an institutional guarantee in the form of the Wage Guarantee Fund[b] which covers, in respect

---

[a] Law of 16 October 1942 stipulating the provisions governing the development of labour regulations (*Boletin Oficial del Estado*, 23 October 1942, No. 246, p. 8462).

[b] The establishment of the Wage Guarantee Fund was approved in 1977 by Royal Legislative Decree No. 17 of 4 March 1977 on labour relations (ibid., 9 March 1977, No. 58, p. 5464). In addition to Article 51 of the Workers' Charter, which provides for a negotiating procedure with workers' representatives in cases of collective redundancies for economic, technical, organizational or production reasons, the main legal standards governing the Wage Guarantee Fund are: (i) Article 33 of the Workers' Charter, the first legal version of which dates from 10 March 1980 and which has the force of law in the redrafted text approved by Royal Legislative Decree No. 1 of 24 March 1995 approving the amended text of the Law on Workers' Status (ibid., 29 March 1975, No. 75, pp. 9654-9688); (ii) Royal Decree No. 505 of 6 March 1985 on the organization and functioning of the Wage Guarantee Fund (ibid., 17 April 1985, No. 92, pp. 10203-10208) which contains the general regulations governing the Fund; (iii) the Ministerial Decree of 20 August 1985 on the implementation of Article 32 of Royal Decree No. 505 of 6 March 1985 on Reimbursement Agreements for Sums Paid by the Wage Guarantee Fund (ibid., 28 August 1985, No. 206); and (iv) Royal Legislative Decree of 7 April 1985 approving the Law on Labour Procedure (articles 235 and 303).

of workers, minimum levels recognized by the social partners as being socially acceptable.

The measures common to many national labour laws and that conform to international labour standards have been complemented in Spain by a new mechanism forming part of a strategy to avoid arbitrary decisions likely to preserve individual interests rather than safeguarding the collective interest of keeping workers in their jobs. This strategy was designed to validate the decisions resulting from negotiations between enterprises and workers' representatives, and, in case of disagreement, to monitor, verify and decide on the measure to be implemented in enterprises whose difficulties would have a collective effect on overall employment.

The new measure consists in using the Wage Guarantee Fund to intervene in an enterprise partially affected by crisis. The Fund acts as a guarantor for the payment of wages and compensation to workers made redundant by enterprises owing to insolvency, suspension of payments, bankruptcy and competing creditors. In such cases, the Fund acts as the "subsidiary" head of the enterprise, in other words, the amounts owing are paid from the Fund in accordance with the law, when an enterprise is in one of the above situations. Thus, the amounts owed to workers are paid out of the Fund, which subrogates to their rights in relation to enterprises in order to recover the debts owing for itself. It defers and pays in instalments the debts of the enterprise concerned so that the latter may continue to operate with the workers who have not been made redundant. Thus, this measure helps avoid the liquidation of assets and the closure of the insolvent enterprise, as well as safeguarding some of the jobs.

The Wage Guarantee Fund is administered by an independent public body under the supervision of the Ministry of Labour and Social Security, which has legal capacity and the capacity to act, and is funded by the contributions – the rate of which is set annually by the Government – paid on a monthly basis by enterprises at the same time as social security contributions.[a] This body is governed by a tripartite Administrative Council and the tasks entrusted to it are carried out by a General Secretariat. The Administrative Council comprises representatives of workers' organizations, employers' organizations and the State. This body[b] is responsible for devising the criteria on which the Fund's activity is based, monitoring the Fund's economic development and making proposals to the Government, under the supervision of the Ministry of Labour, with a view to applying the measures necessary for the accomplishment of the Fund's duties, approving the preliminary draft of the annual budget and monitoring retrospectively budgetary expenditure, and approving the annual activity report of the body administering the Fund.

---

[a] The Fund is financed by the contributions paid by public and private enterprises into a separate account, at a rate of 0.4 per cent of the wages paid to workers. This institution can be defined as an enterprise solidarity fund, containing the contributions made by all enterprises employing workers.

[b] Defined by Article 5 of Royal Decree No. 505 of 6 March 1985.

In addition to this measure, provincial committees monitor the Fund and are headed by the provincial labour director of the Ministry of Labour and Social Security. These tripartite committees comprise three representatives of the public administration, three representatives of workers' organizations and three representatives of employers' organizations. The committees, which meet once every quarter, are responsible for receiving and taking into account the information, guidelines and criteria for action established by the Administrative Council, monitoring the Fund's economic development in the province concerned and its effects in the Fund's field of activity, and for evaluating the activities and operations of the Fund in each individual province.

The General Secretariat of the Fund has a central headquarters and 52 peripheral administrative units (UAPs) responsible for instituting legal proceedings and carrying out subrogatory actions. The structure of the General Secretariat is set by the Royal Decree of 14 August 1979, amended in 1986 to establish the list of positions, then in 1988 to set staff remuneration, and in 1989 to establish the list of positions of the UAPs. The General Secretariat's main tasks are as follows:

— collecting and managing the contributions paid by public and private enterprises;
— paying the wages and compensation owing to workers;
— recovering wages and compensation payments from failing enterprises (as part of competitive, executory, civil and criminal proceedings);
— signing delegation agreements with enterprises; and
— cooperating with judicial authorities.

Close cooperation exists between the Fund's administration, the Labour Inspectorate, the Social Security Treasury and the National Employment Institute.

The General Secretariat has 489 staff members. These officials are subject to the General Statutes on Public Servants for the purposes of appointment, career development and annual performance evaluation. Job descriptions are drawn up in accordance with the regulations in force at the Ministry of Labour. The qualifications required of the officials working in the UAPs are legal and secretarial. Unit heads must be qualified lawyers since they appear before the courts of the Social and Civil Order. At headquarters level, the profiles are more varied and require qualifications in law (social, commercial, civil and fiscal), public and private finance, management, liquidation proceedings and general administration.

The use of information technology for administering the Fund is well established. All officials have the necessary computer equipment. The headquarters of the Fund's General Secretariat and the 52 peripheral administrative units are connected by a network and with the networks of the Ministry of Labour, the Social Security Treasury and the National Employment Institute. Through this system of networks, information is provided instantaneously. Thus, when collective redundancies are made by an enterprise, the employer files the decision with the Labour Directorate of the autonomous community concerned, which conveys this information to the Wage Guarantee Fund and to all the institutions concerned. Information about enterprises' assessed contributions to the Fund is also simultaneously available since the said payments must be made at the same time as social security contributions. Thus, the Fund's administration is informed at all times about which enterprises are late with their payments and which have postponed the payment of their contributions.

The operations of the General Secretariat administering the Fund are financed by money deducted from the capital built up through the contributions paid by enterprises (0.4 per cent of workers' wages) and the interest earned from the investment of this capital. The Fund manages a total capital of 82,270 million pesetas, of which 97.3 per cent represents the amount of benefits paid. The operating budget stands at a little under four billion pesetas, of which about 49 per cent represents staff costs. Financial management is conducted on an annual basis and is detailed in a report submitted to the Fund's Administrative Council after its accounts have been audited.

The activities conducted and the results obtained by the Fund's administration are evaluated by means of statistical instruments and qualitative studies. The statistical data, collected in real time by the computer system, are processed and analysed by the General Secretariat and downloaded into a comprehensive report submitted to the Fund's Administrative Council. As regards the UAPs, the provincial monitoring committees evaluate the activities and results obtained in each province and submit a report to the General Secretariat, which consolidates all the information in its report to the Administrative Council.

In 1997, a total of 79,823 million pesetas was paid to 155,495 workers from 31,788 enterprises in the industrial, real estate, commercial, motor vehicle repair, construction, community social services, transport and communication sectors. In addition, 92,655 jobs have been preserved in the past six years thanks to the Wage Guarantee Fund. The amounts subject to agreements on reimbursement by enterprises declared insolvent (cases in which enterprises have been able to continue their activities with part of their staff by means of "compensation" agreements[a] stood at 56,894 million pesetas and represented an average of 15.9 per cent of the total amount of benefits paid by the Wage Guarantee Fund.

Every year around 15 per cent of reimbursement agreements are not complied with, but this does not always involve total non-compliance followed by the closure of an enterprise. In many cases, payments are not made and the Wage Guarantee Fund does not receive the agreed amounts in any one year, but does not require the agreement to be executed so as not to compromise the number of jobs retained.

---

[a] *"Saneamiento"* in Spanish.

To sum up, the Spanish labour administration's activities are original in that the Wage Guarantee Fund has extended the conditions and methods of payment for wage benefits or redundancy compensation in cases of enterprise insolvency, together with the recovery of an enterprise's debts. In that regard, this activity is exemplary as the measure established provides the possibility of keeping an enterprise running without the need to liquidate its assets, or terminate all work contracts, using a judicial procedure of execution that handles workers' claims separately from those of other creditors. Thanks to the regulations devised by the labour administration in close consultation and cooperation with the social partners, enabling an agreement to be signed between enterprises in difficulty and the Wage Guarantee Fund, it is possible to defer and break down into instalments the debts of an enterprise, as well as granting reasonable deadlines for reimbursement.[a] The entry into force of the agreement leads to the suspension of the activities undertaken by the Wage Guarantee Fund before the judicial authority to which the agreement is sent for temporary archiving of the proceedings, in so far as they pertain to the Wage Guarantee Fund.

The advantage of this measure is that it safeguards a large part of the positions filled in enterprises in difficulty. In addition, the measure has indirect positive effects: firstly, the declared insolvency of an enterprise does not have a negative influence on its market position, since its assets are no longer seized and the enterprise is granted access to external funds or credits; secondly, owing to the transparency of the regulations, the process may be subject to an agreement with the workers themselves from the onset of the crisis. Thus, through partial collective redundancies, for which compensation is paid by the Wage Guarantee Fund subrogating to the workers' rights, it is possible to save the remaining positions and avoid a situation whereby the crisis leads to the enterprise disappearing altogether.

---

[a] Deferral of the total amount without payment in instalments over a maximum reimbursement period of two years, or deferral with payment in instalments of the total amount with a maximum reimbursement period of eight years, and a moratorium of a maximum of six months.

The campaign against clandestine labour

The case of Argentina

Since late 1996, the Argentinian Government has been waging a campaign against clandestine labour, the main goal being to reintegrate these workers into the legal economy. It appears that 41.2 per cent of employed labour, or 3.76 million workers, are not duly registered.

Two years on, the first conclusions that can be drawn are that in spite of its limitations, due primarily to the progressive reduction in the priority assigned to it, the programme has nonetheless made it possible to legalize the situation of a large number of workers; it has also led the federal and provincial authorities to work together for a common goal, an added value which should by no means be underestimated.

This study was carried out on the basis of documents published by the Ministry of Labour and Social Security of Argentina[a] and additional information provided.

Following a meeting of the Federal Council of Provincial Labour Administrations on 20 September 1996 (the Declaration of La Rioja), the Argentinian Government launched the National Programme to Regularize Labour and Social Security (*Programa Nacional de Regularización Laboral y Previsional* (PNRLP)) on 4 November 1996 by signing a Statement of Agreement between the nation and the provinces.

The aim of the Agreement was basically to establish uniform criteria for determining the principles of shared responsibility, cooperation and coordination between the State and the provinces, and to guarantee the efficient and uniform operation of the various inspection services. Moreover, the Agreement asserts the ambition to standardize supervision of the application of labour law provisions, which falls within the competence of the Central Authority and the Supervisory Body of the Labour Inspectorate.

This Agreement also refers explicitly to the provisions of ILO Conventions Nos. 81 and 129[b].

The main characteristic of the organization of this programme is the concept of "cooperative federalism". Given the structure of the Argentinian State, in which the federal provinces enjoy considerable autonomy in numerous fields (including the application of labour laws), the implementation of such a programme involves cooperation between the central and provincial labour services.

---

[a] Information leaflet on the National Programme to Regularize Labour and Social Security (PNRLP) published by the Ministry of Labour and Social Security, March 1998.

[b] Labour Inspection Convention, 1947 (No. 81) and Protocol of 1995; Labour Inspection (Agriculture) Convention, 1969 (No. 129).

This is the first time that planned and coordinated measures in the field of labour inspection are being implemented jointly by the State and the provinces.

The primary objective is to detect and regularize unregistered employment, and there are also two secondary objectives:

— to monitor the use of special contracting procedures; and
— to ensure application of the laws respecting foreign workers.

The programme consists of two joint monitoring operations carried out by the provincial services and the Ministry of Labour and Social Security (MLSS). The Ministry is responsible for planning the operations and provides the provinces with technical assistance and human resources.

The programme can only be successful if the national and provincial authorities work in partnership. To this end, a strategic plan comprising eight specific activities was drawn up in November 1996. The programme furthermore included *an activity aimed at monitoring social contributions*, so as to improve their payment. The legal basis for the programme is defined in the "Urgency and Necessity Decree" of 1996.[a]

Guaranteeing the mobilization of all relevant services

Coordination between the relevant administrations – a main characteristic of the implementation of the programme – is guaranteed by the Supervisory Authority of the MLSS. The National Labour Relations Office, which is dependent on the Ministry, checks that newly regularized workers have been included in the Integrated System of Pensions and Allowances (ISPA) and follows up this activity using information provided by the provincial services.

If a worker's situation has not been regularized, the matter is referred to the General Tax Office (*Dirección General Impositiva* (DGI)) which determines the amount owed by the employer.

The provincial labour inspection services fall within the competence of the provincial governments, which enjoy considerable autonomy with respect to the central Government. This is why it was crucial for the success of the programme that stable relations be maintained with the other services involved: the General Tax Office, the social security and the provincial services. However, no direct participation by trade union organizations or employers' associations was envisaged.

Rigorous implementation planning

At the beginning, three broad phases were defined: November 1996 to March 1997; June to August 1997; and September to December 1997; thus demonstrating a clear will to plan the implementation of the programme.

---

[a] Decree No. 772 of 15 July 1996 conferring on the Ministry of Labour and Social Security the functions of Central Monitoring Authority over the whole country (*Boletín Oficial*, 16 July 1996, No. 28436, p. 12).

The initial objective of the *first phase* was to inspect 10 per cent of the 380,000 employers registered with ISPA.

In order to determine how many inspections were needed, the total number of workers per province was taken into account, on the basis of estimates provided by trade union organizations and the National Institute for Statistics and Censuses. The number of workers targeted was thus set at 300,000.

In view of the experience gained in the first phase of the programme, it was decided that the priority in *the second and third phases* was to check and regularize the situation of the workers. It should be noted that, during the second phase, a special part of the programme was devoted to the National Operation for Inspecting Labour in the road transport sector.

A new orientation for programme implementation was adopted in 1998 taking into account the results of the first phases. The new plan of action – the National Plan for Improving the Quality of Employment (*Plan Nacional de Mejoramiento de la Calidad del Empleo* (PNMCE)) – fixed the number of workers to be inspected at 700,000.

The provincial labour services made use of the coordinated inspection operation, by basing themselves on the results of their activities. The employer was made responsible for presenting up-to-date staff registers for the next inspection. If the workers were not registered, the provincial authority imposed sanctions.

The National Labour Relations Office (*Dirección nacional de relaciones del trabajo* (DNRT)) developed the information papers and the analysis of the operation.

Significant financial and human resources

In conducting the campaign the national and provincial labour inspection services took account of the means available. The central administration lent the provincial services the necessary human and material resources to carry out the inspections, creating 90 teams made up of members of various services and inspectors from the different participating bodies (the DNRT, the National Social Security Agency (ANSES) and the DGI). Moreover, some 50 administrative employees were engaged for a ten-month period. A budget was also set aside for seconded personnel and auxiliary staff.

The operational national statistics service was able to supply the necessary information to follow up on this activity. In addition, it was planned to purchase 40 computers for the provincial services.

A promotional programme about the campaign was carried out, in which ten publicity flyers and other written information were distributed.

The State and provincial budgets guaranteed remuneration of the staff and the provision of equipment. The total amount planned was 8.4 million US dollars, of which 3.2 million came from Ministry funds while the rest was to be contributed by the provinces. A further 61,900 US dollars were to be used for promotional purposes. No information is available as to the amounts actually spent.

Ongoing and realistic evaluation

In March 1998, a provisional overall evaluation was carried out on the basis of incomplete information available at the time.

Throughout the various phases, the process of combating clandestine labour was the subject of ongoing evaluation by the state services.

What was most surprising in the examination of the graphs summarizing the different activities was the highly mixed results across the provinces. Moreover, these disparities varied considerably from one region to the next and also from one phase to the next.

In the first phase (inspection of ten per cent of employers), the average national monitoring rate was 68.3 per cent, that is, 26,000 employers instead of the intended 38,000. During this first phase, an average of 21.9 per cent unregistered workers was ascertained among the 159,296 workers monitored.

The second phase (inspection of workers, including those in the transport sector) covered 105,525 workers, 20 per cent of whom were in the cargo transport sector (that is, 25 per cent higher than the specific objective set). Total cases monitored correspond to an implementation rate of 64.2 per cent of the defined objective. Moreover, the operation in the transport sector made it possible to diagnose the situation there.

The implementation rate of the third phase was a mere 26.3 per cent, that is, 36,383 workers.

These different phases revealed that there was a mean of 23.1 per cent unregistered workers out of a total of 301,204 workers in 51,134 enterprises (including the transport sector). A third of these workers were regularized following the intervention of the labour inspection services. This national average encompasses considerable regional disparities.

It can thus be seen that, in 1997, somewhat less than half the monitoring objective originally set was achieved. The explanations given were reduced mobilization of the services during the latter stages. This reduction was particularly evident in some provinces.

Even if the quantitative objectives were not fully attained, the programme contributed the following:
— greater efficiency in inspection, via the use of statistical information;
— education and information of employers and workers;
— cooperation between project participants; and
— improved results due to the programme for monitoring social security contributions in sectors where the usual methods do not work.

In 1998, a final evaluation of the programme was carried out which reasserted a target of monitoring 700,000 workers. It was estimated that around 20 per cent of these workers still needed to be regularized as part of the national plan for improving the quality of employment.

Lastly, following a number of coordination and complementation agreements between the Ministry of Labour, the Ministry of Social Security, the Federal Administration of Public Finance (*Administración federal de ingre-*

sos publicos (AFIP)), and the General Tax Office (DGI), the National Plan for Social Security Monitoring (*Plan nacional de fiscalización de la seguridad social* (PNFSS)) was drawn up for 1999. This Plan provided for a 40 per cent increase in the operative capacity in terms of human resources, to be distributed across coordinating, monitoring and administrative functions. In addition, a direct link was established with social security databases in all the provincial MTSS agencies around the country, thus enabling computerized supervision of employers' compliance with their obligations.

In the first phase of the Plan, 20,000 enterprises were monitored, that is, a total of 117,000 workers, 32 per cent of whom were not making contributions to the social security system. Approximately 50 per cent of these workers were regularized without any kind of sanction being imposed, by means of an innovative method of monitoring and awareness-raising.

Thus, the new impulse given to this activity cemented the cooperation between the public institutions. As a result, the campaign against clandestine labour has become one of the services' ongoing and routine activities.

Employment, vocational training

The Information Centre

The case of China

To respond to the needs arising from economic reforms and to move beyond a traditional manual data processing system, the Chinese Ministry of Labour and Social Security (MLSS) has sought to transform its computer system from straightforward data processing to a management information system. This action, which set out first to reorganize the MLSS's data processing system to feed into the general policy-making process, should improve the provision of direct services to users such as trade unions, employers and jobseekers in the long term. The latter's number is high due to the period of transition which has led to mass redundancies as state enterprises were placed on a profit-making basis.

The MLSS's Information Centre (IC) was created in 1988 and is responsible for the Labour and Social Security Management Information System (LSSMIS).

Its objective is the provision to the Ministry, through the LSSMIS, of the instruments necessary for general policy-making decisions founded on a reliable analysis of labour market data and to provide central and local governments as well as employers and workers with information suited to their needs. The overall task is to improve the quality of management in the Ministry and in its user services in the fields of labour and social security and especially of employment.

The full implications of this initiative can be seen in the context of the measures adopted by the government in the move from a planned to a socialist market economy, which requires from public institutions in general and the labour administration in particular the establishment of high-quality upstream technical services especially where employment services are concerned.

The retraining of workers made redundant by newly profit-oriented state enterprises concerns some 8 per cent of the adult population, or more than 6.3 million workers. Even though special job placement services must be set up within enterprises with large-scale redundancies, the pressure on the employment services themselves is still very great, and instruments such as an effective LSSMIS are essential for the registration and processing of personal data, unemployment insurance and other benefits, as well as for the provision of a placement and training service that responds to the needs of its clients.

The role of the leading actors

The MLSS is divided into two main parts. The first part includes the so-called administrative departments – legal services, planning and finance, training and employment, wages, old-age insurance, etc. The second part includes institutions such as the Information Centre, the Labour Studies Academy, the Social Security Bureau, and the Professional Registration Centre.

All these institutions and departments enjoy the same degree of autonomy. However, the Information Centre has sole responsibility for the design of the Ministry's general information system and network, while each component part of the structure is responsible, as a subsystem of the general information system, for the provision of its own specific data requirements.

As a section of the Ministry's core structure, the IC's structure, organization, operation and staff all come under the Ministry and it must therefore fit in with the Ministry's organizational system.

It comprises six divisions: Administration, Systems, Operations, Technology, Research and Analysis, and Network Relations. The IC's relations with its users are conducted principally through the Network Relations division.

The IC's principal functions are as follows:
— for internal Ministry users:
  – planning and designing software and operations for the LSSMIS at national level;
  – creation of a computer network and introduction of management systems in the Ministry;
  – design and maintenance of databases at national and ministerial levels; and
  – analysis and promotion of policy-relevant information on labour issues for use by government bodies, workers and employers at the national level.
— for external users:
  – technical and advisory support for provincial and municipal labour offices;
  – planning, designing and implementing a nationwide data network for Job Placement Agencies and for the network's Service Centre.

The LSSMIS is divided into seven fields of activity, namely Employment and Unemployment Insurance, Old-Age Insurance, Maternity and Medical Insurance, Accident Insurance, Wage Management, Labour Relations, and Occupational Development and Training.

The Centre is funded from the Ministry of Labour and Social Security's budget which is provided entirely by the central Government. The entire infrastructure of the Centre, including its premises, equipment and other material is provided by the Ministry, but the budget does not cover all its needs.

Decisions on whether to proceed with major projects are given the go-ahead personally by the Minister, while other decisions are taken by the Centre's Director.

Forty-five per cent of the budget is allocated to staff costs, 15 per cent to administration and 40 per cent to information.

In addition to policy-makers, the main users of the Centre's services are Provincial and Local Labour Offices, Job Placement Agencies, trade unions and employers. The Centre holds regular consultative symposia to improve its ability to respond to their needs.

Implementation

The Information Centre's tasks are directly connected to the MLSS's mission, and its development programme is therefore directly tied in with the Ministry's own planning. The broad outlines of the Centre's ninth Five-Year Plan and its long-term objectives for the year 2010 were drawn up in 1994, but this planning will be reviewed in the light of the recently initiated reform and reorganization of the Ministry.

The LSSMIS was devised by the Centre in 1988 and launched in 1989. It encompasses all fields of activity in the social and labour spheres, which means Provincial and Local Labour and Social Security Offices, and all other basic administrative units, and it provides the elements necessary for effective handling of organization, management, monitoring and evaluation. Management data are organized in four main categories in accordance with the following aims:

— general policy decision-making;
— programme management;
— support for local units; and
— management information for the Ministry.

The Centre's work is coordinated by a Management Group made up as follows:

— the Minister as head;
— the Director-General of the Centre (as deputy);
— the Director-General of Planning and Finance (as deputy); and
— the Directors-General of each Department of the Ministry (as members).

Activities are undertaken on a project-by-project basis. Each project task force comprises a head and staff drawn from the Centre's various divisions.

As an autonomous institution within the Ministry, the Centre is not subordinate to any other structure but must respond to their needs. Within the Ministry it must respond to all requests for technical assistance from the departments, and at service points at local level it provides advice and technical assistance to the Labour Market Information System (LMIS). It also proposes development plans to provincial and local labour offices, on which they must decide in the light of the resources available to them. Outside the Ministry, the Centre has also built up a cooperative relationship with other ministries' information centres and is a participant in the establishment of the national databank for the National Information Centre.

The employment services now have at their disposal computerized information which enables them to provide better service to employers looking for staff and above all to workers looking for a job or for training which might prepare them for a job. The introduction of computers in employment services allows users to have free access to labour market information. However, it would appear that there is a preference for assisted information services because through them valuable personal contact is created and maintained

229

between job placement advisers, jobseekers and employers, all of whom thus obtain a more effective service.

At the time of writing, 40 per cent of the systems in municipal employment offices were linked by network, and were thus able to share information on vacancies and jobseekers within their municipal areas. The four cities which fall directly under the authority of the central Government – Beijing, Shanghai, Tianjin and Chongqing – have established city-wide networks.

The Information Centre employs 34 staff, all but four of whom are professionals – i.e., technical staff responsible for the design, implementation and maintenance of the system and network, for software development and for statistical models of the labour market.

Their status is neither that of civil servants nor of wage-earners protected by the Labour Code: rather they are wage-earning staff working in an institution.

Staff of the Centre are recruited through public announcements and a selection procedure based on competence (knowledge, aptitude and experience). The Centre's staff must be competent in the spheres of operational management, software development or the installation and maintenance of computing equipment. At the time of writing, there were 19 technicians and 15 junior staff (with less than two years' experience) and they had high-level qualifications:

— one Ph.D.;
— five with a Master's degree;
— 15 university graduates in science;
— nine with technical educational qualifications; and
— four polytechnic graduates.

Staff must undergo on-the-job training or attend full-time training courses with a view to future promotion. The Centre's career development programme offers its staff training opportunities ranging from one week to several months, internally or in firms at home or abroad. In recent years, five staff members have completed post-graduate courses.

At the end of each year, all staff must go through a self-evaluation process complemented by group evaluation.

Impact of the measure

All the Centre's services may be inspected and monitored at any time by the various inspection bodies (administration, budget, etc.) The Director-General leads and monitors the activities. He or she in turn submits annually to the Minister a target plan whose progress is reviewed every six months by the Management Group. Finally, the Centre's results are analysed and evaluated monthly and quarterly by the division heads.

The implementation of each project is evaluated by a group of experts. Certain clients or users, such as Employment Offices, can evaluate and choose from the products offered to them in accordance with their needs. The performance and progress of job placement agencies, for example, are analysed by the Information Centre and the Provincial and Local Labour Offices, among others, on the basis of statistical reports produced by the agencies.

After ten years, in 1998, the actions described had had a certain number of positive effects:

— real progress regarding databanks, system management and the information network;

— freeing the Ministry and local office staff from burdensome manual processing of case material and especially of statistical reports;

— long-distance communication over the network has markedly speeded up the exchange of documents between the Ministry and local offices;

— information sharing for all parts of the apparatus;

— mobility of the active population (i.e., jobseekers) greatly facilitated by better access to job vacancy information across regions;

— an improvement in policy setting as a result of appropriate information processing;

— contributing an important element in social development;

— actors have been able to take on greater responsibility through information sharing; and

— the availability of information to all those concerned has produced greater transparency thus placing all users on an equal footing in the face of the competitive environment emerging in the new economic and social circumstances.

The impact of recent economic reforms on the LSSMIS and its ability to respond to the resulting expectations have not been analysed. However, analysis of the activities of the Municipal Job Placement Agency in one provincial capital shows that, following the introduction of the information system in these departments, the amount of information has quadrupled while the placement rate rose from 37.1 per cent to 52.6 per cent.

EMPLOYMENT, VOCATIONAL TRAINING

INFORMATION FOR USERS

An occupation-based statistical system for employment projections

The case of the United States

In the light of the federal Government's desire to equip the country with an integrated system providing users with direct access to labour market information, and of the need for each state to offer efficient services in the place of numerous personalized services which have been ended as a result of budgetary cutbacks, many information tools have been reviewed, improved, or created in recent years. The Occupation-Based Statistical System for Employment Projections offers an example in which the services provided to users (choice of method of information distribution) have been reviewed and their content redefined, as well as an example of collaboration between two different levels of government.

The peculiar features of this programme as compared with systems observed in other countries lie in the involvement of state employment services in data collection, in the contractual agreement between the federal and state governments for its implementation and financing, and in the opportunity it offers of direct free access for all users to this information – information which can be used in making decisions about training, career guidance, the development of a firm, planning of training programmes, etc.

The federal Government first created the Office of Employment Projections (OEP) and its Division of Occupational Outlook in the United States Department of Labor's Bureau of Labor Statistics (BLS) in the late 1940s, in order to provide Second World War veterans with information and career guidance, on the basis of occupational-based employment projections. This remains the objective of the Bureau's employment projections programme, although its projections are now used for a wide range of purposes.

Since 1960, the BLS has developed and published medium- and long-term employment projections, i.e., from ten to 15 years. As of the early 1970s, the projections have been prepared on a two-year cycle. The present projections cover the size and composition of the labour force, economic growth, detailed estimates of industrial production, and employment by industry and by occupation. The information produced is used by those concerned with the course of economic growth and its effect on the job market for specific occupations. They include, among others, labour force advisers, trainers, career advisers to young people, and officials in the spheres of education and training programme planning.

A major change took place during the first half of the 1990s as a result of a request by the Congress to the Secretary of Labor to undertake a complete review of market needs and of existing output as regards labour market information. The study was entrusted to the Employment and Training Administration (ETA) and the BLS in collaboration with a number of Directors of state Labor Market Information Systems (SLMIS), the committee overseeing the Labor Market Information (LMI) of the Interstate

Conference of Employment Security Agencies (ICESA). The report of this working group, dated July 1995, insisted on the need to establish an LMIS based on the following principles:

— focus on the user (including individuals) and responsiveness to the user's needs;

— ease of access and use (state-of-the-art technology);

— link-ups with other information sources; and

— reliability, i.e., the same level of integrity and confidentiality as the information contained in the current system.

This measure paved the way for the design and improvement of four data-banks: America's Job Bank (AJB), America's Talent Bank, America's Career InfoNet and America's Learning Exchange, all grouped together under the joint title of America's Career Kit.

At the state level, governments have felt the need to produce statistical studies of their own in response to specific needs. Due to the major budget cutbacks of the 1980s, they were forced to modify the mission and resources of their State Employment Services, as follows:

— changes in the services provided (i.e., a 50 per cent cut in professional advisory services);

— reduced access of clients to the services themselves (office closures and shorter opening hours);

— staff cuts (24 per cent); and

— changing client profile.

One of the principal ways found by the State Employment Services to preserve the quality of their services in the face of these difficulties was to improve the content of and access to their statistical information output. Client services thus came to be structured around three lines:

— self-service (especially in the form of electronic information);

— assisted self-service; and

— service provided by a professional adviser (on a limited and specialized scale in view of the limited human resources available).

With respect to the improved content of the output, states take advantage of the data collection undertaken by them as mandated by the LMIS and funded by the federal Government by processing the data collected for their own purposes once the federal requirements have been met. Each state organizes the service according to its own needs and priorities. The case of the State of Wisconsin illustrates how this works.

This State is interested in developing occupational projections on account of the investments it needs to make in education and training, and also on account of the labour market information which will be required by the employers and jobseekers who constitute its clientele. (For example, the projections published in September 1997 for the period 1994-2005 forecast that in 2005 there will be 103,201 job openings in the State, of which 59,711 will have been generated by people employed in 1994, who leave their jobs, and another 43,490 will be new jobs created by market expansion.) The occupational projection shows that the openings are of six types:

— occupations with the highest number of jobs;
— occupations with more than 500 jobs where growth is fastest;
— occupations with the highest number of growth opportunities;
— occupations with the highest rate of job growth;
— occupations with the highest number of jobs lost; and
— occupations with the highest number of self-employed.

To avoid leaving job vacancies unfilled for positions that require skilled personnel, these projections are used to plan formal education programmes and also to project training and reskilling programmes for people in employment. New technology and new management methods also mean that currently employed skilled workers will need to learn new skills.

The national employment projections for 1996-2006 published by the BLS in December 1997 provide an overall picture of economic and employment growth, a substantial part of which consists of occupational employment projections.

The role of the leading actors

In 1976, the United States Congress created two committees: the National Occupational Information Coordinating Committee (NOICC) and its state counterpart, the State Occupational Information Coordinating Committee (SOICC). The objective was to promote a coordinated approach to the development and use of labour market information for planning education, training and employment programmes. These committees are supposed to stimulate coordination, cooperation and communication in the development of occupational information. Subsequent amendment of this legislation in Congress added the task of providing career information to young people and adults. Underlying the work of these committees is the premise that by providing users with tools and information, they will be able to make an informed choice regarding education, training and career.

The Bureau of Labor Statistics is the leading agency responsible for the collection, processing, analysis and dissemination of labour market information. It is also responsible for the development of data collection methods and procedures by the states. Responsibility for occupational employment projections lies with the Office of Employment Projections (OEP) within the BLS, which is in charge of the data analysis process. This Office consists of two divisions – Occupational Outlook, and Industry Employment Projections.

At the state level, and returning to the case of Wisconsin, the Governor is assisted in the labour sphere by, among others, three advisory bodies: the most important is the Wisconsin Job Council (on which various interest groups are represented, including employers and workers), in addition to the

EMPLOYMENT, VOCATIONAL TRAINING
INFORMATION AND FORECAST SYSTEMS
ON THE LABOUR MARKET

State Collaborative Planning Team, whose members are mostly state government officials, and the Wisconsin Occupational Information Coordinating Council (WOICC), created by the State Congress and which has brought representatives from the education sector into the management of labour market information. This latter group is composed of representatives of the State Employment Security Agency (known as the Jobs, Employment and Training Service Division in Wisconsin), the Economic Development Agency, the Educational Science Committee, the Employment Training Coordination Council, and the Committee responsible for occupational retraining programmes, and its role being to disseminate information among different agencies and to support the development, maintenance and diffusion of careers information. The WOICC is very eager to encourage direct access for users to information.

The Governor oversees several Departments, including the Wisconsin Department of Industry, Labor and Human Relations. This Department manages a series of divisions, including the Jobs, Employment and Training Services Division, which coordinates the activities of six Bureaus, including the Division of Workforce Policy and Information, the Bureau of Job Service, the Bureau of Workforce Development, and the Bureau of Apprenticeship.

Of these, the Bureau of Workforce Policy and Information is charged with collecting or seeing to the collection of (by the Bureau of Job Service, for example), as well as with processing and analysing, all information required for the production of statistical projections. The BWPI comprises three sections:

— the LMI/Data Collection Section which collects and processes employment data in cooperation with the BLS;

— the Local Workforce Planning Section, which offers technical assistance and staff training; and

— the Workforce Information and Coordination Section which analyses data and disseminates information.

Implementation

State employment services in the United States seem to play a more prominent role in the collection of labour market information than in many other countries, where it is usual for a national, central statistical agency to collect data while the employment services use them and disseminate them. In the United States, the BLS negotiates contracts with each state's employment service for data collection relating to five major programmes. For example, in a State of five million inhabitants the employment service will distribute, collect and analyse some 150,000 questionnaires per year. No other state government agency has access to such a quantity of information on labour markets or on economic activity as a whole.

The responsibilities of the state agencies are standardized as far as data collection is concerned, but states' activities differ in the analysis and distribution of information, depending on policies, priorities and resources allocated by the LMIS.

The federal Bureau of Labor Statistics develops its projections in six stages, each of which has its own models, procedures and solutions:

— the size and demographic structure of the labour force;

— the growth of aggregate economic indicators;

— final demand, or GNP divided into consumer goods and production sectors;

— industrial transactions (input-output);

— industrial production and employment; and

— employment by occupational sector.

The occupational labour force models in industry are complemented by information collected by the State Employment Security Agencies (SESA), of which state job placement agencies form a part. The information collected concerns 250 industries and 500 occupations.

All projections are subjected to a final review prior to publication by internal and external experts with different specializations, who conduct a cross-tabulated analysis.

For their part, the State Employment Agencies generally produce two broad types of statistics: industrial employment, and employment by occupation.

Occupational employment studies (OES) give the level of employment by branch of activity for the secondary and tertiary sectors. In the State of Wisconsin, since the self-employed sample is too small, it is replaced by extrapolations from the BLS's national figures. Thus data are obtained either by the Wisconsin Bureau of Workforce Policy and Information (BWPI) or through methods and statistical models from the BLS.

Employment projections are nonetheless insufficient, especially as regards training needs. While they do provide projections of needs for new and better-trained labour for new jobs, they do not take account of changes in the content of existing jobs, arising above all from new technologies and new methods of quality improvement. It is left to company managers responsible for training programmes and the government to keep a watch over these developments so that training programmes can remain in tune with their needs.

The reliability of projections is evaluated once a target year has been reached, and the results are published. All the projections and evaluations are available on the BLS Website under the title Employment Projections (http:\\www.stats.bls.gov).

The LMIS offers numerous products, including occupational employment projections, to various categories of users:

(a) Employers:

— wage rates;

— additional benefits expected;

— labour supply;

— national and local economic conditions;

EMPLOYMENT, VOCATIONAL TRAINING
INFORMATION AND FORECAST SYSTEMS
ON THE LABOUR MARKET

  — decisions on the choice of a firm's size; and
  — new products and services expected.
(b) Jobseekers:
  — types of job on offer;
  — type of training required;
  — type of training provided;
  — wages on offer;
  — cost of living in the location where jobs are on offer; and
  — growth or decline projection for individual occupations.
(c) Government agencies:
  — economic activity and the state of the economy;
  — unemployment rate;
  — reasons underlying unemployment: industrial policy or international trade;
  — additional labour force training needs; and
  — labour productivity.
(d) Trainers:
  — types of job available after schooling;
  — location of these jobs;
  — skills required by employers;
  — wage rates on offer;
  — jobs likely to be on offer in the future; and
  — training on offer.
(e) Promoters:
  — comparisons with wages offered across the region;
  — availability of workers;
  — skills possessed by available workers; and
  — types of training meeting the workers' needs.

Numerous channels of information are available to users, such as:
— publications (containing employment projections);
— access to local and national electronic databanks, via:
  – free open access electronic sites in Employment Offices;
  – free access on the Internet: at national level, America's Career Info-Net (ACINET), and, at local level, the Wisconsin Career Information System/Career Visions (WCIS).

With the launch of America's Career Kit numerous changes were made to the content of the information service, as information was updated and integrated into a direct access computerized system. For example, the Dictionary of Occupational Titles (DOT) has been reviewed, and will now be replaced by O*NET which will include information on new technologies, new skills and new forms of work organization, while the Standard Industrial Classification System (SIC) will be replaced by the North America Industry Classification System (NAICS). The implementation of these two changes will require substantial training programmes for LMIS staff.

The BLS's Office of Employment Projections employs 47 staff, of whom three hold editorial positions in the OEP's review *Occupational Outlook Quarterly*, two hold administrative positions and the remaining 42 are all economists, including 12 who hold management positions. At the state level, for example in the BWPI, several staff use a specially developed programme to apply the projections forecasting methodology. In both cases, the staff use data generated by other organizational units.

In most states, occupational and industrial projections undertaken by the corresponding department have been funded for the most part by the Wagner-Peyser programme or other revenues, which fund the basic state employment programmes.

A 1998 Act[a] highlighted the role of labour market information in the work-force development system and new processes are under way at both the federal and state levels to better integrate labour market information into the broader workforce development system.

EMPLOYMENT, VOCATIONAL TRAINING

INFORMATION AND FORECAST SYSTEMS ON THE LABOUR MARKET

---

[a] Public Law 105-220 of 7 August 1998 on Workforce Investment (*United States Code Congressional & Administrative News*, October 1998, Vol. 8, pp. 937-1247).

Direct access to information for employment service users

The case of the United States

During the 1980s, federal funds allocated to the operation of the United States Employment Service (USES) were severely cut. As a response to the resulting lack of funds for the provision of an adequate employment service to the public, states' local Employment Services have during the last 15 years launched a series of programmes to reorganize the services they provide, with the intention in particular of broadening the access to the majority of individuals, especially those without a job and employers, to information on the labour market through the production or improvement of appropriate tools, especially electronic ones, like the Internet. The task they faced was to do better with fewer resources.

More recently (1995), as a result of a report to Congress on the improvement of the Labor Market Information System (LMIS), the federal Government had the opportunity to review all initiatives nationwide in the field, including those mentioned above, with a view to build and fund a national LMIS.

This new LMIS now offers a complete array of directly accessible information on current and future (projected) job vacancies, labour supply (personal CVs), training on offer, etc. A user can now, from his or her own home, from the workplace or from a designated service point, survey the steps to be undertaken to bring together supply and demand, and embark upon a particular course of occupational training, or a choice of training paths. All these tools also enable the staff of local employment services to provide appropriate service to the user.

EMPLOYMENT, VOCATIONAL TRAINING

INFORMATION AND VOCATIONAL GUIDANCE FOR JOBSEEKERS

In the United States, two processes have given rise to changes in users' direct access to labour market information in their search for a vacancy, a job, or a choice of training, and in the design of training policy. The first originated in the states' local employment offices, and the second in the federal Department of Labor (DOL).

In the past decade the management of the State Employment Security Agency (SESA) was forced to apply imagination and effort to maintain the quality of service to which its users had become accustomed as a result of significant budgetary cuts and the consequent reorientation of the aims and resources of the United States Employment Service.

At the beginning of the period of change, USES provided four types of service:

— a point of contact between jobseekers and employers with vacancies on offer;

— the administration of tests and occupational counselling;

— enforcement services on behalf of other USES sections or other state institutions (unemployment insurance, social protection, immigration, food stamps, etc.); and

— the collection of information and statistical analysis on the labour market.

During the past 15 years, USES offices have been impacted by:

(a) A change in the types of service provided as a result of:

— a 28 per cent decline in job placements (1980-86) due to a cut in federal support for employment agencies, increased federal support for public sector and not-for-profit intermediaries competing with state agencies, the rapid growth of commercial profit-making employment agencies and of the temporary assistance providers;

— a 50 per cent reduction in professional counselling services between 1980 and 1987 (giving rise to a 34 per cent cut in the number of counsellors) due to a reduction in federal financial support;

— a phasing out in the late 1980s of the large-scale use of aptitude tests (General Aptitude Test Battery (GATB)) whereby candidates' qualifications could be graded for use as a reference in the placement process. In July 1990, the US Department of Labor informed the SESA agencies that, as of the beginning of 1991, the GATB could no longer be used to decide placement priorities;

— increasing duties in compliance-related enforcement on behalf of other agencies, entailing a substantial administrative burden; and

— the heterogeneity of activities and funding sources in the labour market information field. As distinct from a programme designed to produce reliable nationwide estimates, the USDL Employment and Training Administration (ETA) only provided seven per cent of federal funding for such activities.

(b) Restrictions on client access to the services as a result of the 1982 cuts in federal subsidies:

— many local offices were closed or relocated and upkeep or repair work was postponed; and

— opening hours were reduced.

(c) Staff reductions:

— a fall (in 1982) from some 30,000 work-years to 22,800, i.e., a 24 per cent cut arising from a recruitment freeze, staff cuts, internal relocations, doubling up of tasks and the hiring of temporary staff.

(d) A change in the social profile of persons registered with the agencies:

— as a result of legislative changes in the early 1990s the number of economically disadvantaged persons registered declined by 63 per cent, though this was balanced by a rise in displaced workers from the durable goods sector, from the car assembly industry, from steel and from merchant shipping.[a]

As a response to new needs in the midst of these constraints, new strategies and new paths of intervention were first explored at the local level:

---

[a] See ILO: Productivity in Labour Administration (ADMITRA document No. 35, 1993).

— the provision of services to groups, though this turned out to be more costly than their provision to individuals;
— the use of tests, though many of these were abolished in 1991;
— the recourse to associative devices (job-clubs), though the success of these remains unproven;
— registration from a distance, which was already in use in rural areas; and
— the adoption of new technologies in the context of the creation of new "One-Stop" services.

Eventually, this last approach became the axis around which local strategies were designed:
— self-service;
— assisted free service; and
— specialized services provided by professionals.

Given the extreme decentralization of employment services, each state is free to decide how to organize the services provided within its boundaries, and to create "One-Stop" offices where the client has access to these three types of service, the free service being accessible to all via state and federal databanks.

However, the rationalization and slimming down of the employment services meant fewer and fewer staff, especially occupational guidance counsellors. In some states there are none at all for general consultation, except where they have been hired for specific programmes aimed at target groups. Furthermore, the fact that employment agencies were also entrusted with social programmes and with law enforcement harmed their image. Employers believed that the agencies would only provide poorly qualified applicants, while jobseekers believed that the agencies would only guide them towards low-paid jobs. This perception of inefficiency has led to a decline in usage, and the response has been to transfer the dissemination of information and some occupational counselling tasks to computerized career information tools available in employment agencies, secondary schools, colleges, universities and on the Internet.

The objectives were as follows:
— flexibility and adaptability (accessibility);
— reduced staff costs; and
— the shift of responsibility to the users.

The second reason for providing direct access to LMIS users, which normally would be provided by the employment offices, was the creation of an integrated distribution system for labour market information. During the first half of the 1990s, Congress asked the Secretary of Labor to undertake a full-scale review of market needs and of existing labour market information products. The Employment and Training Administration and the Bureau of Labor Statistics of the DOL were then entrusted with this study in collaboration with several state LMIS Directors, with the Committee for Labor Market

Information of the Interstate Conference of Employment Security Agencies (ICESA) and of the National Occupational Information Coordinating Committee (NOICC).

There is little evidence that the social actors at the national level were involved in this consultation process prior to the establishment of the system. At the local level, however, in the setting up of the One-Stop service, advisory groups comprising employers, unions, users, teaching establishments, social groups, etc., were consulted in the establishment of the service.

The role of the leading actors

The investment of money and effort undertaken by the Department of Labor in the dissemination of labour market information, including direct user access to information, arose largely from the Report presented to Congress in July 1995 on the LMIS, the aim of which was to design an overall policy for the creation of a high-quality labour market information system. The report covered:

— user needs and existing products;

— the legislative and funding framework;

— the organization, coordination and management of the system, including the role of the states; and

— an evaluation of the capacity of state and local employment services and the impact on federal funding formulae.

It became clear from the start of the review process that the databank project for the LMIS should have the benefit of the experience and information at state level.

Research and development on the whole system and its components was therefore undertaken through consortia consisting of state agencies, so as to make use of their accumulated experience and of the work already undertaken by them on the job vacancy databank (America's Job Bank), on employment projections, employers, wages, and so on. The Department of Labor therefore invited the states concerned to join in the work and provided a budget to launch the operation. The main lines of the resulting report concerned the following:

(a) *The principles of the LMI system itself:*

— focus on the user and responsiveness to his or her needs;

— ease of access and use (state-of-the-art technology);

— linkages to other systems and information sources; and

— achievement of the same degree of integrity and confidentiality as the existing system.

(b) *Identity of the users targeted:*

— individuals;

— employers;

— intermediaries and counsellors;

— economic development agents;
— teachers and occupational training providers; and
— planners and political decision-makers.

(c) *Description of the various existing systems*

(d) *Recommendations on:*
— products and services to be adopted for users;
— supplementary information needs;
— the technologies required for implementation of the products and services;
— the organizational structure of the LMIS;
— compatibility of technical language and norms; and
— a funding programme.

Implementation

The United States Employment Service and the federal One-Stop/LMI team (ETA) share responsibility for the management and monitoring of the project. The One-Stop/LMI team is also charged with providing the necessary technical specifications for linking up the various databanks built up at state level.

The overall strategic objectives for the databanks arise from the ETA's internal programme and from regular consultation with the states, while the specific objectives and their sequencing in time are determined by negotiations and the consensus reached in the consortium.

In fact, all the databanks are combined under the title America's Career Kit (ACK) which permits easy access to integrated data. These databanks are:

— *America's Job Bank* (AJB) *(an electronic list of job vacancies)*: The result of a joint federal-state effort, it was launched in 1993 as an extension of the Interstate Job Bank (1979) and has been available on the Internet since 1995 (2.1 million visits per working day). It offers direct access to employers, and by April 1998 more than 25,000 employers had registered directly more than 250,000 vacancies. The AJB is managed by the USES, a section of the ETA.

— *America's Talent Bank* (ATB) *(an electronic CV list)*: This instrument was developed by a consortium of 20 states led by Michigan and Missouri. The version launched in the spring of 1998 and which has now been incorporated into America's Job Bank, reflects largely the proposal made by the state members of the consortium. The Internet-accessible databank provides employers with access to jobseekers' CVs, and offers jobseekers access to a vast labour market.

— *America's Career InfoNet* (ACINet): The development of this databank was sub-contracted by the federal Government. It includes a new classification of occupations which has been available in a new version since July 1999 (*Occupational Information Network* (O*NET)). States and

245

other organizations involved in employment and training have been consulted. This instrument is managed by the One-Stop/LMI team at the federal level (ETA).

This Internet databank provides information on occupations. It includes: O*Net which has replaced the Dictionary of Occupational Titles (DOT). O*NET is the primary source of occupational information in the United States. The information is available via occupational codes, keywords or a subject list. It can also provide other information on the following points:

— listing of employers;
— occupational research: general information (classification), wages and relevant training;
— geographical description: regional information on population, unemployment, household income, etc., in relation to any particular occupation;
— complementary resources: information on occupational trade unions, professional associations, a list of enterprises, maps, weather, the educational system, etc.; and
— trends: employment and wage projections by occupation.

— *America's Learning Exchange (educational and training information)*: This has also emerged from a joint approach, and has been developed by the State of Minnesota with prominent participation by educational institutions and by other states. Staff from the National Occupational Information Coordinating Committee (NOICC) were selected to develop this databank, and the final product was due to be available at the end of January 1999. This instrument is already providing useful specialized products for local employment service staff to offer information on training opportunities to employers, jobseekers and students, including hundreds of course descriptions, books, reports, etc. All this material is directed to specialists in the field of employment development, placement, guidance, the dissemination of labour market information, training etc.

The available list of employment-related training attracts more than ten million jobseekers and employers per week.

A large number of educational institutions are already registered, the University of Minnesota being the one hundredth continuing or lifelong education institution to register. Hundreds of training opportunities are now available.

The future management of AJB and ATB is the subject of ongoing discussions between the state and the federal Government. The latter is currently of the view that a not-for-profit organization would be the most appropriate management vehicle for this electronic placement service. A number of proposals have been studied by the Interstate Conference on Employment Security Agencies (ICESA), but no decision has been taken.

The national level management team is small, comprising four full-time staff within the ETA/ OneStop/LMI team, ten people in each regional office and one resource person providing technical support for the various state-level consortia.

The Report to Congress recommended the creation of a Training Institute for ALMIS staff (South Carolina LMI Institute). This would not necessarily have physical premises, but would consist rather of a computerized network providing courses and information and training tools to enable staff to use the resources at their disposal. It also recommended training tools to help data-bank users such as employment advisers working for the employment services.

At the request of Congress, the latest information technology was adopted to facilitate access to information, and it was a stroke of luck that the extraordinary development of the Internet at the same time gave a strong impulse to the decision to provide all the tools of America's Career Kit free of charge. America's Job Bank now lists between 950,000 and one million jobs daily in public employment agencies, directly accessible to all types of users. In September 1998, the number of active CVs increased to 150,000 per week (ATB).

As far as funding is concerned, the 1995 Report to Congress recommended investment in four sectors:

— common services and products, such as staff training, common projections provided by the BLS, etc.;

— the establishment and funding of the activities of seven consortia of states under the leadership in each case of the state responsible for research and development of databanks containing precise data on one of the following subjects:

  – long-term industrial and employment projections;
  – short-term industrial and employment projections;
  – use of unemployment insurance data as a tool of the LMIS;
  – establishment of an employers' database;
  – creation of a LMIS Institute;
  – creation of a system for market research on training providers;
  – creation of a databank on average occupational salaries;

— creation of a computerized network for service delivery and upgrading of existing databanks; and

— financial support to the One-Stop services to ensure that their customers have access to information technology and their products.

Funding for the subsequent years came mainly from Congressional Appropriations, namely allocations for the One-Stop[a] service. Between 1994

---

[a] Law of 6 June 1933 leading to the establishment of a national system of placement and co-operation with the states in view of developing the said system and other purposes (The Wagner-Peyser Act, 1933) (*Legislative Series*, ILO, Vol. XIV, Part 1, pp. 562-572).

EMPLOYMENT, VOCATIONAL TRAINING
INFORMATION AND VOCATIONAL GUIDANCE FOR JOBSEEKERS

and 1998 annual budgetary authorizations rose from 50 million to 150 million US dollars. The last budget was divided between 92.5 million dollars for One-Stop implementation grants and 57.5 million dollars for labour market information investment.

The 1998 Budget (57.5 million dollars for investment) for the Labor Market Information System was broken down as follows, for databanks among other items (in millions of US dollars):

America's Career Kit (AJB, ATB, ACIN, etc.)	13.5 million
America's Learning Exchange (ALE)	2.0 million
Research and development/Consortium Support	4.0 million
Improvement of Consistency between State products	28.5 million
Salary and Consumption Reports	2.0 million
Common support systems for the One-Stop service	2.5 million
Improvement of the One-Stop system	3.0 million
O*Net	2.0 million

The 1999 Budget amounted to 146.5 million US dollars. The 2000 Budget requested the same amount, but subsequently the allocations will decline, especially for the One-Stop system, until they disappear completely.

But under a 1998 Act,[a] funding for local One-Stop delivery systems will come from the required One-Stop partners. All One-Stop partners must agree in a Memorandum of Understanding how each will contribute a fair share of the operating costs of the system and the costs for providing core services to adults and dislocated workers.

Impact of the measure

The impact of the ETA's programmes and interventions is evaluated in accordance with the rules contained in a 1993 Act.[b] The annual budget review is a time for providing data on activity in this field. For the ACK there seems to be no fixed evaluation date.

Evaluation of the employment services takes into account, with respect to AJB/ATB, the number of registered employers and the number of active CVs. It is no longer possible to evaluate the performance of employment services with traditional indicators because the number of jobs found through free information services or through the Internet is not quantifiable. An annual evaluation will from now on be undertaken by asking users about the quality of the service offered.

The numerous sources of information through which users can in some sense short-circuit the services traditionally provided by public employment

---

[a] Public Law 105-220 of 7 August 1998 on Workforce Investment (*United States Code Congressional & Administrative News*, October 1998, Vol. 8, pp. 937-1247).

[b] Public Law 103-62 of 3 August 1993 on Government Performance and Results (ibid., September 1993, Vol. 7, pp. 285-296).

agencies, namely information, guidance, bringing together of supply and demand, have led some people to believe that employment services in the traditional sense are doomed, at least in the most highly developed countries, unless they redefine their value to customers reflecting the raised value floor represented by electronic and self-service vehicles. The movement toward One-Stop services in the United States and the Nordic countries may represent that positive redefinition of adequate services and a way to maintain employment services, at least in countries where technical and financial resources are available.

EMPLOYMENT, VOCATIONAL TRAINING

INFORMATION AND VOCATIONAL
GUIDANCE FOR JOBSEEKERS

Information on job opportunities and vocational training for jobseekers

The case of Germany

Since 1984, the German Federal Ministry for Labour (*Bundesanstalt für Arbeit* (BA)), a public institution, has completely modernized the way in which it deals with its users, employees and employers alike. Efforts have focused both on providing direct access to information relating to the job market and careers guidance.

The most significant aspect of this work has been the marked shift towards new technologies (videodiscs, Internet access, etc.), while still retaining textual aids. In addition, users are encouraged to develop their own research.

This latest technology does not, however, eliminate the intermediary role played by the officials of the Vocational Information Centres *(Berufsinformationzentren* (BIZ)). This development is fully comparable with that which resulted in the network set up by the local public employment agencies in France, designed to receive people and help them obtain information.

The Vocational Information Centres (*Berufsinformationzentren*, (BIZ)) were set up by the German Federal Institute for Labour to publicize job vacancies and offer career advice to users.

Since the early 1970s, it has become clear that the sheer volume of information on careers, employment and training was making it inaccessible to users. The main reasons for this are the transformation of the economy, accompanied by the diversification of occupational activities, and the shift from occupational activities towards service activities, together with the large increase in vocational training and adjustment procedures.

For citizens to be able to exercise their fundamental rights in choosing an occupation, it was vital that they have access to adequate information concerning different occupations, training opportunities and professional choices, as well as on the problems resulting from a career change.

A total of 180 BIZ were therefore established with the intention of making the vast amount of information available in a systematic, comprehensive, clear and objective form, and based on the fundamental principle of "self-service information" by users. Two main groups of users were identified: young people seeking their first job or vocational training, and adults seeking new employment or a new direction. At the same time, it was necessary to take advantage of the opportunity presented by modern methods of communication and use them for the widespread diffusion of the job vacancies available and all the information regarding the different occupations by facilitating access to this information.

For young BIZ users in particular, the system is designed to enable them to recognize the context of the occupation in which they are interested and make their own alternative choices.

To satisfy clients' needs for information, the quality of services offered by the local employment agencies had to be improved. The system was first tested in a few large cities and, from 1984 onwards, was gradually extended to the rest of Germany on the authorization of the BA's central authorities, in accordance with its supervisory and administrative councils on which the social partners, such as the Federal Labour Ministry, are represented. A secondary concern was how to best use BA's own resources in the face of increasing demands from users.

The aim of BIZ

Internally, the organizational unit acts as an information gathering point for the team of advisers working in the local employment agencies and, externally, as an information provider for the clients who use these agencies. Five main tasks fall within the scope of BIZ competence:

— *Providing help in using the various methods of promoting* information relating to employment and training issues requested in writing, over the telephone or on-site, usually with the help of "KURS" *(Datenbank für Aus- und Weiterbildung)*, a database containing information about basic and further vocational training.

— *Ensuring the acquisition and mastery of the data processing systems* made available to users. The funding of BIZ activities is managed in-house.

— *Supporting activities linked to career guidance:* in cooperation with other training institutions, BIZ employees offer information sessions on the different topics within the field of career guidance. These topics are defined and managed in conjunction with employment advisers from other departments of the local employment agency.

— *Providing documentation concerning different occupations:* information materials relating to specific occupations and training procedures are collected and adapted, and made available to the staff of the employment agencies; users are assisted in their research and answers are given to their questions concerning the different occupations.

— *Promotional campaigns* to acquaint users with the services provided by BIZ and the employment services as a whole.

In order to obtain a complete picture of all the resources, vacancies and facilities available, the BIZ have the following aims: teenagers and adults who are faced with career choices must be made aware of the need both to take and strengthen their *own initiatives*, their *sense of responsibility must be encouraged* and their *decision-making capacity* enhanced. Thus, the BIZ must endeavour to provide such individuals with opportunities to inform themselves. This service, which is provided through self-service information facilities, must be complemented by the employment agencies which should advise and guide users and act as an intermediary.

EMPLOYMENT, VOCATIONAL TRAINING

INFORMATION AND VOCATIONAL GUIDANCE FOR JOBSEEKERS

A modern organization using modern technology

The BIZ are generally located within local employment agencies and are equipped by the BA. Additional information is provided by mobile information centres, information stands and the regional labour institutes. Consequently, the BIZ have relatively little financial autonomy.

The size and number of staff working in an employment information centre are firstly determined by the number of inhabitants in the town where the local employment agency is located. The number of school leavers is also taken into account. On the basis of these criteria, the BIZ have been put into four categories which comprise between two and nine employees working in an area that ranges from 350 m^2 to 1,150 m^2. Throughout Germany as a whole, these centres employ a total of 700 people who usually receive training from the Federal Institute of Labour on the resources and organization of the BIZ, and more particularly on the target population. Their tasks and the extent to which they cooperate with other employees of the local employment agencies have been defined. Regular training sessions enable them to update their knowledge of different careers. They are classed either as intermediate-level civil servants or, in the case of the largest centres, partly as high-level civil servants. They have high-level university training, which guarantees them autonomy and initiative and enables them to form a relationship with their clients.

The BIZ are generally organized in a similar manner:

— a media library offers free access to all information media. Places for both individuals and groups to read and consult documents, audiovisual resources (slides and films) and opportunities for consulting information on-screen are made available to users. BIZ employees are on hand to provide help and answer questions relating to training and careers;

— the internal databases of the employment office, such as the "KURS" system which provides information on basic and further vocational training establishments, can also be accessed;

— information on Europe is likewise available;

— rooms equipped with audiovisual resources are available for groups such as school groups, students, parents of pupils, teachers, or for the organization of occupational information sessions by various work groups on all topics related to the job market; and

— in-depth documentation can be found in the documentation centre to which access can be granted on request. Career briefs corresponding to approximately 800 occupations and types of training contain information relating to tasks and activities, the level of training required, and employment and promotion prospects. This information is edited for all of Germany and is supplemented by local information. More than 700 videos lasting between five and six minutes and 350 sets of photographs present a brief picture of various work situations. These videos can be consulted directly by users of the centre.

More and more frequently, information relating to jobs is being supplied externally; thus, there are mobile information agencies, and documents about the employment information centres and the services which they provide are distributed by information stands in shops and firms.

The speed at which innovations emerge in the field of media requires that sources of information be updated very reactively. Consequently, under the "Employment Services 2000" project, the networking of employment agencies and BIZ was being set up so that users can access the vacancy announcements and information on the Internet. The BA's Intranet is also being improved. The purpose of all this is to allow users to carry out research with as little need for help as possible from agency employees, thus enabling the latter to provide specific information more rapidly. Depending on their size, the BIZ are therefore equipped with three to seven computerized workstations to give users direct access to information.

In addition to providing information relating to job vacancies and different occupations, the BIZ also provide information concerning the network of addresses of employment agencies for training or employment purposes. Users of the information centres can therefore apply for jobs directly without going through the employment officers, by using the Employment Information System (*Stellen Informationssystem* (SIS)).

Employers can also benefit from the information collected by the BIZ: by obtaining information on job applicants using the same network, provided that laws concerning the right to protection of the individual are respected. The advantage of the modern method of intermediation is that it enables more rapid contact between employers and jobseekers, thus reducing the costs resulting from the use of several intermediaries.

Improvements in advertising job vacancies in even the smallest local offices have enabled six million contacts to be made annually by means of 5,000 sources of information; these figures will increase still further with diffusion on the Internet. Job vacancies are advertised by companies on a regional or national basis; if a company does not wish to put its name on the server, it is not obliged to do so; nevertheless, jobseekers will be able to obtain this information from the employment services.

The BA seeks to ensure transparency in the job market and the quality of vacancies advertised through these means; in 1997, 50 per cent of companies were aware of this interactive system, and offered some 250,000 jobs in September 1998. Large companies prefer to use this system for reasons of cost and efficiency, that is, fewer administrative formalities and more interesting applicants who are found more quickly. These companies are more willing than before to use the services of the BA. Small companies, however, remain indifferent or reticent, pointing out certain disadvantages: the disappearance of individual contact leads to a larger number of unsuitable applicants who do not have the right or sufficient qualifications. Moreover, such companies are subject to intense lobbying on the part of enterprises hiring out workers.

Despite these disadvantages, companies are resorting more and more often to the services of the local employment agencies.

EMPLOYMENT, VOCATIONAL TRAINING
INFORMATION AND VOCATIONAL
GUIDANCE FOR JOBSEEKERS

High level of client satisfaction

Feedback on the way in which the services are received as well as on their level of success is extremely important for an institution like the BIZ, whose main aim is to satisfy the needs of its clients.

Since 1988, a rotating survey has been carried out on groups of users every three years. The last survey in 1997 included the BIZ of the "new Länder" (the eastern regions of reunified Germany). Ten thousand questionnaires were filled in, reflecting a very comprehensive study. The replies revealed that a third of the seven million registered visitors came to obtain more information about a specific occupation or type of training. Another third were interested in information on training and the job market; they indicated that they were often interested in finding out about training and hiring conditions, their chances of success in the job market and further training possibilities.

The level of visitor satisfaction is high or very high (78 per cent), with most on-site consultations lasting between one and three hours, which correlates with the rate of visitors (75 per cent) having found the information they were looking for.

For the last ten years, the high proportion of visitors under the age of 20 (78 per cent) expressing satisfaction with their visit to the BIZ has remained unchanged. The most preferred documentation resources are the computer facilities and teaching-related materials.

Users who took part in the survey gave BIZ employees an average mark of 1.8 on a scale of one (excellent) to five (unsatisfactory), thus showing that, in addition to the documentation provided, personal contact is still an important part of customer service. The majority of visits were instigated by parents, teachers or career advisers, even though a large number of visitors stated that they had come on their own initiative.

Making information on employment and various occupations accessible to users, that is to clients of the public employment services, is the culmination of efforts of an organization that uses modern communication methods but has also continued to adapt and train the staff responsible for dealing with users. Naturally, the initial investment had to be combined with effective ways of bringing the organization up to date. The role of the public employment services has thus been strengthened by its ability to supply services that are effective and adapted to the needs of its users, be they employees or employers.

Placement of the unemployed

The case of the Hong Kong Special Administrative Region of China

---

The Job Matching Programme

The Job Matching Programme (JMP) is a proactive employment action of the Hong Kong (China) labour administration providing unemployed persons with comprehensive employment services comprising in-depth interviews, counselling, active job matching and, where appropriate, referral to tailor-made retraining.

First introduced by the Public Employment Services (PES) in April 1995, the JMP operates through a case officer approach. Each JMP registrant is attended by a placement officer who will follow him or her through the jobseeking process until the registrant settles on a new job or is referred to attend a retraining course to enhance his or her employability. The JMP has proven to be an effective means of helping the unemployed to find gainful employment; it has achieved very good placement results and thus far has a success rate of 60 per cent.

The Interactive Employment Service

The Interactive Employment Service (IES), applying the latest Internet technology, was introduced in March 1999. It builds on the huge computerized databank maintained by the Public Employment Service (PES), i.e. the jobseekers pool and vacancies pool, and uses a search engine to conduct automatic job matching.

Employers and jobseekers can access the information 24 hours a day, from home, office, and just about any part of the world. Users can contact their counterparts directly or through the PES.

The IES enhances the efficiency, effectiveness and transparency of the PES and has proven to be extremely popular among the better-educated jobseekers. In the first two and a half months of operation, it attracted 11,231 jobseekers with 315,198 hits, searching mostly for managerial, professional, skilled, technical and related posts as well as clerical posts.

EMPLOYMENT, VOCATIONAL TRAINING

PLACEMENT

The Asian financial crisis

As a result of the Asian financial crisis, the unemployment rate in Hong Kong, China, reached a record level of 6.3 per cent between February and April 1999. Altogether, 216,000 persons were out of a job. The number of vacancies shrank from 47,200 in the first quarter of 1997 to 25,350 in the fourth quarter of 1998. Hong Kong had not experienced such a serious unemployment situation in over three decades. A high-level Task Force on Employment chaired by the Financial Secretary of the Hong Kong Government instituted monthly meetings in mid-1998 to promote job creation and to monitor the employment situation. The PES was under unprecedented pressure to innovate and deliver.

Mission

The mission statement of the Hong Kong Labour Department's PES has been updated to "provide a responsive, client-oriented, efficient and cost-effective employment service for employers and jobseekers to meet the changing needs in the labour market". This has been set against the background of the five values of the department, namely professional excellence; proactive approach; client-oriented service; partnership, and participation.

Job Vacancy Processing Centre

Hong Kong, China has a vibrant free market economy. Despite the recession, new vacancies come up in the market every day. Efforts have been directed to facilitate employers in reporting vacancies to the PES. A central Job Vacancy Processing Centre (JVPC) was opened for employers in February 1999.

The JVPC receives hundreds of vacancies a day, mostly by fax. Information is verified and entered into the computerized PES databank within 24 hours, and made available to all job centres. The PES conducts regular analysis of the wage levels of the vacancies received and shares the information with all placement officers. Officers are therefore in a better position to advise employers where the terms offered are significantly below the market rate.

Telephone Employment Service

The rise in unemployment resulted in an upsurge of jobseekers visiting the job centres daily. Despite additional staff resources, jobseekers sometimes had to be turned away because the appointment books were all full. Efforts were therefore made to develop a more user-friendly system.

This was introduced in February 1999. A jobseeker not requiring an appointment on the same day could register at any job centre by completing a simple form supplying personal particulars, skills and work experience. The information is entered into the computerized PES databank. On the following day, the jobseeker calls the newly introduced Telephone Employment Service. A staff member can put the jobseeker immediately into contact with the prospective employer, carry out job matching and arrange job interviews.

Open job orders

Developing a user-friendly service means providing more options for both employers and jobseekers. Since June 1998, employers have had the option of opening up their vacancy orders for direct application from jobseekers. This was an important step forward from the traditional approach where the identity of employers would remain anonymous and all applications for a job had to be arranged through the PES. Open job orders simplify the procedure and speed up the recruitment process. The service has become more and more popular among both employers and jobseekers. In less than a year, the percentage of employers opting for open job orders increased from around 30 per cent to over 50 per cent.

Self service and semi-self service

The latest job vacancies are displayed in job centres and accessible via the Internet. Jobseekers can screen the vacancies displayed and make their own selection. They can contact the employers either directly, in the case of an open job order, or through a placement officer in the job centre. Self service and semi-self service are speedy and efficient.

Job Matching Programme (JMP)

A more intensive and personalized service has been offered through the Job Matching Programme to jobseekers facing greater problems in their search for employment. The JMP was first introduced in April 1995 when the unemployment rate rose to 2.8 per cent with more than 50,000 unfilled vacancies in the labour market, while many jobseekers were unable to find a job on their own. The anomaly put into doubt the previous assumption that jobseekers should be able to look after themselves as long as there are sufficient vacancies available in the market.

The Job Matching Programme incorporates job counselling, job matching, referral for job interviews and, where applicable, referral to appropriate retraining courses funded by the Employees Retraining Board. The JMP has a higher success rate than self service. However, as jobseekers have to book their appointments a few days in advance, most tend to opt for the faster route of self service or semi-self service. The JMP provides a fall-back position for jobseekers.

The increasing popularity of the Job Matching Programme and the very heavy demand on staff resources prompted the introduction in mid-1999 of a group briefing session and a workshop before jobseekers are interviewed individually and referred for interviews. The JMP scheme is regularly reviewed and revised in the light of practical experience and client feedback.

Referral to retraining provides an alternative to jobseekers who are identified during the briefing session and the workshop as not fully ready for immediate placement or who would stand a better chance of pursuing their preferred choice of career after retraining. Having identified the retraining needs of JMP registrants, placement officers would refer them to training bodies for retraining courses. There are standing arrangements in place whereby training bodies of the Employees Retraining Scheme would give priority to JMP registrants in need of retraining to attend full-time training courses. Most people are able to find gainful employment after retraining, either through the placement service of training bodies or the JMP.

Group briefings

Group briefings under the JMP are conducted on a regular basis for major job categories: professional, skilled, clerical, service-oriented, construction, real estate management, low-skilled jobs, and so on. Briefings are conducted

EMPLOYMENT, VOCATIONAL TRAINING

PLACEMENT

257

by experienced placement officers in the job centre. Participants have to submit, at registration, personal details and particulars regarding education attainment, work experience, job preference and salary expectations. A profile of participants is prepared to help the instructor address the problems encountered by them and to highlight the latest market opportunities available. The briefings cover the latest market information, job requirements, wage levels, working conditions, career prospects, and free retraining opportunities available. They also cover basic jobseeking skills such as self-analysis, market positioning, networking, interviewing skills, access to public and private employment services, access to retraining courses, and learning to bridge the gap between subjective expectations and market realities through a systematic collection and interpretation of market information.

Workshops

A workshop follows the briefing session. Participants are divided into small groups. The workshop focuses on job search, market adjustment and interviewing skills. There is experience-sharing among group members in their recent jobseeking experiences, what problems they have encountered, what mistakes can be identified and how they can do better. There is also an exercise in the analysis of the market trend of a particular job based on vacancies advertised in a popular newspaper. The objective market information is used in a case study to adjust a jobseeker's salary expectations. And practical problems such as how to make ends meet are tackled. More than one placement officer will be involved, as tutors, in the workshop. The tutors will make notes on the performance and the perceived strengths and weaknesses of individual participants and produce another profile of the participants.

Based on their performance in the workshop and the perceived level of motivation in job search, participants will be grouped under three categories: those who are ready, those not quite ready and those requiring further personal assistance.

Job matching

With the benefit of the observation of individual jobseekers' actual performance during the workshop, the placement officer is in a better position to identify suitable job vacancies from the computerized databank. For participants in the "ready" group, the placement officer will keep on making referrals for the jobseeker until he or she lands a job. For participants in the "not quite ready" group, one or two referrals will still be made, if they so wish, for less demanding jobs. But they will be advised of the retraining opportunities available to them. For participants in the group requiring further assistance, the placement officer will open a case file for each individual jobseeker and provide one-to-one intensive counselling and job matching service until he or she has found a job.

Promotion

A specialized team assigned to the Employment Information and Promotion Programme is responsible for the promotion of the Public Employment Service, including the JMP. It stages various publicity and promotional activities to introduce the programme to jobseekers and employers. These activities include holding job bazaars, organizing exhibitions, conducting briefing sessions and recruitment seminars, and publishing pamphlets and information leaflets. Recruitment seminars are organized so that employers can meet jobseekers face to face to present vacancies in their respective industries and establishments. Focus-group discussions were introduced in mid-1999 to improve communication with major end users of the PES, and to seek their advice on the future development of the PES. Responses from end users have been most encouraging. The team also introduces details of the PES to employers' associations, personnel managers and human resources executives through briefing sessions and major seminars. These promotional activities are very important in winning the support of employers, jobseekers and the public for the programme.

Administration

Hong Kong, China's governmental agency responsible for formulating employment policy is the Education and Manpower Bureau (EMB). In respect of employment policy formulation, the work of the Bureau is to define, develop and review policies, programmes and legislation in respect of employment including workforce planning, training and retraining, labour importation schemes, labour relations, employees' rights and benefits, and health and safety at work. The Bureau assumes policy responsibility for the services provided by the agencies within its purview, among which is the Labour Department. Provision of public employment services is one of the four programme areas of the Labour Department. The Education and Manpower Bureau has direct policy lead on the PES and the latter is also accountable to the Bureau for its performance and implementation of employment service policies.

The PES falls within the purview of one of the Assistant Commissioners who is responsible for, among other things, formulating policies in respect of various types of employment services delivery. It is composed of two main divisions, namely the Employment Services Division (ESD) offering employment service to employable jobseekers, and the Selective Placement Division (SPD) offering specialized employment service to jobseekers with disabilities.

The Employment Services Division is the major service provider of public employment services. Free placement services are provided to jobseekers through a network of nine employment centres under its Local Employment Service (LES). It provides free recruitment assistance to employers and employment services to employable jobseekers. This Division is the major provider of PES and served some 190,000 jobseekers in 1998.

EMPLOYMENT, VOCATIONAL TRAINING

PLACEMENT

The Selective Placement Division (SPD) is the major service provider of public employment service for jobseekers with disabilities. A one-to-one counselling, placement and follow-up service is provided for every jobseeker. The service is even more intensive than the JMP in terms of time and attention given to each individual jobseeker. The service is free and the Division works in close collaboration with the Employees Retraining Board and non-governmental organizations offering specialized services to people with disabilities. The Division served 3,598 jobseekers in 1998, and 1,455 of them were successfully placed in the open job market.

It is the policy of the Hong Kong, China Government to require government agencies to lay down their own performance pledges and make them known to the public, so that the public can monitor their service quality. As far as the employment service for able-bodied jobseekers is concerned, its performance pledges are:

— put vacancy information on display within 24 hours of receipt;
— attend to jobseekers within 30 minutes of the appointed time;
— provide written guidelines to every fresh registrant on employment service; and
— provide an in-depth career counselling session to Job Matching Programme registrants within one week after registration.

The performance pledges of the employment service for jobseekers with disabilities are:

— attend to jobseekers with disabilities for counselling or pre-referral interview within 15 minutes of the appointed time;
— provide a vocational assessment interview to jobseekers with disabilities within two weeks upon receipt of request for employment assistance;
— provide a follow-up service to the employer and employee for three months after placement to ensure successful job settlement;
— send replies by fax to hearing-impaired jobseekers within one working day upon receipt of enquiries by fax; and
— deal immediately with requests from non-governmental organizations and schools for a free loan service of employment related videos.

The senior management of the PES is entirely made up of government officials who have in their careers been trained as labour administrators. These officers have wide exposure in labour administration and hence have rich experience in the fields of labour relations, employee rights and benefits, and employment services. Their experience enables them to formulate policies on employment services delivery from the perspective of labour administration. In operational terms, this means that due care will be taken to ensure that jobseekers are given assistance in finding jobs that guarantee appropriate rights and benefits.

The PES service outlets, including the Local Employment Service (LES) offices, are each managed by an office manager. The office manager is responsible exclusively for activities carried out by the centre. These include general administrative work, supervision of staff, quality of services provided and quantity of work accomplished. The manager supervises a team of staff, each of whom is assigned specific duties such as office administration, placement work, or provision of support services. All these officers are accountable to the office manager for their own performance. The office manager makes annual evaluation reports of individual staff members. These reports have direct bearing on the promotion prospects of the officers concerned. Where necessary, the office manager can also take disciplinary action against officers who fail to attain the standards laid down. As the performance of each service outlet is the aggregate efforts of all staff working there, the leadership and supervisory role of the office manager is very important.

All permanent staff in the PES are civil servants who are recruited centrally. The Asian financial crisis led to an upsurge in the demand for service. The number of jobseekers registered in the PES rose from 8,878 in January 1998 to 23,522 in May 1998. Temporary staff, who are not civil servants, have been engaged on month-to-month contracts to cope with the additional workload. They received special on-the-job training which enabled them to give exemplary service to jobseekers. The managers of the service outlets are labour administrators with university education who have acquired extensive exposure in the labour administration field before being promoted to the rank of manager. Their immediate assistants are also university graduates but with shorter service and experience in the department. However, their firm commitment to placement work and their updated knowledge of labour market movements will help build up their expertise in delivering good employment services. Under this group of supervisory officers is a team of operational staff whose main duties are to refer jobseekers to interviews with prospective employers. These operational staff have generally completed upper secondary education. Most of them have worked as placement officers in the PES for some time and thus have sufficient knowledge about requirements of different types of jobs in the labour market.

The level of pay for PES officers strictly follows the pay scale laid down by the civil service. Generally speaking, it compares favourably to the market rate. Officers in general are highly committed to their jobs, partly because they see the value of their contribution, especially during the economic downturn, and partly because of team spirit. Key performance indicators of the 11 LES offices and the three SPD offices are released internally on a monthly basis. They cover the numbers of jobseekers, vacancies, referrals and successful placements, and caseload per staff member. Each office can check its own ranking in the league table. Offices with good performance are singled out for mention in monthly management meetings. Individual officers with exceptionally good performance are singled out for commendation and a mention is made in their annual evaluation reports.

Each LES office has ten to 20 staff members, depending on the number of users in the geographical districts that it serves. However, the number of staff has lately been increased to provide service to the greatly increased number of jobseekers following the Asian financial crisis. All placement

EMPLOYMENT, VOCATIONAL TRAINING

PLACEMENT

officers have a computer terminal connected to the main database network. They also have their own telephone extension. Jobseekers requiring employment service are seen by the placement officers who will perform job matching or call up employers to arrange job interviews. This face-to-face contact facilitates immediate clarification of jobseekers' qualifications and preferences where necessary, and enhances communication between employers and jobseekers before an interview actually takes place. Upon confirmation of job interviews, a computer printout is be given to the jobseeker as a referral letter.

As the LES offices are highly computerized, each officer is provided with ample training so as to be conversant with the application and input methods of the computer system. Since placement officers may need to receive clients speaking different languages, they are also required to be fluent in both Chinese and English. As far as Chinese is concerned, most officers can communicate in Putonghua (the official Chinese dialect) in addition to Cantonese, the dialect most commonly used in Hong Kong.

The PES is highly automated, which is also a characteristic of local businesses. All LES offices are connected by a computer network and share a common database of vacancies and jobseekers. Any LES office can access this database to retrieve vacancy and jobseeker information. This system greatly facilitates job matching work. It also breaks the previous geographical limitations of different LES offices as the information of all vacancies and jobseekers is pooled and can be used by placement officers in all districts. Jobseekers can register in any LES office; most of them either come to those nearest to their residence or the one most easily accessible.

Computerization also has another significant impact on the PES service. It helps to break the traditional mode of service delivery. Before the LES was computerized, information on jobseekers and vacancies was kept on paper records, which made information sharing very difficult or inefficient. Computerization of the LES in early 1998 has made the process much easier. Employers can now send their vacancy information to the LES via the Internet. The LES has posted a specific vacancy order form on its web site. Through the Internet, employers can fill in the form and send the vacancy information on to the LES. Once it has been entered into the LES database, the information can be accessed by jobseekers performing simple job matching either on the Internet or through the self-service computer terminals located in all LES offices. This system thus provides for a much wider scope of vacancy information distribution.

The 11 LES offices are connected by an online computer network. The network first came into operation in April 1998. The network links up the data of vacancies and particulars of jobseekers available at all the employment service offices. In addition, jobseekers have access to all the vacancies available in the LES through self-service computer terminals installed in each office. Using these terminals, jobseekers can perform simple job matching by themselves. They can also obtain the most up-to-date vacancy information through the Internet.

To enable the JMP to perform more effectively, in December 1995 an additional funding of 2 million Hong Kong dollars was obtained to install a local area computer network system at LES offices. From January 1996, each placement officer was provided with a computer for the purpose of inputting registrants' records and performing computerized job matching. The network allows data to be distributed to different work stations. This system facilitated JMP vacancy information updating and better communication among LES offices. It was replaced by an upgraded and further enhanced network upon computerization of the LES in early 1998.

Although an active service deliverer itself, the PES of the Labour Department does not work alone in pursuit of its goals. The Local Employment Service works closely with the Employees Retraining Board for identification of training needs and referral of displaced workers. It also maintains very close contact with employers to seek vacancies. To further enhance this function, an Employment Information and Promotion Programme was launched in mid-1998 to develop relations with major employers and canvass vacancies actively. On the part of workers, the service liaises closely with trade unions to be informed about changes in the labour market. When employers need to recruit a large number of workers, trade unions are also resorted to as they are important source providers of skilled workers.

The Job Matching Programme as well as overall activities of the PES are funded from the annual budget of the Labour Department. The total expenditure of the Department for 1998-99 was 703.3 million Hong Kong dollars, up from 507.2 million in 1996-97. The computerization of the Employment Services Division, including those functions responsible for the implementation of the Job Matching Programme, amounted to 28 million Hong Kong dollars.

The performance of the PES is always under close scrutiny. Such scrutiny can be regular or ad hoc, by the public or by the Government itself. All these serve as monitoring mechanisms for the effective operation of the Hong Kong PES.

Regular monitoring

There are a number of standing mechanisms to keep track of PES performance. Some of these come from inside the Government and some from outside. For internal monitoring, each job centre issues monthly reports on the number of jobseekers and vacancies registered, referrals made and placements achieved. A new measure introduced in 1999 is the empowerment of managers in job centres to make operational decisions best suited to local circumstances. At the same time, there is increased transparency and accountability. A monthly league table of the performance of all job centres is released to all job centres for reference. The results are also reviewed at the monthly management meeting. A more in-depth review is conducted at six-month intervals, covering improvements achieved by each office during the period, and comparing their past performance with that of other offices. The Labour

EMPLOYMENT, VOCATIONAL TRAINING

PLACEMENT

Department has to submit bi-weekly performance statistics to the Education and Manpower Bureau. Through these performance statistics, the Education and Manpower Bureau is able to monitor the performance of the PES and give policy directives where appropriate. The Labour Department is also accountable to the Education and Manpower Bureau for its own performance, including that of the PES. If the PES fails to meet its expected target, it is obliged to explain to its policy bureau the reasons behind the shortfall and suggest measures to be taken to eradicate it. This mode of monitoring from within the Government is management oriented. It is an initiative on the part of the central Government to ensure that proper use has been made of the resources allocated to a programme. And where performance falls short of expectation, the mechanism will enable the responsible policy bureau to be alerted on a regular basis so that corrections can be made.

Apart from monitoring from within the Government, external checks are also in place. All government agencies are required to set out their annual budget estimates and their performance targets. These budget estimates and proposed performance indicators are circulated to members of the legislature. Before the beginning of each financial year, members of the Hong Kong, China Legislative Council (LegCo) raise questions they have in relation to Government spending. They can also query government agencies on their performance in the past year, or the proposed performance indicators for the coming year. The purpose of this process is to hold government agencies accountable for the way they spend public monies and to link up performance with spending. This yearly exercise enables legislative members to make use of this mechanism to raise questions concerning the performance of government departments. Therefore, government agencies are usually very cautious in ensuring that they can keep up with their committed performance targets. The PES, likewise, has to undergo the same scrutiny process by the legislature. The major performance indicators it lays down are mainly those of the number of jobseekers and vacancies registered, the number of placements, and the number of young persons participating in careers activities. These indicators have formed important yardsticks for measuring the effectiveness of the PES.

Other than quantitative monitoring, there is also a mechanism to keep track of the service quality of the government agencies. As mentioned above, it is the policy of the Hong Kong, China Government to require government agencies to lay down their own performance pledges and make them known to the public, so that the public can directly monitor the service quality of these agencies. The Labour Department publishes each year a list of results it has been able to achieve in the previous year.

Another new measure introduced by the Labour Department in 1999 was the focus group meetings with its major clients. The first meeting was held on 2 June 1999 with representatives from 20 Government departments who are major users of the PES. Together, they generated a total of around 9,000 placements in 1998. The PES introduced them to the new management philosophy as well as the new services to end users. The end users pointed out what their major concerns were and what they expected from the PES. Innovative ideas were generated during the discussion. This led to a clearer and better interface between recruiters and the PES. The meeting was so fruitful that clients have requested quarterly meetings instead of the proposed half-yearly meetings. Similar focus group meetings will be held with major users in leading employment sectors such as retail trade, restaurants, hotels and manufacturing to solicit user feedback as a means to further improve the PES. Focus group discussions will also be held with major trade unions to solicit their views from the point of view of jobseekers.

There is also a mechanism designed specifically for monitoring the performance of the PES. The Committee on Employment Services of the Labour Advisory Board was set up to advise the Labour Department on matters relating to employment services in Hong Kong in general, and in particular the work of the Local Employment Services, the Careers Advisory Service and the Selective Placement Division of the Labour Department. Members of the Committee on Employment Services of the Labour Advisory Board are appointed by the Commissioner for Labour. Each year, the PES submits to this Committee reports on its work and listens to the views of its members on how the PES could be further improved.

Apart from regular monitoring, there is also ad hoc monitoring on the activities of the Government. In Hong Kong, the Legislative Council can raise questions or make proposals to the Government on various items. In addressing LegCo members' concerns, policy bureaux and departments have to provide the relevant facts or give official responses to questions raised or proposals submitted. Experience shows that it is almost the norm for the legislature to question the Government on the effectiveness of the PES whenever the unemployment rate escalates. In such events, the PES has to ensure that its performance can stand up to public scrutiny.

All the abovementioned mechanisms knit together to hold the PES accountable for its own performance, whether to the public, the legislature, or the central Government. Some of these monitoring mechanisms are more effective in one way while some are more effective in another. However, they serve to make the PES administrators more alert in delivering its service, and prepared at all times to be accountable for their own performance.

Results achieved by the Job Matching Programme

Statistical data on results obtained by the Job Matching Programme shows that the JMP is successful in terms of helping those who have problems finding jobs. Of all jobseekers registered under the programme as at end-1995, about two-thirds were females who had a lower secondary or below educational level. The 30-39 and 40-49 age groups accounted for more than 40 per cent of all registrants. Slightly over half of them came from the manufacturing sector.

This profile of JMP registrants has gradually changed over the years. Among the 15,599 JMP registrants in 1998, the 30-39 and 40-49 age groups

EMPLOYMENT, VOCATIONAL TRAINING

PLACEMENT

together made up 52 per cent of total registrants. Compared to the 86 per cent of jobseekers aged between 30 and 49 registered in 1995, jobseekers now seeking assistance from the JMP are younger. The proportion of registrants from the manufacturing sector also decreased from 49 per cent in 1995 to 22 per cent in 1998, which shows that economic restructuring no longer affects just the manufacturing industries but has also extended to the service industries. Moreover, the educational level of jobseekers has improved. In 1998, slightly more than 59 per cent of JMP registrants had an upper second-ary or above educational level, compared to 35 per cent in 1995. This subtle change shows that JMP registrants have become more diversified. More job-seekers who have experienced difficulty in finding employment on their own would now think of using the JMP. This trend should not be considered sur-prising because a new form of economic restructuring has been taking place. During this restructuring process, workers with single or lower skills lost their jobs to those with multi- and higher skills. This new restructuring is sweeping through the economy as a whole. Workers affected hence not only include displaced factory workers but also younger people who are better educated or even have highly sophisticated experience in a certain field. Hence the JMP is facing even greater challenges in the years ahead because of the wide range of unemployed jobseekers who require special placement assistance.

In the first year of implementation of this new programme, of some 5,500 jobseekers registered with the JMP, a total of 3,870 job offers were obtained for them, representing a success rate of 70 per cent. At the same time, it was noted that 1,261 registrants out of the total of 5,500 were able to find jobs on their own after counselling by the placement officers.

Of the total placements obtained by JMP placement officers, 35 per cent of the registrants were placed in clerical and related jobs while 30 per cent went into the sales/service sector. As regards the time lag between registration and placement, about 80 per cent of registrants were placed within the first month of registration and another 16 per cent were placed during the second and third months.

As regards the level of retention, according to a snapshot survey of the placed registrants in 1995, it was found that 72 per cent had remained in the same employment for three months or more. This reflects that, apart from a high success rate, the effort of JMP in placing the unemployed into jobs is also highly sustainable.

From its inception to the end of 1998, the JMP had registered a total of 36,810 unemployed jobseekers. A total of 141,480 job referrals had been made for them and, as a result, 22,512 job offers were obtained, representing a success rate of 61 per cent. In addition, 7,314 registrants had managed to find a job on their own after receiving counselling.

Skills assessment

The case of France

This practice was confirmed by legislative provisions and regulations in 1991 after numerous experiments. It concerns the use of a new tool for managing careers and individual projects, which provides the opportunity for workers – employees or jobseekers – "to analyse their occupational skills and personal abilities as well as their talents and motivation, with a view to defining an occupational project and, where necessary, a training project".

The practice involves the participation of private service providers (subcontracting) which back up the labour administration.

The scheme studied below is referred to in both legal and general terms as "skills assessment".

Although it is defined within a specific legal and regulatory context, this service can be implemented in various ways, the adjustment variable being the source of funding, depending on whether the skills assessment is carried out by an employee, a recent or long-term jobseeker, an unskilled young person under 26 years of age, or an unemployed executive.

This scheme is the result of the convergence of two types of concern: that of the State, which, since 1986, has been seeking to develop a whole series of initiatives aiming to promote labour market fluidity, and that of the social partners which, operating within the negotiating bodies of the Ministry of Labour, Employment and Vocational Training, have sought to promote the legitimacy of these experiments in the eyes of employer and trade union organizations.

These common concerns focused on two specific subjects in particular: vocational guidance and the recognition or validation of occupational experience. In view of rising unemployment (a 68 per cent increase in the number of registered jobless from 1976 to 1988 and an increase of 17 per cent between 1984 and 1988), from the mid-1980s onwards, the National Employment Office (ANPE) strove to develop its services for users, in particular by experimenting with assistance in the assessment of vocational skills. However, in view of the workload and the specialization of the tasks involved, the Office called in external partners to set up and implement these new "services". The initiatives of the labour and vocational training administration in this context were initially focused on the creation of 15 pilot bodies known as Vocational and Personal Assessment Centres.

The mission of these Centres was to put into effect the theory of the need to optimize assessment and counselling tools and methods used in vocational guidance or recognition of experience. From 1989 onwards, on the basis of the conclusions of this first experimental phase, the State took steps to extend the establishment of these centres throughout the country at the rate of one centre per *département* or administrative division, called Inter-institutional Skills[a] Assessment Centres (CIBCs).

The negotiation of the Inter-Trade Agreement of 3 July 1991 enabled the social partners to take on board the results of the two phases of this experiment. Since their role was not to express an opinion on the creation of operational structures but rather on the forms of eligibility of training expenditure, they incorporated the skills assessment into their agreement as a service to be financed in the same way as individual educational leave and chargeable to the company's training scheme.

The State thus incorporated the terms of that agreement into the framework of the Act of 31 December 1991,[b] with only minor differences. Real negotiation "on the substance" enabled the partners in the tripartite system to agree on a common outline of methodology and ethics. This consensus was eventually reflected in the regulations contained in the Labour Code through a State Council decree of 2 October 1992.[c] That was when the scheme really developed in enterprises. The skills assessment is intended primarily for two main categories of user – salaried employees and jobseekers – with a view to enabling them "to draw up a project which will lead to vocational development and advancement".

The role of the main actors

The legislative basis for the "skills assessment" scheme lays down voluntary access to this type of procedure as a fundamental principle. Not only is there no obligation involved, but the scheme is also covered by the confidentiality rule (Article 378 of the Penal Code). Its promotion depends essentially on the public authorities (the joint bodies having the possibility of launching any public relations campaign they may consider necessary and suitable). The advantage of the scheme lies in this flexibility, of which the user is, in the final analysis, the main beneficiary, for he or she can take the initiative of undergoing skills analysis, choosing a service provider and, where necessary, a means of transferring the results of the assessment to a third party (employer, employment or vocational guidance services, or training institution, etc.).

Since the "skills assessment" scheme is integrated into Book IX of the Labour Code, which deals with "further training in the context of continuing education", it is governed by common law provisions. It is thus subject to the same regulatory mechanisms as those of all continuing vocational training measures defined by Article L.900-2 of the Labour Code. Consequently, the

---

[a] The term "skill" gradually became established in human resources management practices during the same period.

[b] Law No. 91-1405 of 31 December 1991 respecting vocational training and employment (*Journal officiel de la République française, Lois et Décrets*, 4 January 1992, No. 3, pp. 168-178).

[c] Decree No. 92-1075 of 2 October 1992 on skills assessment, and amending the Labour Code (Part II: State Council decrees) (ibid., 6 October 1992, No. 232, pp. 13866-13869).

General Delegation for Employment and Vocational Training (DGEFP) is the only body competent to carry out supervisory operations.

On the other hand, the implementation, piloting and management of the scheme are subject to various practical procedures which are entirely related to the target groups involved. Three types of organization are involved: the State, the partners and the service providers.

The State

The state departments, including the DGEFP, are responsible for follow-up control and regulation of the activities of the joint bodies as well as for organizing services for jobseekers. The system includes:

— an internal monitoring department, which carries out follow-up monitoring of the real impact of services in the field and the regularity of their financing; and

— the definition of quality standards and means of evaluating the bodies in order to draw up quality charters at the regional level.

As of January 2000, the National Employment Office has been managing the funds related to skills assessment intended for jobseekers who used to be administered by the DGEFP.

In this capacity, the Office's task is to develop better linkage between skills assessment and the beneficiaries' process of building an individualized career path.

The Regional Directorates for Employment and Vocational Training (DRTEFP) distribute the funds and mastermind quality policy. They are backed up by:

— an internal (follow-up) monitoring department; and

— a Regional Steering Committee on Skills Assessment composed of the main funders and sponsors.

The partners

Joint fundraising bodies authorized to operate in the field of individual educational leave (known as OPACIF) are responsible, among others, for monitoring activities on the authority of the State.

The service providers

The CIBCs are autonomous structures. There are 110 such centres and they are funded by many different sources, although the State plays an important role in this financing (almost 60 per cent of the total turnover of the CIBCs through the purchase of assessment services for jobseekers).

The bodies providing services are certified by the OPACIFs. There are some 700 such bodies, which are private service providers operating in a free market according to the rules of supply and demand. Only certain accounting rules are imposed on them.

EMPLOYMENT, VOCATIONAL TRAINING
SKILLS ASSESSMENT

With regard to the services derived from skills assessment such as the skills assessment leave and training scheme, the State has chosen to confer a primary role on the joint structure in the OPACIFs. These joint bodies are, by definition, authorized to draw up for each department a list of bodies providing services which can carry out skills assessment for employees.

In the case of jobseeking target groups (except for executives), the CIBCs are the only bodies authorized to provide jobseekers with free services. To do so they benefit from agreements which are awarded by the ANPE's regional directorates on the basis of precise specifications.

In addition to the monitoring arrangements mentioned above, the State has vested itself with various means for evaluating the skills assessment scheme: annual statistical and financial monitoring of the activities of the bodies responsible for carrying out the skills assessments, identification of the financing of this type of service by enterprises, inspection missions of the Social Affairs Inspectorate General, and external audits.

As regards social partner involvement, it may be found at practically every level of action. Like the public authorities, the social partners are responsible for encouraging, coordinating and evaluating the activities of the skills assessment scheme as a whole.

The OPACIFs are central to the system for regulating the supply of skills assessments for employees. The CIBCs have tripartite management boards, and the state departments are responsible for follow-up monitoring and regulation of the activities of the bodies providing services and for organizing services for jobseekers.

Furthermore, the State has set up a working party within the Standing Committee of the National Council for Vocational Training, Social Advancement and Employment (the tripartite body for negotiation on vocational training policy), assigning it the task of monitoring the development of the scheme. This group has a joint structure and is chaired by a state representative.

Process management

The skills assessment activity cannot be said to be strategically planned. However, as regards the state budget earmarked for this scheme, it must be stated that the share of public funds allocated each year is structured and negotiated on the basis of an appraisal of the activities of year "n-2".

There are two sources of funding allowing the skills assessment activities to develop: the state budget and private funds (individual educational leave and company training scheme).

The amounts allocated by the state are determined on the basis of criteria which are intended to be objective. In the case of funding related to individual educational leave, the joint bodies are the only ones authorized to specify the share of the funds collected which is to be reserved for skills assessment. Enterprises are absolutely free to decide whether or not to finance these services for their employees.

The CIBCs receive their operating budget from the State; it is calculated according to the appraisal of year "n-1" (maintenance and project engineering costs, as well as costs of financing the number of skills assessments carried out). In addition, there are other resources for measures commissioned by the Regional Councils, enterprises or other bodies sponsoring assessments.

The service providers finance their activities by selling their services. The overall turnover involved in these activities was 316 million French francs in 1998.

Any private or semi-public body responsible for carrying out skills assessments is subject to the rules of supply and demand; it offers a service (service facilities, methods of implementation, price) on a market where there are numerous competitors (almost 1,000 bodies in 1998). Only the 110 CIBCs, by virtue of their mission as a public service, have a "captive market" such as jobseekers from the National Employment Office, who enjoy special remuneration conditions (see above).

As soon as the scheme was set up, the labour administration departments devoted efforts to commissioning a series of studies, whose purpose was to define the standard profile for a "skills assessment consultant".

In the experimental stages, this function was carried out by staff members from the various institutions composing the CIBCs: professional Employment Office consultants, labour psychologists from the Adult Vocational Training Office (AFPA), and continuing training consultants from the state education system.

Three types of reference system were defined as a result of this preliminary work: an occupation reference system, which is also referred to as the vocational activity reference system, various training reference systems, and a certification reference system for each university that proposes its training course.

Currently, each structure that provides skills assessment enjoys complete freedom in recruiting.

However, the financial backers greatly value an approach where emphasis is laid on team competence combining a variety of professional consultants. Thus, each body systematically has a labour psychologist.

Each service provider is responsible for managing its own personnel. If a body is independent, it applies its own human resources management policy. If it is part of a larger structure – Skills Assessment Centres of the state education system or the AFPA – it is subject to the common law rules governing the network to which it belongs, while adhering to the management criteria imposed on the other CIBCs. In the latter case, the few centres which are still part of large structures will soon have to be converted into independent bodies.

As the skills assessment scheme has gradually emerged, tools for assessing and guiding the persons concerned have developed (study of behaviour in simulated exercises, analysis of vocational and personal experience, multimedia tools, broadening of the person's vocational ideas, research methods and data processing on working environments).

The decisions on the purchase of tools or on staff training are taken at different levels:

EMPLOYMENT, VOCATIONAL TRAINING
SKILLS ASSESSMENT

271

— the Regional Directorates for Labour and Employment manage a budget which is reserved for furthering the quality of the network of service providers (specific training courses, assessment-related public relations measures, development of tools for specific target groups);

— the annual priorities in staff training are defined on the basis of the regional report of the scheme's strengths and weaknesses. This is derived from evaluations conducted as part of the quality improvement initiative; and

— furthermore, each Directorate of the Assessment Centre must guarantee that the collective competence of its team in the field of assessment, evaluation and guidance is maintained.

Initiatives to improve the scheme's quality

In 1996, the State took the initiative to institute a policy on skills assessment quality. The objective of this initiative was twofold: to improve the harmonization and coherence of practices, and to regulate supply at the regional level.

This policy resulted in the implementation of quality charters in most regions, a document that can be imposed on any body that wishes to develop activities in skills assessment; quality charters are subject to monitoring to ensure the quality of the signatory bodies.

Furthermore, the State wished to improve the vocational objective of skills assessment, leading to the creation of communication tools during the year 2000 that feature:

— a liaison form between service beneficiary and provider so that post assessment monitoring can be linked;

— a handbook for service providers; and

— a register guide for users on the important criteria to take into consideration in choosing a service provider.

Conclusion

The skills assessment scheme enlists the services of a large number of partners for the benefit of the users. This diversity is the guarantee that the scheme will last, even if there is a risk that the services provided will be dissimilar. It would be to the advantage of the scheme if it were more fully integrated into the range of services which are currently being developed as part of the employment policy.

Retraining of workers

The case of China

This measure was introduced by the Chinese Government to facilitate the re-employment of workers made redundant in the wake of the decision to make state enterprises profitable.

The recent decision by the Chinese Government to change the economic system and adopt a socialist market economy has seriously disrupted the entire employment sector. As a result, the Government has been obliged to give top priority to worker re-employment in the coming years.

As of May 1998 all employment-related institutions and especially the system of labour administration have been enlisted in the effort. They have been given ambitious targets for the re-employment of workers who have lost their jobs in the context of collective redundancies.

Once the Chinese Government had taken the decision, in September 1997, to transform most of its large and medium-sized state-owned enterprises into profitable concerns within a three-year period, it also had to change the rules of management. The measures adopted to help them overcome their critical condition involved supporting mergers, allowing bankruptcies to take place, surplus employees to be dismissed and guided into new jobs, the introduction of competition through job cuts and the pursuit of profit, and finally, an improvement in re-employment programmes – all in pursuit of a competitive system in which only the fittest enterprises would survive.

Anxious to preserve a minimum of social security protection and to establish re-employment programmes for redundant workers, in May 1998 the central Government called on all levels of government to give top priority to the re-employment of redundant staff. In an official document dated 9 June 1998[a], the Government established a set of targets to be achieved in the years to come:

— the number of redundant workers re-employed each year should exceed the number made redundant in that year;

— during 1998, 50 per cent of the workers already made redundant (before 1998) and 50 per cent of those made redundant during that year were to find new jobs; and

— within five years, a social security system and an employment service adapted to the socialist market economy were to be created.

---

[a] Notice of the Central Committee of the Chinese Communist Party and the State Council concerning the special attention to be paid to basic social security protection and to the re-employment of redundant workers (*Zhongfa*, 1998, No. 10).

273

The scale of the task

This decision has far-reaching implications. It concerns the entire country, it is a challenge to the management of enterprises as a whole, and especially the management of human resources, and it threatens with exclusion a large part of the country's labour force on account of their inadequate skills.

Redundancies arising from enterprise reorganization in order to achieve profitability took place across the entire country, including both industrialized and less advanced regions. The number of workers affected was enormous: 6.3 million, or 8.8 per cent of the total number of workers in state-owned enterprises. It was therefore a widespread economic problem and one which furthermore was set to worsen during the next three years, until 2000. Although all areas of economic activity are affected, some, such as trade and industry, are particularly badly hit.

In centrally planned economies, the obligation imposed on enterprises by the government to employ more than the necessary number of staff, without considering profitability, led to over-employment, and China, as a country where the supply of labour exceeded demand, was no exception. The clash between this over-employment and the market economy's requirement that each worker should operate efficiently, inevitably led to an imbalance between staffing needs and actual enterprise employment levels. Another contributory factor was the need for enterprises to improve and diversify their output to face competition which, when combined with changes in industrial structure, led to a need for a different and more highly skilled workforce.

If enterprises had to dismiss workers, those workers had to find new jobs. But, accustomed as they had been to a planned economy where unemployment was unknown, these people (especially the women) had serious psychological problems in facing their dismissal, fearing the judgement of others and also fearing that they might lose their next job. As a result, they lost their confidence and were often not in a position to take on a new job. Furthermore, their skills tended to be low-level, outdated or over-specialized, thus hindering their mobility. Most of them were women and older workers who could offer little in the way of comparative advantages (skills) in the "new" labour market.

The measures envisaged by the Government, therefore, are aimed at workers who have lost their jobs in the original enterprise for more than three months and have not been redeployed or re-employed for reasons related to the production and operation of their original enterprise (or elsewhere), and have retained an employment relationship with that enterprise. They mostly come from state enterprises or collectively owned municipal enterprises.

Given the number and characteristics of the people made redundant and the weakness of the current support system for them – inappropriate insurance and social assistance systems to deal with all these problems – re-employment has become a monumental task requiring mobilization of efforts on a comprehensive scale.

Intervention strategies

At the national level, the Ministry of Labour and Social Security (MLSS) and the State Economics and Trade Committee have been made responsible for implementing new measures. All local governments are empowered to adopt and set up similar structures.

Overall, the role of the State is to encourage initiatives in all ministries and social organizations. The global strategy adopted involves:

— strengthening the leading role played by certain bodies such as the MLSS;

— creating re-employment centres in enterprises where redundancies are taking place;

— strengthening support for re-employment policies for persons made redundant through:

  – the accelerated development of the national economy and opening up of new re-employment sectors;

  – the development of the tertiary sector;

  – the development of small and medium-sized enterprises especially through bank loans;

  – the development of private enterprise and self-employment;

  – the encouragement of profitable enterprises to hire redundant workers;

  – accelerating the reform of the system of social security (unemployment insurance, old-age pensions, minimum wage, etc.); and

  – improving employment services and strengthening training programmes for re-employment.

The role of the main actors

The scale of the changes and the extent of the actions to be undertaken require the involvement of all actors (political, economic and social) of the ministries with the redundant workers. New practices have had to be adopted in the fields directly related to labour administration, in particular employment.

As the Ministry jointly responsible for the operation as a whole and in charge of re-employment, the MLSS has been given the following tasks:

— ensure the involvement of other ministries and departments whose activities are related to the process. This means collaborating with these institutions and also coordinating directly the drawing up of policy and the corresponding legislation. For example, the policy statement on enhancing the management of redundancies and the operation of Post-Redundancy Re-employment Training Centres has been jointly drawn up by:

  – the Ministry of Labour and Social Security (MLSS) itself;

  – the State Committee for Economics and Trade;

EMPLOYMENT, VOCATIONAL TRAINING
RETRAINING OF WORKERS

275

- – the Ministry of Finance;
- – the National Statistical Office; and
- – the National Trade Union Federation.
— implement concrete employment measures such as:
  - – establishing policy on minimum living standards, social insurance and re-employment;
  - – organizing and coordinating the implementation of these policies in local level Departments of Labour and Social Security;
  - – ensuring the proper functioning of labour relations;
  - – working towards a solution to the social insurance problem through a reform of the system and organization of the labour market;
  - – ensuring speedy re-employment of redundant staff through occupational information, and job placement and induction services programmes;
  - – encouraging enterprises to create favourable conditions for the hiring of redundant staff; and
  - – encouraging people made redundant to look for jobs themselves within the framework of the measures proposed.

Following on from the initiatives and directives from the central Government concerning re-employment policies and measures or any other available assistance, local governments have also adopted at their level a series of measures to encourage re-employment in accordance with local needs.

Provincial and municipal governments have set up specific working groups to clarify the responsibilities of all departments. Given the importance of the operation, these groups are placed under the highest political authority, namely the Governor or the Mayor. For example, following the lead of the changes made to the National Statistical System by the MLSS, they have changed the provincial and municipal statistical systems, thus enabling them to undertake studies and research at all levels of government.

Provinces and municipalities have also set up their own training programmes and several municipalities have set up special employment services to speed up re-employment.

At the enterprise level, the trade unions have immediately joined in the consultative processes concerning redundancy proposals. In general, they have joined with women's and young people's federations so as to present proposals to the various levels of government. In particular, they have set up training courses dealing with changing attitudes and ways of thinking among redundant workers and re-employment, and have also set up job placement services and psychological support courses for the transitional period.

All state enterprises who make workers redundant are obliged to set up re-employment service centres. Profit-making enterprises finance all the projects which directly concern them, while loss-making enterprises can apply for state co-financing, whereby the Ministry of Finance and local sources such as the unemployment fund each provides one third. The enterprise which is making workers redundant must provide the remaining third. In the worst affected areas, the central Government provides additional special assistance. The responsibilities of the Re-employment Centres are as follows:

— to make social benefit payments equivalent at least to the level of unemployment insurance payments to persons made redundant. After three years of unemployment, redundant staff lose their employment relationship with the enterprise and are entitled to unemployment insurance or social assistance, depending on the case;
— to pay old-age insurance;
— to pay health insurance;
— to pay unemployment insurance;
— to provide occupational information or re-employment training programmes; and
— to monitor the progress of redundant staff and help them to find a new job.

All enterprises must follow the same procedure when making staff redundant:
— give a 15-day prior redundancy notification and undertake discussions with the trade union;
— prepare a redundancy programme which must be approved by the trade union and create a re-employment service centre;
— identify the workers who will be affected in case of partial redundancy; and
— fill in an official redundancy document for the local institution in charge of labour and social security.

The impact of the measures

This major experiment is still too recent (dating from only May 1998) to be evaluated. So far, all that has been achieved is the mobilization of the actors concerned.

The overwhelming majority of redundant staff have registered with the Re-employment Service Centres, thus becoming entitled to the various benefits available. They have taken part in the courses on offer and, after receiving guidance and information, have started their own businesses or have looked for a job themselves.

Most of the people over 40 years of age who have been made redundant have taken advantage of the retirement arrangements on offer.

When an evaluation is conducted, the Government's objectives concerning the number of people who ought to be re-employed, for example in 1998, should be taken as points of reference, as should the target period of five years for the implementation of reforms of social security and of the employment services.

A few figures produced by the tightly targeted programmes give some idea of the activities undertaken in the wake of the measures adopted:

277

— there has been a 20 per cent increase in the rate of re-employment of redundant staff in one municipality as a result of the organization of training courses;

— by the end of August 1998, more than 85 per cent of those made redundant in the whole country had registered with a Re-employment Service Centre and had received their basic benefit; and

— by the end of August 1998, more than 4.5 million redundant staff had joined private enterprises.

The early warning system

The case of Austria

Introduced within the framework of a preventive proactive employment policy, this is an early warning system *(Frühwarnsystem)* to be activated in case of staff reductions. The regulation, administered by the Federal Ministry of Labour, Health and Social Affairs (FMLHSA), stipulates compulsory notification of all staff reductions only when they exceed a certain proportion of the total workforce employed in firms of a certain size. The aim is twofold: to improve coordination of personnel management within enterprises with the opportunities provided by employment promotion policies to enable them to maintain the highest possible level of employment, and to give timely information to workers threatened by dismissal and help them find new jobs (unemployment benefit, placement assistance, guidance, counselling, the creation of training jobs, and financial support).

The early warning system grew out of a sense shared by all actors involved in the labour market that the shake-up of economic structures had forced individuals to change jobs or occupations in order to adapt to the new conditions of production and marketing, but that at the same time it was necessary to provide the workers affected with longer-term employment prospects.

The system was introduced following negotiations among the social partners and then between the social partners and the Government in 1976, with Article 45a of the Labour Market Promotion Act.[a] The new regulatory system, which aimed to set up preventive measures to avoid long periods of unemployment and to provide support for rapid and smooth retraining for the unemployed, arose from the effects of the first "oil crisis" which, in Austria as elsewhere, imposed long-term adjustment to new demand conditions and led to the restructuring of industrial sites, production, etc.

This preventive policy entered a new phase in 1993 with the implementation of the Agreement on the European Economic Area (EEA) and the enforcement of Community Law.[b] The Austrian National Council adopted this initiative on 9 July 1993 in the framework of the Employment Security Law, setting 1 August 1993 as the date for the implementation of the early warning system in accordance with the Agreement on the EEA so as to take into account the particular situation of older workers. The early warning system remains in force as set out in that version.

The aim of this regulation is to give the Employment Service (*Arbeitsmarktservice* (AMS)) time to examine the possible solutions and to look for

[a] Act of 12 December 1968 respecting labour market promotion (*Bundesgesetzblatt für die Republik Österreich*, 21 January 1969, No. 7, Text No. 31, pp. 465-479), as amended by the Act of 7 July 1976 (ibid., 30 July 1976, No. 115, No. 388, pp. 1345-1399).

[b] Council of Ministers Directive 75/129/EEC of 17 February 1975 on the harmonization of legislation among member states in relation to collective redundancies (*Official Journal of the European Communities*, 22 February 1975, No. L 48, pp. 29-30), as amended by the Council's Directive 92/56/EEC of 24 June 1992 (ibid., 26 August 1992, No. L 245, pp. 3-5).

EMPLOYMENT, VOCATIONAL TRAINING
RETRAINING OF WORKERS

the best way to respond to the needs both of the employees affected and of the economy as a whole.

The role of the leading actors

Despite initial reluctance among employers, this regulation eventually was the subject of an agreement between the social partners and the Government based on the AMFG Act, thus bringing together a rule derived from employment management and labour legislation. In 1976, together with the introduction of the early warning system, the social partners and the Federal Employment Office *(Bundesanstalt für Arbeit)* of the time – in its role as the Ministry's main intervention agent in the labour market – agreed that this mechanism paved the way for the establishment of various measures in advance of possible redundancies and the resulting unemployment:

— consultations with management, the works committee and the workers affected concerning likely redundancies;

— discussion with the management and the works committee on measures to be taken to avoid redundancies, including those in the social pro-grammes, pre-integration training and measures facilitating labour market integration;

— provision of information to workers concerning their entitlements to unemployment benefits and assistance in starting a new job; and

— drawing up personal occupational re-entry plans for the workers affected (proactive placement, skills training, etc.).

The system has been implemented in the old structure of the Federal Employment Office for the following reasons:

— the dense network of employment agencies and offices allowed contacts, consultations, negotiations and information meetings to take place on the spot and without delay (one agency for each Land, or State, overseeing a varying number of local offices, based on needs); and

— the close association of the social partners with consultations and key decision-making concerning employment promotion measures. The labour market policy in Austria, like social policy in general – labour relations as well as income distribution issues – is characterized by close cooperation between the social partners and the Government. With regard to employment, this cooperation has a long history: employment promotion policies comprise unemployment insurance as well as all proactive measures such as counselling, placement, labour market re-entry assistance, etc.

Before 1994, this association among the partners took the form of consultation, with the partners being represented at all levels of the Ministry. By transforming the federal Employment Office into an Employment Service (AMS), the 1994 Act[a] preserved and even broadened the participation of the

---

[a] Employment Service Act of 28 April 1994 (*Bundesgesetzblatt für die Republik Österreich*, 21 April 1994, No. 97, Text No. 313, pp. 3241-3270).

social partners, turning it into a full joint decision-making process. Under this Act, the federal Employment Office ceased to be a service provided by the federal administration, becoming instead a statutory service-providing body.

The current organization of the Service is as follows:

— the Ministry
  – sets the AMS's objectives;
  – oversees and monitors the Service's activities; and
  – has overall responsibility for the Service's budget.
— *the Employment Service (AMS) at the federal level is managed by:*
  – a Board of Directors (which oversees the work of the AMS and formulates general federal directives on the implementation of labour market policy). This tripartite body has three representatives each from the Government, the workers and the employers. The Board has several committees, including a management committee made up of two people.
— *the Employment Service (AMS) at Land level is managed by:*
  – a Directorate in each Land (responsible for general supervision of the AMS at that level, and for the formulation of directives specific to each Land for the implementation of labour market policy under federal directives). The Directorate includes Land administrative staff and two representatives each of workers, employers and the Government. It has committees dealing with the provision of subsidies, unemployment insurance and policy on the employment of foreign workers. The administration consists of two people who undertake tasks at Land level and oversee the AMS's regional offices.
— *the Employment Service (AMS) at regional level is managed by:*
  – the regional Consultative Committee (which implements employment promotion policy at the district level *(Bezirk)*). It is composed of a regional administrative director and two representatives each of workers and employers. It also has subcommittees as at the Land level.

The information, counselling and conciliation tasks involved in the early warning system have been transferred from the old Federal Employment Office and integrated into the Employment Service. The first responsible body to be consulted, and therefore the decisive instance for authorizing collective redundancies (as prescribed by the Act) is the Regional Agency of the Employment Service, with the support of the Land agency in cases where the redundancy affects a strategic site.

The regional agencies, with the support of the Land agencies, advise and inform both management and the workers affected. When a large-scale intervention is required for a site to be preserved, coordination is undertaken at the federal level under the aegis of the Ministry of Labour, Health and Social Affairs, which has the relevant employment promotion powers, together with the Ministries of Finance and Economic Affairs so as to ensure a consistent and coordinated approach on the part of all the institutions concerned, including those at Land level.

EMPLOYMENT, VOCATIONAL TRAINING
RETRAINING OF WORKERS

Implementation

The detailed implementation of the system is governed by an Employment Service general directive which spells out all the aims and procedures to be applied.

Official notification of impending job losses is compulsory only where they exceed a certain threshold, and are required from employers only for employment policy-related job losses (thus excluding retirement, resignations, etc.). Failure to comply with the early warning system entails the annulment of redundancies as laid down in the labour legislation.

These notifications by the employer or the employer's representative are addressed in the first instance to the managers of the regional employment service offices, and more particularly to their staff in charge of early warnings of redundancies. The institutional framework guarantees the right of all the parties to collective agreements to take part in consultations between employers, the works committee and the Employment Service. The legislation requires immediate consultations between employers' and workers' representatives party to the collective agreements, as well as the immediate intervention of the works committee which, according to Austrian tradition, has close links with the union. This compulsory participation of employers and workers is meant to ensure that redundancies will be kept to a minimum as a result of an appraisal of their social consequences, and that all possible and imaginable measures will be taken to protect jobs, in partnership and in agreement with the Employment Service and the relevant political authorities.

The early warning system at regional office level (the Employment Service is comprised of one authority at federal level, nine at provincial level, 96 at regional level and 14 branch offices) simplifies administrative procedures for seasonal enterprises.

The early warning system is usually implemented as follows:

— the firm contacts the AMS regional office by telephone or in writing before issuing the formal notification. The office then provides information and advice on the notification and proposes alternative solutions;

— the firm submits the formal written notification;

— the office proceeds with formal examination of the notification to ensure that all the information required by law has been provided;

— after receiving the notification the regional office manager must decide, on the basis of the employment promotion policy, on the advisability of consultations to avoid redundancies or limit their number. If necessary, the office then contacts all the interested parties;

— a special examination is undertaken in cases where an employment contract is terminated prematurely without the 30-day legal warning period; and

— the procedure initiated by the AMS regional office is designed to maintain employment, and it therefore proposes appropriate measures in each case (training, partial layoffs, time-sharing).

If no solution is found to protect the jobs threatened, services must be recommended to enable the redundant workers to re-enter the labour market immediately. The regional office then provides:

— the usual Employment Service services;
— a set of labour market integration measures;
— information to groups of workers;
— guidance to groups of workers;
— group activities with financial support from the employers (labour market reintegration); and
— business start-up guidance.

The Service also arranges the involvement of "integration foundations". This term is used to refer to an employment promotion vehicle, and has little to do with the usual meaning of the word "foundation". It refers to any body with a juridical personality of its own (such as an association) or indeed without such status (where integration measures are contracted out to an external institution, for example, an occupational training establishment, or an agency involved in economic and employment promotion). These foundations, envisaged in the Unemployment Insurance Act,[a] are recognized by the Employment Service when the firm concerned makes available to its redundant employees the services of an institution possessing certain objective, personal, financial and organizational conditions, and which takes on responsibility for the planning and implementation of job-creation measures.

The implementation of this system is constraining for the Employment Service's agencies. Their internal regulation at both Land and regional levels clearly specifies the responsibilities of all departments and employees responsible for the implementation of the system, and these receive continuous training devoted especially to the relevant provisions of labour law and its amendments concerning the early warning system.

The number of staff devoted to the implementation of the early warning system is small, reflecting its secondary role in the battery of instruments at the disposal of the Employment Service. There are fewer than 25 in the whole country (not including staff gathering redundancy notifications through electronic media). Once a notification has been received, the staff launch the necessary actions and coordinate them. The total staff of the Employment Service stands at around 4,200. Usually, people charged with implementing the system also have other responsibilities, but the standard practice is for them to react immediately on receipt of a redundancy notification from an employer, so as to avoid delays which might undermine the effectiveness of remedial measures.

EMPLOYMENT, VOCATIONAL TRAINING RETRAINING OF WORKERS

---

[a] Unemployment Insurance Act of 1958 (*Arbeitslosenversicherungsgesetz* (AIVG)). An updated version of the Act was published in *Bundesgestzblatt für die Republik Österreich*, 21 December 1977, No. 182, Text No. 609, pp. 3917-3938.

Selection and recruitment of staff are undertaken in accordance with the general recruitment procedures of the Employment Service when a post provided for in the budget becomes vacant. Once recruited, staff undergo a basic systematic training programme, followed by more specialized training related to the field to which they will be assigned, namely unemployment insurance, counselling, placement, and the Employment Service's measures to ease reintegration into the labour market. This training is provided within the framework of broader-based courses imparting the knowledge and skills indispensable for any Employment Service staff member: labour law, social law, techniques for counselling and for approaching clients, complemented by information on the relations between institutions operating in social affairs and their various tasks, with special emphasis on the interface between them and the Employment Service – such as medical insurance funds, pension funds, the federal Office for Social Affairs and the Disabled, social assistance offices and collective bodies. After this initial training programme staff are introduced to the early warning system.

A staff member assigned to the early warning system receives further training in the relevant computerized instruments.

The early warning system makes use of computer technology. In a section specific to the Austrian information system – the application of databases to enterprises – certain data entry fields have been defined by the legislation, and these must compulsorily be filled in. These fields are used to support the compilation of essential information for decision-making and planning measures, and concern the individual enterprise: location, number of employees, type and method of production, number of jobs threatened, the knowledge and skills possessed by the employees, their occupational experience, their labour law and social law status, as well as social and demographic information. Other parties to negotiations and representatives of social partners are similarly profiled.

Every employee of the Service has the necessary computer equipment and the Employment Service's own internal network allows permanent real-time information exchange throughout the country.

The financial provision for employment promotion policy enables the Service to respond to needs as they arise, and, among other things, allows an extension of unemployment insurance payments beyond the period prescribed by the Unemployment Insurance Act.

The budget, which is laid down as a special budget by the annual Federal Finance Act passed by Parliament, is funded mostly by employers and workers, on an equal basis, together with unemployment insurance contributions (currently 6 per cent). Furthermore, in accordance with the responsibilities of the federal Government in the employment field, there is a further federal subsidy, though it represents only a tiny proportion of the total budget.

After its transformation into a statutory body, the Employment Service also received a special budget for staff and equipment expenditures, in the framework of employment policy. This framework also covers expenditures incurred by staff assigned to the implementation of the early warning system as well as current expenditures, for example, on computer equipment.

Like all other expenditures on employment policy, expenditures for the system are budgeted annually and are permanently monitored. A complex audit system has been set up by the Employment Service and the federal Ministry of Labour, Health and Social Affairs for this purpose. Finally, the Public Accounts Court audits accounts after the end of each financial year.

The impact of the measure

The value of this system has been proven particularly in the context of numerous structural adaptations and of the creation of the integration funds.

A series of statistics covering the last three years showing the frequency of use of the system show that redundancy notifications cover all sectors of the economy, even if special circumstances have meant that some sectors sent in more notifications than others, often in the context of long-term restructuring (for example, public and private infrastructure works, construction and related activities, and wholesale and retail trade).

As yet no scientific evaluation has been conducted on the effect of the early warning system. Evaluation does not seem to have a high priority. The evaluation of effects in terms of success or failure of the system seems to occur at the implementation level where the associated social partners in charge play a central role. The effectiveness of the system is evaluated in the light of feedback from the Länder concerning the applicability and adequacy of federal directives, accompanied by recommendations for more suitable legislation.

The coordination among social partners and the Employment Service has led those involved to the conclusion that the system provides several opportunities:

— timely collection of information on the enterprises targeted;

— based on that information, arranging a basis which all those involved, including local communities and other bodies, can use to develop concrete measures to overcome the problems;

— timely introduction of preventive measures for the benefit of employees affected so as to avoid redundancy (partial unemployment, reorganization of working time); and

— envisaging measures which will help the workers affected to enter new jobs or training (integration foundations, regional integration measures or a concerted job placement effort). The Unemployment Insurance Fund has also been able to save money thanks to the speed with which redundant workers find a new job. Evaluation expenses are integrated into the general operating budget.

EMPLOYMENT, VOCATIONAL TRAINING
RETRAINING OF WORKERS

Contract policy for development in the field of vocational training: Training Development Agreements (EDDF) and Contracts for Prospective Studies (CEP)

The case of France

> The contract policy for developing employee training, which was introduced in 1984, is defined by Article L.951 5 of the Labour Code. Its aim is to promote action that anticipates skills favourable to employment and to develop employees' qualifications.
>
> This policy is based on the drafting of contracts binding the State, the professional or inter-trade organizations and employers seeking to become involved in these measures.
>
> There are two separate types of contract:
>
> - *Training Development Agreements (EDDFs)* are designed to promote and support companies' investments in training as an integral part of their strategy for economic development and adaptation to change. They are granted state aid, which complements employers' contribution in the field of training for vocational development and qualification of employees. Sectoral or regional agreements define the priorities for action specific to the branch or area concerned;
> - *Contracts for Prospective Studies (CEPs)*, introduced in 1988, are designed to launch forward-looking employment, labour and vocational training measures within an occupational branch. A survey is carried out on a particular branch of activity with its specific economic, technological, organizational and social characteristics as parameters in order to determine the foreseeable trends in jobs and occupations, defining the skills needed and orienting training policy. These contracts are also state-financed within the framework of an agreement concluded with one or several signatory union organizations.
>
> In addition, this policy falls within the scope of a permanent dialogue with the social partners at the inter-trade, sectoral or local level on the strategies for developing skills and qualifications.

The contract policy is part of the history of continuing vocational training. Designed initially to correct the adverse effects of the legal obligation for employers to finance continuing training for their employees (particularly inequalities regarding access which were to the detriment of the least skilled workers), it soon became the focus of the debate on management planning of human resources, employment and skills (GPPEC).

This policy was actually justified from the outset by the will of the public authorities to move from a system of obligation to one of incentive, since most employers see the compulsory contribution towards the financing of vocational training which was instigated by the 1971 Act[a] as additional taxation

---

[a] Act No. 71-575 of 16 July 1971 respecting the organization of continuing vocational training as part of further training (*Journal officiel de la République française, Lois et Décrets*, 17 July 1971, p. 7035 ff.).

rather than an incentive measure. The purpose of creating this scheme was to change the image of further training, which the "candidates" considered to be the driving force behind company competitiveness. With the EDDFs, the State thus undertakes to promote a strategic vision of access to continuing training.

Initially, the declared target was to accompany the introduction of new technologies with training. Contract policy consequently focused on large enterprises that were leaders in the technology industries. However, given the development of industrial policy, the labour administration reoriented its action towards employees with the least skills in all enterprises and sectors with a view to developing GPPEC measures. This shift, which came about in 1988, was to give rise to the second tool of contract policy, the CEP, which is designed to enable the State and the social partners to develop their ideas on employment and vocational training in a forward-looking vision of economic, technological and organizational change. The CEP is thus intended to integrate complementary factors such as those of the employment market and the observations noted in the development of occupations or skills.

In parallel, the EDDFs took on a new role correcting the continuing training scheme with a view to improving social cohesion. The State thus defined priorities concerning the choice of branches of activity, giving precedence to those where pressures were stronger in the economic, technological and human resource field (the metal industry, the construction and public works sector, the agro-food industry, the textile sector, etc.).

The scheme is currently clearly oriented towards, on the one hand, sectors which hold promise in terms of job creation or are undergoing structuring, as well as small and medium-sized enterprises (SMEs), and, on the other hand, the development of skills training for employees.

The general objectives of contract policy can be summarized as follows:

— to maintain and develop the principles on which state intervention is based, i.e., the analysis of needs, negotiation, the definition of common goals and measures to build up means;

— to target measures more specifically according to their exemplary nature, their impact, and the degree to which they can be transferred to SME/SMIs;

— to promote the validation of training measures instigated in the context of the schemes used and to develop methods for recognizing or certifying the skills acquired; and

— to improve the linkage between the national, regional or department levels regarding the objectives of the contracts and the conditions for achieving them (management, respect for priorities, etc.).

The role of the main actors

The contract policy scheme is thus by definition a partnership scheme. Whether in the case of EDDFs or CEPs, the action involved is joint action, the purpose of which is to enable the social partners, enterprises and public services to anticipate change more effectively and to orient their policy and decisions accordingly.

The joint framework within which contract policy is implemented makes it possible to highlight the basis of a possible compromise between the interests of enterprises and those of employees. But it also facilitates the emergence of needs that have not been satisfied in respect of either the vocational qualification of employees with the least skills or training in new skills for specific categories of employees.

In general, it can be said that contract policy contributes considerably to the dynamism of social partner action, sometimes even inducing the social partners to reconsider existing collective agreements.

Implementation

A working party of the Standing Committee of the National Council for Vocational Training, Social Advancement and Employment chaired by a competent key figure participates in the definition of the priority guidelines for contract policy and issues an opinion on the EDDF and CEP projects.

The social partners are involved in the development of the requirements for the prospective studies or the draft EDDF agreements in the context of the National Joint Committees on Employment.

Where necessary, the State offers prior technical support to branches that request it.

More generally, the method of application of contract policy must be examined on the basis of the principal current use of the two schemes.

Training Development Agreements (EDDFs)

This intervention measure is implemented within the framework of the conclusion of agreements with the branches of industry at the national level, while the specific projects are implemented at the level of the region or area.

National framework agreements give precedence to the functions of providing general specifications, orientation, and monitoring and evaluating the measures to be taken in enterprises. Their objectives and content differ depending on the characteristics of the sectors involved:

— in the case of sectors which are becoming involved in this type of measure for the first time, the primary aim is to promote the vocational qualification of employees and their employability in connection with the strategies for developing human resources and the development of the organization of the enterprises concerned; and

— in the case of sectors requesting the extension of a previous agreement, the conclusion of a new EDDF can provide an opportunity for further developing the initial measures and reorienting training practices to take account of the conclusions drawn from the evaluation of earlier agreements; if this opportunity is taken, the objectives of the new EDDF will be more ambitious and at the same time more streamlined; action will also be targeted more specifically, and particular importance will be attached to the exemplary aspect and transferability.

The objectives of the programmes launched at the regional level are different:

— to reach targets which have not been reached through national planning, particularly in emergent sectors or those where structures are weak;
— to organize the grouping of enterprises; and
— to strengthen consulting services and decentralized accompanying measures, particularly for SMEs.

Enterprises can thus conclude an EDDF:

— in the context of a sectoral project on which an agreement is concluded at the national or regional level;
— in the context of collective area inter-trade projects concerning an employment area; and
— in a bilateral context for enterprises which cannot be included in a sectoral or an area agreement.

The rate of state subsidy is between 30 and 40 per cent of expenditure in line with the measures eligible for the EDDF.

Contracts for Prospective Studies (CEPs)

The CEP method of application is marked by the declared will of the State to establish partnerships with the occupational sectors which, in most cases, have to be provided with methodological tools in order to promote genuine involvement in the definition of training and employment policies. The strategic choices of the public authorities mainly concern sectors which have few structures or where major changes are taking place.

Since it is important to vest the social partners in the branches of industry with a permanent tool for providing aid in the negotiation of the measures they are implementing in the employment and vocational training field, the General Delegation for Employment and Vocational Training (DGEFP) has encouraged the creation of occupation, employment and vocational training observatories.

The studies are conducted on the basis of a project specification which is drawn up jointly by the State and the social partners and specifies:

— the field covered by the CEP;
— a presentation of the branch of industry;
— a statistical study pinpointing employment and training;
— the issues at stake and the priorities of the sector;
— the main operational objectives of the CEP;
— the methods of investigation proposed to operators;
— the means mobilized by the sector;
— the schedule of activities; and
— the steering committee.

The operators are selected jointly by the State and the branch after a call for tenders, and the work is co-financed by the State and the trades concerned.

Analysis of the impact of contract policy

Provision has been made for monitoring and evaluating the measures carried out and the results obtained by mobilizing the internal resources of the trades on the one hand, and by resorting to independent external service providers on the other.

Explicit provision is made for "internal" evaluations of each EDDF in the project specifications drawn up before the draft agreements or agreements are signed. They define the monitoring methods employed throughout the duration of the agreement and lead to the examination of the interim assessments carried out in the steering group context.

The external evaluations are systematically entrusted to public or private external operators specializing in consultancy or in the study and development of training projects. They are subject to a call for tenders under ordinary law, and their purpose is to analyse both quantitative and qualitative results.

Taken as a whole, the results for 1996 in terms of trainees and financing reveal that:
— of the 318 million French francs raised, 6 million were allocated to CEPs, 20 million to accompanying measures and expert evaluations, and 292 million to training measures for employees;
— the total state contribution for EDDFs amounted to 292 million French francs as against 727 million French francs payable by the enterprises, i.e., 28 per cent of the operating costs of the training measures carried out, and 14 per cent if pay is included;
— almost 200,000 trainees were trained in approximately 3,700 enterprises, 66 per cent of whom were blue-collar and white-collar workers.

In 1999, the funds raised for CEPs and EDDFs as part of the Vocational Training and Social Advancement Fund amounted to 335 million French francs. The contract policy measures were co-financed under the objectives of the European Social Fund (ESF) from 1994 to 1999.

Conclusion

Evaluation of the contract policy measures reveals that:
— the CEPs favourably influence the ability of the social partners to take account of the link between training and employment in collective bargaining; on the other hand, this scheme has little direct impact on company policy; and
— the EDDFs have a multiplying effect on the development of training measures within an occupational branch and they trigger and accelerate measures in SMEs. The limits observed concern difficulties in reaching enterprises in emergent sectors and/or sectors where structures are weak,

EMPLOYMENT, VOCATIONAL TRAINING
DEVELOPMENT OF TRAINING

the correction of inequalities regarding access to training, and the implementation of measures providing genuine qualifications.

The guidelines and priorities underlying future contract policy measures take these observations into account. They were decided during a series of discussions with the social partners at the end of 1998 about the project for reforming vocational training.

The priority objectives and the targeting of state intervention have been specified as follows:

— to support the elaboration and implementation of training schemes which are articulated and consistent with the strategies for developing human resources, organizing enterprises and introducing advanced technologies; and

— to promote the implementation of measures for improving the level of occupational skills, developing skills and qualifications, in branches of activity and enterprises or for categories of employees whose level of involvement in vocational training is low.

In terms of branches of activity, the objective is to reach enterprises which have little structure as regards industrial relations and work organization and whose development is based on the professionalization of their activities. These various characteristics apply more specifically to activities in the service sector.

In terms of size, enterprises employing fewer than 250 workers are targeted in particular, irrespective of the branch of activity; these enterprises are characterized by operating methods which are not conducive to the implementation of measures for developing human resources. Furthermore, specific adaptations of the intervention scheme are intended for collective approaches in the sectors or regions.

In terms of target group, the aim is to reach employees who are subject to various forms of insecurity in their occupational activity due to their qualifications, employment contract, age or work history.

The underlying concern in these guidelines is to give state intervention a real leverage effect in influencing company policy to promote employees' access to training and vocational qualification.

Labour administration and the informal sector: The importance of the Informal Sector Support Fund (FASI)

The case of Burkina Faso

This employment aid programme, which was set up in 1994 and initially managed by the labour administration, is used to finance small-business projects through small-scale repayable loans.

The administrators of the Informal Sector Support Fund (FASI) accompany small entrepreneurs, providing them with access to the traditional banking system which is not normally interested in financing this type of operation; this action thus allowed beneficiaries to become structured and move beyond the informal sector.

The Fund became independent in 1998.[a]

One of the main reasons why self-employed workers remain within the informal sector is that the lack of financial security bars their access to banking services. The State therefore proposed to fund the start-up phase of small-business projects with small-scale repayable loans and, in a second phase, once the project is functioning effectively, to guarantee a link with the banking sector.

This scheme originates partly from research into the reasons for the failure of the Employment Aid Fund for SMEs and microbusinesses (FONAPE) in 1991: that project, which offered loans to young people, often students, in order to finance their return to and establishment in the countryside in a pilot village, failed owing to its highly interventionist character and hasty implementation.

It was, however, necessary to launch new schemes which would help to find a possible way out of the informal economy in Burkina Faso, and in particular in Ouagadougou.

The FASI was therefore set up initially as a financial aid programme; its main aim was to provide help in the form of repayable loans to small entrepreneurs operating in the informal or "non-structured" sector.

Objectives of the Fund

The FASI programme had both educational and economic objectives: on the one hand, for small entrepreneurs to familiarize themselves with modern credit tools and to try to make their activities financially viable and, on the other, for Burkina Faso to take steps towards strengthening its economic fabric while reintegrating economic players into the structured economy.

---

[a] This case study was compiled mainly from information prepared at the request of the ILO by Mr. Zaïdi, the current head of FASI.

The following *strategic objectives* were defined:
increasing national production and improving its quality and competitiveness;
— increasing the absorption capacity of the workforce and stabilizing current real jobs in the sectors concerned;
— increasing the contribution of the informal sector to national production with the aim of replacing imports;
— promoting better distribution of income for the benefit of poor and vulnerable sections of Burkina Faso's population; and
— accelerating the modernization process of a number of minor trades, the activities of which are placed upstream or downstream from the modern sector, in order to facilitate their transfer into the sphere of the SMEs/SMIs.

Specific objectives relating to economic, sectoral, technological or commercial concerns were defined with a view to:
— improving productivity, notably in the manufacturing industry;
— increasing the rate of employment of informal sector players in the urban or semi-urban environment;
— creating conditions for developing the export of products specific to Burkina Faso;
— encouraging the use of local materials and the recycling of by-products;
— promoting the use of basic technologies that are better adapted to local conditions;
— modernizing and rehabilitating large consumer commodity production sectors (shoe-shiners, grilled food street vendors, restaurant owners, fruit-sellers).

The role of the actors

The FASI was established following a meeting between the Head of State and those responsible for the social and professional sector of Burkina Faso in June 1994. The Ministry of Employment, Labour and Social Security was chosen to supervise the technical aspects, while the financial aspects came under the jurisdiction of the Ministry of Economics and Finance.

At first, the FONAPE was chosen to implement the FASI programme. However, after three years, the FASI came to need its own structure, principally because the FONAPE was no longer able to ensure its own stability (due to the non-repayment of loans to which it had agreed), and thus put the FASI programme at risk.

During 1998, the FASI was in the process of becoming legally established[a] after having operated for three years as part of the FONAPE; it became

---

[a] Decree No. 98-053 PRES/PM/METSS of 24 February 1998 on the support fund for the informal sector (*Journal officiel du Burkina Faso*).

independent from the FONAPE (which has since stopped operating) on 18 March 1998 and has its own Management Board and Budget Committee.

The social partners, who essentially represent the formal sector of the economy, have not been involved at all either with administering the Fund or with defining its objectives, but were very much in favour of such a mechanism being established.

The FASI aims were to develop a partnership with already operational ground structures (to oversee the implementation of projects) and joint, public or private bodies working in areas which are of interest to the FASI, as well as with financial backers who may view the FASI as a way of achieving specific objectives.

FASI resources

The procedure for preparing, filing and processing applications is intended to be simple and instructive.

1. A model showing the steps to be followed when presenting a project document is sent to the applicant.

   The following information is attached to the application:
   — FASI's field of intervention;
   — interest rate by sector of activity;
   — maximum amounts of FASI support according to whether the project is presented by one or more people, or an association;
   — deferred repayment deadlines; and
   — maximum credit allocation period.

2. A project promoter files his or her project document with the FASI, which duly acknowledges receipt thereof.

   The project document is processed according to the field of activity envisaged by an expert, who gives an opinion after having studied the document.

   The experts together form the Internal Technical Committee: this committee preselects the applications which meet the requirements regarding form and substance defined by the FASI and prepares them for the Credit Committee.

   The Credit Committee selects the applications approved for funding.

3. When the financing of a project is agreed, a legal and administrative file on the promoter is compiled (identity, Burkinese nationality, no financial commitments with local financial institutions, certificate of approval for associations):
   — the conditions of the loan are explained;
   — together with the promoter, a disbursement schedule (each instalment depends on the gradual implementation of the project) and the repayment conditions (length, delay, frequency of repayments) are set; and
   — a minimum security for the project is settled: joint surety bond and notarized deed for the loan.

EMPLOYMENT, VOCATIONAL TRAINING
STRUCTURING INFORMAL LABOUR

Human, material and financial resources of the Fund

At the outset, the FASI programme functioned with one person in charge of monitoring operations under the responsibility of the FONAPE Director-General together with four collection officers in the provinces. Applications were studied and on-site visits were carried out with technical support from the other divisions within FONAPE which, in 1997, comprised approximately 20 officers, four of whom were government officials seconded by various administrations pending the establishment of a specific statutory framework.

Some officials have been hired specifically for this programme on the basis of a recruitment test. However, due to a lack of funding, it has not been possible to implement a training programme. It should be noted that the absence of a regulatory framework within the FASI has made it difficult to evaluate the performance of individual officials (who come from different administrations).

The lack of specific office and computer resources has probably limited the large-scale development of the Fund's activities, but is not a major problem with regard to its objectives. There is, however, a software application for calculating loan repayments. A study of investment in software is currently under way (for accounting purposes, managing loans and assisting project studies) in order to be able to process information in a reliable manner and reduce the time needed to finance a project, thus increasing the credibility of the project with external partners likely to finance the FASI.

The continuing funding of this scheme is a crucial problem: the first (and to date only) stage of the Fund was guaranteed by the state budget within the context of cooperation between Burkina Faso and China (Taiwan). The structure currently being established anticipates the discontinuation of state funding, with the Fund being financed with the aid of the repayment of the loans that have already been granted. A triennial budget should be implemented.

Scheme evaluation and prospects

Administered by some 20 people, seven of whom have managerial status, the FASI programme was given an initial sum of 350 million CFA francs; this amount financed 166 microprojects at the rate of 2 to 7 million CFA francs per operation, resulting in the creation of 600 jobs.

The rate at which the loans granted during the first stage are being repaid is a good indicator of the success of the scheme; after one year of operation, a third of the monies lent had already been reimbursed. However, the large number of applicants for this type of loan come up against the limited resources of the Fund. Thus, 1,900 applications were awaiting funding in 1997.

Given the lack of previously set criteria regarding success, FASI officials are often asked questions relating to those benefiting from the scheme as well as to the financial integrity of the FASI. However, the insufficient financial and institutional backing of the Fund makes precise evaluation difficult.

Nevertheless, questions concerning the services provided by the Fund, its financial capabilities and customer satisfaction were examined and gave rise to the following responses when the FASI was restructured in 1998:

— gradual implementation of statutory and institutional instruments;

— downward revision of the maximum amount of aid provided;

— the need to use computers with suitable management software;

— strengthening of the collection and legal department; and

— creation of an internal supervisory department.

Moreover, the FASI Management Committee has adopted a procedural manual as part of the current restructuring of accounting procedures, expenses, client payments, asset management, the granting and management of financial aid, and human resources management.

The scheme run by the FASI is therefore interesting in that, like other micro-finance schemes in other parts of the world, it shows that it is possible to supplement individual initiative and to consolidate it at low cost, thus enabling individuals to stabilize their personal situation and permitting them to become more established in the formal economic sector.

The risks hanging over the continuation of the scheme are the result of insufficient public funding due to the narrow margins within which the Government operates, even if the method by which the scheme functions appears to guarantee a satisfactory rate of repayment from benefiting businesses. Moreover, within the present context, the FASI does not foresee a link with the implementation of a scheme to provide minimum social protection which could complement the project.

EMPLOYMENT, VOCATIONAL TRAINING
STRUCTURING INFORMAL LABOUR

297

Promoting entrepreneurship

The case of Poland

The very rapid increase in the number of unemployed people in Poland in the early 1990s, following the restructuring and privatization of the state sector, led the Government to consider that job creation by the unemployed should be strongly encouraged. This required a large-scale transformation of the employment services, which began in 1990 with the assistance of the ILO. Among the numerous activities conducted by the employment services, a system of start-up loans was made available to potential entrepreneurs and to employers wishing to hire staff.

The involvement of the Labour Ministry's local offices enabled this procedure to be effectively implemented, and at the same time its use helped to enhance entrepreneurship and also to strengthen the skills and abilities of Ministry employees.

Numerous local bodies have continued the work undertaken and complemented the Government's activities with the effect that in today's Poland, the vast majority of private activities are conducted by very small enterprises which make a significant contribution to the country's Gross National Product (GNP): the term "snowball effect" can therefore be used when referring to these activities.

EMPLOYMENT, VOCATIONAL TRAINING

EMPLOYMENT AND BUSINESS CREATION

The large increase in unemployment between 1990 and 1993 (three million unemployed at the end of 1993) pushed the labour administration services to attempt to develop entrepreneurship, in particular among young people, in order to "activate" the expenditure earmarked for unemployment.

However, unclear legislation with regard to job creation, difficulties for individuals in obtaining bank loans, high indirect labour costs, low productivity and a mentality reluctant to take business-related risks were all significant obstacles to the implementation of this policy.

The policy seeks to arrange for loans to be granted both to unemployed people wishing to set up a business and to small employers looking to recruit, as well as to encourage and train those interested in setting up small enterprises.

Its legislative framework[a] has been more precisely defined as the assessment of its application has developed. The stated aim is mainly to encourage the unemployed and small employers to create or strengthen their activities, by providing them with the financial resources to create their own (or new)

---

[a] The foundations of this framework include: Law of 23 December 1988 respecting economic activity (*Dziennik Ustaw*, 28 December 1988, No. 41, pp. 609-613); Law No. 298 respecting the privatization of state enterprises, 13 July 1990 (ibid., 1 August 1990, No. 51, pp. 695-700); and Law of 9 November 1990 respecting the expansion of privatization, as amended by the Law of 16 October 1991. Article 18 of Law No. 1 of 14 December 1994 respecting employment and combating unemployment (ibid., 6 January 1995, No. 1, pp. 1-7) defines the exact procedures and expands the scope of the framework to include workers affected by mass lay-offs during the notice period.

jobs. From the outset, the Government considered that the wave of unemployment generated by the restructuring and disappearance of state enterprises could be absorbed by the large-scale creation of SMEs.

In order to achieve this aim, it was essential to awaken the entrepreneurial spirit which had been inhibited during the previous decades.

The role of the Labour Ministry's local offices

The network of labour offices, which are decentralized authorities of the Labour Ministry, was chosen to implement this policy. Established in its current form on 1 January 1993, the network is based around the National Labour Office, whose Chairman is appointed by the Prime Minister on a proposal by the Labour Minister following consultations with the National Employment Council, and comprises 49 regional directorates and 365 local offices whose representatives are appointed at the regional level.

These services do not have any structural links with the autonomous local bodies which also develop structures to promote job creation.

This activity forms part of the tasks of the local employment services. It is not carried out by isolated individuals. The labour offices system includes 20,000 employees, 400 of whom are responsible for managing loans, but this is not their only function.

The majority of these employees have undergone enterprise creation training as part of an ILO programme designed to enhance the capacities of the employment services; they have also received other forms of technical training.

Increasingly stringent conditions for implementation

Following an initial period during which no precise criteria of eligibility for loans existed, thereby leaving local offices a broad degree of autonomy as the authority responsible for initiating the relevant procedures, the conditions of allocation have been standardized in order to avoid any failures or abuses resulting from insufficient initial processing.

The vague initial conditions gave rise to a wave of loans which were also linked to the novelty effect (there was a pool of potential entrepreneurs) prevalent in 1990, followed by a much lower regular annual flow.

Other parallel measures, designed to promote job creation and targeted at different types of people, have been introduced:

— subsidized employment in enterprises;

— measures for young school leavers; and

— vocational training for young people as part of an apprenticeship.

Since 1995, activities targeted at the most disadvantaged groups, for example the disabled, women and rural populations, have been introduced.

In each of these cases, the local offices pay the wage costs either partially or in full.

The most original activity is the start-up loan scheme for unemployed people setting up enterprises:

— general information was made widely available to users when the scheme was introduced in 1989-90;
— local employment offices take active measures to provide information and to promote activities: they explain the regulations, which have been clarified, and provide free legal and professional advice to applicants; and
— initiation training for setting up an enterprise have been provided.

The latest version of the procedures for obtaining loans, issued in 1998, is as follows:

— eligible parties: the unemployed, surplus staff, those being served with redundancy notice;
— an application is filed at a local employment office indicating the amount of the loan applied for, the planned activity, a forecast budget, the desired reimbursement period and whether any delay in the repayment should be envisaged at the beginning of the period.

The loan is calculated on the basis of the average cost of employment rather than on the basis of the projected investment cost. For each job created, a loan may not exceed 20 times the average national monthly wage. A delayed reimbursement may be granted during the first six months and the total duration of a loan may not exceed four years. The interest rate is particularly favourable, since it is limited to 30 or 50 per cent of the current interbank rate.

Where necessary, after two full years of actual activity, a loan beneficiary may ask for the amounts outstanding to be written off.

The conditions governing employment creation loans for employers are similar. A loan is based on the number of jobs created. There is no limit on the number of such jobs, but if it exceeds 20, the opinion of the local Employment Council is required. In this case, there must not have been any redundancies in the previous 12 months; however, an employer may not have the remaining debts written off, either wholly or partially.

Allocation procedure: a description of this procedure emphasizes the involvement of the different levels of the labour administration services.

A loan application is registered by a local office which verifies whether it can be accepted. It is then examined by a Committee for Employment Fund Loans, comprising a representative of the local Employment Council (a tripartite body), the head of the local employment office and a member of the team responsible for loans.

The legislative framework and procedure have been revised on the basis of the conclusions of a project conducted by Switzerland and the ILO, which has enabled the training of staff setting up individual loans to be improved and the procedure to be rationalized, in particular by defining the precise allocation criteria which were lacking, following an experiment conducted in six administrative districts.

EMPLOYMENT, VOCATIONAL TRAINING

EMPLOYMENT AND BUSINESS CREATION

Reviews are conducted by local offices during the loan period: reimbursements are effectively monitored and on-site visits help verify whether the new enterprise is actually carrying out its stated activities.

Multifaceted cooperation between different institutions

The social partners work together to verify the implementation of this policy as part of the local or regional Employment Councils which are "tripartite" consultative organizations and are peculiar in that they involve four different partners: the State, local communities, employers and trade unions. Within this institutional framework, the local communities, with a broad degree of autonomy, participate in the work of employment offices. As tripartite bodies, the local Employment Councils are involved in the loan allocation scheme.

Cooperation between the different partners interested in improving the employment situation has led to an increase in the number of authorities which promote the creation of small enterprises: the services of the Labour Ministry are no longer alone in providing start-up loans for different activities.

The introduction of start-up loans has been accompanied by a willingness to involve the social partners and, in addition, the different players, be they institutional or otherwise, of economic life. A new kind of cooperation with the local authorities has been introduced: these authorities have actively promoted the setting up of structures which continue and expand the activities of the Labour Ministry services, including the establishment of "business incubators," vocational training centres, businesspeople's clubs, guarantee funds, non-governmental employment promotion agencies, etc., and give rise to cooperation agreements between the institutions involved and local employment offices.

This network of relations has helped foster a climate favourable to the development of individual private activities. In addition to the public employment service, there are now 59 enterprise support centres which offer practical training, 31 Enterprise Development Foundations, set up by a World Bank programme, and 24 "incubators" which provide technical support for budding enterprises. It should be noted, however, that the territorial distribution of this network is uneven.

There are also the Entrepreneurs' Development Foundation, the Regional Funds, the Social and Economic Development Banks, the State Fund of Rehabilitation of the Disabled and the Agricultural Funds, all of which offer loans to stimulate job creation.

Considerable initial resources and sustained public funding

The introduction of the programme has meant that computer technology is necessary to ensure that loans are set up and managed correctly, and that legal and professional advice is provided. The creation of a database, dissemination of information, provision of statistics and forecasting have been facilitated by the setting up of a computer network which has reached a satisfactory level of operation owing to cooperation programmes conducted with the World Bank, the ILO, the European Union's PHARE[a] programme, and bilateral cooperation.

The network of local employment offices is financed firstly by the State budget and, secondly, by employers' contributions.

The Labour Fund is state-managed and is now responsible for paying benefits to the unemployed and funding employment policies. The creation of an Unemployment Insurance Fund, which would be responsible for funding unemployment benefits, was being studied in 1998.

The decline in the absolute value of the Fund's resources, from 7.5 billion zloty in 1996 to seven billion zloty in 1997, has not adversely affected the level of active expenditure to combat unemployment; its proportion appeared to have increased from 10 per cent in 1996 to 17 per cent in 1997, of which a small portion was devoted to start-up loans.

The recovery rate for start-up loans relating to enterprise activity varies between 70 and 90 per cent depending on the region, thereby constituting a marked improvement on the initial period. It may be considered that changes in prices, which are still considerable, make it easier to honour reimbursements.

Since the budget allocated to start-up loans has not been increased, this scheme appears to be well established or even to have reached a ceiling. In addition, it should be noted firstly that loans are now provided by different organizations, since the Ministry certainly does not claim to have a monopoly on them and, secondly, the economic context makes it ever more difficult to start a new business, due to increasing competition. Furthermore, the selective nature of the loan allocation procedure has intensified as employees processing applications have become better trained.

A gradually defined evaluation

On the basis of the sufficiently numerous data available showing similar trends, it can be considered that the activities conducted have satisfied their basic aims:

The number of beneficiaries of start-up assistance (jobseekers and employers) between 1990 and 1997 was around 140,000, which led to the creation of approximately 300,000 jobs essentially in the services and trade sectors. Compared to the number of unemployed (three million in 1993) which has been decreasing since 1994, this result is quite considerable. The annual number of applications ranges between 8,000 and 10,000, and the number accepted between 3,000 and 4,000.

The profile of beneficiaries is relatively homogenous. They are men between the ages of 35 and 45, with between one and 20 years' previous professional experience in a large state enterprise which has been restructured or

---

[a] European Union-coordinated aid operation for Poland and Hungary: assistance for economic restructuring (PHARE).

closed, living in a large urban centre, and who have been unemployed for more than ten months. By contrast, there are few beneficiaries in non-urban regions. The vast majority of the activities chosen are in the services and trade sectors.

The structure of Polish industry has changed radically in the past ten years: small and medium-sized enterprises make up more than 90 per cent of the total number of enterprises and, of those, 90 per cent have five or fewer salaried employees (2.4 million enterprises including 2.3 million in the private sector; 2.1 million SMEs of which 90 per cent are micro-enterprises): the SMEs employ more than half of the 11.1 million salaried employees in the private sector and contribute 40 per cent of GNP.

There does not appear to have been any precise strategic plan, the only measure being the budget made available for the scheme. However, the stated aim of the Polish Government was very clear. The evaluation criteria defined on a gradual basis have shown that this policy was effective.

No criteria seem to have been defined beforehand. However, the financial stakes of this policy have led the Government to evaluate its effectiveness on a continual basis, prompting several successive revisions of the technical regulations.

Numerous studies conducted by independent institutes on behalf of both the Government and the social partners have produced a large amount of information allowing the impact of the policy to be assessed. These studies have made a direct contribution to the successive adaptations of the scheme by enabling the Government to improve the selection of beneficiaries while making the scheme less easily accessible.

An internal evaluation process was generalized in 1997 based on local experiences. The first indicator – which is the most widespread – is the rate of loan reimbursement. Two other indicators – analysing the cases of failure and the cost of creating a new job – are not sufficiently generalized for relevant comparisons to be made between the regions.

As regards the beneficiaries: economically, they have managed to create their own jobs, enter the competitive market and earn income from their own activities; the status of the entrepreneur has been greatly enhanced. Socially, the programme has enabled them to break down the psychological barrier generated by their period of unemployment and to develop their self-confidence. The learning capacity of the unemployed in the open economy has increased. Finally, the scheme has helped to establish a middle class.

As regards the Government: the major objective of increasing the number of jobs has been achieved. The opportunity presented by the loans granted has encouraged individuals to find employment and has helped to transform passive benefit expenditure into active expenditure. In the medium term, these activities lead to a rebalancing of the budget by reducing the number of unemployed receiving benefits and by increasing the tax receipts generated by activities subject to VAT. Finally, the creation of very small enterprises is an essential basis for local development.

Ripple effects which relate directly to the role of labour administration: the enhanced ability of the Labour Ministry authorities to provide users with a service, in particular by providing legal and business management advice, together with the actual involvement of the social partners in these procedures, have led the labour administration to play a pivotal role in the transformation of the economy.

Furthermore, the labour administration has been directly involved in the international cooperation projects implemented (PHARE, ILO and the World Bank) which have provided concrete results.

The success of the scheme constitutes experience which may be of use to less advanced countries engaged in a similar transformation process.

EMPLOYMENT, VOCATIONAL TRAINING
EMPLOYMENT AND BUSINESS CREATION

Promoting employment in small and medium-sized enterprises (SMEs)

The case of Japan

SMEs play a very important role in the Japanese economy. To support them and to encourage their development so as to preserve existing jobs and create new ones, at the beginning of the 1990s the Government adopted a series of measures concerning assistance for the improvement of human resources management in the existing SMEs through business cooperatives.

Following the economic upheavals in recent years, it was observed that human resources management in SMEs needed to be improved further so that they could play a real role in employment creation; the State has already introduced a second series of measures, some of which are in the area of personnel management, so as to attract workers to this type of enterprise.

In Japan, the various levels of government – national and prefectural – provide numerous support services to SMEs in the form of subsidies, financing, guidance and advice. The various forms of support provided for in the 1991 Act[a] were intended to improve the attractiveness of jobs in these enterprises through improvements in working conditions such as shorter working hours, improved workplace environment and better social protection.

At the time, the Government believed that by preserving or even stimulating the level of activity in small enterprises which played an important role in the economy, it would contribute to overall economic revival and to promoting the well-being of workers. The gap between the levels of working conditions and social protection in large corporations and those prevalent in small enterprises was such that the latter were caught in a vicious circle: unable to provide good working conditions, small enterprises could not attract highly qualified workers; this put limits on their own development, and thus on their ability to improve working conditions to the point where those workers would be interested in working for them.

The 1991 Act was based on the conclusions of a group of experts brought together at the request of the Director-General of the Employment Security Bureau of the Ministry of Labour. In response to changes occurring in the labour market, their report raised employment security in small enterprises as the first priority of the labour market policies. The Act was passed by Parliament after consultation with some consultative bodies composed of experts and representatives of workers and employers.

This law has since made a major contribution to employment protection in SMEs. However, following the recent restructuring of industrial organizations as a result of globalization and deregulation, Japanese industry and

---

[a] Law No. 57 of 2 May 1991 respecting the improvement of employment management in small enterprises to protect the workforce (*Kampoo*, No. 61, 2 May 1991, pp. 22-24).

SMEs in particular have had to face new and severe problems, which have led to closures, production reorientation, and so on. Once again, the Government made labour mobility a top priority. Numerous measures were adopted to allow many workers to move smoothly – that is, without an intervening period of unemployment – from one industry or firm to another. A balance had to be found between facing the difficult employment situation on the one hand, and maintaining employment stability for workers on the other. Furthermore, job creation became a priority issue on account of the decline in job openings for young people, in spite of the long-standing policies designed to facilitate access to employment.

It was thus necessary to create new employment opportunities by setting up new businesses or through innovations such as opening up new fields of activity in existing businesses, given the saturation point which the labour market had reached. Small and medium-sized enterprises, which were expected to open up new fields of activity, simply found themselves unable to do so. They could not bring about the changes required without causing unemployment, and did not hire young workers graduating from the education system for three principal reasons:

— the workers themselves seemed uninterested in working in SMEs, preferring to work in large corporations;

— the SMEs' recruitment methods were not very effective; and

— SMEs had great difficulty attracting either highly qualified or highly creative workers.

To create new jobs, it was necessary to provide support to improve employment management in SMEs, in particular staffing. The Government's primary objective was therefore to create jobs by supporting the improvement of SMEs' activities in the development and motivation of their labour force and in the promotion of work in this sector.

Thus, in order to protect and develop employment and provide more stimulating jobs, the Government proposed amendments to the 1991 Act which were passed by Parliament after consultations with Tripartite Advisory Committees and experts. The amended law provides for new measures for SMEs concerning their human resource management, in addition to those already existing through business cooperatives.

The role of the leading actors

The various measures envisaged by the law are implemented by the prefectures, the Public Employment Security Offices and the Employment Promotion Corporation (*Koyo Sokushin Jigyodan* (KSJ)) – a statutory body under the jurisdiction of the Ministry of Labour, whose local offices and the Employment Promotion Centres are located in each prefecture.

The law lays down the role of national and prefectural governments as well as that of the Public Safety at Work Offices and the KSJ. Detailed information on this point is provided to the prefectures and the KSJ in directives issued by the Ministry of Labour. The law stipulates that the national government sees to the promotion of employment measures and that the prefectures apply them.

In order to obtain the greatest possible support from the social partners for the measures undertaken, the various levels of government consult workers' and employers' representatives at the national and prefectural levels when drawing up and implementing measures. Workers' and employers' associations therefore play an important role in promoting these measures.

Implementation

All this activity takes place in the context of a job creation policy. It is carried out according to specific directives issued by the national government based on the law and on officially approved regulations. The content of the directives – whether when first promulgated or amended – are the subject of prior consultation among the administrative bodies concerned and with advisory Committees on which workers' and employers' organizations are represented.

The main contents of the directives relate to:

— methods of management and employment in SMEs;

— the content of measures aimed at improving human resource management in SMEs; and

— other important aspects that SMEs should take into account in order to improve their human resource management.

The budget for these activities, which comes from the unemployment insurance fund, as well as planning and action programmes are all drawn up and approved on an annual basis.

The different stages of the process are the following:

— business cooperatives and SMEs in search of assistance must prepare a project setting out measures they wish to take to improve human resources management, the workplace environment or the education and training of highly qualified or trained staff with a view to protecting their workforce. Prefectural governments and the KSJ provide services (such as advice) to help in the preparation and presentation of projects;

— the project is presented to the Governor of the Prefecture authorized to provide assistance if the project meets the prevailing criteria;

— prior to authorization, the prefectural governments check that the project fulfils the criteria contained in basic guidelines;

— the KSJ provides assistance (budget) and advice in accordance with the rules contained in its procedure handbook to launch the project; and

— national and prefectural governments can also provide advisory and guidance services for particular projects.

The main support measures provided by the labour administration to SMEs are as follows:

— subsidies to employers for the recruitment of workers indispensable to the initiation of new activities; the subsidies help to pay part of the wages of these workers and part of the wages of extra workers for one year;

— subsidies for the purpose of improving worker skills; these subsidies are intended to pay part of the costs, such as wages during training periods, so as to improve skills through exchanges (such as secondments to research institutes or the hiring of training experts from large corporations), vocational training, etc.;

— subsidies for the improvement of the workplace environment; these subsidies cover some of the costs of services and/or of the installation of equipment for SMEs employing new workers or wishing to improve the quality of the workplace environment in respect of air-conditioning systems, lighting, work space, health, cultural activities and childcare;

— subsidies for securing the workforce; these pay the cost of research and consulting services provided by business cooperatives on improvement projects authorized by the prefectures; and

— financing for employment promotion; employers seeking to improve employee welfare through services such as housing, the provision of canteens, nursing stations or vocational training services may receive a long-term, low-interest loan.

As a rule, an employer cannot ask a third party to recruit staff for him or her without permission from the Ministry. However, as an exception, an employer can do this if the third party is an authorized business cooperative, i.e., a business cooperative whose plans for improvement of employment management have been authorized by the Governor of the prefecture. Furthermore, workers in SMEs which are members of cooperatives that have recruited personnel for them, have priority in renting property managed by the KSJ. This measure concerns workers who need to relocate in order to take up a new job and who have thus received the approval of the Public Employment Office.

All these activities are undertaken in coordination with various national and prefectural bodies – the Employment Promotion Corporation (KSJ) – and are integrated into the normal managerial and administrative activities of the responsible bodies. It is for the Governor of each prefecture to prepare and approve the improvement plans, and for the KSJ to undertake the necessary consultation with the grant-making planners, to provide advice and assistance, etc.

This policy is promoted at all levels of government through a widespread publicity campaign, including the publication and distribution of brochures.

Impact

These measures were implemented too recently for an evaluation to be made. However, the law provides that the Governor of the prefecture may require that the cooperatives and SMEs report on the progress of the implementation of the authorized improvement programmes.

Internal audits are undertaken both before and after so as to monitor the proper use of funds, and external audits, carried out where necessary by the Audit Council, are also possible.

EMPLOYMENT, VOCATIONAL TRAINING

EMPLOYMENT IN SMES

Industrial relations

Conciliation of collective labour disputes

The case of Belgium

In Belgium, conciliation of collective labour disputes is based on the principle of voluntary conciliation. It is conducted by joint commissions which are statutory bodies generally chaired by social conciliators, civil servants from the Collective Labour Relations Service in the Federal Ministry of Employment and Labour. One of the particular features of the Belgian system is that it introduces a prior conciliation procedure; in other words, the procedure is set into motion even before a dispute is declared.

Historical background

Bipartite social collaboration extended to all employers and workers in the Belgian private sector was established in 1945.[a]

The strategy of the Belgian system is based on the autonomy of the social partners in negotiating collective agreements and on the prevention and conciliation of collective labour disputes in order to maintain social harmony. The objective is to avoid any collective labour dispute and when a dispute does arise, to reach a solution acceptable to each of the parties through conciliation and thus allow the resumption of social relations in a calmer atmosphere.

The system is derived from the joint commissions established by a 1968 Act which complemented the legislative decree of 1945.[b] Article 38 of the 1968 Act assigns important responsibilities to representatives of employers' and employees' organizations, in particular:

— to conclude collective labour agreements;
— to prevent or mediate in any dispute between employers and workers;[c]
— to give their views to the Government and other bodies on matters within their purview; and
— to fulfil any other mission assigned to them by law.

Institutional framework

As the joint commissions were created by the State, they are statutory bodies which, in addition to their role of conciliation and conclusion of collective agreements, have public law powers only, such as withdrawing protection from members of company boards, or prevention and welfare boards, and

---

[a] Legislative Decree of 9 June 1945 entrenching the status of joint commissions (*Moniteur belge*, 5 July 1945, No. 186, p. 4338).

[b] Act of 5 December 1968 respecting collective labour agreements and joint commissions (*Moniteur belge*, 15 January 1969, No. 10, p. 267 ff.).

[c] The principle being voluntary and not compulsory conciliation.

the maintenance of essential services. This illustrates the Belgian system of collective relations in which the State plays a supplementary role, i.e., it only intervenes in the case of disagreement between the social partners.

In addition to the hundred or so joint commissions organized by sector of activity, there are some 60 joint sub-commissions, many of them autonomous.[a] Each joint commission or sub-commission can take account of the situation and problems inherent in a geographic or economic sector of the country. In order to follow social and economic development, and to some extent steer it, joint commissions meet with great regularity to adapt the texts of collective labour agreements or plan new measures.

In addition to their "legislative" activities, the joint commissions play a major role in cases of collective disputes in an enterprise or a sector.

One of the particular features of the Belgian system for the conciliation of collective labour disputes is that it introduces a prior conciliation system whereby the head of a company, even if not a member of a representative employers' organization, a trade union delegation or the chairperson of a joint commission may, if he or she considers it useful, ask for the convening of a conciliation panel before a dispute is declared, even if there is only threat of litigation or even a simple difference of opinion (for example, to interpret a clause in a collective labour agreement).

Responsibility for the functioning of the joint commissions lies with the Collective Labour Relations Service in the Ministry of Employment and Labour. The Service is primarily responsible for setting up joint commissions, i.e., defining the scope of their powers, examining the representative nature of the candidate organizations, appointing, by the Minister on the recommendation of the employers' and employees' organizations, the members of the joint commission and their replacement. Joint commissions[b] are generally chaired by social conciliators who are civil servants from this Service.

The secretariats of the joint commissions are made up of registrars in the Collective Labour Relations Service. They are responsible for drafting reports, preparing the texts of collective agreements and the royal decrees making them binding. Several hundred royal decrees are prepared annually.

The Service is also responsible for preparing royal decrees on the establishment and composition of each joint commission.

Apart from these activities directly linked to the functioning and activity of the joint commissions, the Collective Labour Relations Service carries out other administrative tasks and studies, such as:

— registration of collective agreements, including company collective agreements (a total of over 3,090 agreements filed in 1996);

— analysis, revision and submission of these agreements for ministerial approval when mandatory enforcement by royal decree is requested or required;

---

[a] Autonomy means that the joint subcommission can conclude collective agreements on the same basis as the joint commission without having to obtain its prior consent.

[b] Ninety-eight per cent of joint commissions are chaired by social conciliators.

— examination of requests for dispensation from the application of the regulations concerning wage bargaining, youth training and early retirement; and

— issue of opinions concerning the competent joint commission.

Methods of implementation

In the case of conciliation of collective labour disputes, the conciliation panel of the joint commission, after hearing the parties, makes a recommendation aimed at achieving a solution satisfactory to each of the two parties. If this fails, the chairperson of the joint commission, who is often also a social conciliator, may act alone as conciliator. The conciliation activity may constitute, depending on the sector, a quarter and sometimes a third of the work of social conciliators.

The recommendation of the conciliation panel or the proposal by the conciliator aims to reach a solution acceptable to each of the parties and allow the resumption of social relations and activities in a calmer atmosphere. In no case will the point of view of one of the parties be imposed on the other. Such a method would be liable to humiliate one of them, which would be prejudicial to the restoration of a healthy social climate.

The objective of the Collective Labour Relations Service is to ensure that collective agreements, which vary in length, are filed and made binding and to ensure that they are reviewed. The actual schedule is maintained on computer by the social partners. In particular, the trade unions have every interest in maintaining these schedules properly as failure to renew collective labour agreements could give rise to legal uncertainty and social instability. In addition, the Collective Labour Relations Service sets qualitative targets which relate essentially to preventing legal difficulties during renegotiations.

The service provided to joint commissions is laid down by law and is thus mandatory. It also consists of several services where officials draw up draft royal decrees and sometimes the texts of collective agreements negotiated between the parties.

The Ministry of Labour regularly publishes brochures, booklets and reviews containing information on social cooperation, the work of joint commissions and the results achieved. In addition, as the media are becoming increasingly interested in the means used by the State to maintain social harmony, information on the conciliation of collective labour disputes is increasingly made known to the general public. Moreover, as the organizations of social partners in Belgium have large staff and resources, they inform their own members about all the legal conciliation procedures, thus providing conciliation training to their members.

In the context of continuous economic growth, apart from carrying out their administrative duties related to the filing of sectoral collective agreements, social conciliators work independently in their sector, while reporting on the results of their work to the Minister of Labour and the General Administrator of the Collective Labour Relations Service. At the present time, because

INDUSTRIAL RELATIONS
COLLECTIVE DISPUTES

317

of the growing complexity of society, regular meetings[a] are held between social conciliators, the management of the Collective Labour Relations Service and the Minister's office to explain the implications of government decisions or legislation concerning collective relations and their effects on the ground. The same goes for the rulings of the courts and tribunals and the European Court of Justice.

The social conciliator is independent of the social partners, but remains subject to the authority of the Minister, under Article 40 of the Act of 5 December 1968, which provides that the chairperson of the joint commission shall exercise his or her office under the direct authority of the Minister responsible for labour. Moreover, the royal decree of 23 July 1969 which stipulates the status of the staff of the Collective Labour Relations Service, provides that in exercising their functions, social conciliators are accountable to the Minister responsible for labour. In practice, however, social conciliators enjoy autonomy because they decide on the recommendations they submit.

Most recommendations formulated by the conciliation panels of the joint commissions are the result of unanimous deliberation by the representatives of the social partners. It is exceptional for the chairperson of a joint commission or a social conciliator alone to formulate a recommendation without the approval of the organizations with which he or she collaborates; it happens only in the case of exceptional disputes.

Management of human resources

As the tasks of social conciliators were set by the royal decree of 23 July 1969, a job description is not necessary. According to the decree, conciliators have the task of preventing and resolving social conflicts. They may, in addition, be assigned to chair joint commissions. Because of the way legislation has evolved, they increasingly carry out specific tasks (tasks which are of a more administrative nature) laid down in more recent laws, as in matters of industrial apprenticeship, for example.

The Collective Labour Relations Service has a total of 140 staff, including 24 registrars. The conciliation activities are carried out by four senior social conciliators, nine social conciliators and 11 assistant social conciliators. They have the status of civil servants and are appointed by the King.

As regards the recruitment of social conciliators and assistant social conciliators, the decree of 23 July 1969 only laid down conditions of age and experience (35 years of age and 10 years' experience). As a result of social and economic change, other qualifications have proved necessary. A royal decree of 10 January 1994 introduced the requirement for a diploma alongside the age and experience conditions. For example, the candidate must hold

---

[a] When specific clarification on a particular issue is considered useful to the participants, experts from outside the labour administration are sometimes invited to these meetings. For example, a professor from the University of Liège came to talk to social conciliators about recent judicial developments concerning occupation of work premises by strikers, as well as picket lines to dissuade volunteer workers in the case of work stoppage.

an upper secondary school diploma coupled with 12 years' experience in handling social problems, at least eight of them in social relations between employers and workers, the age limit being lowered to 30 years. Alternatively, holders of a university degree need only eight years' experience in social relations between employers and workers, with the same age requirement.

Although there is no explicit training policy, social conciliators receive training through participation in seminars.

In the past, there was no system for evaluating the work of social conciliators. However, as the Belgian Government seeks to evaluate the work of all its staff, a system of work performance evaluation has been introduced for assistant social conciliators, which will ultimately be extended to the whole body of conciliators. The senior social conciliators have been given responsibility for evaluating the assistant social conciliators. Moreover, social conciliators, like all civil servants, are subject to administrative sanctions in the event of proven professional misconduct. These sanctions are imposed by the Minister of Labour.

Information technology

All collective agreements have been entered into a computer application by the registrars and the registry of the Collective Labour Relations Service. The system can be accessed by the social partners. In addition, each social conciliator has a workstation and is appropriately trained.

Partnership

The social partners (employers' and employees' organizations) are the primary players in the Belgian conciliation system. Indeed, the joint commissions are composed exclusively of representatives of employers' and employees' organizations, and are chaired by a civil servant (often a professional conciliator) from the Collective Labour Relations Service in the Ministry of Employment and Labour.

Financing

The financial resources necessary for the conciliation of collective labour disputes come from the national budget. The budget of the Collective Labour Relations Service is an integral part of the budget of the Ministry of Employment and Labour and is managed in accordance with the Ministry's financial regulations. The budget is approved annually by Parliament, and is subject to follow-up checks, as in the case of all government services, by the Belgian Court of Auditors.

Evaluation

Given the nature of conciliation work, the evaluation of the results of the Collective Labour Relations Service is achieved through political control and

INDUSTRIAL RELATIONS
COLLECTIVE DISPUTES

319

comments (Government and Parliament), for example during the debate in Parliament on the budget of the Ministry of Employment and Labour.

Results

The results achieved by the Collective Labour Relations Service are as follows:

— in 1995:   835 meetings of joint commissions (mainly to renew sectoral collective agreements);
368 conciliation meetings; and
446 meetings on other work carried out by the Service.
— in 1996:   619 meetings of joint commissions;
385 conciliation meetings;
380 other meetings; and
3,090 agreements filed.

More than 4,000 members of joint commissions appointed.

It should be noted that more than two-thirds of conciliation meetings related to prior conciliation.

Settlement of individual labour disputes

The case of Chile

Extrajudicial conciliation by appearance

In an effort to speed up the settlement of individual labour disputes and therefore to allow employees whose contracts have been terminated to receive their wages and compensation quickly, the Chilean labour administration offers employees the chance to make a claim with the labour inspectorate before the case goes to court. This practice is known as extrajudicial conciliation and involves the conflicting parties being summoned to appear so as to seek an agreement or a negotiated solution.

This practice, the procedures of which are not subject to explicit legal regulations and which results from the interpretation of various national labour law provisions, has proved to be not only judicious but also swift and economical both for employees and employers, as well as the labour courts. It has produced significant results in that 75 per cent of disputes are settled out of court, thereby reducing the number of cases brought before the courts.

This practice has been established by the labour inspectorate which has set up Hearings Units for this purpose and issued a Procedural Manual for claims and appearance hearings.

In Chile, the role of labour administration in settling individual labour disputes is based on a large number of regulatory mechanisms stemming from national labour legislation. These mechanisms make it possible to settle problems likely to arise during the execution of or after the termination of the employment relationship between an employer and an employee, and to prevent these difficulties from being brought before the courts. Extrajudicial conciliation by appearance is one such mechanism, whereby the labour inspectorate may summon the employer and the employee to appear. It falls under Article 29 of Legislative Decree No. 2/1967 relating to the creation and organization of the Labour and Social Welfare Ministry. This provision stipulates that "the Labour Directorate and its officials may summon employers, employees, trade unions or representatives thereof to appear (...) in order to find a solution to cases that may be assigned to them in the course of their duties or which would ensue from the implementation of legal or regulatory provisions, or to prevent possible disputes".

Extrajudicial conciliation by appearance has been established as a result of an internal practice of the Labour Directorate stemming from interpretation of the aforementioned Article and of a certain number of provisions of the Labour Code and provisions governing the functions of the labour inspectorate.[a] This practice has been formalized in a Procedural Manual for claims

INDUSTRIAL RELATIONS

INDIVIDUAL DISPUTES

---

[a] These provisions make it possible to exercise control and issue orders, to indicate obligatory reforms with immediate application and to apply sanctions and other penalties.

and appearance hearings drawn up by the Labour Directorate.[a] Although there is no precise standard establishing it as such, this practice ensues from a specific measure, namely the summons to appear, which is absolutely obligatory for the parties. Upon receiving the summons, they must present themselves before the labour inspectorate in an attempt to reconcile their points of view. Failure to appear is punishable by an administrative fine.

With this practice, the Labour Directorate's strategy is to arrive not only at a better application of labour legislation, but also to help redundant workers receive their salaries and compensation more rapidly after termination of their contracts, and to substantially reduce the number of cases brought before the courts. In the long term, the aim is to streamline user services and to develop a culture in which workers learn to interpret the law governing their employment relationship themselves and "find the applicable law on their own".

Article 168 of the Chilean Labour Code holds that an employee whose contract has been terminated for one of the reasons indicated by the Labour Code and who believes that the application thereof is unjustified, unwarranted and inadmissible, or whose contract has been terminated with no mention of the legal grounds, may submit a claim to the labour inspectorate before the matter is taken to court. The object of the claim is to verify the situation surrounding the redundancy, the circumstances in which it has occurred and, consequently, ensure that the worker's rights have been respected. It is therefore a method of control and as such makes it possible to note offences and to apply the sanctions laid down by legislation.

The claims are investigated by hearings inspectors belonging to the "Hearings Units" of the labour inspectorate services. In Chile, the labour inspectorate comes under the Labour Directorate, which is a decentralized public technical service and enjoys the status of a corporate entity in its own right. This Directorate is under the administrative authority of the Under-Secretary for Labour and its organizational structure is laid down by Legislative Decree No. 2/1967. The services of the labour inspectorate have public offices which provide information and set up consultations with users concerning national labour law provisions and to direct those persons wishing to make a claim. These claims represent approximately 10 per cent of all enquiries made by people using these offices. Moreover, "legal aid agencies"[b] provide free assistance to employees wishing to initiate court action. These cases concern a (non-quantified) fraction of the 25 per cent of claims that are not settled during the appearance hearing.

The Hearings Units devote most of their time to registering and processing the claims they receive. According to the Procedural Manual for claims and appearance hearings, their aim is to "obtain reconciliation as the main

---

[a] A study carried out in 1995 by two consultants (Ramírez and Jofré) to obtain the opinion of users and partners of the Labour Directorate concerning the activities of the labour inspectorate in matters of conciliation proved favourable to the Labour Directorate with regard to the procedure of extrajudicial conciliation by appearance.

[b] "Las Corporaciones de Asistencia Judicial".

method of settling differences or controversies that arise in relation to individual labour relations and, in general, oversee rigorous application of labour and welfare provisions once the employment relationship has been terminated". The other objectives laid down by the Labour Directorate are: (1) out-of-court settlement of the majority of claims; and (2) reducing the average time limit between submission of the claim and the appearance hearing by making the summons procedure more flexible and optimizing resources (the time limit was 15.5 days in 1997).

The involvement of the Hearings Unit is triggered by the claim, through which the former employee requests the intervention of the labour inspectorate to ensure that he or she receives the sums deemed owing to him or her by the former employer following termination of the employment relationship. The hearings inspector, who has complete independence, sets the date and time of the hearing and summons the parties to appear (the employee is automatically summoned to appear when he or she files a claim). The employer's summons indicates the documentation that he or she should bring to the appearance hearing for examination by the inspector and also indicates that he or she may instead send a representative who, under these conditions, should be provided with a simple proxy giving him or her the right to make a deal and to make commitments on behalf of the employer. In line with the aforementioned Procedural Manual, the hearings inspector should inform the parties about their rights and obligations, attempt to convince them of the benefits of a rapid solution and the disadvantages of lengthy litigation, and then complete the appearance procedure by sending the file to the court. The Hearings Unit is charged specifically with:

— evaluating whether social and welfare obligations have been respected by the employer when these are the subject of a former employee's claim;
— reconciling the parties concerned by explaining their rights and obligations and convincing them of the advisability of a rapid solution to the disagreement; and
— sanctioning violations of labour and welfare provisions discovered during the processing of the claim.

During this procedure, a number of facts are first ascertained, such as the date when the employment relationship began, in order to determine the length of service. This helps to determine the seniority allowance and to verify that payments for the period preceding the termination of services have been made correctly and social security contributions paid for the entire working period, as well as to ensure the payment of other charges and benefits owing to the employee, such as compensation for holidays outstanding or for public holidays worked.

At the time of the hearing, the labour inspector may intervene to confer a more solemn character on the "final discharge",[a] a document in which the parties determine the sum of allowances due and put an end to reciprocal claims.

---

[a] The final discharge is governed by Article 177 of the Labour Code.

INDUSTRIAL RELATIONS
INDIVIDUAL DISPUTES

This means that once it is signed, the obligations and rights that could be claimed will be extinguished. For this "final discharge" to have due legal effect, the formalities indicated in the standard document must be fulfilled. By submitting their "final discharge" to the labour inspector and confirming the terms thereof, the employee and the employer fulfil the formalities necessary for this instrument to become legally binding and cancel the obligations between the parties. This condition of ratification is a means of control aimed essentially at ensuring that the inspector may effectively ascertain that the rights of the worker are protected. This procedure is therefore part of the so-called protection of social rights incumbent upon the State.

The report drawn up by the hearings inspector is binding when, according to established jurisprudence criteria, the obligations that it covers are enforceable legally or by virtue of a contract, provided that the nature of the debt is determined fully and clearly without possibility of error, the method of payment for the compensation claimed is clear and that said compensation is liquid or can be transformed into cash. If the hearings inspector notes that labour or welfare legislation has been violated, he or she is required to apply the appropriate administrative sanctions to the employer.[a] In this case, the inspector must also draw up a report detailing the welfare debts.

As regards human resources management, the Department of Human Resources of the Labour Directorate has had available since January 1998 a document defining the qualifications required from hearings inspectors. This document indicates that the hearings inspector should pursue the following aims:

— contribute to solving labour disputes through mediation and agreement between the parties in a fair and equitable manner;

— allow labour disputes to be settled without initiating major legal proceedings; and

— ensure that social and welfare standards are respected throughout, be it in establishing controls or levying sanctions.

The qualifications required to be a hearings inspector are: sound knowledge of labour and welfare legislation, of administrative jurisprudence (decisions taken by the Labour Directorate) and a basic knowledge of accountancy. In addition, the hearings inspector must be able to summarize and express the result of the appearance hearing in a report, and must have good interpersonal skills. A hearings inspector must also be polite and courteous towards the parties, act fairly in relation to the interests at stake and be able to assert himself or herself so as to draw conclusions and establish agreements.

The services of the labour inspectorate are financed solely by the public Treasury. Labour Directorate officials with access to computer equipment have used, since 1999, software enabling them to register the debts ascertained

---

[a] In Chile, it is the inspector who applies the sanction and it is possible for the subject to file a claim through administrative or legal proceedings.

by the hearings inspectors in relation to agreements ultimately concluded between the parties.

The activities of and the results obtained by the Hearings Units are evaluated internally using statistical tools and externally by means of studies and surveys carried out either at the request of the Labour Directorate or by public evaluation organizations. The statistical data are collected monthly.

Internal evaluation

The results of processing claims received by the labour inspectorates are grouped statistically into three categories: "settled", "unsettled" (referred before the courts) and "unfounded, withdrawn and abandoned claims". This last category, which each year represents approximately 20 per cent of all cases, groups disputed situations which have one thing in common: there is no appearance hearing.

The number of claims filed increased from 78,504 in 1990 to 101,182 in 1997. Seventy five per cent of cases giving rise to an appearance hearing regularly end in conciliation between the parties. In only one quarter of cases, does the inspector recommend that the employee pursue the case through the courts. Between 1995 and 1997, the sector of economic activity in which conciliation was the least successful was the transport sector with a total of 72.3 per cent of claims being settled, while the sector in which conciliation was most successful was the financial sector in which more than 79.8 per cent of cases leading to an appearance hearing were settled. Claims are generally filed as a result of non-payment of redundancy money, unpaid salaries, sums owing for unrecognized statutory holidays, non-payment of welfare contributions (which are deducted from each pay period) and failure to make documentation available (which in the majority of cases means that there was no "final discharge").

The labour inspectorate registers only the total amounts paid to employees as a result of appearance hearings. In 1997, the total sum paid to employees as a result of 59,672 claims ending in conciliation was 10,530,313,322 US dollars. To conduct a more rigorous analysis of the results of extrajudicial conciliation, the Labour Directorate, in 1999, installed software for registering debts noted by the labour inspectors in relation to agreements ultimately concluded between the parties.

External evaluation

As part of an external study conducted by Ramírez and Jofré in 1995 to evaluate extrajudicial conciliation, some 30 legal aid agencies were consulted regarding conciliation activities carried out by the labour inspectorate, and 32 labour magistrates were asked to give their opinion on the basis of the cases referred to them.

In general, the legal aid agencies have a good opinion of the work of the inspectorate brought to their attention. Given the fact that the outcome of this

INDUSTRIAL RELATIONS
INDIVIDUAL DISPUTES

work, of which the agencies are aware, consists of the reports established during the appearance hearings, overall unfavourable opinion was shared by only 26.7 per cent of people questioned. A large share of the criticism (46.7 per cent) concerns the fact that the inspectors do not provide employees with clear information concerning the time limits, deadlines and jurisdictions involved in judicial proceedings; it is also indicated (36.7 per cent) that they are exceedingly brief and that errors occur in the identification of the defendant (26.7 per cent). In the case of employees who request assistance from these legal aid agencies and for whom the intervention of the labour inspectorate ended in an unfavourable result (since these employees failed in their attempt to assert their claims during the appearance hearing), it is interesting to note that, for 36.7 per cent of agencies, these employees had an average or good image of the labour inspectorate. Naturally, the majority have an unfavourable image of the inspectorate; 46.7 per cent of criticisms report that the employees perceive the appearance hearing as a useless formality and 10 per cent affirm that employees question the integrity of the labour inspectors.

The opinion of the magistrates shows that an overwhelming majority is in favour of the activities of the labour inspectors. In 71.9 per cent of replies, the appearance reports are held to be generally average or good, while negative opinions are expressed in only 6.3 per cent of cases. The most frequent criticism levelled against these reports (25 per cent) is the lack of clarity or errors. Among magistrates, 18.8 per cent even claim to have found no faults whatsoever with these reports. As with the legal aid agencies, employees calling on the courts have an unfavourable image of the activities of the inspectorate. Only 40.6 per cent of magistrates believe that employees have a good or average opinion of the labour inspectorate.

The difference in opinion between the magistrates and the legal aid agencies is due to several factors. A first explanation lies in the fact that the magistrate, who relies not only on the report but also on some other means of information, including his or her own opinion, takes into greater account the content rather than the form of the hearings report, while the legal aid agency that has to prepare the claim is also extremely concerned with the formal aspects. In the case of the magistrate, although the appearance report is not invested with the legal features of presumption concerning its content, it is evaluated together with other evidence included in the file (testimonies included), while for the legal aid agencies, this report is very often the only document used to prepare the lawsuit and establish the claim.

A study of national socio-economic characteristics (CASEN) carried out in 1996 by an independent organization at the request of the labour administration sought to explain the increase in claims and to analyse the correlation between the increasing number of claims per region[a] and certain features that might be important in each of these regions. The following variables were noted: percentage of salaried employees; percentage of contractual salaried

---

[a] From 1990 to 1997, the number of claims filed increased from 78,504 to 101,182.

employees; percentage of the working population with basic or low-level education; percentage of the working population in companies employing fewer than ten salaried workers; percentage of the population living above the poverty line; ratio of unionized workers to salaried employees; ratio of unionized workers to the total working population. The results of this study showed a significant correlation (equal to –0.5) only between the increase in claims and the number of contractual salaried employees, that is, the feature corresponding most to the filing of claims by salaried employees whose employment relationship has been terminated is the actual precariousness of this employment relationship. This study also showed that the level of education, poverty and unionization of salaried employees had no bearing, whether positive or negative, on the increase in claims.

Lastly, another external study carried out in 1997[a] by the Economic Commission for Latin America and the Caribbean (CEPAL) showed that the most significant economic growth between 1994 and 1997 took place in the transport (23.5 per cent), trade (22.1 per cent), mining development (19.9 per cent) and construction and building sectors (18.2 per cent), sectors in which the increase in claims evolves differently. Growth in production was weakest in services (5.5 per cent), agriculture (7.5 per cent) and electricity (8.7 per cent), which are precisely the sectors where the greatest differences in the number of claims were noted. Moreover, the relative frequency of the issues claimed is almost constant over the two periods comprising the period for which statistics are available; only a minor above-average increase can be observed concerning the non-respect of statutory holidays and the handing over of documentation, while there has been a remarkable drop concerning unpaid social contributions. This last result is particularly significant since, although Chilean legislation permits the employer not to declare and pay social contributions deducted from the employee's pay immediately, breaches of social welfare legislation account for 34 per cent of all breaches registered by the labour inspectorate for all its activities.

The analysis carried out by the author of this case study[b] concerning the attitude of the hearings inspectors with regard to current practice reveals the existence of two apparently contradictory bodies. The first body emphasizes the value of the appearance hearing as a means of ensuring that social and welfare legislation is respected and even talks about a "monitoring of office activities". According to this vision, the main task appears to be that of registering the sums due in a strict manner, leaving any chance of agreement essentially in the hands of the parties. The other body places emphasis on the actual conciliation work, which does not mean that the sums due are not registered, but that the inspector is given a much more active role in seeking an agreement between the parties. This latter concept, which conforms more to the aims pursued by the Labour Directorate, is the more widespread among the hearings inspectors. The fact that 75 per cent of claims dealt with at the

INDUSTRIAL RELATIONS
INDIVIDUAL DISPUTES

---

[a] *Estudio economico de América latina y el Caribe*, 1996-1997.
[b] Interviews were conducted by the author with a representative sample of hearings inspectors.

appearance level end in conciliation shows clearly that the Chilean labour inspectors are extremely effective as conciliators.

In short, the extrajudicial conciliation work carried out by the Chilean labour inspectorate plays an important role in providing an alternative, rapid and economical solution to legal disputes that may occur at the termination of an employment relationship between an employer and a salaried employee. This conciliation activity has filled and will continue to fill a very significant function in favour of salaried employees during and following the termination of their employment relationship. It also relieves the labour courts of an enormous amount of work.

Labour administration activity: The organization of collective bargaining

The case of Hungary

The Hungarian Government has introduced measures to provide facilities to users of the labour administration services in the field of collective bargaining. Since 1988, it has set up institutions and mechanisms designed to develop negotiation between the social partners.

Firstly, the creation of a tripartite body, the National Interest Conciliation Council (ICC,) helped to institutionalize a forum for exchanges and negotiations; its influence has been highly significant, even while the social partners were in the midst of restructuring.

In parallel with the creation of this institution, which was a major innovation in the post-planned economy political landscape, certain occupational sectors began to develop the practice of collective bargaining.

In addition, an arbitration and mediation service was set up in 1996 to settle labour disputes before industrial action was used.

These processes are still at an embryonic stage of their development. They have not spread to all occupational groups nor are they present throughout the country, but remain confined to the national level and to certain sectors at the moment of their privatization. Nevertheless, they illustrate the potential role of the labour administration in strengthening previously unknown procedures.

It can but be hoped that the very recent restructuring of the government apparatus, which has led to the distribution of the functions of labour administration among three different ministerial departments, will reinforce these new practices.

Note: The information provided below applies to the structures operating up to June 1998, when a new government took office and the Ministry of Labour was dismantled.

Establishment of the National Interest Conciliation Council (ICC)

In 1988, during the final period of the socialist government, a "National Interest Conciliation Council" was established at the instigation of the Government. Its membership represented the various social bodies of the socialist regime. Its objective was to develop mechanisms for social collaboration at a time when the central system of wage regulation was being abandoned, and was in particular charged with establishing an institutional framework for negotiating a minimum wage. But "the structure of the ICC did not reflect the then already emerging pluralism and its composition was strongly influenced by the heritage of the past", as noted by M. Lado in 1995 *(Continuity and changes in tripartism in Hungary)*.

During the summer of 1990, the new Government relaunched this institution and revitalized the tripartite forum as the "Interest Conciliation Council", broadening its objectives, strengthening its organization and opening up its membership to a broader range of social partners. The political and economic considerations were the same as those leading to the establishment of the first tripartite forum two years earlier. The renewal of the tripartite body was accompanied by a number of changes: it was renamed, all the existing trade unions and employers' organizations were invited to join the forum (and they did so); attempts were made to integrate the ICC into the macro-level decision-making mechanisms; and a new organizational structure was designed accordingly.

The ICC's creation was the result of an agreement between the Government and the social partners, and not of a law. Subsequently, it was enshrined in the Labour Code and its internal procedural regulations were published in the *Official Gazette*.

Other bipartite and tripartite forums for interest conciliation have also been established, in particular a **Labour Market Committee** and, for the civil service, a Public Sector Interest Conciliation Council (specifically for institutions funded by the State budget) responsible for the negotiation of public sector wages, with the civil service statute as their reference.

The ICC's basic mission is to prevent labour disputes through an institutional framework which encourages the exchange of information and tripartite consultations. The ICC has the authority to negotiate tripartite agreements on minimum wages and salary scales in the private sector. It must be consulted in advance on social or economic draft legislation of interest to the social partners and can examine the basis of such proposals, and it must be consulted on social problems of national importance. Its agreement must be obtained on decisions relating to minimum wage, hours of work, paid holidays and collective redundancies. It lays down its own operating procedures.

The Interest Conciliation Council has a secretariat and several permanent committees. The Ministry of Labour provides the resources for the secretariat to function and other ministries are responsible for the secretariats of its specialized committees. The ICC adopts its policy positions in plenary sessions, which take place at least once a month, and in smaller sessions, which are somewhat more frequent. In fact, there is a meeting of one or another of the ICC's bodies every week.

The Labour Market Committee, which was formerly one of the ICC's committees, was transformed in 1997 into the Labour Market Steering Committee. It is a tripartite body independent of the Government, and its principal mission is to regulate the allocation of employment policy funds, which are managed by the Labour Market Fund, itself an independent agency.

On account of its specific character, the ICC involves the social partners and the Government closely and directly in its management. The employers are represented by nine national organizations and the workers by six.

The fact that the Government is obliged to consult the ICC in advance makes it an unavoidabe link in the legislative process. It also has the power to scrutinize any issue which seems to come within its remit, to pronounce upon such issues, and to make recommendations.

The ICC normally plans its work on a six-month basis, both for plenary sessions and for the specialized committees. Some items come up regularly, such as government consultation on its forthcoming annual budget, bills proposing changes in taxation, and issues on which consultation is required, such as bills in the social field to be examined by Parliament. The ICC's work programmes are regularly published in the Official Gazette.

The secretariat of the ICC consists of eight officials seconded by the Ministry of Labour. The secretariats of the plenary sessions and of the specialized committees are staffed by officials loaned by the ministries or agencies involved (such as the Ministry of Labour, the Labour Market Fund, the Ministry of Finance), and are appointed on proposal by the groups.

The ICC has organized numerous training courses and study trips for its members and experts, with significant support from the Government or the European Union's PHARE programme. The ICC is a tripartite body: its members are representatives of each employers' and workers' organization as well as their advisers. The number of members varies according to changes in its regulations. Each party chooses its own representatives, which raises the question of the representation of the social partners.

The question of the representativity of ICC members has yet to be resolved. The Government has set out a series of criteria to determine the organizations representing the workers, but such a system has not yet been laid down for employers. Some mergers are expected among employers' organizations. Changes in the Government have led to changes in the list of organizations deemed to be representative.

The ICC's annual budget (40,000 US dollars) forms part of the Ministry's overall budget and covers wages and operating costs.

The ICC does not produce an annual report such as might be considered an evaluation of its policies. Nevertheless, there are many studies undertaken by independent researchers and journalists.

It should be emphasized that for the last ten years the ICC has been involved in an intense process of reflection and debate which has heavily influenced government decisions on economic and social matters. It could even be said that its interventions, especially those of the Labour Market Committee, have held back much needed economic reforms or have stopped the Government from taking decisions, preferring a broad consensus instead.

It is still too early to evaluate the relations between the new liberal Government and this singular institution.

Collective bargaining (1992): The early stages

The Labour Code, as amended in 1992, provides for the independence of each party and does not place particular emphasis on collective bargaining, even if it does create a procedure for the extension of collective agreements. It was only in 1995 that the promotion of collective agreements became one of the priorities of the Ministry of Labour. A change introduced into the Labour Code in 1995 contains a reference to collective agreements for the regulation of overtime; and the incorporation into Hungarian law of the European Directive on transfers of companies provides for the use of collective

INDUSTRIAL RELATIONS
COLLECTIVE BARGAINING

331

bargaining and the transfer of the collective agreement in case of a change of employer.

The Labour Inspectorate has the authority to check that the standards governing collective agreements are adhered to and to ensure that they are registered; the existence of a collective agreement in a company is a criterion for firms' eligibility to receive employment aid.

The conditions for the extension of collective agreements is that they be signed – by workers' and employers' representatives – and that a joint request for their extension be presented. Collective agreements may be extended by a specialized department of the Ministry of Labour, the Department of Industrial Relations.

Furthermore, this Department keeps a register of sectoral collective agreements, which are the only ones to be filed and verified. The verification relates to the authenticity of the signatures, but not their legal character.

However, the Department has no set work programme. Its limited resources restrict it to the role of registration and do not allow it to promote collective bargaining, especially in the private sector. It works in close collaboration with the labour regulation agency.

Its staff consists of six people whose responsibilities cover all matters related to collective agreements: registering agreements, advising negotiators, etc.

The Department of Industrial Relations is part of the state administration and does not have a budget of its own. It has, however, received a specific budgetary allocation in order to computerize its operations and register collective agreements.

Its main dealings are principally with the social partners. Although the latter are not themselves responsible for the extension procedure, their role is nevertheless decisive according to whether they seek to impede or support it. Thus several unions have set up training programmes in collective bargaining for their members.

Although there is no formal evaluation mechanism of the collective bargaining process, it is nevertheless possible to list the achievements of the last ten years.

There is no doubt that Hungary was the first Eastern European country to set up and implement a collective bargaining system.

A total of 27 collective sectoral agreements were signed in 1997 in industry. Collective agreements are far more numerous in the public sector: 2,000 in 1997. The extension procedure has been tried only in three sectors (electricity, bakery, and hotel and catering) and has only been concluded in two of them. Moreover, this outcome was the result of the particular situation of these sectors: since the privatization process had not yet begun, the social partners (the State as employer and the unions) had a common interest in preserving as far as possible the existing conditions of employment and wages, since in the above-mentioned three sectors, it was understood that the extension of a collective agreement would offer protection against the spread of unfair competition through the employment of illegal workers.

The weakness of employers' organizations and the fact that they do not seem to be mandated to negotiate collective agreements on their members' behalf, and the problems of union representation hinder the development of collective bargaining.

However, the social partners and the Government do seem to agree on the need to combat illegal labour: a rapid increase in such practices will only be prevented by a strengthening of collective agreements with the currently measured government support.

Establishment of a Labour Mediation and Arbitration Service (LMAS)

Created by the ICC on 1 July 1997 (regulation published in the Government's *Official Gazette*) after a long period of preparatory work dating back to 1993, and supported by the European Union's PHARE programme, the LMAS has the task of resolving labour disputes. Its objectives are to speed up the settlement of these disputes, to contribute to the preservation of social harmony nationwide and in the different occupational sectors, and to encourage the development of an industrial relations culture in Hungary.

The LMAS is not strictly speaking an autonomous institution. Its authority is based in principle on the submission of joint requests from the parties to a dispute. It maintains a list of qualified mediators and arbitrators, trained by the Service itself. It may also make recommendations in a bid to prevent conflicts.

The creation of the LMAS was not a response to the number of strikes, which was particularly low during the transition period, but rather a recognition at the political level of the need for a professional conciliation and arbitration body.

The remit of the LMAS does not include intervention in individual legal disputes, which fall within the remit of the labour tribunals, which are themselves swamped with cases despite the introduction in 1997 of the possibility of mediation in individual conflicts before they reach the courts.

The social partners are closely involved in the supervision of the LMAS, in so far as it is placed under the direct supervision of the ICC, to which it reports, but they may not intervene in its operations. Although the LMAS can offer assistance, there is no obligation for parties to conflicts to have recourse to it and it cannot intervene of its own volition. The novel character of this institution and the slow growth of its activity account for the small number of cases processed in its first two years of operation.

The LMAS has informal, but constant, links with the Ministry of Labour, especially the Labour Regulation Department and the Department of Industrial Relations, without prejudice to the rules guaranteeing its operational autonomy. Registered mediators are independent and receive no instructions, so as to maintain their impartiality.

The 98 experts registered in 1998 on the list of mediators underwent a selection procedure conducted by a tripartite selection committee (360 applicants), and satisfied highly demanding recruiting criteria: a university degree

INDUSTRIAL RELATIONS
COLLECTIVE BARGAINING

and five years' experience in industrial relations or labour law. After recruitment they undergo further specialized training. Usually they have a professional activity of their own and act as mediators when called upon by the LMAS. Their remuneration cannot exceed eight days' work per dispute. They are bound by the rules of professional confidentiality.

The resources available to the LMAS are modest, in spite of the significant effort made by the Government at the time of its establishment. Two full-time officials, a director and a secretary paid by the Ministry of Labour run the LMAS secretariat. This staff manages the work of the Service and prepares an annual report for the ICC.

The State has set aside a budgetary item for the LMAS. This contribution is approved by the ICC. This budget, amounting to some 45,000 US dollars per year, is enhanced by resources from bilateral and multilateral technical cooperation, and pays the salaries of the two permanent officials and the honoraria of arbitrators and mediators, as well as administrative costs. The National Audit Office oversees the proper expenditure of these funds.

Evaluation of LMAS's operation and effectiveness is undertaken essentially on the basis of its annual report, which is presented to and debated by the ICC, and is published.

In its first year of existence, the LMAS's level of activity was lower than expected (18 cases examined and six submitted to mediation in 1996); in fact, its main activity that year consisted of setting up and training the network of conciliators and arbitrators. Subsequently, the Service's conciliation activity grew as it became better known: 89 cases were examined in 1997, of which 62 related to collective agreements.

Most of these cases were, however, requests made unilaterally by the unions, and the Service attempted to change them into joint union-employer requests.

As in the case of collective bargaining, it is necessary to look for the causes of this low level of activity, and especially of the reluctance of employers to reach agreements with their partners, even when negotiations are conducted under the aegis of a third party. The annual report concluded that only with patience and time will the LMAS be able to exert significant influence on industrial relations in Hungary.

Before concluding, particular mention should be made of the **role of the National Audit Office**: this is the body responsible for the accounts of all labour conciliation bodies, though its remit extends far beyond the labour sector. It oversees, on Parliament's behalf, the activities of the tripartite bodies. Its role has the same importance as the Constitutional Court with respect to supervision of the new democratic institutions, except that it is mainly concerned with overseeing the propriety of public expenditure (monitoring the appropriateness of expenditures, absence of corruption, etc.) rather than being concerned with the impact analysis of the use of public funds.

On this basis, the Audit Office severely criticized the Labour Market Fund, because its members – the social partners – had not limited themselves to deciding the principles and broad direction of the Fund, but had also intervened directly in its operations, taking decisions about the allocation of resources which in the end restricted the Government's freedom of action in defining employment policy. The Fund's operating mechanisms were therefore changed in 1996 in order to restore effective decision-making power to the Government.

Conclusion

An industrial relations system has been emerging and taking root over the last decade in Hungary. Even though it has yet to be integrated into the everyday reality, especially at the local level, its development in the framework of specialized institutions at the national level, constantly reinforced by the labour administration and the international community, is an example to all countries in transition.

The role of labour administration in countries emerging from armed conflict

The case of Mozambique

The past few decades have been marked by numerous civil armed conflicts; the settlement of these conflicts – sometimes after many years of war and destruction – leads to the establishment of reintegration and reconstruction projects in the countries concerned.

In general, the urgent tasks to be undertaken relate to humanitarian assistance, demobilization of soldiers, return of population groups, employment, training, rebuilding of infrastructures, etc. A large part of these activities directly or indirectly involve the institutions working in the field of labour administration, that is, employment, labour market information (statistics), vocational guidance and training, etc.

Based on the experience of Mozambique, the following examination attempts to highlight the effective role of labour administration in the process of reintegration and reconstruction in a country emerging from armed conflict.

When the General Peace Agreement (GPA) was signed in October 1992 in Mozambique, the country's domestic situation was disastrous: the economy was almost paralysed; some 5.7 million people – nearly a third of the total population – were either displaced within its borders or living as refugees in the neighbouring countries; unemployment rates were high; and, every year, some 100,000 young people arrived on the labour market.

Following the ratification of the GPA, 92,928 soldiers were demobilized from service units, adding to the 16,000 soldiers already demobilized by the Government outside the framework of the Agreement.

Such was Mozambique's social climate when the process of socio-economic reintegration of demobilized soldiers began.

Soon after the end of the negotiations, the GPA was incorporated into the country's legal system when it was ratified by the former People's Assembly.

The GPA stipulated the establishment of the Commission for Reintegration (CORE), bringing together representatives of the Government, the National Mozambican Resistance (RENAMO) – the armed group which fought against the Government for 16 years – and of the guest countries, as well as a United Nations representative, who chaired the Commission, and representatives of other international organizations.

CORE's mission was to implement socio-economic reintegration programmes for demobilized soldiers and, to this end, to take measures for planning, organizing and regulating procedures, and for directing, supervising and monitoring the reintegration.

As part of its operating strategy, the Commission set up a small group consisting of representatives from the two parties and the United Nations, responsible for examining and debating various issues on the CORE agenda in order to best prepare its delegations.

Reintegration programmes

Programmes under CORE

CORE set up the following programmes:

— **Reintegration Support Scheme (RSS)**

Under this scheme, each demobilized soldier received 24 months' salary corresponding to his rank at the time of demobilization. The first salary was paid immediately and the rest over the 23 months following demobilization, in the area where he had chosen to settle.

The Government paid six months' salary, and the balance was covered by the international community.

— **Information and Referral Service (IRS)**

Set up by the International Organization for Migration (IOM), this service was introduced throughout Mozambique to perform the following functions:

– provide demobilized soldiers with information and advice to facilitate their access to the benefits offered by ONUMOZ (joint United Nations and Mozambique programme) and the Government; and

– provide demobilized soldiers with information and referrals on employment and training opportunities.

— **Occupational Skills Development Programme (DHO)**

The main aims of this programme, which was carried out in collaboration with the ILO, were to provide training for demobilized soldiers under the GPA and to distribute vocational kits to them. When the CORE mandate expired, the National Institute for Employment and Vocational Training (INEFP)[a] was entrusted with the task of implementing this programme.

The programme was operated by a director, INEFP's National Director for Vocational Training, a principal technical adviser, an ILO specialist, and two experts from the ILO, respectively in charge of developing training programmes and vocational kits. National experts were engaged in other fields of activity, in particular vocational training, credit and educational training.

Under this programme, 9,245 demobilized soldiers were successfully trained, 8,554 kits were distributed and 2,457 jobs were created.

— **Provincial Fund (PF)**

This fund helped pay for vocational training activities for 25,511 demobilized soldiers. Like the IRS, the Provincial Fund was coordinated by the IOM.

---

[a] INEFP, an entity with a legal personality as well as financial and administrative autonomy, was instituted by the Council of Ministers' Legislative Decree No. 37/92 of 27 October 1992 (*Boletim da Republica*, October 1992, No. 42, pp. 26-29). The INEFP comes under the Ministry of Labour and carries out its activities throughout Mozambique.

— **Open Fund for Reintegration (FARE)**

Managed by the GTZ (German Technical Cooperation Organization), FARE provided funding directly to the officers in charge of carrying out the job creation projects. It operated in four provinces.

FARE collaborated in 319 projects resulting in the creation of 8,073 jobs.

During the CORE mandate, only the first two programmes and a minimal part of the third programme were effectively implemented. The other programmes were carried out during the post-election period, that is, after the appointment of the elected government.

Other programmes

After signing an agreement with the Italian Embassy, INEFP, in collaboration with the *Istituto sindacale per la cooperazione allo sviluppo* (ISCOS), an Italian non-governmental organization, set up a project dealing essentially with vocational training and the distribution of kits to demobilized soldiers and other unemployed persons. ISCOS worked in Maputo, Gaza, Sofala, Manica, Tete and Nampula.

This NGO trained 1,598 persons, distributed 1,215 kits and subsidized 653 jobs.

Another Italian NGO, the *Comitato di coordinamento delle organizzazioni per il servizio volontario* (COSV), focused its activities on training and the distribution of kits to disabled soldiers in Maputo and helped train 149 disabled soldiers.

Coordination of programmes

When the CORE mandate expired, the coordination of activities conducted by the various officers was entrusted to INEFP, through the intermediary of the PCU (Programme Coordination Unit) at the central level and the PPCU (Provincial Programme Coordination Unit) at the provincial level.

The PCU's mandate was to ensure that the various reintegration projects for demobilized soldiers were complementary and effectively coordinated so as to avoid duplication and establish a reintegration programme.

In December 1993, on behalf of the INEFP, the Ministry of Labour signed an agreement on employment promotion with the Italian Embassy, not only for ex-combatants but also for other population groups, covering six of the country's 11 provinces and relying on a strategy of vocational training and management of small enterprises, essentially in occupations that lend themselves to self-employment. Once they had completed their training, the persons who were job-ready and determined to engage in an independent income-generation activity were given vocational kits while the others were directed towards the formal sector of the economy, either through the usual process of replying to a job vacancy or through incentives to firms (subsidized employment).

This project has been entirely managed by INEFP while the Employment Centres have implemented recruitment, selection and job reintegration into

INDUSTRIAL RELATIONS COUNTRIES EMERGING FROM ARMED CONFLICT

both sectors as well as supporting people who have found a job. INEFP used the six Vocational Training Centres available at that time to train people and signed contracts with other public and private bodies when necessary.

The project conducted with ISCOS – which was also jointly funded by the Italian Embassy (the sponsors, being reluctant to fund government institutions only, most often collaborate with a national NGO) – focused mainly on the logistical aspects, in particular the acquisition of equipment (vehicles, computers, kits and other), while the running of the project was entrusted to the labour administration bodies, at both the central and provincial levels.

It should be noted that ISCOS plays a consultative role in the fields that do not fall within INEFP's authority, in particular employment promotion. This relatively recent body does not yet have all the capacities required.

The project led jointly with ISCOS has acquired a number of vehicles and computers and financed the renovation of a few Employment Centres in order to improve the working conditions of civil servants at the Labour Ministry.

INEFP's 22 Employment Centres, located throughout the country, have continued to be in charge of placement in the labour market for the above-mentioned project and for the Occupational Skills Development Programme as well as for other situations, either as part of the process of reintegrating ex-combatants or in their everyday operational context.

The Government was represented on the Commission for Reintegration by a delegation that included Mr. Guilherme Mavila, Deputy-Minister of Labour, Mr. Alcino Dias, INEFP General Coordinator, and Mr. Francisco David Jovo, Head of the Vocational Training Department.

The Provincial Labour Directors represented the Ministry of Labour on the provincial Commissions for Reintegration.

A Labour Ministry senior official was integrated into the parallel structures of the Ministry of Labour at the provincial level, created during the United Nations mission (for example, the Information and Referral Service) to ensure that activities conducted by the said structures continue.

Selected INEFP experiences in vocational training and employment of demobilized soldiers

When the CORE mandate expired, the DHO was entrusted to INEFP under which a similar programme had already been established jointly with ISCOS and funded by the Italian Government.

As a programme funded by the international community under CORE, the DHO was under a lot of pressure to reintegrate the greatest number of demobilized soldiers within the shortest possible time in order to reduce tensions among them and maintain the still fairly fragile peace process. These pressures have to some extent hampered the usual process of studying, planning, implementing and evaluation.

The process was carried out as follows:

— Identify the occupations that would most likely result in revenue-producing activities and that were generally based on self-employment, in each area where training activities were planned.

— Select the institutions likely to provide training activities. In addition to the traditional vocational training institutions, in particular vocational training centres and technical schools and institutes, production units of all sizes and craftspeople were used, thus covering a large part of the country.

— Select professionals with solid technical skills and provide them with educational training so that they can become apprenticeship masters.

— Select applicants for training on the basis of the following criteria:

  – minimum school education required to assimilate the apprenticeship programme of the desired occupation;

  – confirmation through an interview of the willingness to comply with the training procedure and the models defined for the chosen occupation; and

  – immediate availability to undertake training.

— Provide vocational training complemented by basic concepts of management of small enterprises.

— Sell at a symbolic price a kit to the demobilized soldiers who, after successful completion of their training, could demonstrate that they were capable of creating their own jobs based on the occupation that they had learned.

A small part of this training programme was centred on formal employment, either to respond to a job vacancy or to encourage firms, through subsidized employment, to hire the duly trained demobilized soldiers for a six-month period. Their wages were paid by the programme, based on the minimum wage rate.

Many of the demobilized soldiers who were in this group became indispensable to the firms and were hired permanently by them at the end of the six-month period.

— Provide support to the graduates for one semester, after they have received the kit or after they have been hired by an enterprise, so as to provide the former with technical and management support, and to be kept informed of the subsequent progress of both groups.

— Ask and/or encourage interested institutions to grant a small fund or a credit to part of this group, in particular to people who have shown the initiative to help their business prosper.

Impact

Although the process of reintegration of demobilized soldiers can be viewed as an overall success, a number of points must be made:

— The process of reintegrating demobilized soldiers has benefited from the participation of various actors, from CORE to the NGOs, including the Government and other organizations, without any prior coordination on fields of activity, type of programme and methods of operation. Thus, a

INDUSTRIAL RELATIONS
COUNTRIES EMERGING FROM ARMED CONFLICT

number of groups were given assistance at several levels while others received none at all. The PCU later intervened in the process in an attempt to correct this lack of rational coordination.

— During the CORE mandate, state institutions were excluded from programme implementation; this gave rise to parallel structures which prevented the national institutions from consolidating their capacities in terms of resources and know-how, a situation which was detrimental to the continuity of the programmes during the last phase of the CORE projects.

— In parallel with the CORE programmes, it should be noted that a large part of the reintegration occurred naturally, within the communities where the ex-combatants had settled.

— Given the situation in Mozambique, it is important to ensure that the process of reintegration of demobilized soldiers does not go on forever and to ensure that these ex-combatants are taken care of by programmes intended for all the other disadvantaged groups, in order to avoid the creation of elite groups, which would contribute to excluding demobilized soldiers from society.

— When the programmes set up by CORE expired, the parallel structures disappeared and some of their resources were transferred to INEFP. However, given their poor state, they constituted a problem rather than a solution.

— This situation, combined with the fact that the community of sponsors had considerably reduced the funding for this type of programme, turned out to be rather constraining. Indeed, the general public viewed this reduction in funding as a lack of interest on the part of the elected Government and considered foreigners to be the only ones in a position to give such support because they had much more effective and healthy managerial methods.

— With regard to preparing staff for reintegration activities, the existing capacities were reinforced with seminars on vocational training, mostly led by ILO experts. It should be stressed that trainers as well as experts on employment and vocational training generally had the training and experience required. However, for plant workers and craftspeople destined to serve as apprenticeship masters, two-week training courses on the "apprenticeship-teaching" process were organized via INEFP's training trainers' cell (*Núcleo de Formação de Formadores*).

Evaluation

Performance evaluation in labour administration

The case of the Province of Quebec (Canada)

All departments and government agencies of the Province of Quebec have internal procedures for the evaluation of their activities and results. In the case of external evaluation, like all departments and government agencies, the Department of Labour and its subordinate agencies are subject to periodic evaluation by the Auditor General of Quebec. Staff appraisal procedures, where they exist, do not always have a direct influence on staff members' careers, but are rather used as sources of motivation and incentives to staff.

The labour administration system

In Quebec's system of government, a distinction must be drawn between agencies under the responsibility of the Minister of Labour – the majority – and those for which other ministers are responsible. Agencies under the Minister of Labour are generally grouped under two main categories according to the way they are financed: budgetary agencies, financed directly by the Department of Labour itself, and so-called non-budgetary agencies, which are self-financing. The *budgetary agencies* for which the Minister of Labour is responsible are: the Department of Labour, the Pay Equity Commission, the Quebec Building Board,[a] the Advisory Council on Labour and Manpower and the Pay Research and Information Institute.[b] The *non-budgetary agencies* under the Minister of Labour are: the Quebec Construction Commission, the Occupational Health and Safety Commission, the Labour Standards Commission and the Essential Services Council. In addition, there is an institution peculiar to Quebec, the joint committees, independent bodies (29 in all) which, under a 1934 law,[c] have particular responsibility for monitoring and enforcing collective bargaining agreements applied by decrees.[d]

---

[a] Although under the Minister of Labour's responsibility, the Quebec Building Board's data have not been included in this study because the agency's mandate falls outside the definition of labour administration contained in ILO Convention No. 150. Its mission is to ensure the quality of work in the construction of a building and, in some cases, of a facility intended for public use and safety for members of the public who have access to the building or facility (Annual Report, p. 33).

[b] The Pay Research and Information Institute was until recently an independent agency, financed by the Department of Labour, with the mandate of carrying out research and informing the public about civil servants' pay and that of other salaried employees in the main sectors of the Quebec economy. The data for this agency has not been included in this study because a law has just been passed to cancel its mandate. The mandate has been transferred to the new Quebec Statistical Institute, created by the same law. The Pay Research and Information Institute has therefore ceased to be an agency of the labour administration.

[c] Collective Agreements Decrees Act, 1934.

[d] In North America, only the Province of Quebec has a procedure of extension of collective agreements by decree.

LABOUR ADMINISTRATION AND ITS COMPONENTS

345

The budgetary agencies under other ministers are, for the Minister of Employment and Solidarity, the Department of Employment and Solidarity, Emploi-Québec (which is an autonomous service unit within the Department) and the Commission of Labour Market Partners; and for the Minister of Culture and Communications, the Commission for the Recognition of Artists' and Producers' Associations.

All Quebec's departments and government agencies have internal procedures for the evaluation of their activities and results. However, these procedures vary from one agency to another mainly by virtue of their varying degrees of independence. In the case of external evaluation, like all departments and government agencies, the Department of Labour and its subordinate agencies are subject to periodic evaluation by the Auditor General of Quebec. Staff appraisal procedures, where they exist, do not always have a direct influence on staff members' careers, but are rather used as means of motivating and of providing incentives to staff.

Internal evaluation

Department of Labour[a]

Some ad hoc evaluations are commissioned after the introduction of a new law or, for example, to verify the time taken to respond by the Office of the Labour Commissioner General. Some laws contain so-called "sunset" clauses which require the Department to evaluate the laws in question at a given time. Strategic plans also provide for the obligation to carry out an annual or specific evaluation in accordance with the requirements and specific procedures of the legislation concerned. The Department of Labour also conducts user satisfaction surveys and research, primarily to ascertain the relevance of the services provided by the Department. Lastly, the Department has a group of market researchers who go out and contact users in the regions to ask about the relevance of services provided locally. Internal evaluation is the responsibility of the Division of Policies and Research and the Division of Labour Relations. The Division of Human Resources is responsible for the implementation and monitoring of policy on performance management.

The policy on performance management is intended to ensure that evaluation contributes to the achievement of the Department's goals, appropriate use of human resources and the professional development of all Department staff. Under this policy, all staff members are given targets by their immediate

---

[a] The Department of Labour's task is: to promote the establishment or maintenance of harmonious relations between employers and employees or the associations representing them; to carry out or commission and publish such studies, research and analyses as it sees fit; to collect, compile, analyse and publish available information on labour relations, labour standards, work organization, labour markets and working conditions; to represent the Government or collaborate with other ministries or agencies on certain intergovernmental issues such as the North American Free Trade Agreement (NAFTA), the Canadian Association of Administrators of Labour Legislation (ACALO), representations to the International Labour Organization (ILO) and intergovernmental or international cooperation programmes.

superior and are evaluated on the basis of the results achieved. Performance evaluation is a continuous process which requires constant communication between the manager making the evaluation and the employee, so as to allow regular appraisal of the results achieved and to take remedial action in a timely manner.[a]

Pay Equity Commission[b]

As this commission has only recently been set up and is of modest size (three commissioners and about 20 staff), the concern for evaluation exists but it is carried out by the Commission itself. The commissioners and the management committee made up of the heads of department carry out the internal evaluation themselves. The method used is monitoring rather than evaluation. Based on the minutes of the Commission and the management committee, the Secretary of the Commission records on a management chart the instructions for what has to be done, by whom and when.

Quebec Construction Commission[c]

The internal evaluation section evaluates the activities of the Commission and the customer coordination section evaluates its own service provision. As in the Pay Equity Commission, the method used is monitoring. However, the Construction Commission carries out a review of its activities, drawing up a balance sheet of its operations within the framework of government strategic planning as well as defending its budget in the National Assembly.

Occupational Health and Safety Commission[d]

Evaluation of activities is the responsibility of a project evaluation section in the Planning Department. In addition, the Division of Statistics and Information Management is responsible for the internal audit of operations and

---

[a] Source: *Policy on performance management for civil servants* (CT 157 191 of 25 June 1985, adopted 25 January 1993), pp. 1-2.

[b] The Pay Equity Commission's task is to "monitor the establishment of pay equity plans and ensure the maintenance of pay equity" in Quebec. For this purpose, the Commission is assigned several functions: assistance to enterprises through the development of tools and support for employees involved in the pay equity process; information to clients affected by the Act, i.e. employers, male and female employees, women's groups and the general public; research, studies and advice to the Minister on all matters related to pay equity; handling disputes and complaints from employees and employers to encourage a settlement between the parties; powers of investigation.

[c] The Quebec Construction Commission monitors the maintenance of coherent labour relations and is responsible for workforce management in the industry. It is also responsible for the introduction of an integrated system of vocational training and qualifications, and administers the universal social benefits scheme.

[d] The functions of the OHSC are to propose and implement policies relating to the health and safety of workers so as to ensure better working conditions. The OHSC is accountable to the Government for the occupational health and safety plan. For this purpose, it runs programmes on prevention and the compensation scheme for victims of industrial accidents and of occupational diseases.

EVALUATION

LABOUR ADMINISTRATION AND ITS COMPONENTS

347

monitoring of activities. Finally, section XII of the Commission's Rules of Procedure provides for an audit committee composed of two representatives each of the employers and the employees. The audit committee reports to the Executive Board and ensures that the financial statements give a true and fair view of the Commission's financial state of affairs, activities and results.

The internal management information system provides information on monthly variations in the number of compensation payments in the form of summary indicators. Regional parameters are also evaluated. The Project Evaluation Section in the Planning Department seeks to improve services and programmes and helps managers to identify ways of improvement. The section also provides for the evaluation requirements of the units themselves for the purposes of short-term evaluation of their actions. The evaluations focus on the quality of service provision to users, reducing the costs of the scheme and improving productivity.

The Commission also evaluates services by indicators for compensation payments, the number of injuries and payments for medical treatment. It carries out surveys among its staff (using the Intranet), customer surveys and focus groups. Finally, the audit committee studies the report of the internal audit division and the Auditor General, and the follow-up actions taken.

The OHSC does not have its own staff appraisal scheme. The evaluations carried out are the same as those for the Quebec civil service. Each manager is responsible for completing an annual evaluation form for each staff member.

Labour Standards Commission[a]

This body has probably one of the most developed systems of evaluation of activities and results of all those studied. The Division of Quality Control and the Division of Internal Audit are responsible for internal evaluation. Staff evaluation is left to the discretion of each service manager.

The Commission has two main internal evaluation systems: performance reports and quality assurance. Performance reports cover 15 topics, including:
— management;
— relevance of activities;
— adequacy of resources;
— achievement of expected results;
— evaluation of customer satisfaction;
— service unit costs;

---

[a] The role of this Commission is to monitor the introduction and application of labour standards in Quebec, i.e., the system of minimum working conditions, and the application of the *National Holiday Act*. In order to play its role effectively, the Commission must provide clear and consistent information to the public, deal with employees' complaints quickly and promote fair settlement of disputes between employees and employers with a minimum of delay. Finally, the Commission must formulate recommendations to the Minister for more effective application of the *Labour Standards Act*, the *National Holiday Act* and a number of regulations.

— productivity;
— secondary effects;
— working environment, etc.

Senior managers must report on their respective services three times a year. A guide to communication of performance evaluation was produced for this purpose some years ago.

The second system is quality assurance. Since December 1996, the Commission has had ISO-9002 certification. A customer service contract, which sets out precise standards, is now applied. The Commission's specific commitments to its customers contained in the contract are not only targets to be achieved but also indicators of success. Checks are made to see whether the various types of complaints are dealt with in the specified and published time limits, and whether the list of open cases is in line with forecasts. It is also possible to provide productivity indicators in terms of the number of cases handled by each staff member per year and to monitor those numbers. The data prove very useful in evaluating the costs of processing the various types of complaints submitted and the legal proceedings instituted by the Commission.

As well as other forms of evaluation, the Labour Standards Commission uses various types of customer and staff surveys. Two such surveys[a] were conducted recently, as well as checks on customer satisfaction with the information service and arbitration services. In addition, the Customer Relations Service deals with complaints from customers about the quality of service provided by Commission staff. Finally, team leaders regularly check the quality of information provided by each employee in customer services. In addition, to ensure and continually improve the quality of the arbitration service, a survey in the form of a questionnaire is given to the parties by the arbitrator after the proceedings.

In the case of staff evaluation, the Commission does not have any specific policy. Staff appraisals, which are left to the discretion of individual service managers, take place once a year using a form similar to that of the Quebec civil service.

Essential Services Council[b]

Given the agency's small size, the method of evaluation is simple and direct. The Chairman and Managing Director carries out the internal evaluation himself, sometimes calling in external consultants to ascertain better the views of the staff. The Council evaluates activities through staff meetings and a periodic report on its activities, as well as emerging trends. By systematically

---

[a] A survey on the working environment, using a questionnaire distributed to staff, and a survey on customer satisfaction.

[b] The Council is primarily an administrative tribunal with the mandate of ensuring that the public continue to enjoy at all times the services considered to be essential and to which they are entitled, in particular when workers exercise their right to strike in certain public services and in health and social service institutions.

EVALUATION

LABOUR ADMINISTRATION AND ITS COMPONENTS

reviewing all the Council's services, the Chairman and Managing Director is able to see if the targets have been met. The principle of self-assessment is also used.

In the case of staff evaluation, the Council systematically conducts annual interviews with all staff and Council members. The Minister of Labour conducts the evaluation of the Chairman and Managing Director.

Department of Employment and Solidarity[a]

The Department of Employment and Solidarity has its own evaluation methods. However, in exercising its mandate relating to the administration of active employment measures, it is also subject to a special evaluation procedure laid down in the Canada-Quebec Agreement. The Division of Research, Evaluation and Statistics, the Division of Employment Promotion and departmental heads within the Department are responsible for internal evaluation.

The Department evaluates the achievement of its targets and the effectiveness of its programmes by submission of reports, by user surveys, by conducting on-site evaluations at the point of delivery of services and by compiling information provided by the office of information and complaints. Finally, the Department also evaluates the effectiveness of employment measures.

In the case of staff evaluation, the Department has adapted the civil service evaluation standards. The evaluation thus covers performance, respect for confidentiality of information obtained by officials according to the code of ethics and, bearing in mind the sums of money involved in the Department's work, the integrity of the staff.

External evaluation

There are two main types of external evaluation. First, there is the evaluation common to all departments and government agencies, carried out by the Auditor General of Quebec. He/she is directly responsible to the National Assembly, which gives him/her great authority and independence. The Auditor General's mandate extends far beyond financial audit. Secondly, there is the evaluation conducted by various external agencies, at the request of certain bodies, either for specific reports, or financial audits. This applies particularly

---

[a] The Department's function is essentially to promote the development of manpower and employment and to combat poverty. More specifically, it has the mandate of promoting the economic and social inclusion of individuals by: promoting employment and the development of manpower; providing financial support to people with insufficient resources; and providing resources aimed at promoting social integration of individuals. This mission accounts for the two main elements of its actions: firstly, it provides overall administration of programmes related to the labour market (recruitment, proactive measures, vocational guidance, skills acquisition) for both the unemployed and people who have a job but wish to change; secondly, it administers social assistance programmes and pays benefits to those on welfare. The unification of these two major elements within the same Department is intended as a firm expression of the will to promote the return to employment of the most deprived.

in the case of the Quebec Construction Commission and the joint committees, which are outside the scope of the Auditor General. They must submit annual financial statements audited by a recognized firm of accountants to the Department of Labour.

The Auditor General of Quebec

The Auditor General of Quebec is appointed by the National Assembly for a term of ten years, on the proposal of the Prime Minister, which must be accepted by two-thirds of the members of the National Assembly. The Auditor General is responsible exclusively to the National Assembly and can only be removed by it. He/she has the necessary latitude in carrying out audit work and decides the content of his/her report. This discretion applies to any matter related to his/her audit or investigation, and to any opinion on the financial statements or documents containing financial information.

What distinguishes the Auditor General from other government sector auditors is that he/she is not part of the Administration and is exclusively at the service of the National Assembly. His/her work can be compared to that of the external auditor of a company who reports on decisions taken by the management to the board of directors and to the shareholders. In the same way, the Auditor General reports on government administration to the National Assembly.

Mandate of the Auditor General

The Auditor General's mandate is to verify the optimal use of resources and to look at the methods established to manage resources in an economic and efficient manner, and to evaluate the effectiveness and existence of management structures. The Law on the Auditor General defines economy, efficiency and effectiveness. *Economy* means the acquisition, at the best price and in a timely manner, of the financial, human and material resources of appropriate quantity and quality. *Efficiency* is the transformation of resources into goods and services for the best productivity. *Effectiveness* means achieving to the maximum degree the objectives or other goals of a programme, an organization or an activity.

The Auditor General's work thus covers all government departments, agencies and enterprises. He/she can also audit the use of any subsidy granted to an establishment, institution, association or enterprise. The Auditor General audits the majority of government agencies and enterprises. In the case of other entities audited by a private firm, the Auditor General has the right of review to ensure a degree of uniformity of information submitted to the National Assembly.

Financial profitability is not the only evaluation criterion for the performance of such agencies and enterprises. The accountability of these agencies and enterprises to the shareholder, i.e., the Government, may extend beyond financial appraisal. They are also subject to verification of compliance and, in some circumstances, to maximization of resources.

EVALUATION
LABOUR ADMINISTRATION
AND ITS COMPONENTS

351

Report of the Auditor General

The Auditor General's report indicates any matter or case arising from his/her audit or the exercise of his/her right of review which, in his/her opinion, should be brought to the attention of the members of the National Assembly. The Auditor General also informs the heads of the audited entities of his/her main findings. In the report, the Auditor General sets out his/her audit findings and adds any recommendations he/she considers appropriate in order to bring about improvements in the management. The recommendations indicate the objective to be achieved. The Auditor General is not, however, responsible for enforcing the procedure necessary to give effect to the desirable improvements. The Auditor General may be questioned on his/her report by a parliamentary commission, under the rules of procedure of the National Assembly.

The report of the Auditor General on the financial statements of the Government (Public Accounts) and of government agencies and enterprises audited by him/her, takes the form of an opinion. This is based on an audit carried out in accordance with generally accepted auditing standards. The opinion also focuses on the compliance of the format with accounting principles in force in government administration and on the consistency of their application. In addition, the Auditor General expresses an opinion on their appropriateness.

The Auditor General's methods of work

The Auditor General has developed an integrated planning process which covers his/her mission, the nature of his/her audit procedures and the type of work required. The certification of financial data, exercise of the right of review and the examination of the annual reports of entities all involve annual audits. Other audits, such as compliance, optimization of resources or use of subsidies, are carried out as priorities permit. Such audits may be carried out on a sectoral basis or in the context of a government mandate when the audited activities and the types of audit apply to several entities. The Auditor General gives priority in his/her audit work to sectors with the greatest scope for improvement.

Consequences of evaluation

In the *Department of Labour*, internal and external evaluations are used to redirect the Department's objectives and priorities and to check whether targets have been met. They can also lead to proposals for changes in the law, or serve to establish a restructuring plan or adjust targets in the light of budget cuts. Staff evaluations allow opportunities for promotion or performance bonuses.

In the *Pay Equity Commission*, internal and external evaluations provide evidence of efficiency. The methods used allow swift adjustment of targets based on decisions taken by the Commission and also provide rapid information to employees.

In the *Quebec Construction Commission*, a marked increase can be seen in the number of appeals handled by the agency and its clients receive a reply more promptly than was the case previously. There has also been an improvement in methods. Internal and external evaluations often become priorities in improving the agency's efficiency and effectiveness. The Chairman and Managing Director regularly asks for follow-up reports on the effects of the evaluations.

In the *Occupational Health and Safety Commission*, the evaluations allow comparisons with other government agencies which also have a role in paying compensation to the public, such as the Quebec Automobile Insurance Company, the Quebec Health Insurance Board and the Quebec Pension Board. These comparisons have a bearing on customer relations and procedures, and also involve agencies in the Province of Ontario. They are all aimed at reducing paper and administrative procedures and making customer relations more friendly. The Commission has introduced a programme of continuous improvement of customer reception, and measures aimed at taking greater account of the needs of cultural communities.

In the *Labour Standards Commission*, performance audits provide information to the Commission and allow adjustments where the need is felt. They can lead to administrative reorganization or modifications to the Commission's goals, objectives, methods and procedures. The introduction of a quality assurance system and ISO-9002 certification is being watched with interest by many government agencies. Information and training sessions have therefore been provided to various federal and provincial government agencies. The Commission regularly submits reports and recommendations to the Minister of Labour. Several of its recommendations have already resulted in changes in the law or an extension of its scope. Finally, the performance audit has little influence on the career of staff members. In this regard, it serves more as an incentive and source of motivation to staff.

In the *Essential Services Council*, evaluations keep the Council informed about the status of all the items under scrutiny and whether the objectives have been attained or not. The evaluations pointed to an increasingly judicial nature of proceedings. Toning down this tendency seems a more promising path and the Council's recommendations reflect this opinion. Staff evaluations also demonstrate an employee's potential for future promotion.

In the *Department of Employment and Solidarity*, internal and external evaluations provide evidence of efficiency since they give an accurate view of the Department's staff, measures and programmes. The resulting recommendations, relating to both departments and individuals, have an impact on the subsequent career of staff, since a poor evaluation could prevent the promotion of a professional to a management post. However, given the ageing of the Department's staff, a good evaluation does not necessarily lead to promotion up the salary scales, because most staff are already at the top rate. In the case of the organization and functioning of the administration, the evaluations can lead to administrative reorganization and adjustments to programmes, or the development of new programmes that better reflect customer needs. Specific

EVALUATION

LABOUR ADMINISTRATION
AND ITS COMPONENTS

353

recommendations for implementation elsewhere may also be derived from the evaluations. This is the case with checks on people dependent on income support and the agreement on active measures financed by the Federal Government and the other provinces. The Department of Employment and Solidarity publishes its findings and remains receptive to what is being done in other provinces or countries in order to improve its own methods. The Department also receives observer missions from other provinces and countries who come to see what is being done.

Organization of internal evaluation: The General Inspectorate of Social Affairs (IGAS)

The case of France

> The French Ministry of Labour has an internal evaluation body which, since 1967, has been merged with the health and social affairs inspectorate: the General Inspectorate of Social Affairs (IGAS).
>
> This body is charged with evaluating the operation and the policies carried of the Ministry. It examines, either on the Minister's instructions or as part of its own annual agenda, the policies' relevance in the fields of labour and employment or vocational training, and of health and social affairs, as well as the operation of the public or private bodies responsible for implementing these policies.
>
> Thus, in 1996, IGAS carried out a survey of the decentralized services of the Ministry of Employment, entitled "The transfer of services of the Ministry of Labour".

IGAS was established in 1967.[a] It is a monitoring, evaluation and assessment body which looks not only into the Ministry(ies) of Labour and Social Affairs (there may be one or several depending on changes in the composition of the Government), but also into various parapublic organizations, or even those which are legally independent of the Ministry but which receive public funds or appeal to the generosity of the public in order to carry out the duties entrusted to them.

A 1996 Act[b] established that IGAS's powers of intervention covered all institutions in the field of social services, including charity associations, and gave legal status to the annual report procedure.

IGAS is generally charged with evaluating public policies implemented by the social services ministries. It monitors public or private bodies responsible for providing social protection in the broadest sense of the word. It also carries out surveys that inform the Government about the current situation and enable proposals to be made concerning changes in public activities. It also carries out assessments of the internal operation of the services concerned, upon their request.

A think tank was set up in 1999 to examine the methods of evaluating managerial and executive staff and promotion proposals. Until 1999, these activities were carried out together with the technical directorates concerned.

Being a general inspectorate, IGAS occupies a special place in the organizational chart of the social services ministries: it depends directly on the Minister. Therefore, it has no hierarchical link with the ministerial technical services which could restrict its freedom of judgement. Nevertheless, it is not

---

[a] Decree No. 67-390 of 11 May 1967 on bringing the general inspection services of the Ministry of Social Affairs under the General Inspectorate of Social Affairs (*Journal officiel de la République française, Lois et Décrets,* 14 May 1967, p. 4805 ff.).

[b] Act No. 96-452 of 2 May 1996 respecting health, social and statutory measures (ibid., 29 May 1996, No. 23, pp. 7912-7922).

EVALUATION

LABOUR ADMINISTRATION AND ITS COMPONENTS

an independent or autonomous agency and its officials are employees of the labour and social affairs administration.

IGAS has a small structure comprising a few "permanent assignments" such as that of "methodology training". However, the majority of its activities are organized in the form of assignments lasting several months and which do not take the particular specializations of its members into account.

Moreover, IGAS inspectors are placed under the authority of the Supervisory Committee for Mutual Companies and Provident Institutions, an independent administrative authority, in order to help the Committee carry out its own on-site monitoring. This activity is becoming more and more important.

A follow-up committee examines the consequences of the recommendations made by the inspectors approximately one year after the filing of their reports.

IGAS may also intervene at the request of the Prime Minister or other members of the Government, but may not initiate by itself an investigation that would fall outside its jurisdiction.

A wide field of intervention

IGAS assignments are determined by the texts under which it was established. These texts also set out the powers of the inspectors; in particular, the latter have free access to all State administrations and public organizations, services, establishments or institutions falling within the scope of IGAS. These bodies are required to offer their assistance.

Each year, the head of IGAS defines the programme of activity in collaboration with the central administration heads and on the basis of the observations made in previous years. This annual programme is approved by the Minister(s) of Labour and Social Affairs.

In addition, specific assignments are decided by the Minister when there is a major malfunction in a service or institution falling under IGAS jurisdiction. IGAS may also be entrusted with a joint inspection assignment with another of the state inspection services such as the General Finance Inspectorate, the General Administration Inspectorate and the General Inspectorate of Judiciary Services.

Finally, an annual report is published which recounts part of the activities and results of the work carried out by IGAS.

In order to assess the operation of a service or system set up by the authorities, IGAS inspectors carry out an evaluation following a traditional method: interviews with those in charge of the system being investigated, interviews with the officials charged with its implementation, and most often with those benefiting from the services, examination of administrative and accounting documents, reconciliation of different sources of information, a possible statistical survey followed by the drafting of a provisional and confidential report. This report mainly puts forward proposals aimed at improving the system or disposing of it if it is clearly ineffective with regard to the objectives set. The report is submitted for comments to those in charge of the system.

Once these have been recorded, the report is referred to the requesting party (usually the Minister of Labour) who may then take decisions on the basis thereof. As a rule, IGAS reports remain confidential, in particular when they involve judicial procedures. The Minister may decide to have them published or circulated among the people or organizations concerned.

Until 1999, IGAS also participated in the process of evaluating officials in charge of the decentralized employment and social affairs services. IGAS inspectors conduct in-depth staff interviews based on an evaluation rating; assessments are moderated to take account of possible bias on the part of the assessor. These evaluations mainly take place when an official is put forward for promotion. They may also be requested by an official who feels that he or she has not been fairly evaluated by the manager during an annual appraisal.

This procedure is carried out in close cooperation with the labour administration and social affairs administrative directorates and with all the central and regional services working in the field of labour and social affairs.

Today, the role of IGAS in the evaluation of those in charge of the decentralized labour and social affairs services is being re-examined. The reform of this procedure, in consultation with those responsible for managing the employees being evaluated, should lead to a better assessment of the capabilities of this managerial staff.

Specialized and highly qualified personnel

IGAS officials are senior civil servants belonging to a body specialized in evaluation and monitoring assignments. The General Inspectorate of Social Affairs was given independent status in a 1990 decree.[a]

IGAS officials, classed in the upper echelons of the French civil service, are divided into three levels: deputy inspectors, inspectors and general inspectors. There are around 80 in current service; half of them are graduates of the *Ecole nationale d'administration* (ENA) – training college for senior French civil servants following recruitment through a competitive examination – while the rest are employees of the other social services ministries: the labour inspectorate, the decentralized departments of health and social affairs, hospital directors, etc.

The performance of inspectorate officials is evaluated by the head of the service under the usual conditions for evaluating managerial staff employed by the Ministries of Social Affairs. The evaluation may affect their premiums.

In addition to the training offered to all officials employed by the Ministries of Social Affairs, IGAS inspectors benefit from a training programme in

---

[a] Decree No. 90-393 of 2 May 1990 on the special status of the General Inspectorate of Social Affairs (*Journal officiel de la République française, Lois et Décrets*, 13 May 1990, No. 111, pp. 5742-5746).

line with their duties both when they initially take up their post and subsequently according to their needs, notably with regard to all matters concerning accounting procedures within the organizations being monitored, a large number of which follow those in the private sector.

Inspectors who have recently joined the service are assisted by their more experienced colleagues when undertaking field assignments and are appointed deputy to the head of IGAS according to a rota, thus acquainting them with all the activities of the service.

Human and budgetary resources

IGAS is administered by the head of the service who is assisted by an administrative team of around 30 officials. IGAS as a whole employed some 120 officials in 1998.

The uniformity of the body and its limited numbers allow staff management based on retirement forecasts to ensure a good balance in the age pyramid. The scope of this practice is, however, limited by strict budgetary constraints with regard to staff.

In order to carry out their duties, inspectors have access to modern tools (laptop computers, document databases, Internet access, and so on) but the activities of IGAS are not organized in accordance with these techniques.

IGAS has a running budget corresponding to the number of authorized positions. Given the nature of its assignments, the budget for travel expenses per official is greater than in other sectors of the Ministries of Social Affairs. Since it is not a body which provides public money, it does not have an operational budget.

The use of its budget is subject to ordinary public accounting procedures (this is the responsibility of the financial comptroller appointed by the Ministry of Finance, as in every ministerial department).

The social partners are not involved in the operation of IGAS on the organizational level. However, on the national level, the employers' and workers' organizations are in regular contact with the Minister. They may draw the Minister's attention to any difficulties arising from the operation of services or concerning any policy which has been unsatisfactorily implemented in order to prompt intervention by IGAS.

Annual report

The IGAS annual report is drawn up by the operational inspectors and coordinated by the head of the service. The topics discussed in the annual report may give rise to a summary of several investigations on various aspects relating to the main subject of the report. The report also takes up selected excerpts of the work carried out during the previous year.

Since the beginning of this publication procedure (1962), all the issues falling within the purview of the social services ministries and other institutions in this field have been regularly investigated by IGAS.

Its intervention generally remains an internal affair concerning only the administration and the organizations under scrutiny. Nevertheless, certain in-depth investigations have had considerable repercussions for the general public: in the field of employment, the 1994 study on the merging of the two organizations responsible for placement and unemployment compensation gave rise to the establishment in 1997 of a "one-stop service" for the compensation of jobseekers who were previously obliged to complete the same bureaucratic formalities with both organizations. As regards charitable projects in the field of medicine, a thorough investigation of a fund-raising agency for cancer research became notorious when it gave rise to legal proceedings for embezzlement.

The permanent nature of the evaluation and monitoring tasks assigned to IGAS and the regularity of its reports, which are made public and produced annually, guarantee its function of internal evaluation and give it a certain standing in the eyes of the Minister(s) of Labour and Social Affairs.

Evaluation in labour administration

The case of the United Kingdom

These elements are taken from Jason Heyes'[a] study of the national system of labour administration carried out for the ILO in 1998 and updated in 1999. They show that the evaluation of services provided by the labour administration was introduced as a major indicator of the "new administration" in order to make it more accountable to its users, the "clients". The UK labour administration is characterized by a fragmentation of its functions in several ministerial departments and a great number of parapublic bodies.

There is, in particular, a great diversity of evaluation mechanisms. Evaluation can be either internal, that is, conducted by the internal services of the entity involved, or external, conducted by another administration department, or even completely outside, that is, conducted by a private firm. The growth of evaluation is not specific to the field of labour administration. Indeed, these procedures have been developed in the entire UK administration system at the same time.

However, it is still too early to judge whether the systematic use of evaluation has had positive effects on labour and employment services in the United Kingdom.

Introduction

The principles of departmental management introduced by the Conservative Government in the 1980s and 1990s placed emphasis on the promotion of "economy, efficiency and effectiveness".

Efficiency reviews, designed to reduce operating costs and promote more effective management, were introduced in 1979. These were accompanied by "fundamental reviews" designed to force departments to consider whether activities should be continued or whether they should be delivered through new organizational structures. The Financial Management Initiative (FMI), introduced in 1982, gave departments responsibility for the management of budgets and activities.

Increasing emphasis has been placed on the identification of objectives and targets in an effort to import elements of private sector practice into government. The rhetoric of delegation and greater accountability has accompanied these developments, although doubts have been raised about the extent to which effectiveness in public service provision and policy-making has been encouraged. Thus, Williams[b] maintains that:

> ... in practice it has often proved problematic to establish objectives and targets in relation to policy work which contain sufficient rigour and quantification to be useful, but sufficient flexibility to cope with the uncertainties and rapid changes characteristic of such work. The result is increasing emphasis on those elements of the work

---

[a] Jason Heyes: *Labour administration in the United Kingdom*, ILO 2001, GLLAD/Department for Government and Labour Law and Administration, p. 78.

[b] N. Williams: "The changing face of Whitehall: Open government, policy development and the quest for efficiency", in *Political Quarterly*, Vol. 69, No. 9, pp. 258-266.

which better lend themselves to such approaches, creating potentially perverse incentives to focus on what is capable of being measured and managed at the expense of what may be more important but is less certain and less capable of being planned in advance.

The Conservative government also introduced principles of "market testing" which called upon departments and agencies to select activities which could potentially be contracted out to external providers.[a] The real estate maintenance function of the Department for Education and Employment (DfEE) represents one example of a service which has been contracted out.

From 1995 to1997, government departments produced Efficiency Plans and submitted these to the central Efficiency Unit. The Efficiency Plans provided a statement of aims and objectives for the subsequent three-year period and indicated how these were to be achieved within the budgets set, including the areas where efficiency savings might be made. With the 1997 election of the Labour government, the requirement to produce Efficiency Plans was dropped. The Government has instead focused on efficiency savings in the context of a Comprehensive Spending Review. Completed in 1998, the review has determined expenditure levels for the period until the next general election.

Principles of resource accounting that are currently being implemented should simplify the process of identifying departmental assets, such as property and land, for potential sell-off. By the new millennium, departments will have to present end-of-year financial statements on an accrual basis, providing an account of revenue and expenditure including the values of current assets and liabilities. Resource accounting will also require departments to produce an analysis of their spending according to both financial and *non-financial* objectives. It represents the latest in a string of initiatives aimed at improving value for money in service provision.

Internal evaluation methods

The Citizen's Charter programme

Originally introduced by the last Conservative government, the Citizen's Charter attempts to establish normative standards for public services. The Charter, which applies to public services at both local and national levels, identifies performance principles in six areas: *standards* (including the setting and monitoring of standards and the publication of actual performance); *information and openness*; *choice and consultation* (particularly with end-users); *courtesy and helpfulness*; *putting things right* (including the rapid provision of a full explanation for why things went wrong); and *value for money* (emphasis on efficiency, economy and effectiveness combined with independent validation of performance).

---

[a] R. Pyper: *The British Civil Service*. London, 1995, Prentice Hall/Harvester-Wheatsheaf.

EVALUATION

LABOUR ADMINISTRATION AND ITS COMPONENTS

The Citizen's Charter programme itself is being re-launched by the Labour government and this is likely to have an impact on the evaluation process.

In April 1997, six central government standards of customer service were introduced for all government departments. While these are intended to apply to the services which departments provide directly to the public, they can also apply to specialist services, such as those delivered through the DfEE's Overseas Labour Service. Those services which are delivered indirectly (e.g., through Jobcentres and Training and Enterprise Councils (TECs)) are covered by the standards of customer service adopted by those organizations. There is an expectation, however, that agencies incorporate the standards within their operating plans.

The six standards commit each department to:

— answering letters clearly and within 15 working days of receipt;
— seeing individuals within ten minutes of any pre-arranged time for appointments at departmental offices;
— providing information about services and a public enquiry point for telephone callers;
— consulting users regularly about services and reporting on findings;
— having a complaints procedure and providing information about the procedure to the public on request; and
— taking all reasonable steps to making services available to all (including those with special needs).

The departments produce an evaluation of their performance against these standards through a number of media, including the Internet.

Audit and evaluation

Evaluation of DfEE programmes is overseen by an Evaluation Steering Group. In developing the evaluation programme, the Group takes into consideration the need to assess the effectiveness of new and changing policies. Research projects, designed to evaluate the effectiveness of the policies implemented by the Government, are commissioned from independent external contractors.

The Internal Audit Division of the DfEE aims to provide an assurance to the Accounting Officer that adequate internal controls are in place. The Division also assists managers through auditing specific systems and functions. In 1997-98, 121 audits were conducted. The DfEE evaluates the effectiveness of the audit by judging how plans are achieved, evaluating the delivery of individual audits, checking the extent to which recommendations have been accepted, and by reviewing client satisfaction surveys.

The Department of Trade and Industry (DTI) conducts a series of surveys designed to monitor the resolution of employment rights disputes. One such survey of Industrial Tribunal applications is used to assess the effectiveness of various forms of dispute resolution, including the Advisory, Conciliation and Arbitration Service (ACAS), and as a means of monitoring the satisfaction of end-users with the Industrial Tribunal service.

Staff evaluation

Departments operate Personal Action Plans for individual staff members. These are reviewed on an annual basis. They are drawn up at the beginning of the year and can be amended as the objectives of the Directorate develop. These feed into the end-of-year annual reports. The system has become increasingly standardized across departments over time. Emphasis has increasingly been placed on tying individual pay and promotion prospects more closely to the achievement of performance objectives. Major and Stevens[a] describe the relationship between individual performance and rewards in the following way:

> ... Performance is assessed annually on a scale which usually has five or six points ranging from outstanding to unsatisfactory. Since 1988 these markings, which are based on the achievement of goals agreed at the beginning of the year, updated if necessary, have been used to make the annual allocation of pay increases performance related. Staff judged to have performed best move further and faster up their pay scales than those whose box markings are no better than average ... Another way to reward performance, with much larger consequences for remuneration at all levels, is by promotion. There is a necessary link between the achievement of agreed objectives and rapid promotion, but the "can-do" culture which has become prevalent in recent years tends to favour those who can demonstrate an ability to deliver what is most wanted by ministers and senior officials.

Evaluation and research

Both the DTI and the DfEE operate research programmes designed to inform the development of policy and evaluate the effectiveness of existing programmes. External bodies are often commissioned to undertake research projects which have been identified as priority areas. The Employment Relations Research Committee is responsible for allocating DTI research programmes in employment. Thus, the main element of the programme for 1998-99 was the fourth Workplace Employee Relations Survey which has involved interviews in approximately 3,300 workplaces and questionnaire responses from approximately 30,000 employees in the same workplaces. According to the DTI, the results of the survey published in September 1999 will set a benchmark on the state of employment relations in the United Kingdom prior to the introduction of the Government's new legislative measures.

The DfEE's research programme is overseen from within the Financial & Analytical Services Directorate. Over the period 1999-2000, the DfEE expected to spend 7.4 million pounds sterling on research (funds are moreover provided to the Employment Service (ES) to commission research from

---

[a] M. Major and H. Stevens: "Measuring the impact of new public management and European integration on recruitment and training in the UK civil service," in *Public Administration*, Vol. 75, pp. 531-552.

external bodies). The DfEE is currently reviewing its research priorities and invites members of the external research community to express their views.

Evaluation of executive agencies

Each executive agency operates according to the terms set out in a framework document which establishes the responsibilities of ministers and the Chief Executive, as well as the financial regime and responsibilities in the area of personnel. The framework document is reviewed regularly and at each review the agency is subjected to the same prior options test that it faced at its inception. The prior options test for agencies considers whether the service is required at all, and if it is required whether it should be delivered by the Government, privatized or subjected to market testing.

Performance reviews, evaluating the effectiveness of the agencies established under the Next Steps programme, are published annually as the Next Steps Review. This document includes results for each agency over the preceding three-year period. It measures agency performance, efficiency, benchmarking, service quality and Investors in People issues.

Chief executives are responsible to their parent department for the performance of the Agency, and often an element of their salary is linked to the achievement of specified targets. Full costs and income expenditure accounts are required to be submitted for scrutiny. The Chief Executive is the accounting officer for the Agency and thus bears responsibility for demonstrating that public funds have been spent in a way which secures value for money in service delivery.

In the case of the Employment Service, a set of targets is produced each year by the Secretary of State for Education and Employment and published in the form of an Annual Performance Agreement. Coinciding with the publication of this Agreement, the ES produces an Operation Plan which specifies the ways in which it will attempt to achieve the targets set as well as setting out its priorities for the coming year. The ES's performance is reviewed by ministers on a quarterly basis.

At the close of each year, the ES publishes its annual report and accounts in which actual performance over the preceding year is compared with the targets set.

The standards of service the unemployed can expect from Jobcentres are laid out in the agency's Jobseeker's Charter launched in October 1996. The standards contained in the Charter are agreed between the ES and the Benefits Agency and apply in equal measure to Benefits Agency employees working in Jobcentres. Standards of service are monitored through a practice dubbed "mystery shopping" carried out for the ES by an independent research company. Service standards are evaluated regularly and the results are posted in each Jobcentre. ES districts covering approximately 150 Jobcentres have also been awarded with Charter Marks, which are a nationally recognized award for service quality.

The Internal Audit Service of the ES is in the Corporate Governance Division. The coverage of the audit and the specific performance measures are decided upon by the Internal Audit Committee. This is chaired by the Chief Executive of the ES. The internal audit procedures are as follows. The Chief Executive has responsibility for:

— ensuring that appropriate arrangements are put in place for internal audit of the ES and its management information systems and that quality assurance is maintained in the organization;

— appointing an appropriately qualified head of internal audit to report to the Chief Executive as Accounting Officer. The appointment is determined following consultations with the DfEE; and

— ensuring that the internal audit conforms to the standards specified in the Government Internal Audit manual. This manual describes the relationship between DfEE and ES internal audits.

Like the ES, the Employment Tribunals Service also has a Charter stating standards that end-users can expect. This was published in April 1997, coinciding with the launch of the agency.

Some have argued that the pressures emanating from public expenditure constraints and organizational value-for-money pledges for economy and efficiency within government have resulted in a relative sacrifice of effectiveness in service delivery. There is a clear tension between the objective of achieving quality in service delivery and the Government's desire to restrict public funding. One result of this tension has been for executive agencies to tend to set low performance targets in the hope of ensuring a high success rate.

Evaluation of performances and executive agencies

A benchmarking exercise was conducted from June to December 1996 involving the Next Steps Team, the British Quality Foundation and 30 agencies. The Business Excellence Model (BEM), which was developed by the European Foundation for Quality Management, was used for the purpose. The BEM has nine criteria covering: leadership; policy and strategy; people management; resources; processes; customer satisfaction; people satisfaction; impact on society; and business results. All of the agencies involved in the experiment developed plans with the aim of improving the key areas identified through the process.

A new phase of the benchmarking project began in late 1997, involving two further groups of agencies using an independent body, Total Quality Management International (TQM International), to conduct an external validation. By October 1997, 45 agencies and non- departmental bodies had volunteered for a total of 87 assessments. A database of results, managed by the Civil Service College, was compiled from the benchmarking project. It is anticipated that the database will form the most comprehensive record of public sector assessment in Europe.

EVALUATION

LABOUR ADMINISTRATION AND ITS COMPONENTS

365

The ES has been using the Business Excellence Model and other quality models in parts of the organization and is now recommending the BEM to the entire organization. Since April 1998, all new Training Expertise Council licensing arrangements have had to include TECs using the BEM so as to allow TECs to benchmark themselves against one another and against other organizations.

External audit

The accounts of government departments, executive agencies and non-departmental public bodies are audited and certified by the National Audit Office (NAO). The NAO, which employs around 750 people, is independent of the Government. It was established in 1983 after 20 years of calls for "effective and accountable state audit". It is headed by the Comptroller and Auditor General who has responsibility for authorizing the provision of public funds to government departments and other public bodies. The NAO also has statutory authority to report to Parliament the results of value-for-money examinations which evaluate the "economy, efficiency and effectiveness" with which the various departments and other organizations use their resources. The organizations subject to audit have opportunities to discuss with the relevant area director of the National Audit Office how value for money is to be defined.

At the close of each financial year, each department compiles an appropriation account for each "supply estimate" (or vote). The accounts demonstrate against a range of subheadings the finances provided and the actual amount spent. Any significant variations must be explained. The appropriation account is signed by the accounting officer for the vote who accepts responsibility for the expenditure itself and for the accounts provided. The account is scrutinized by the Comptroller and Auditor General of the NAO who then presents it to the Government. The account is subjected to an examination by the Public Accounts Committee (PAC) of the House. The PAC is empowered to summon accounting officers to appear before it.

At the request of the Treasury, and through agreements between the relevant Minister and organizations, the Comptroller and Auditor General conducts audits of a number of non-departmental bodies including Training and Enterprise Councils. There are also annual accounts, termed White Paper Accounts, which are separate from departmental accounts but which are presented to Parliament in a similar fashion. The authority for the preparation of accounts is generally to be found in the legislation governing the service to which they relate. This legislation either allows for the Comptroller and Auditor General to scrutinize and certify the accounts or, alternatively, provides for the appointment of commercial auditors. Several bodies within the National System of Labour Administration (NSLA) are affected thus: ACAS, the Commission for Racial Equality (CRE), the Health and Safety Commission/ Health and Safety Executive (HSC/HSE), and the Equal Opportunities Commission (EOC).

Concerns have been raised about the effectiveness of the PAC and the ability of committee members to evaluate the management of public sector services. According to Roberts and Pollitt,[a] the enabling legislation for the National Audit Office and its relationship with the PAC means that the scope of its work "remains predominantly financial, so that management issues tend to be pursued only to the extent that their relationship to expenditure issues remains obvious. Inevitably, this imparts a certain 'slant' to NAO discussions of broader management issues, perhaps especially those which are nowadays termed 'human resources management', where questions of motivation and job satisfaction may be paramount".

Fragmentation of government, brought about via contracting out, privatization, the creation of agencies and "quangos" ("quasi governmental organizations", or semi-public bodies) has resulted in declining strategic coordination and control over implementation from the centre and, despite the rhetoric, may have served to reduce rather than enhance public accountability. Nor is it clear that auditing procedures result in improvements in the effectiveness of policy and service provision within the NSLA. The reports of the NAO rarely include a detailed indication of the measures which departments and other audited bodies should take to rectify perceived deficiencies in their performance.

Parliamentary Select Committees

Parliamentary Select Committees are bodies with a relatively permanent membership drawn from across the political spectrum. They are intended to investigate areas of policy and to produce reports as a result of their investigations. These Committees are provided with powers to choose their area of inquiry and also have the right to summon individuals to appear before them to submit themselves to questioning.

The extent to which the powers of the Select Committees encourage true accountability is, however, questionable. Richards[b] has argued that:

> ... far from taking the opportunity to modernize the doctrine of ministerial responsibility and develop new forms of public accountability, the [Conservative] Government has chosen to adopt the line that agency chief executives, as civil servants, cannot be personally accountable for the exercise of their stewardship, requiring them to speak to Parliament (through select committees) only on behalf of their ministers, even when they give evidence on their own domain.

[a] S. Roberts and C. Pollitt: "Audit or evaluation? A National Audit Office VFM study," in *Public Administration*, Vol. 72, pp. 527-549.

[b] Richards, S: "New Labour – New Civil Service?," in *Political Quarterly*, 1996, pp. 311-320.

EVALUATION
LABOUR ADMINISTRATION
AND ITS COMPONENTS

Evaluation of non-departmental public bodies within the NSLA

Training and Enterprise Councils (TECs)

The amount of funding the TECs receive from the Government is performance related. Resources are allocated according to the number of trainees rather than to the relevance, quality or results of training. Concerns have been raised about the standards of training delivered through the TEC system. In response to these concerns, the Government established a Training Standards Council (TSC) in April 1998 to carry out inspections of the companies and educational institutions responsible for providing training funded by the Government. The TSC reports directly to the Secretary of State at the DfEE.

The DfEE has recently put in place new procedures for the evaluation of government-funded vocational education and training (VET) provision. The new practices are based on proposals provided by the TEC National Council and include:

— the creation of a Training Standards Council (as above) to oversee and ensure the independence of training inspection;

— the creation of the Training Inspectorate to coordinate a national programme of inspection;

— the piloting of training inspection; and

— the creation of fully qualified teams of regional inspectors.

The inspection arrangements cover England alone. The Training Inspectorate is to report on the quality of government-funded VET provided through contracts with TECs. In addition, training inspection will apply to VET provided under the Government's New Deal initiative (opportunities for the unemployed to leave welfare and enter employment). The Training Standards Council is expected to provide an annual report to the Secretary of State for Education and Employment and to the TEC National Council.

Advisory, Conciliation and Arbitration Service (ACAS)

ACAS's performance is measured according to the following performance indicators:

— costs of individual conciliation cases settled or withdrawn;

— percentage of individual conciliation cases settled or withdrawn;

— unit costs of answering public enquiries;

— percentage of collective conciliation cases where a settlement was achieved or significant progress was made;

— unit costs of collective conciliation cases where a settlement was achieved or significant progress was made;

— unit costs of completed advisory mediation projects; and

— unit costs of arbitration.

368

Unit costs are calculated by dividing the cost of all cases by the number of those with a successful outcome. ACAS submits its annual report to the DTI at the end of each year. In February 1994, ACAS became the first multi-site civil service body to gain recognition as an "Investor in People" (IIP). ACAS was re-accredited in March 1997.

Certification Officer

The Office of the Certification Officer is subject to audits of its procedures by the DTI Internal Audit.

Equal Opportunities Commission (EOC)

The accounts of the EOC are subject to the auditing procedures of the Comptroller and Auditor General. Like other bodies, the EOC operates a prompt payment policy. Sample tests during 1996 suggested that 96 per cent of invoices for purchase orders were paid within the target time. In its Corporate Plan for 1997-2001, the EOC states one of its principal aims as being to provide "effective and efficient service". To this end, it was working towards gaining IIP status by 1999/2000 and is introducing customer service standards across all EOC units, departments and offices. The organization is also working to "improve accessibility of services and develop new systems to ensure the cost effectiveness of our service delivery".

Commission for Racial Equality (CRE)

The accounts of the CRE are audited by the Comptroller and Auditor General. It is currently working towards IIP status.

Health and Safety Executive (HSE), Health and Safety Commission (HSC)

The performance of the HSE as measured against a number of target objectives, ranging over personnel, energy conservation, inspections and contacts with firms is reviewed in the organization's annual report (and in the annual report of the Department of the Environment, Transport and Regions). The HSE has obtained IIP accreditation for 20 of its 21 sections.

The Department of the Environment has carried out prior options reviews into various functions of the HSE. The HSE itself has carried out a benchmarking study to evaluate its performance compared to the provision of similar services in other European Union Member States. During 1996-97, a new set of 30 performance measures was introduced into the HSC/HSE in preparation for the implementation of resource accounting and budgeting principles.

Conclusion

What is mainly demonstrated by this case is that as a result of the strong political will which has had a significant impact for a number of years, evaluation has developed rapidly throughout the United Kingdom administration

EVALUATION

LABOUR ADMINISTRATION
AND ITS COMPONENTS

and the departments responsible for labour have been directly involved in it. Indeed, without ongoing effort, administrations do not willingly agree to an internal or external evaluation. The other lesson to be drawn is that the evaluation applied is not specific to labour administration: the same methods would be applicable to any organizational entity. It is therefore up to the labour administration to use this process to check whether its available resources are appropriately allocated in relation to the objectives set.